PRIESTS OF OUR DEMOCRACY

Priests of Our Democracy

*The Supreme Court, Academic Freedom,
and the Anti-Communist Purge*

Marjorie Heins

NEW YORK UNIVERSITY PRESS
New York and London

NEW YORK UNIVERSITY PRESS
New York and London
www.nyupress.org

Some of the material about loyalty oaths originally appeared in Marjorie Heins, "A Pall of Orthodoxy: The Painful Persistence of Loyalty Oaths," *Dissent*, summer 2009. Material about oaths also appeared in Marjorie Heins, "Guilt by Association: Georgia's Anti-subversive Test Oath," Free Expression Policy Project, 2010, http://www.fepproject.org/commentaries/georgiaoath.html; Marjorie Heins, "What Makes a Conscientious Objector? Ohio's Anti-terrorist Oath," Free Expression Policy Project, 2009, http://www.fepproject.org/commentaries/ohiooath.html.

References to Internet websites (URLs) were accurate at the time of writing.
Neither the author nor New York University Press is responsible for URLs that may have expired or changed since the manuscript was prepared.

LIBRARY OF CONGRESS CATALOGING-IN-PUBLICATION DATA
Heins, Marjorie.
Priests of our democracy : the Supreme Court, academic freedom,
and the anti-communist purge / Marjorie Heins.
p. cm.   Includes bibliographical references and index.
ISBN 978-0-8147-9051-9 (cl : alk. paper)   ISBN 978-0-8147-4464-2 (ebook)
ISBN 978-0-8147-7026-9 (ebook)
1. Academic freedom—United States. 2. United States. Supreme Court. 3. Freedom of speech—United States. 4. Public schools—Curricula—Censorship—United States. 5. Universities and colleges—Law and legislation—United States. 6. Anti-communist movements—United States. 7. Teaching, Freedom of—United States. I. Title.
KF4242.H45   2013
344.73'078—dc23   2012032821

New York University Press books are printed on acid-free paper,
and their binding materials are chosen for strength and durability.
We strive to use environmentally responsible suppliers and materials
to the greatest extent possible in publishing our books.

Manufactured in the United States of America

10 9 8 7 6 5 4 3 2 1

This book is dedicated to the memory of Robert Pascal Boalch

July 21, 2005–March 29, 2011

To regard teachers—in our entire educational system, from the primary grades to the university—as the priests of our democracy is not to indulge in hyperbole. It is the special task of teachers to foster those habits of open-mindedness and critical inquiry which alone make for responsible citizens.

—Justice Felix Frankfurter, *Wieman v. Updegraff*

CONTENTS

Introduction

New York, 1952

Harry Keyishian was a junior at Queens College, New York City, in the fall of 1952 when the Senate Internal Security Subcommittee came to town. Investigations of suspected communist or ex-communist teachers were nothing new by this point in America's Cold War history, but by 1952 they had reached such a pitch of intensity that the Senate subcommittee (commonly known as the SISS) was just one of multiple government and private bodies competing in a crowded field of political investigators. One of the subcommittee's primary purposes in coming to New York was to persuade the local Board of Higher Education (the BHE) to be more aggressive in rooting out allegedly subversive faculty from the city's free public colleges.

The first Queens professor to be called before the SISS was the economist Vera Shlakman, an officer in the left-wing Teachers Union, whose campaigns against low pay, poor school maintenance, and racially biased textbooks had antagonized city officials since the early 1930s. Shlakman was the author of a much-praised book, *Economic History of a Factory Town*, and had been at Queens since 1938, after a PhD at Columbia, a research fellowship at Smith College, and a teaching stint at Sweet Briar. She had found the college "wonderful" when she arrived—the faculty full of European intellectuals, refugees from Nazism, and the students diligent and eager.[1] Like many beleaguered academics in the early 1950s, she objected to legislative probes into her political beliefs, and when the time came, she refused to tell the SISS whether she had ever been a Communist Party member. Despite her 14-year tenure at Queens, the BHE fired her two weeks later.

Harry Keyishian, who wrote a column for the student newspaper recounting humorous bits of campus news, and who had up to this point been more interested in girls than politics, joined a committee to protest the peremptory firing of a popular professor.[2] From this modest beginning, Keyishian became, 15 years later, a protagonist in the U.S. Supreme Court's most important ruling on academic freedom. But now, in 1952, he was just one puzzled and indignant member of the protest committee, whose faculty advisor, the literature scholar Oscar Shaftel, was to be the second person fired from Queens.

The SISS, a subcommittee of the Senate's powerful Judiciary Committee, was back in Washington, D.C., when Shaftel testified in February 1953. Like Shlakman, he refused to answer questions about his political beliefs or activities, but he did tell the SISS that he thought communists could be competent teachers: "I cannot imagine an academic administrator of any sense and magnitude and dignity saying to Sean O'Casey, who has been generally associated with Communists, 'You may not teach the drama,' or tell Picasso, 'You cannot teach art.'"[3] The BHE scheduled a meeting to vote on firing him, a campus newspaper condemned the attack on "a well-loved, respected professor,"[4] and students distributed leaflets protesting another imminent dismissal.

At the BHE meeting in March 1953, Shaftel lectured board members on the importance of intellectual freedom and the malignancy of their "surrender to expediency" in following the SISS's commands. He concluded by quoting from John Milton's poem "Lycidas":

> Blind mouths! that scarce themselves know how to hold
> A sheep hook, . . .
> What recks it them? What need they? They are sped; . . .
> The hungry sheep look up, and are not fed,
> But, swollen with wind, and the rank mist they draw,
> Rot inwardly, and foul contagion spread.[5]

Neither Shaftel's erudition nor his students' protest saved the jobs of professors caught in what has often, without exaggeration, been called the witch hunt of America's Cold War years. It was not until the early 1980s that the BHE apologized to Shlakman, Shaftel, and five other then-elderly professors (and the estates of three who had died) and offered compensation for what were by then recognized to be unjust dismissals.

Academic Freedom from *Adler* to *Keyishian*

Well before the SISS arrived in Manhattan in 1952, there had been years of debate all over America—in the courts, in educational institutions, and in the press—about whether the First Amendment principle of free speech protected suspected communists and, more specifically, about whether the concept of academic freedom barred political inquisitions against teachers and professors. Libertarians urged that laws and policies that disqualified communists from teaching were direct assaults on freedom of inquiry; those who supported loyalty programs insisted on just the opposite: that all communists were mental slaves of Moscow and therefore incapable of independent thought; hence, it would only advance academic freedom to get rid of them.

The Supreme Court confronted the question in a case that challenged New York State's 1949 Feinberg Law, which required detailed procedures for investigating the loyalty of every public school teacher and ousting anyone who engaged in "treasonable or seditious acts or utterances" or joined an organization that advocated the overthrow of the government by "force, violence or any unlawful means." It was a typical Cold War–era loyalty law; hence, *Adler v. Board of Education*, the Supreme Court's 1952 decision upholding it, had nationwide repercussions.

In *Adler*, a majority of the Supreme Court found no First Amendment problem with the Feinberg Law. Embracing the anti-communist fervor of the time, the Court said that teachers have no right to their jobs; and because they work "in a sensitive area" where they shape young minds, the authorities are entitled to investigate their political beliefs. "They may work for the school system upon the reasonable terms laid down by the proper authorities. . . . If they do not choose to work on such terms, they are at liberty to retain their beliefs and associations and go elsewhere."[6] The decision did not suggest any limit to the power of public employers to hire and fire based on political views. Instead, it followed the simplistic philosophy articulated many decades earlier by Oliver Wendell Holmes, Jr., when he was a justice on the Massachusetts Supreme Judicial Court, that a man might have "a constitutional right to talk politics" but does not have "a constitutional right to be a policeman."[7]

Even at this unfortunate moment for free speech, however, the Court was not unanimous: Justice William O. Douglas wrote a fiery dissent in the *Adler* case. Douglas said the Feinberg Law "proceeds on a principle repugnant to our society—guilt by association"; furthermore, it "turns the school system into a spying project," with the ears of students, parents, and administrators "cocked for tell-tale signs of disloyalty." The law would "raise havoc with academic freedom," he predicted; "a pall is cast over the classrooms."[8] Fifteen years later, in 1967, Justice William Brennan borrowed Douglas's image of a pall hovering over education, in a case that overturned *Adler* and invalidated the Feinberg Law.

That 1967 case began at the Buffalo campus of the State University of New York (SUNY). The SUNY trustees had decided to make all employees sign a "Feinberg certificate" affirming that they were not members of the

Communist Party and that if they ever had been, they had disclosed this fact to the state university president. The Feinberg certificate was a classic "test oath"—that is, a demand for political or religious loyalty as a test of job fitness. Test oaths are usually worded in negative terms, as denials or disclaimers of disfavored associations or beliefs, but affirmative oaths—to support the king, the church, or in more modern times, the Constitution—are also tests of loyalty.[9] Although condemned by the Supreme Court after the Civil War, disclaimer oaths such as the Feinberg certificate were a common feature of the Cold War landscape.

In the fall of 1963, some 300 SUNY-Buffalo professors voted their opposition to the Feinberg certificate. But *Adler* was still the ruling precedent, and despite the protest, caution and the desire for job security prevailed. In the end, only four faculty members refused to sign the certificate; a fifth, the poet George Starbuck, declined to answer a question about subversive associations on a civil service form. The five rebels were aware of the ruling in *Adler* but hoped that both the times and the Supreme Court had changed; in 1964, they filed suit to challenge the entire Feinberg Law.

Harry Keyishian, who since his graduation from Queens College had attended graduate school, served in the navy, and started his professional life as an English instructor at Buffalo, was one of the five. He jumped at the chance to challenge the system of loyalty purges that had cost his alma mater valued professors a decade before; it would be his "revenge on the '50s."[10] He became the lead plaintiff in *Keyishian v. Board of Regents*.

Some Supreme Court decisions over the previous decade had cautiously chipped away at loyalty programs, but Justice Brennan, writing in *Keyishian*, rejected wholesale the idea that restrictions on expression, ideas, and political associations are permissible under the First Amendment as conditions of public employment. And because the Feinberg Law targeted teachers, Brennan had particular words to say about education. "Our Nation is deeply committed to safeguarding academic freedom," he wrote, "which is of transcendent value to all of us and not merely to the teachers concerned. That freedom is therefore a special concern of the First Amendment, which does not tolerate laws that cast a pall of orthodoxy over the classroom."[11]

What had happened in the 15 years between *Adler* and *Keyishian*? Of course, the political landscape had changed: the "haunted '50s"[12] had given way to the more libertarian '60s. The toll taken on public and private life by two decades of loyalty programs and blacklists was palpable. Popular opinion had finally rejected the demagoguery of opportunists like Senator Joseph McCarthy of Wisconsin, who had jumped on the already speeding anti-communist bandwagon in 1950 and given his name to the recklessness that characterized much of the Cold War Red Scare. And liberal Supreme Court justices had replaced more conservative ones, although even in the heady year of 1967, *Keyishian* was decided by a narrow 5–4 vote, over a blistering dissent by Justice Tom Clark.

Ornery Professors, Then and Now

Why did Vera Shlakman, Oscar Shaftel, and hundreds of others refuse to cooperate in the political inquisitions of the witch-hunt era? After all, the totalitarian Soviet Union was a threat to U.S. security; some American communists had passed classified documents or otherwise engaged in espionage for the USSR.[13] If you were an honest citizen, so the argument went in the 1950s, you had nothing to hide. If you had been a communist during the tumultuous 1930s, when the poverty of the Depression, the ruthless racism of the American South, and above all the threat of fascism in Europe inspired people to join the Party, but you had since seen the error of your ways, you should admit it, instead of hiding behind claims of constitutional privilege which all too often seemed disingenuous and evasive.

Certainly, some teachers—like others who refused to cooperate—were communists, and truthful answers would likely have cost them their jobs. For others, who had been Party members in the past, self-interest was mixed with principle: cross-examining citizens about their reading habits and political beliefs, as legislative committees and educational boards inevitably did, was a disturbing spectacle. If a witness was not sufficiently hostile to the USSR or sufficiently supportive of U.S. forces in the Korean War or was favorable to racial integration or had marched in a May Day parade, these were all grounds for suspicion. The questions not only violated privacy; they intimidated the population and persuaded all but the most intrepid to avoid politically progressive activities.

There was another unseemly aspect to cooperation. Even those who were willing to go through the ritual of professed repentance for their communist past usually did not want to identify others they had worked with on political issues or seen at meetings or on picket lines. Yet many inquisitors believed that "naming names" was the only good evidence of a sincere break with communism. This presented profound moral dilemmas not only for ex-communists but for liberals and "fellow travelers" of the Party who had been active in civil rights and other causes of the 1930s and '40s and who thus inevitably came into contact with the communists who shared in and often led these campaigns. The saga of five New York City teachers who admitted their own communist pasts but refused to name names (told in chapter 9) is a cautionary tale about the excesses of heresy hunting and its sometimes unintended effects.

Many people who had made the difficult break with communism, or who had never been communists, simply did not want to collaborate in the Red hunt—its super-patriot rhetoric, its methods of exposure and disgrace. Harry Keyishian and his fellow plaintiffs in their challenge to the Feinberg Law exemplified this disinterested objection to the loyalty oaths and investigations that warped American political life during the Cold War. Even fervent anti-communists at the time were embarrassed by the crudeness and stupidity of some legislative inquisitors such as the House Committee on Un-American Activities (HUAC); they wanted a kinder, gentler witch hunt. Others understood that it was not possible—that it was the very nature of the enterprise that threatened the free speech on which democracy depends.

The fates of Vera Shlakman, Oscar Shaftel, and hundreds of others affected by loyalty programs in academia, both in New York and nationwide, may seem like ancient history. But these events, and the Supreme Court's eventual recognition of First Amendment academic freedom in response, are stories with resonance today. Battles over free speech on campus, and over the purpose and meaning of education, continue to bedevil our national politics. Today's war on terrorism has replaced Cold War anti-communism as a justification for limiting civil liberties, both on campus and off. Although contemporary fears of a return to the repressive zealotry of the late 1940s and early '50s—the legislative inquisitions, loyalty investigations, and test oaths—are overblown, we do face threats to academic freedom in the 21st century, both institutionally and in the courts. Often, these threats arise from a habit of mind, long prominent in American politics, that seeks simple answers to complex problems, that shuts out nuanced or radical critique, and that demonizes dissent, especially from the left. It was this habit of mind, in large part, that allowed the anti-communist purge of the 1950s to flourish as long and intensely as it did.[14]

The Meaning of Academic Freedom

The Supreme Court in *Keyishian* spoke of academic freedom as a "special concern of the First Amendment" but did not define the term or delineate its scope. In the next few decades, judges often applied the language of *Keyishian* broadly, leading one scholar to complain that, "lacking definition or guiding principle," First Amendment academic freedom "floats in the law, picking up decisions as a hull does barnacles."[15] As the federal courts became more conservative, this "hull-and-barnacles" critique gained adherents.

Courts began to view the First Amendment concept of academic freedom, if they recognized it at all, as a right belonging to the university as an institution, not to individual professors. And some commentators began to argue that academic freedom, although important as a principle of educational policy, has no basis in the Constitution. After all, they pointed out, the First Amendment, like the rest of the Bill of Rights, generally only stops government entities—legislatures, boards of education, public university trustees—from abridging "the freedom of speech," but academic freedom should apply at private and public institutions alike.[16]

Obviously, academic freedom has limits, with or without its First Amendment baggage, and William Brennan's stirring words in *Keyishian* left myriad questions unanswered. Professors must teach the subjects assigned, for example, and not spend their time in a chemistry class lecturing about history or literature (which does not mean they should be punished for occasionally straying from the assigned topics). There are limits, too, on how unconventional or provocative their speech can be: how, for example, do we balance rules forbidding sexual and racial harassment against the freedom to express controversial views? Is the teacher who uses the term *wetback* in the course of describing U.S. attitudes toward Mexicans discriminating or simply exercising academic freedom? (The question arose in 2007, when Brandeis University declared a professor guilty of harassment for using the word and placed a monitor in his classes.)[17] Does a public university that demotes a professor who made anti-Semitic remarks at an off-campus event violate his First Amendment rights? (A court in 1994 said yes but later revised its opinion in response to a Supreme Court decision that cut back on public employees' free-speech protection.)[18] What about a professor whose writings deny the Holocaust or the theory of evolution—can she be fired on grounds of incompetence? Or is she protected by the First Amendment as long as she does not try to teach her misguided views in class?

And what of Professor Ward Churchill, who was fired by the University of Colorado because of an essay he wrote after September 11, 2001, in which he attacked the stock traders who worked at brokerage firms in the World Trade Center as "little Eichmanns" because, he argued, they were part of a "technocratic corps at the very heart of America's global financial empire" and were complicit in the damage caused by American military operations?[19] The university understood that the First Amendment protected his hyperbolic remarks and so, responding to pressure to get him off the public payroll, searched for other reasons to fire him. It found some instances of alleged "research misconduct"; a jury concluded that they were pretexts; but the trial judge decided that Churchill should lose his case in any event, because the university committee that recommended his firing was immune from suit.[20] Such are the consequences, even in the courts, when professors engage in angrily provocative speech.

But why should the university have had to look for pretexts? Should Churchill's constitutional right to express his political views with an outrageous metaphor have protected him from academic retribution? More broadly, should academic freedom even be a special concern of the First Amendment or of educational policy? Are teachers an élite, with free-speech rights greater than everybody else's? They are not, but as Justice Felix Frankfurter explained in a 1952 case that invalidated a test oath required of professors in Oklahoma, teachers are "the priests of our democracy" because it is their "special task . . . to foster those habits of open-mindedness and critical inquiry which alone make for responsible citizens."[21] The point was that academic freedom is necessary not because teachers are smarter or better than the rest of us but because they impart the skills to think critically and thus to participate meaningfully in the great, if often flawed, American experiment in political freedom.

Chief Justice Earl Warren reprised this theme in 1957, in an opinion voiding the contempt conviction of a Marxist scholar who had refused to answer questions about a lecture he had given. Warren noted "the essentiality of freedom" in universities and the dangers of "an atmosphere of suspicion and distrust." Teachers and students cannot be put in "an intellectual strait jacket," he said; they "must always remain free to inquire, to study and to evaluate, to gain new maturity and understanding."[22] It was the same vision of academic freedom that Brennan was to celebrate a decade later in *Keyishian.*

In none of these cases, though, did the Court say whether—and if so, how—academic freedom should apply below the college level. In *Keyishian,* Justice Brennan made no distinction between schools and universities when he spoke of "a pall of orthodoxy over the classroom." Many high school students are on the verge of adulthood, and it would shortchange them, their teachers, and the community to relegate their education to rote learning and to eliminate free inquiry from the mix. As the American Association of University Professors (the AAUP) points out, high school is, for virtually all Americans, the necessary prerequisite to college, and students will surely be limited in their ability to pursue higher learning "if their previous education has ill-prepared them."[23]

Yet public schools *are* different from universities; one of their purposes is to inculcate civic values. Conflicting philosophies—inculcation (or indoctrination) versus free inquiry and critical thinking—continue to drive battles in the United States over educational policy. In the late 1960s, the Supreme

Court leaned toward free inquiry, remarking in one famous case that students are not merely "closed-circuit recipients of only that which the state chooses to communicate,"[24] but more recently, the courts have drastically narrowed that principle and have stripped students and teachers below college level of almost all First Amendment rights in the context of school activities. This book argues for renewed constitutional protection for free inquiry not only in universities but in public schools.

The Arc of the Narrative

Priests of Our Democracy traces the political, cultural, and legal events that gave rise to academic freedom as "a special concern of the First Amendment." It shows how loyalty purges at schools and universities during the worst years of the Red Scare eventually produced monumentally important Supreme Court decisions. Although some of this history transpired before the Cold War, and there is also much to recount after 1967, a natural framework for the book's central chapters is the Supreme Court's response to teacher loyalty programs in the 15 years between its 1952 decision in *Adler* to uphold the Feinberg Law and its 1967 decision in *Keyishian* to strike it down.

These were years when the Court evolved from a generally passive body, approving oppressive loyalty regimes, to an activist one, applying the Bill of Rights to limit government overreaching. Although the Supreme Court led by Earl Warren has been much criticized, and its role in the "rights revolution" of the '60s may be a rare exception to the traditionally conservative stance of the judiciary, in times of political crisis courts are critical players not only in protecting free speech but in enriching the literature of democracy. So, while we should not ignore academic freedom as a matter of good educational policy governing private as well as public universities, I argue that we must also defend the First Amendment principle of academic freedom as a limit on what government officials, including administrators of public institutions, can do to their teachers and students. The history I recount—the inquisitions of New York professors and teachers, the Supreme Court's response, and its eventual dismantling of loyalty programs in *Keyishian*—will show where First Amendment protection for academic freedom comes from and why it remains important.

But *Priests of Our Democracy* is not simply a legal history. Indeed, the Supreme Court does not become a major player in the story until chapter 4. The book aims to tell social and human stories, to connect the policy issues and the court cases to the people who lived them—those who were targeted by the witch hunt, those who pursued them, and those who started, like

Harry Keyishian, as bystanders but eventually found a way to participate. The characters in this saga range from radical intellectuals like Oscar Shaftel and Vera Shlakman, impassioned about their scholarship and teaching, to public school teachers like Irving Mauer and Julius Nash, who could not find it in their consciences to "name names" of former comrades and were punished by the New York City Board of Education for 18 years thereafter. There are energetic Cold Warriors like Harry Gideonse, the truculent head of Brooklyn College, ambivalent ones like Ordway Tead, head of the BHE, and aggressive inquisitors like Saul Moskoff, who directed the Board of Education's investigations of elementary and high school teachers and engaged his subjects in heartrending debates about the meaning of justice under Jewish law. There are conscientious objectors: Quakers and other non-communist protesters whose refusal to sign loyalty oaths led to major Supreme Court decisions. There are people caught in excruciating dilemmas—professors who chose to perjure themselves before New York State's Rapp-Coudert investigating committee in 1941 when their legal arguments against the inquisition failed. All were complicated individuals; none were angels; all gave flesh and context to the legal rulings that emerged from their struggles.

In New York City and State, these struggles were particularly intense. The overwhelming majority of left-wing teachers and professors targeted by the Boards of Education and Higher Education were Jewish; so were some of the leading inquisitors. Anti-Semitism, Jewish-Catholic tensions, battles over educational policy and race discrimination, and turmoil within the city's Jewish community provide the background against which the courts and the state's administrative apparatus wrestled with questions of free speech, union busting, and ultimately, the Board of Education's unseemly policy of requiring teachers who admitted past CP membership to "name names" or lose their jobs.

In the nation's largest, most ethnically diverse city, the passion and idealism of radicals eager for social justice clashed with legions of both super-patriots and liberals. The super-patriots wanted to use anti-communism as a wedge against progressive reforms; the liberals either were trying to prove their anti-communist credentials, and so undermine Republican Party claims to monopolize the issue, or were so fiercely hostile to communism that they were willing to condemn people who had once been attracted to radical causes unless they publicly and lavishly recanted past enthusiasms. New York plays a special part in the story not only because the Supreme Court's Feinberg Law cases arose there but because, as one scholar said, "no other state has shown so continuous a sense of insecurity" about revolutionary sentiments among its residents.[25] In New York City especially, left-wing radicalism had strong roots, and in reaction, the anti-communism of Cold War America played out with particular ferocity.

Part 1 of the book traces the origins of academic freedom as an American ideal and describes the radicalism, and the Red Scares, that characterized New York politics in the first half of the 20th century (chapters 1 and 2). It concludes with the 1940–42 Rapp-Coudert investigation of New York's public schools and colleges and the trajectory of the city's higher-education establishment, from resistance to acquiescence, in response (chapter 3).

Part 2 begins with New York City in the late 1940s and early '50s—its remarkable Teachers Union, its battles over the Feinberg Law, and the particular aggressiveness of the anti-communist purge undertaken by its Board of Education (chapters 4 and 5). Chapter 6 focuses on the Cold War Supreme Court, led by the affable but intellectually underwhelming Chief Justice Fred Vinson, which not only upheld the Feinberg Law but, with a few minor exceptions, turned back all constitutional challenges to loyalty programs, blacklists, and Red-hunting legislative investigations across the nation. The ambivalence of two brilliant intellects on the Court, Robert Jackson and Felix Frankfurter, solidified the anti-civil-liberties majority: both Jackson and Frankfurter had deep reservations about loyalty purges but feared, for political reasons, to try to stop them by judicial fiat. Prophetic dissents from Hugo Black and William O. Douglas, on the other hand, provided the rhetoric and the arguments that kept free-speech debates alive in these years and prepared the ground for landmark decisions in the 1960s, when the intensity of Cold War anti-communism had abated.

Part 3 recounts the clash between rebel professors and the SISS not only at Queens but at Brooklyn College, where President Harry Gideonse continued to battle radical students and to seek ways to oust popular, activist professors such as the literature scholars Frederic Ewen and Harry Slochower (chapters 7 and 8). Chapter 9 explores the excruciating dilemma of informing that confronted teachers at both the public school and college level, and the city Board of Education's demand that people name names as a condition of employment.

In part 4, I trace the progress of the Court, now led by Chief Justice Earl Warren, from cautious incursions on some of the witch-hunt era's more drastic practices to its breakthrough decisions of June 17, 1957—so-called Red Monday—and the retrenchment that followed (chapter 10). The story then moves into the 1960s, when Justice William Brennan emerged as a leader on First Amendment issues. Three cases involving teacher loyalty oaths—from

Florida, Washington, and Arizona—set the stage for *Keyishian*, which was essentially the death knell for statewide anti-subversive programs (chapters 11 and 12).

But all was not settled, by any means, by *Keyishian*. (It never is, in politics or constitutional law.) Part 5 recounts the later adventures of Vera Shlakman, Frederic Ewen, and other actors in the story, including, ultimately, apologies and vindications for the wrongs they suffered (chapter 13). The courts have wrestled with myriad variations on the themes sounded in *Keyishian*; as chapter 14 relates, contemporary universities face serious questions about the future and meaning of academic freedom, as a matter of both policy and First Amendment right. Chapter 15, finally, looks at the academic-freedom issues that have arisen since September 11, 2001, both in the schools and in the courts. The issues include new loyalty oath controversies, pressures against outspoken professors and against Middle East studies, and broad uses of the word *terrorism* to silence dissent.

Home Is Where One Starts From

Personal motivations always play a role in projects as daunting as writing a book. I grew up in Brooklyn in the 1950s, the child of a schoolteacher (but not an activist one), in a liberal household where there was only muted talk of left-wing friends who had lost their jobs. I absorbed enough of the anti-communist mania around me to be fearful, when I went to college, of involvement in the civil rights movement, which was said to be communist dominated. I did not know what this meant, but I knew it was bad.

I had heard of New York City's municipal colleges but was taught to aim for the Ivy League; I had no inkling of their remarkable history, their tradition of radical activism, or their social importance in providing free higher education to the poor and working classes of the city. I never saw Brooklyn College until I visited its archives in 2010 in connection with research for this book. The research has been—to maul only somewhat the words of T. S. Eliot—a return to where I started, to "know the place for the first time."[26]

In college, like so many of my generation, I was inspired by the movements for civil rights and against the war in Vietnam. I joined the New Left but had no idea what the Old Left had been. More sophisticated activists, including those who had been "Red diaper babies," spoke meaningfully of the errors of the Old Left, in particular its adherence to communist ideology or to an often indefensible "Party line." But again, I had no historical context for these pronouncements. Certainly, the New Left made its own share of grievous errors.

As the New Left disintegrated, I began to wonder why there was so little tradition or historical memory of political radicalism in America. Certainly, we did not learn in my Brooklyn high school about such landmarks of U.S. history as the anti-fascist Popular Front of the late 1930s or the nearly one million votes in the 1912 presidential election for Eugene Debs and the Socialist Party.

Why, I also wondered, did the Supreme Court not do more to support free speech during the heresy hunts of the 1950s? After all, the Constitution gave federal judges life tenure in order to remove them from the pressures of politics. But as I read more, I began to understand that this "least dangerous branch" of government rarely gets too far ahead of majority political sentiment; often, it lags behind. Even in its progressive moments, the Supreme Court will usually move only incrementally around the edges of political repression.

Historians have explored why many thousands of intelligent people joined the Communist Party in the 1930s and '40s, despite its flaws: it was simply the most effective advocate on a multitude of important issues, from race discrimination to labor organizing. The tragedy of the American left is that all this energy and commitment was linked to an organization whose leadership was repressive and beholden to the needs and commands of the Soviet Union. The 1917 Bolshevik Revolution had sparked wild hopes around the world, but totalitarianism and mass murder soon descended on the USSR. It took too many American leftists too long to break with the hopelessly compromised Communist Party, but their errors were not the sole, or even the major, reason for the demise of a credible radical movement in America. Political repression did that, and its legacy is an impoverished political discourse that persists in the United States to this day.[27]

This book, then, is also a cautionary tale. It is critical of the choices made by many ex-communist and communist teachers, even while comprehending their dilemma. It weighs the argument so often made in the 1950s that the First Amendment should not protect communists, and it tries to bring balance and common sense to today's continuing debates about the scope of academic freedom.

"The freedom of speech" is mentioned but not defined in the First Amendment. It is generally understood today to protect not only the academic-freedom values of open inquiry, critical thinking, and challenge to conventional beliefs but the propagation of ideas that are evil and wrong. Of course, free speech has limits, but the presumption—the "default" position, as it were—is that even bad ideas are protected. One reason is that the cost of repressing them is too high—that the people in power will inevitably try to squelch the ideas they think dangerous to their hegemony; yet these may be the very ideas needed for progress and social justice. Academic freedom is a "special concern of the First Amendment" because genuine education is not only liberating in itself; it is the basis of a successful democracy. If not all teachers fulfill their high calling as priests of that democracy, it is all the more important to encourage those who do.

PART I

Prelude to the Deluge

1

"Sifting and Winnowing"

Professors under Siege

Academic freedom was not a coherent concept in America before the late
19th century. But as the nation's universities evolved from sectarian institutions drilling young gentlemen in Latin and Greek into something approach-
ing the modern ideal of scholars united in a quest for knowledge, conflicts
over the role of professors, the powers of trustees, and the very nature of the
academic enterprise began.

The notion of college teaching as a profession and of the university as a
venue for scholarly research and critical inquiry was just developing. Guild-
like academic associations began to replace the less exclusive "learned societies" that dominated intellectual life before the Civil War.[1] Literature professors formed the Modern Language Association in 1883; historians formed
the American Historical Association in 1884. The American Economics
Association followed in 1885, the American Political Science Association
in 1903, and the American Sociology Association in 1905.[2] Along with the
new societies came a new élitism: as one historian put it, academics began to
speak mainly "to each other rather than the general public."[3] But at the same
time, new fields like economics and sociology incorporated social activism:
these scholars wanted their work to make a difference in the real world.[4] Professors gained social status because of their reform activity and government's
increasing use of experts; as another author notes, "the new type of professor, the practical man, was winning public approval," while "the humanistic
scholar more often felt elbowed aside."[5]

The last few decades of the 19th century saw fierce battles between rob-
ber-baron capitalists and their exploited workers. There was revolutionary
rhetoric and sometimes violence on the workers' side, and greater violence
by the owners in response. The Great Railroad Strike of 1877 paralyzed trans-
port, was brutally suppressed, and seemed a harbinger of full-dress class war.
Charismatic labor leaders like Eugene Debs, soon to found the Socialist Party,
caused panic among the middle and upper classes.[6] As the turmoil continued

into the 1890s, with nearly 500 strikes per year,[7] some professors, particularly in economics and other branches of the new social sciences, spoke out on the side of labor and reform. University boards of trustees, populated largely by corporate executives, were not happy with the activist scholars.

Economics professor Edward Bemis was a prime example of the new academic. He wrote popular articles on local government, tax policy, working conditions, labor strikes, socialism, and religion.[8] He began teaching at the University of Chicago in 1892 after stints at Amherst and Vanderbilt but was ousted three years later because of his politics. Bemis sympathized with labor during the 1894 railroad strike against the Pullman Company of Chicago. In a speech, he seemingly excused unlawful acts by the strikers, or at least suggested that the companies "must set an example" if they expect their workers "to be law-abiding."[9] The speech "was considered nothing short of treasonous" by Chicago businessmen, and the university president obliged them by warning Bemis to "exercise very great care in public utterance about questions that are agitating the minds of the people."[10] Bemis was fired the following year and went on to serve as superintendent of the Cleveland, Ohio, Water Works where, over protests from the local Democratic machine, he replaced party hacks with a merit system of employment, reduced water rates, and crusaded for higher tax valuations on corporate property.[11] Given these accomplishments, one might think that his loss to academia was a gain for society, but it is telling that at the time, at least some universities were less hospitable to ideas about social reform than were major public employers like the City of Cleveland.

Professor Richard Ely had been Bemis's mentor and was even better known for social-reform views. An economist whose philosophy mixed Christian piety, redistribution of wealth, and the rights of labor, Ely promoted his ideas through an accessible writing style rather than the obfuscatory prose that was coming to dominate academia.[12] His "trial" at the University of Wisconsin in 1894 became the defining moment for academic freedom in its early years.

Wisconsin was a crucible of social-reform ideas when Ely arrived there in 1892. There were municipal reform movements across the state, with a core of dedicated professors contributing to the "Wisconsin idea" of an activist government staffed with a merit-based civil service and relying on many expert commissions.[13] But two years later, unemployment and labor war, most notably the long, bitter Pullman strike, left the country in turmoil. The *Nation* magazine condemned the strike, and socialism in general; it then criticized "the common practice among Christian and other socialists and utopians of abusing nearly everybody who succeeds in life as an enemy of the human race, and the existing constitution of society as an engine of fraud and oppression." Instead, the *Nation* editors cautioned, it was "the solemn duty of all writers, preachers, and professors, who are engaged in the work of reform, to refrain from denunciations of the existing society and social arrangements."[14] Wisconsin superintendent of public instruction and ex officio university regent Oliver Wells wrote in support of this laissez-faire viewpoint, in a letter that the magazine published under the headline "The College Anarchist." The *Nation* continued its attack the following week, reporting sardonically that "a few years ago Prof. Ely sent forth his platitudes on socialism, ethics, and labor from Johns Hopkins University, but that institution was able to spare him when he desired to extend his usefulness over the wider field of the boundless West."[15]

Wells's letter accused Ely not only of writing "glittering generalities and mystical and metaphysical statements" but of pressuring a local printer to use exclusively union labor and threatening to take his business elsewhere if the printer did not comply. Newspapers reprinted the letter; the university regents appointed a committee of three prominent citizens to investigate the charges.[16] Ely proclaimed his innocence, and the printer backed him up, testifying that although the professor had repeatedly urged him to unionize, he had not made any threats.[17] Ely did not cite free speech in his defense; in fact, he said that if the charges were true, they would have shown him "unworthy of the honor of being a professor in a great university." But his supporters saw an opportunity to argue for a professor's right to off-campus political activity, and on the last day of the hearings, university president Benjamin Andrews told the Board of Regents that if they fired Ely it would be "a great blow at freedom of university teaching in general and at the development of political economy in particular."[18]

The board agreed. Its September 1894 report not only exonerated Ely but sang the praises of academic freedom as a necessary component of "a university with over one hundred instructors supported by nearly two millions of people who hold a vast diversity of views regarding the great questions which at present agitate the human mind." As regents, they said, "we could not for a moment think of recommending the dismissal or even the criticism of a teacher even if some of his opinions should, in some quarters, be regarded as visionary."[19]

The report's rhetorical climax was a sentence that, 16 years later, was reproduced on a plaque that sits at the entrance to the university's main administration building. "Whatever may be the limitations which trammel inquiry elsewhere," the regents proclaimed, "we believe that the great State University of Wisconsin should ever encourage that continual and fearless sifting and winnowing by which alone the truth can be found."[20] The regents thus "turned a trial in which academic freedom had scarcely been mentioned into an occasion for a bold assertion of the right of free inquiry and expression."[21] Ely was at best a reluctant hero of the proceedings: he accepted the assumption that the regents had the power to censor his views and off-campus activity, and he soon began to retreat politically.

Professor Ross and Mrs. Stanford

Other Ely acolytes had academic-freedom crises. John Commons, one of his star students when Ely was a professor at John Hopkins, went on to lose jobs at Indiana and Syracuse Universities in the 1890s because of his reformist views. Through Ely's efforts, Commons joined the Wisconsin faculty in 1904.[22] Edward Ross, another protégé from Hopkins, was hired by Stanford but offended the widow of the university's founder, who now constituted a one-person board of trustees. Ross defended socialism, supported public ownership of utilities, and railed against big companies' use of immigrant Asian labor in terms redolent with the racist stereotypes that were common even among progressives at the time. "Perhaps Leland Stanford, had he been alive, would have tolerated the iconoclasm of the professor," write Richard Hofstadter and Walter Metzger, authors of the major history of academic freedom in its early years, "but his wife had all the prejudices of her class, and they had been hardened by her ignorance into absolutes." She wrote to the university president, David Starr Jordan, that Ross had scandalously stepped "out of his sphere, to associate himself with political demagogues," "exciting their evil passions" and "play[ing] into the hands of the lowest and vilest elements of socialism": "I must confess I am weary of Professor Ross, and I think he ought not to be retained at Stanford University."[23]

Jordan protested that Ross was "one of the best teachers" and neither "an agitator nor a socialist," but Jane Stanford was adamant and, in 1900, forced Ross to resign. Ross issued a public statement; the press picked up the story, and the activist professor soon became a national symbol of academic resistance to what one student of the case aptly called "the arrogance of economic power."[24] Even the *Nation*, which had set off the campaign against Richard Ely six years before, was quiet, and its owner at the time, the *New York Evening Post*, which in 1894 had campaigned to stamp out socialism in the universities, supported Ross.[25]

Stanford now faced a crisis. An esteemed senior professor, George Howard, called Ross's firing "a blow" to academic freedom and therefore "a deep humiliation to Stanford University."[26] When Mrs. Stanford forced Jordan to fire Howard as well, seven more professors resigned in protest, among them philosopher Arthur Lovejoy. Lovejoy went on to help found the AAUP, largely as a response to the continuing interference by trustees with the free speech of scholars. Although an alumni committee attempted to calm the waters by reporting that Ross was dismissed for unprofessional behavior, an outside report by a committee of leading economists came to the opposite conclusion.[27]

With Ely's help, Ross was eventually hired by the University of Wisconsin, where he remained controversial. In 1910, the feminist and anarchist Emma Goldman spoke at the campus Socialist Club and the local YMCA. Ross was accused of anarchism by local newspapers and, as he put it, by "certain financiers and capitalists on the Board of Regents" after he announced Goldman's lecture to his classes and escorted her around the campus.[28] This time, he kept his job and, unlike Ely, did not move politically rightward with the passage of time: his research and writings provided a basis for later laws on factory safety, child labor, maximum working hours, and minimum wages.[29]

Scott Nearing and the AAUP

Scott Nearing, since 1906 an economics professor of at the University of Pennsylvania's Wharton School of Finance and Commerce, was among the best known of the Progressive era's muckraking intellectuals. The left-wing critique of society propounded by such scholar-activists as Nearing had by 1915 gained some traction among both working- and middle-class Americans. The socialist periodical *Appeal to Reason* commanded a national circulation of more than 700,000; Socialist Party leader Eugene Debs received nearly a million votes for president in 1912—6% of the total; socialists won state and local offices; Wisconsin and New York elected socialists to Congress.[30] In New York City, socialism was a means of "transition and acculturation" for immigrants, writes the critic Irving Howe, especially for Jewish workers. At union meetings, they learned how to make speeches, to conduct meetings, and to follow *Robert's Rules of Order*.[31]

Nearing was an immensely popular teacher: his introductory economics course, with more than 400 students, was the largest class in the university.[32] He had just left Philadelphia for summer vacation in June 1915 when his secretary called to tell him of a letter from the provost advising that his contract would not be renewed. No reason was given, but the decision was not a surprise: Nearing had recently been active in drives for decent wages and an end to child labor, and a group of business-oriented alumni had been pressuring the university's Board of Trustees for the past several years to fire him on the

The young Professor Scott Nearing.
(University of Pennsylvania archives)

ground that his "unsound" and "radical" views "tended to arouse class prejudice" and to lead to "fallacious conclusions."[33]

Nearing, like Edward Ross before him, was an excellent publicist: he
quickly sent a mailing to about 1,500 newspapers and prominent individuals.
The summary dismissal of a well-known activist intellectual, and the outraged reaction among faculty and students at Penn and around the country,
inspired a media blitz that lasted several months.[34] The *World*, the Pulitzer
paper in New York, wrote satirically that the trustees would do well "to state
with absolute clearness the rules to be obeyed" in the future; "it is not yet
too late to bar all intruders who may incline to offenses against the only true
Pennsylvania faith."[35] The *New York Times* bucked the trend with a more conservative reaction, editorializing that "there is altogether too much foolish
babbling on the part of some professors."[36] Hundreds of telegrams went to
the governor urging him not to sign a $1 million appropriation bill for the
university until the trustees had satisfied him that their dismissal of Nearing
was not a payoff for the votes of state legislators beholden to businesses that
used child labor.[37]

The firing of Scott Nearing triggered nationwide debate on the nature of
universities. Were they like businesses, which could hire and fire employees
at will, or was there some other sort of relationship, necessitated by the principles of higher education? Nearing did not regain his job, and after a stint as
a dean at the University of Toledo, Ohio, which was cut short by his opposition to America's entry into World War I, his teaching career was over.[38] But
the incident, and similar ones at state universities in Utah, Colorado, and
Montana, pushed the newly organized AAUP into investigating the case and

drafting its founding document: the 1915 "Declaration of Principles on Academic Freedom and Academic Tenure."[39]

The idea of a national organization that would unite professors across disciplines had been brewing at least since Stanford had fired Edward Ross in 1900. But not much happened until 1913, when a joint committee of the American Philosophical Association and the American Psychological Association undertook an investigation of the forced resignation of a Lafayette College professor but was unable to get any cooperation from the high-handed president. The snub, write Hofstadter and Metzger, "underscored the inability of the learned society to muster enough power and prestige to persuade administrators to cooperate with it."[40]

When 18 Johns Hopkins professors sent out a call for a conference to discuss the creation of the AAUP, their main goal was to establish that academics were not like other employees, and universities were not simply business corporations.[41] Professors from seven universities—Clark, Columbia, Cornell, Harvard, Princeton, Wisconsin, and Yale—answered the call and came to the organizing meeting. Among them were John Dewey and Charles Beard of Columbia, Richard Ely of Wisconsin, and Arthur Lovejoy, now of Johns Hopkins. There followed a broader invitation, still to an élite list; this "was not, as first envisioned, 'one big union for all,' but a union of the aristocrats of academic labor."[42]

The AAUP was almost immediately inundated with calls for help from professors under siege by hostile administrations. Subcommittees were sent to different campuses to investigate complaints, while a new "Committee A" of nine top professors, led by Columbia's Edwin Seligman and including Lovejoy, Ely, and Harvard Law School's Roscoe Pound, went to work drafting a document that would set out basic principles of the academic profession.

The resulting 1915 "Declaration of Principles" explained that while there are some institutions of higher learning that are dedicated to promoting particular beliefs and are not designed "to advance knowledge by the unrestricted research and unfettered discussion of impartial investigators," a true university "is a great and indispensable organ of the higher life of a civilized community." Its trustees therefore "have no moral right to bind the reason or the conscience of any professor." Once appointed, "the scholar has professional functions to perform in which the appointing authorities have neither competency nor moral right to intervene. The responsibility of the university teacher is primarily to the public itself, and to the judgment of his own profession."[43]

There followed an explanation of academic freedom as the defining characteristic of a university. The explanation derived from Germany, where thousands of American professors, including Ely, had studied. They had come home to create graduate schools on the German model, introducing such novelties as lectures, seminars, libraries, and laboratories and promoting the German idea "that knowledge can be advanced only in a climate of absolute intellectual freedom."[44]

The Germans defined academic freedom by two interlocking concepts: *lehrfreiheit* (freedom to teach) and *lernfreiheit* (freedom to learn). The fledgling AAUP, focused as it was on professors, mentioned *lernfreiheit* only in passing.[45] As for *lehrfreiheit*, the committee proposed a three-part definition: "freedom of inquiry and research," "freedom of teaching within the university," and "freedom of extramural utterance and action."[46] It considered this third aspect, "expression outside university walls," to be the most vulnerable: all the cases it had recently investigated involved, "at least as one factor, the right of university teachers to express their opinions freely outside the university or to engage in political activities in their capacity as citizens."[47]

The declaration was cautious, though: "there are no rights without corresponding duties." Thus, scholarly writings "must be the fruits of competent and patient and sincere inquiry, and they should be set forth with dignity, courtesy, and temperateness of language." Classroom teaching, when touching on controversial subjects, should "set forth justly, without suppression or innuendo, the divergent opinions of other investigators." And professors, "in their extramural utterances, . . . are under a peculiar obligation to avoid hasty or unverified or exaggerated statements, and to refrain from intemperate or sensational modes of expression."[48] But the basic principles remained beneath the caveats, and it followed, for the AAUP, that scholars must not only be free to research, write, and teach without ideological constraints; they must also participate in university governance and, in particular, decide who among the rising generation is qualified to join their ranks.

In the first years of the AAUP's existence, the great national question was whether the country should remain neutral or join the world war then decimating Europe. President Woodrow Wilson was reelected in 1916 on the slogan "he kept us out of war" but soon changed his mind and, to persuade the public, created a formidable propaganda machine to demonize the German enemy and to heighten enthusiasm for the battle. This pioneering approach to molding public opinion was so successful that by 1917, when the United States entered the war, even the mildest expression of dissent was considered disloyal, if not treasonous. Under the 1917 Espionage Act and amendments passed by Congress the following year (the Sedition Act), pacifist leafletters, obscure revolutionists, and anti-war activists including Eugene Debs were jailed for their dissenting opinions.[49]

The conflict between anti-war attitudes and mounting war hysteria proved particularly intense in New York City, where, as Irving Howe recounts, the 1917 mayoral campaign of the socialist Morris Hillquit triggered a backlash among some of the city's "newly prosperous and respectable" Jews, who feared that they "would be smeared as radicals and war 'shirkers.'"[50] Hillquit did well despite the backlash, although he lost the election. But conflicts over radicalism and patriotism were to be a continuing theme in the Jewish community and resurfaced with a vengeance in the 1950s when inquisitors like the Board of Education's Saul Moskoff locked horns with left-wing Jewish teachers.

Professors were hardly immune from World War I fever. Although there were notable exceptions, such as Columbia anthropologist Franz Boas, academics were among the war's greatest enthusiasts. In Wisconsin, Professors Ely and Commons urged "the dismissal of any professor unwise enough to oppose, criticize, or in other ways undermine the nation's war effort."[51] In New York, Columbia University president Nicholas Murray Butler announced that "what had been tolerated before becomes intolerable now" and promised the prompt firing of any professor who "opposes the effective enforcement" of the laws or who "acts, speaks, or writes treason."[52]

Carol Gruber, whose book *Mars and Minerva* details the challenges to academic freedom during World War I, comments that "although scholars have treated [Butler's] pronouncement with the disapproval it deserves, they have not noted that the initiative for it came in part from faculty members." Butler acted on the recommendation of a faculty committee headed by AAUP co-founder Edwin Seligman that investigated the indictment of three students for publishing a draft-resistance pamphlet. The committee criticized fellow professor Henry Dana for participating in a meeting of an anti-militarist organization and warned, "If in the future . . . [Dana] or any other colleague of ours acts in any way contrary to the letter or spirit of the President's declaration, we shall be prepared to bring him before the authorities of the university for necessary discipline."[53]

Dana and a colleague were subsequently fired for violating President Butler's ban on dissent; Charles Beard, one of the country's most influential historians, resigned from Columbia in protest, and other objecting faculty, including John Dewey and Franz Boas, asked the newly formed AAUP to investigate. But the AAUP turned out to be equally infected by wartime intolerance. Responding to numerous complaints of university retribution for anti-war views, the AAUP's report "Academic Freedom in Wartime" attempted to distinguish between discussion of policies not yet adopted by the government, which should be permitted, and statements that might

undermine the draft, the military, the conduct of the war, or even volun-
teerism in support of the war, which should be grounds for firing any professor who uttered them. The report's few efforts to strike a free-speech balance
were far outweighed by its insistence on suppression and punishment of pacifist or other anti-war views. As for professors of "German or Austro-Hun-
garian birth or parentage," the AAUP proposed that to avoid any suspicion
of disloyalty, they should "refrain from public discussion of the war; and, in
their private intercourse with neighbors, colleagues, and students, avoid all
hostile or offensive expressions concerning the United States or its government."[54] Gruber observes:,

> An association that constituted the sole organizational defense of academic
> freedom might reasonably have been expected to believe that its function
> was to protect professors from anticipated assaults, and not to go even
> further than the state in limiting their freedom. In effect, the AAUP was
> opening the floodgate of repression, or at least was stepping aside, when
> it might have been expected to make every effort to hold back the water.[55]

At Wisconsin, as at Columbia, the administration went to extremes. The university president was on the defensive after a Wilson administration official
criticized the campus ambiance as insufficiently patriotic. He wrote Wilson an
eight-page rebuttal, "describing in detail the wholehearted and total mobilization of the university community in support of the war." Professor Ely delivered a patriotic speech that maligned all Germans, while Commons worked
to defeat the socialist Victor Berger's 1918 Senate bid "by crudely implicating
Berger in treason."[56] In 1918, Ely became president of the Wisconsin Loyalty
Legion's Madison chapter, whose purpose was to undermine the state's popular senator, Robert La Follette, because he opposed the war and the repressive
Espionage Act. A university committee, responding to charges that the faculty's failure to repudiate La Follette was a stain on its patriotism, circulated a
petition denouncing the senator as a traitor; 90% of the faculty signed.[57]

La Follette survived, but most dissenting politicians—and most dissenting
professors—were silenced. The repression not only intimidated academics
and other opinion leaders; Gruber believes that it prolonged the bloodiest
conflict to date in Western history. American professors "evaded the issue
of the real savagery and horror" of the war—"the still-stunning casualties of
the stalemated, technological conflict—and succumbed to the easy path of
outrage and indignation against Germany."[58]

Some professors abandoned scholarship entirely. Through a "National
Board for Historical Service," historians created syllabi that were essentially

coarse propaganda—unbalanced, inaccurate, and emotionally manipulative, with "grossly oversimplified arguments and crudely drawn historical analogies."[59] Ten years after the war, *American Mercury* magazine documented how historians had propagated "the most violently distorted fulminations of war propagandists" and "presented example upon example of witch hunts conducted against professors who were suspected of disbelief in the Holy Cause, witch hunts which had been undertaken with the sanction of their colleagues" and the AAUP.[60]

The First Red Scare

Only a few prophetic souls considered the First Amendment a wedge against political repression in the years before World War I,[61] but the harsh criminal prosecutions and long prison terms handed out to anti-war dissenters—some as long as 20 years—led to the Supreme Court's first pronouncements on the subject. Free speech did not prevail in these early cases, but Justice Oliver Wendell Holmes, Jr.'s "clear and present danger" test for measuring the validity of government censorship created a standard, at least in theory, against which to measure repression in later years.[62] Academic freedom was not viewed as a First Amendment concern, largely because of the legal principle, also memorably articulated by Holmes, that "there are few employments for hire in which the servant does not agree to suspend his constitutional rights of free speech as well as of idleness by the implied terms of his contract."[63] According to this reasoning, since a job is a privilege, not a right, the government can impose any conditions on the job that it chooses. This "right-privilege distinction" persisted in constitutional law, but eventually, and largely in response to the Cold War anti-communist purges, the Court finally recognized that depriving people of their jobs for exercising their right to free speech actually does implicate the First Amendment.

Laboring under no such restraints in the years just after World War I, the United States embarked on the most politically repressive period thus far in its history. As early as 1917, New York passed a law that required the removal of any teacher or other public school employee "for the utterance of any treasonable or seditious word, or the doing of any treasonable or seditious act or acts."[64] The law remained on the books until 1967, when the Supreme Court struck it down in *Keyishian v. Board of Regents*.

Political repression intensified in response to the 1917 Bolshevik Revolution. The revolution energized but also splintered the American left, as socialists and other varieties of dissenters either avidly supported it, by creating two separate communist parties in 1919, or remained at a critical distance from the new prophets in Moscow. The Socialist Party fractured and never recovered its pre-war strength. But the new communist parties caused alarm out of proportion to their numbers. (Estimates—probably inflated—of their combined membership ranged from 20,000 to 40,000.)[65] As one historian sums up the national mood, "real or imagined" American agents of the new Soviet government "became a cause for great worry in certain circles," creating a "state of mind that bordered on hysteria."[66]

The New York legislature's contribution to this first American Red Scare was a committee created in early 1919 and spearheaded by freshman state senator Clayton Lusk. Like its successors in the 1940s and '50s, the Lusk Committee stoked fears that communist ideas would infect young people: shortly before the committee's creation, New York City suspended a teacher for alleged Bolshevik teachings, and an ex-FBI agent told a U.S. Senate committee that many universities were hotbeds of sedition.[67] The *New York Times* supported the Lusk Committee with an editorial deploring the alleged existence of "rich, native boudoir Bolsheviki" who were aiming "to poison the young with their fatal teachings."[68]

In March 1919, the Lusk Committee set up headquarters in New York City and began a publicity campaign designed to generate public panic about an imminent revolution. It announced that it had evidence of a well-organized plan by the Russians "to seize the reins of government in this country."[69] Just before May Day, the labor movement's annual celebration, the panic was heightened by the discovery of postal bombs addressed to government officials and prominent capitalists such as J. P. Morgan and John D. Rockefeller. Actual bomb explosions in early June, including one outside the home of Attorney General A. Mitchell Palmer, set the stage for raids by the Lusk Committee in June 1919 and then by Palmer's agents later in the year and early in 1920. Hundreds of federal and state agents swept into immigrant and radical meeting places in these "Palmer raids," rounded up thousands people, and seized tons of documents.[70]

The Lusk Committee initially focused its attack in June 1919 on the Soviet Bureau office in New York City. The new Russian government had established the bureau to encourage trade with U.S. corporations. An impressive list of American firms expressed interest, but the committee's agents raided the bureau's headquarters, arrested its officers, seized its records, and quickly forced it out of business.[71] Buoyed by this success, Lusk and his cohorts next aimed their sights at the Rand School for Social Science, founded in 1906 by (among others) Scott Nearing, Charles Beard, and Socialist Party leader Norman Thomas. The Rand School was a flourishing socialist institution, not revolutionary in any violent sense, with more than 5,000 enrolled students, not

counting evening lectures and correspondence courses. It offered both workers' education and classes for the general public on subjects ranging from
science and philosophy to music, drama, public speaking, and hygiene and
counted among its teaching staff such luminaries as Jack London, W. E. B.
Du Bois, and William Butler Yeats.[72] But the Lusk Committee and the state
attorney general, Charles Newton, wanted it closed; in late June, they staged
what the New York Times called "the biggest raid of its kind in the history of
the city,"[73] then filed suit for an injunction. They relied, among other seized
documents, on an article that proposed an organizing drive among African
Americans, claiming that the school had "a detailed plan for the spreading of
Bolshevik propaganda among Negroes of the South."[74]

Although the tactic of linking civil rights with communism was to be a
continuing theme in American political investigations, in this case it was
counterproductive. The Rand School attracted wide public support, including free legal services from the respected establishment lawyer Samuel
Untermyer, who hated socialism but said that he had "never known anything
as lawless as the Lusk Committee."[75] Untermyer countered Attorney General Newton's motion for an immediate injunction to shut the school with
a request that the case be tried as soon as possible; Newton expected a trial
date in October and was not prepared to fight the case on its merits. After
three more weeks of lurid headlines, the trial date arrived; Newton sought
a postponement on grounds of "new, potentially damaging evidence." The
judge was not impressed and dismissed the case.[76]

The Lusk Committee next turned to legislative hearings and in March
1920 proposed a series of repressive laws. One, aimed at the Rand School,
required anybody conducting a private school in the state (excepting religious institutions) to apply for a license, which could not be granted unless
"the instruction proposed to be given will not be detrimental to the public
interest." Another bill mandated "Americanization" classes at factories and
community centers. A third—the "teachers' loyalty bill"—required all public
school teachers to obtain a certificate of character attesting that they were
"obedient to" and would "support the constitutions and laws" of the United
States and New York and that they were "desirous of the welfare of the country and in hearty accord and sympathy with" both the state and federal governments.[77] The New York Times endorsed the teachers' loyalty bill because it
thought there was "only too much evidence of the success of the Socialists in
imparting their fatal doctrines to young and ductile minds."[78] The Lusk laws
passed by large margins in both houses of the state legislature.

But Governor Al Smith vetoed them, with a stirring statement on academic freedom. It was "unthinkable," he said, "that there should be delegated

to any body of men the absolute power to prohibit the teaching of any subject of which it may disapprove." The legislation would "unjustly discriminate" against teachers, depriving them of "freedom of thought" and limiting the profession "to those only who lack the courage or the mind to exercise their legal right to just criticism of existing institutions."[79] One Smith biographer surmised that the governor's modest origins in New York City's ethnic neighborhoods endowed him with sympathy for exploited immigrant workers and an understanding of the anger and discontent that attracted them to socialism.[80]

Al Smith was narrowly defeated for reelection in the Republican sweep of 1920; the legislature passed the Lusk laws again the following year, and the new governor, Nathan Miller, signed them. But the laws were unpopular and only desultorily enforced; those who were working for repeal occupied a broad political spectrum that included the Catholic bishop of western New York and the state's Episcopal diocese. The Rand School refused to apply for a license; Newton did not seek to close it. Smith was reelected in 1922, on a platform that prominently featured repeal of the Lusk laws; and in 1923, by a close legislative vote, he was able to keep his promise.[81] "Freedom of opinion and freedom of speech were by these laws unduly shackled," Smith said in signing the repeal measures, "and unjust discrimination was made against the members of a great profession."[82]

2

Radicalism and Reaction in the 1930s

The Appeal of Communism

Anti-communist zealotry in the years after World War I weakened but did not crush political and labor radicalism in America. In the early 1930s, with the country suffering a brutal economic depression and with fascism triumphant in Italy and Germany, socialism again began to attract Americans willing to question existing arrangements of power and property. "The reality of soup lines," one historian writes,

> of Hoovervilles that sprang up on the outskirts of countless cities, of families scavenging for food, of an army of young men and women roaming the country in a desperate search for jobs, and of millions living on the edge of starvation while bumper crops rotted in the fields shattered the American dream and the philosophy of self help, and raised for many serious questions about the future of capitalism itself.[1]

Although the Socialist Party of America was also active, it was the Communist Party that organized Unemployed Councils, fought foreclosures and evictions, restored disconnected gas and electricity, and organized hunger marches. The CP was also the first majority-white political organization to campaign for racial equality—"a considerable departure from the Left's traditional lack of concern" with the brutal racism of America, both North and South.[2]

As one young communist recalled, the CP "was the one organization that was really doing something" about racism and poverty: "the campaign against Jim Crow," for example, or "putting people who had been evicted by the city marshal back in their buildings." It was a heady experience to join the movement: Party members had a huge range of conversation and interests. "They could talk about music. There was a Marxist analysis of music. They could talk about art. There was a Marxist analysis of art. They could talk about the international situation."[3]

Joseph Papp, who went on to found New York City's Public Theater and the free New York Shakespeare Festival in Central Park, had a similar experience growing up in Brownsville, Brooklyn, where young communists would fight evictions, often in the dead of winter:

> The word *Communist*—which sounds so reprehensible to many people today . . .—was a beautiful word to me. To me, in the 1930s, it represented a fearlessness, a stand against appalling social conditions, a way of creating a world that was free of injustice. I joined the Young Communist League when I was about 16. . . . I began to speak on street corners and at rallies about conditions on the block and to learn about the theory of communism.[4]

The Party greatly expanded its influence in the mid-1930s by abandoning the dogmatic sectarianism that plagued its early history and building alliances with non-communist progressives, especially in the labor movement. The inspiration for the change was the growing menace of fascism. This new style of coalition politics became official policy when the Seventh Congress of the Communist International in Moscow called for a worldwide Popular Front against fascism. The American CP responded by creating mass organizations or "fronts" that focused on specific issues. Among the most prominent were the National Negro Congress, which initiated battles against race discrimination that would come to fruition in the 1960s; the International Labor Defense, which found lawyers and mounted campaigns to help political prisoners; and, as the Spanish Civil War came to its bloody conclusion, the Joint Anti-Fascist Refugee Committee, dedicated to assisting refugees from the new fascist rule of Francisco Franco. The fronts were effective because hardworking communists joined with liberals, independent leftists, and others who, in the words of the historian Harvey Klehr, were "not willing to join the Party but agreeable to working under Party leadership."[5] CP activists won political office: in the early '40s, two of them, Peter Cacchione and Benjamin Davis, were elected to the New York City Council.

Young teachers in New York were particularly drawn to the Party. Many of them grew up poor and Jewish, with a neighborhood tradition of labor organizing and street-corner socialism. Despite hard work and education, during the Depression most of them had very restricted job options because of both the stagnant economy and pervasive anti-Semitism. Public school teaching was one option for educated Jews, but if they managed to find work with the Board of Education, they were often consigned to labor indefinitely as substitutes earning a fraction of regular teachers' wages.[6]

Harry Adler, a high school shop teacher who was to be suspended by the Board of Education in the early '50s for refusing to cooperate with its anti-communist interrogations, explained to his questioner then that he joined the Party because during the Depression, he saw his family evicted twice and began to ask himself "how it came about that here was I with a skill that I felt was important, usable, and—well, I was unemployed." He finally found work as a substitute, but "there was very little security in the teaching game in those days," so, he said, "I became attracted to a party which in my opinion worked for social measures which were calculated to alleviate such conditions—we now call it social security, unemployment relief, and so on." The interrogator at this 1954 interview was Saul Moskoff, on loan to the Board of Education from the city law office (the Corporation Counsel). Moskoff responded to Adler, "Aren't you giving us the Democratic program?" Adler explained, "Perhaps the Democratic program today, but in those days, this was the program of the Communist Party," while "on the international scene there was a madman let loose in the world, a guy by the name of Hitler, who announced as a clear statement of government policy the extermination of people of my race." Adler was "determined to merge with a group who in my opinion were capable of leading the fight against that sort of menace."[7] The CP meanwhile was loudly proclaiming its patriotism. The hall at its 1936 convention was festooned with portraits of Washington, Lincoln, and Jefferson and a banner touting communism as "20th century Americanism."[8] "At the height of its strength," writes one historian, the Party "drew tens of thousands" to New York City's annual May Day parade "and filled Madison Square Garden with 20,000 cheering spectators."[9]

But the Party had fatal flaws, which grew more glaring as the decade progressed and, paradoxically, as it achieved ever greater success with its Popular Front campaigns. Inspired by high hopes for the presumed socialist utopia in Russia, the CP continued to take direction from Moscow and to change its Party line to conform to Soviet demands. One of the most poignant examples of the delusion that afflicted even sophisticated intellectuals with communist sympathies was a May 1938 "Statement by American Progressives" supporting Stalin's purge trials of former revolutionary comrades, which appeared in the *New Masses* magazine; its more than 100 signers included the writers Nelson Algren, Dashiell Hammett, Lillian Hellman, Langston Hughes, Dorothy Parker, and Irwin Shaw. The statement asserted that "the sheer weight of evidence" established the defendants' guilt and that critics of the trials only "obscure the truth about the achievements of the Soviet Union," which included "the peaceful and progressive solution of the problems of all minority peoples and nationalities within its borders; the magnificent gains in industry and agriculture; [and] the increase in the standard of living" that resulted from forced collectivization, among other policies.[10] With propaganda like this, and unwillingness to confront the crimes of Stalin, American communist sympathizers became easy targets for heresy hunters in the decades to come.

Secrecy was another drawback. Although communists in the 1920s and early '30s were "hardly bashful" about their politics and affiliations, writes Klehr, by the Popular Front period of the late '30s, they "became harder to differentiate. Not only did they try to look and sound like liberals, but many deliberately concealed their true affiliations."[11] The concealment may have been understandable, given the risks of stigma and job loss, but it was out of place in the open spaces of a democracy and left them vulnerable to exposure when the political temperature changed in the late '40s and early '50s.

As the 1930s progressed, and as word spread of the homicidal effects of Stalin's rule, it took increasing levels of either rationalization or denial to remain in the Party. Many people left, but many others remained, committed both to the good causes that the Party supported and to the social and cultural community of fellow radicals that sustained them. One New York activist recalled that rank-and-file communists were too busy with local struggles in trade unions, consumers' groups, and parent-teacher organizations to pay much attention to policy manifestos from Party leaders. "A constant flow of directives from headquarters reflect[ed] the leadership's concern with international affairs, but these were often received with a pious 'Amen—file and forget' by hard-pressed local union or community leaders."[12] Academic communists meanwhile varied in their commitment: the investigation files of New York's Rapp-Coudert Committee in 1940–41 note one ex-communist informer describing an instructor whose "feeble interest in the party" was "exemplified by the fact that during meetings, he would work out mathematical problems instead of attending [to] the speaker"; other members, similarly, showed "greatest loyalty to scholarship."[13]

Local activists and academic Marxists may have tried to ignore the Party leadership's shifting policies and loyalty to the needs of the Soviet state, but the Russians were also trying, occasionally with success, to recruit American communists to pass classified information. What, if any, damage was caused by this ideologically inspired espionage is debatable, but screaming headlines about "Red spy rings" in the late '40s and early '50s obscured the fact that most Party members were neither saboteurs nor spies; they were dedicated reformers who believed that ultimately the inequities of capitalism would be eliminated only by class struggle and a socialist revolution (not necessarily a violent one) but who meanwhile spent countless evenings at meetings, walked miles in street demonstrations, and doggedly distributed copies of the Party's paper, the *Daily Worker*.

This tension between the reformist grass-roots organizing of CP members and the Party leaders' obeisance to directives from Moscow has been much debated by historians of the left. Early histories focused too much on the leadership and its often-shifting Party line; later ones concentrated on social history, community organizing, and the courage and achievements of local activists, sometimes underplaying the fact that the CP was a dictatorial, Leninist organization. For a balanced view, both aspects of American communism need to be acknowledged.[14]

The spread of fascism in Europe had two contrary outcomes in the United States. On the one hand, it inspired homegrown imitations: anti-Semitism peaked in the 1930s, and fascist groups such as the Christian Front prospered, especially in New York City. But it also inspired the Popular Front against fascism, built by the Communist Party. Fascism both foreign and domestic obviously had particular resonance for Jews, and thus for New York City's increasingly Jewish teaching ranks. Teachers and professors joined in opposition to Franco's victory in Spain and worked to help Jews—sometimes their own family members—who were fleeing Germany and eventually other parts of Nazi-occupied Europe. Although there were few Jews among the first generation of communist professors, by the late '30s, writes the historian Ellen Schrecker, "at least half if not more of the Party members in the academic community were Jewish."[15]

The New York City Teachers Union (the TU) exemplified the spirit of 1930s radicalism. Founded in 1916 by Henry Linville and Abraham Lefkowitz, the union initially counted only about 600 members; most of the city's 20,000 teachers, even those sympathetic to labor organizing, worried that joining a union might undermine their professional status.[16] But salaries and working conditions in the city schools were sufficiently miserable that, by 1940, the TU—Local 5 of the American Federation of Teachers (the AFT)—was the largest organization representing teachers in the city, with 6,034 members, and one of the most dynamic and unusual teachers' organizations ever to emerge in America.[17]

The TU was attractive because it fought such exploitative Board of Education practices as keeping qualified teachers in a long limbo as underpaid substitutes, without job security or benefits. It tackled what its first historian, Celia Zitron, aptly called the "caste system of education,"[18] including racism in textbooks and staff assignments, and it pushed for community participation in school reform. It worked with literary celebrities like Langston Hughes and Richard Wright to improve the curriculum so that it would emphasize rather than denigrate African American achievements. Another author concludes that the TU thus "forced city officials to pay attention to problems they preferred to ignore, solutions to which were both fiscally and politically expensive."[19] Teachers also took direct action: half a century later, one of them told documentary filmmakers that she was so outraged by a history textbook that depicted "happy slaves" that she gave her pupils scissors to cut out the offending pictures.[20]

In 1935, Local 5 organized the Harlem Committee for Better Schools; Alice Citron, an elementary school teacher, community activist, and dedicated communist, was a founding member. She later became one of the first to be purged by the Board of Education for refusing to cooperate with Saul Moskoff's investigation. The Harlem committee fought to improve deplorable conditions in neighborhood schools and persuaded the board to promise five new school buildings—the first in Harlem since 1900. Although U.S. entry into World War II caused a halt in construction, the TU's Harlem Committee continued to push for replacement of racist textbooks and to sponsor courses for teachers on African American history and race relations, while other activists organized street demonstrations and public meetings around such issues as evictions, unemployment, and defense of the Scottsboro Boys, young African Americans falsely accused of rape and facing execution in Alabama.[21]

The radical activism and militant tactics of a growing "rank and file" caucus within the TU caused conflict with Linville and Lefkowitz, the union's founders. After losing a fight for control in 1935, the two led a walkout of about 700 members and formed the rival Teachers Guild. They then lobbied the AFT, unsuccessfully, to expel the TU and to affiliate with the Guild instead.[22] The TU continued to thrive; by 1937, it was big enough to justify the creation of a separate Local 537 of the AFT, the College Teachers Union. A battle for control followed, which the communists won.[23]

Bella Dodd, a former instructor at Hunter College, the women's branch of New York City's free municipal college system, was the TU's legislative representative in the late 1930s and early '40s. Dodd worked on bread-and-butter issues: the exploitation of substitute teachers in the primary and secondary schools, the pitiful salaries paid to instructors at the college level. She was soon drawn into the communist movement, where, as she later recalled, she could mingle with "real proletarians—longshoremen, painters, plumbers, shipping clerks, and sailors." She "marveled at the sacrifices" made by her communist friends, who "would go without lunch to buy paper and ink and other items for propaganda leaflets. . . . It was an infectious thing, this comradeship, for so often it helped [those] in dire need."[24]

May Day parade, 1938, New York College Teachers Union contingent.
(Morris Schappes Photographs Collection, Tamiment Library, New York University)

Dodd was a brilliant organizer of mass protest meetings, telegram campaigns that inundated the offices of state political leaders, and delegations of teachers to the state capital in Albany.[25] By the late '30s, she had helped build Local 5 and its higher-education counterpart, Local 537, to a membership of about 10,000. She later estimated that the Communist Party, at its peak, had 1,000 members inside the Teachers Union.[26] Although Dodd's memory was not always reliable once she was ousted from the Party, experienced a religious conversion, and became an anti-communist witness for Red-hunting committees in the 1950s, there is no question that the TU was the most significant teacher organization in the city.

But nagging questions about the Moscow purge trials, with their lavish coerced confessions, and then, in August 1939, Stalin's turnaround from Popular Front anti-fascism to a non-aggression pact with Hitler, disillusioned communist sympathizers and sparked a new Red Scare. In 1941, after New York's Joint Legislative Committee to Investigate the Educational System—more commonly known as the Rapp-Coudert Committee—had generated sensational headlines about communist leadership in the union and its allegedly nefarious effects on youth, the Teachers Guild finally persuaded the AFT to expel the TU on charges of communist domination and practices "inimical to democracy." Two years later, the TU became Local 555 of the United Public Workers, a left-led member of the CIO that was soon to face its own problems with Red hunters.[27]

Largely in reaction against the Hitler-Stalin Pact, prominent liberals including Columbia's John Dewey formed the Committee for Cultural Freedom, which was to become a haven for anti-communist intellectuals. One of its most active members was the economist Harry Gideonse, who became president of Brooklyn College in 1939. Gideonse was a fierce communist hunter and was to provide lurid testimony to the Rapp-Coudert Committee.

The U.S. Communist Party responded to the Pact by swiftly, and in transparent obedience to Moscow, switching its line from bellicose anti-fascism to isolationist-tinged opposition to American participation in World War II. Although some communists rationalized the Pact as a military necessity, buying time for the Soviet Union to prepare its defense against an inevitable Nazi invasion, others were "devastated by the image on the front page of every newspaper of [German foreign minister] Ribbentrop and Stalin toasting to Hitler's health."[28] The Party lost half its membership in the next two years.[29] As one ex-communist said, "From one day to the next Roosevelt and Churchill were transformed from the saviors of peace and civilization to devilish warmongers."[30] More significantly, the Party lost its alliances with other progressive groups. The Popular Front against fascism that had done so much to legitimize communism in the late '30s was at an end.

The City Colleges

Both the Teachers Union and the Communist Party were active at all four of the city's public colleges—Brooklyn, Hunter, Queens, and particularly City College of New York (CCNY), the oldest of the four. Founded in 1847 as the Free Academy, the first free public college in the nation, CCNY initially occupied an undistinguished building in mid-Manhattan, but in 1895, it moved uptown to a campus in Harlem. It was a combination prep school and college that offered poor and working-class students, including many recent immigrants or children of immigrants, access to higher education on the basis of academic merit rather than religion, wealth, or social connections. The founder, Townsend Harris, proclaimed, "Open the doors to all. . . . Let the children of the rich and the poor take their seats together and know of no distinction save that of industry, good conduct and intellect."[31]

"Children," however, did not include females, and in 1870 Hunter College for women opened in Manhattan. Like CCNY, it was a commuter school: students often traveled long distances from the Bronx, Brooklyn, and Queens. Brooklyn College came next, in 1930, to accommodate the overflow from CCNY. Initially, its 2,800 day and 5,000 evening students attended classes at three crowded buildings in downtown Brooklyn; in 1937, a beautiful campus opened in Flatbush, deep inside the borough. The students were overwhelmingly first-generation Americans and overwhelmingly Jewish; about 40% of their parents had not progressed beyond elementary school or had never been to school at all.[32] Queens College, like Brooklyn coeducational, opened in 1937 on a leafy site that had previously been a home for delinquent boys.[33]

Although the Free Academy began as a predominantly Protestant institution with some German Jews, the student body became predominantly Jewish as immigration accelerated from eastern Europe. Economic necessity, anti-Semitic quotas at private colleges, and the drive for higher education in Jewish culture all contributed to the unique demographic.[34] Some of the most brilliant students in the country attended City College, generating such nicknames as "Harvard of the Proletariat." Oscar Shaftel, who attended as an undergraduate and went on to a PhD at Harvard, recalled the social difference: CCNY was "rowdy," and students would brazenly challenge professors. Intellectually, "a teacher took his life in his hands at City College."[35]

Alongside brilliant scholarship and intellectual aggression came political radicalism. Although most of the students were not politically active (many were too busy with school and part-time work), there were sufficiently large contingents of differing left-wing sects—among them, Trotskyists, Stalinists, democratic socialists—to generate heated daily debate in the alcoves of the college cafeteria. In the 1930s, writes one memoirist, City College was a heady mix of impassioned political debate in the "dark, Dostoevskian" alcoves and bristling pursuit of existential questions in the classrooms.[36]

Discrimination in academic hiring meant that young Jewish PhDs also gravitated to the municipal college system or to public school teaching.[37] Some of their parents had been socialists before World War I, and they were ready to carry on the tradition. But CCNY's president in the early '30s, Frederick Robinson, was pompous, rigid, and reactionary: he is most vividly remembered for having attacked students with his umbrella during an anti-ROTC protest in 1933. In 1936, he fired Morris Schappes, a popular young teacher of English and an open communist. Schappes had offended his department chairman by reading a revolutionary excerpt from Percy Bysshe Shelley's poem "The Mask of Anarchy" to his class. (The chairman thought Schappes had been reading Marx.) About 500 students staged a sit-in to protest Schappes's dismissal, and 2,000 participated in a mock funeral for academic freedom. Faculty protested too; Robinson fired 12 of them, all union activists or members of the college's Anti-Fascist Association. The Board of Higher Education, led by Ordway Tead, reinstated Schappes and 12 others.[38] It was a victory that Edward Bemis or Scott Nearing would have relished, but the board's defense of academic freedom was not to survive the 1940–41

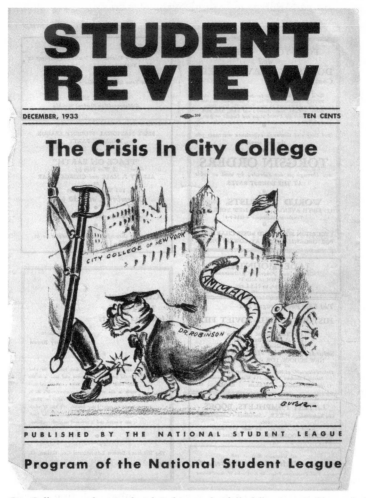

City College president Frederick Robinson dutifully following a jackbooted officer and wagging the tail of Tammany Hall: cartoon on the cover of the *Student Review*, December 1933. (Archives, The City College of New York, CUNY)

assault of the Rapp-Coudert Committee, and Schappes was to become the committee's most strenuously punished witness.

The BHE, meanwhile, was looking for a new Brooklyn College president who would be a strong leader and boost its academic standing. Harry Gideonse, then teaching at Barnard, had excellent credentials but was known as a scrapper, having crossed swords with University of Chicago president Robert Maynard Hutchins while teaching economics there in the early '30s.[39] Gideonse made his anti-leftism clear before the BHE hired him: as he told the board, he did not intend "to live in peace with the Teachers Union." It would be "open war from the word go, and it will get worse as time goes on."[40] Evidently, this was just the combination of brains and combativeness that the BHE was looking for: the previous president, William Boylan, had been ineffectual, and ill for much of his tenure.[41]

One of Gideonse's goals was to erase what he perceived as the insular, uncouth culture of the Jewish students. As one of his deans, Thomas Coulton, wrote in an ideologically charged history of the school that reads as a brief for Gideonse, the student body "lacked as a group many of the opportunities afforded most students on other American campuses to acquire social poise and broad cultural experience"; the pressures from home "to succeed scholastically emphasized the importance of intellectual values" at the expense of "recreational or social opportunities." Gideonse thus "understood that even if the barriers of discrimination were to disappear, the Brooklyn College student would still have to become less insulated and more cosmopolitan in outlook."[42] The wording was indirect, but the coded language evoked traditional anti-Semitic attitudes: intellect would not be enough for success; one needed social graces, as defined by mainstream America.

Once in office, Gideonse sought to undermine the influence of those he believed to be communist sympathizers on the editorial board of the *Vanguard* student newspaper, in student government, and in organizations such as the American Student Union (the ASU). *Vanguard* had begun in 1936 while the college was still located in downtown Brooklyn; its first editorial announced its progressive orientation, "for Brooklyn College students have shown that they realize the necessity of working for the establishment of peace, the maintenance of academic and civil freedom and adequate educational facilities for all."[43] Gideonse, arriving three years later, was unable to distinguish these sentiments from communist manipulation; he carried on a running battle with *Vanguard*, and in 1950 he was to shut it down entirely.[44]

Although the communist contingent at Brooklyn College probably never numbered more than 75 students, Gideonse felt they had inordinate influence because of their hard work and energy.[45] In the spring of 1940, his administration scheduled student government elections to take place during class time so that a larger percentage of students would vote and thus dilute the prominence of the left-wingers. The ASU and the Peace Continuation Committee organized a largely unsuccessful class walkout and peace demonstration an hour before the balloting began; both groups were punished with suspension for the rest of the semester. Subsequent protests escalated to picketing of Gideonse's house and incidents of harassment that he soon vividly described to the Rapp-Coudert Committee.[46]

It was the radical students who initially recruited teachers into the Communist Party at Brooklyn College. Their first convert was philosophy instructor Howard Selsam, who agreed to become faculty advisor to the ASU in 1933. Selsam, with English teachers Frederic Ewen and Bernard Grebanier, had already formed the campus Association of Instructors, Tutors, and Fellows, representing the young scholars who labored at the bottom of the professorial hierarchy and pay scale. Both Ewen and Grebanier soon joined the Party as well.[47] The communists on the faculty were a small group: probably, not more than 30 were CP members or close to the Party ideologically even at its peak in the late '30s.[48] But they worked tirelessly to alert the public to the dangers of fascism (at least before the Nazi-Soviet Pact), and their weekly campus newspaper, the *Staff*, was Gideonse's most vocal critic.[49]

Thomas Coulton's history of the college acknowledges that some of the communists "were teachers of unique and outstanding ability" and that "all of them refrained from spreading overtly propaganda in their classrooms," but he says their influence was nevertheless insidious because they came in contact with students outside class and encouraged them "in creating disorders, in disregarding regulations," and even in "abuse and vilification, innuendo and scandal mongering."[50] Coulton does not document these charges, and one person's vilification may be another's passionate argument, but there is no question that the attacks on Gideonse were not always polite. (Neither were his responses.) The regulations that radical teachers allegedly encouraged students to disregard, moreover, were created by an administration determined to crush free speech by left-wingers on campus.

Gideonse recognized that Brooklyn College had a reputation as "the little red schoolhouse" and that, in part because of its largely Jewish student body, the communist label only stoked the already virulent anti-Semitism in sections of the borough and, indeed, throughout the city. The Brooklyn priest Edward Cullen was fully as anti-Semitic as the pro-fascist national radio personality Father Charles Coughlin.[51] By the beginning of World War II, as one scholar recounts, New York City had experienced "a steady stream of anti-Jewish propaganda, rallies, and even physical attacks on Jewish schoolchildren."[52] Gideonse's biographer notes that the *Tablet*, newspaper of Brooklyn's Catholic diocese, "was as rabidly anti-Semitic as the worst of the German-American Nazi publications."[53] The Christian Front, inspired by Father Coughlin, held viciously anti-Semitic outdoor meetings in the Bronx and Brooklyn; "incitements to pogroms" that caused panic in many neighborhoods; and street riots where demonstrators shouted "Buy Christian," "Heil Hitler," and "Get rid of the Jews" and "parad[ed] near Jewish-owned stores, in order to prevent their business activities."[54] The *Tablet* defended Father

Coughlin, while condemning Jews as "communists, international bankers and war mongers."[55]

It would be simplistic to characterize Brooklyn's political climate in the '30s as solely a Jewish-Catholic battleground: far from all Jews were left-wingers, and although the Catholic Church was far right politically, Catholicism also had a tradition of social reform. But tensions clearly existed: Catholics were Brooklyn's biggest religious denomination, with a population of almost 1.4 million. Jews were second, with more than 800,000; by 1940, "nowhere in the world were more Jews living in one place."[56] And Jews composed the majority of CP membership in New York City.[57]

Gideonse worried about the effect of all this on public opinion and on his students' prospects for good jobs and admission to graduate and professional schools. By 1939, Brooklyn College had 13,700 students, almost 80% of them Jewish and first-generation American. They were, as Coulton acknowledged, "the most markedly able group, intellectually, to be found on any American campus of similar size."[58]

The Roots of Rapp-Coudert

Partly in response to the radicalism of the '30s, and under pressure from patriotic societies and the Hearst press, states and localities throughout the country enacted loyalty oath requirements, especially for teachers. Ten states had teacher oaths in 1931, and 11 more adopted them in the next few years, as the American Civil Liberties Union reported, "in a burst of flag waving."[59] Not all were negative oaths, requiring disclaimers of seditious views and associations; some were worded in affirmative terms, but they were hardly less repressive of dissenting views. In Ohio, for instance, teachers had to swear to "teach by precept and example respect for the flag" and for "law and order."[60]

The ACLU study recounted that since World War I, more laws had been passed "interfering with teaching in public schools than in all our previous history," more college professors had been dismissed or disciplined, and more student newspapers and clubs had been censored. It was "hazardous in most communities for teachers to discuss in the classroom, and often outside," not only communism and Soviet Russia but socialism, pacifism, trade unions, government regulation of industry, dishonest banking, racial equality, or birth control. Yet, as the ACLU and other commenters observed, oaths are "an obvious failure" as a means of detecting disloyalty: "Any really disloyal teacher would take such an oath without qualm. The laws penalize only those conscientious and wholly loyal teachers who object to being coerced into a meaningless declaration which they well know is intended to cripple their independence."[61]

New York's 1934 loyalty oath bill for teachers was typical of the times. Governor Herbert Lehman vetoed it, but the legislature reintroduced it in broader form the next year, now requiring an oath of teachers in not only public schools but private schools operating on tax-exempt land. It was not a negative-style disclaimer oath; it merely demanded that teachers swear support for the constitutions of the United States and New York. But education groups and the ACLU objected because it singled out teachers—precisely the people whose essential function demanded freedom of thought. This time Governor Lehman signed the bill into law.[62] In the 21st century, the "Ives Loyalty Oath" is still required of teachers at private and public schools in New York State.[63]

In early 1936, state senator John McNaboe introduced legislation to fund an investigation of "un-American activities allegedly being carried on by students and faculty in New York schools." McNaboe had been a Red-baiter since the early '30s, when, as a member of a legislative committee investigating pervasive corruption under New York City mayor Jimmy Walker, he had tried to obstruct the investigation by accusing its supporters of socialism and communism.[64] His bill passed, although authorizing $15,000 in expenditures rather than the $150,000 that McNaboe wanted. The McNaboe committee held no hearings that year, but the demagogic senator made "a welter of unsubstantiated charges of a thoroughly sensational and irresponsible character," writes the historian Lawrence Chamberlain. According to McNaboe, Cornell, Columbia, and NYU were all "hotbeds of communism."[65]

More controversy about "un-American" activities erupted in May 1938 after Manhattan borough president Stanley Isaacs hired an open communist, Simon Gerson, as his director of press relations. A coalition of religious and veterans groups petitioned Governor Lehman to oust Isaacs because his hiring choice "flagrantly outraged . . . the patriotism, morals and public decency of American citizens." Among the petitioners was the Catholic activist and lawyer George Timone, later to lead the Board of Education's crusade against suspected communist teachers. Lehman declined to intervene, explaining that the appointment was legal and that he could not be swayed by "public clamor."[66]

Governor Lehman's refusal to force the firing of Simon Gerson prompted the state legislature to pass another loyalty law in 1939. This one denied public employment to anyone who "wilfully and deliberately" advocated the overthrow of the government of the United States or any state "by force, violence or any unlawful means." Unlike New York's 1917 law, which barred "seditious" persons from employment in public education, this one applied to all government workers. Gerson resigned, and the legislation was not legally challenged until 1949, when both it and its 1917 predecessor were incorporated into the Feinberg Law.

To supplement the vigilance of New York's legislators, the first of the federal anti-communist investigating committees descended on the state in 1938. This was HUAC, also known as the Dies Committee, after Martin Dies, its Texan chairman, and it was looking for communists at the city colleges. Many people condemned Dies as a bigot and a demagogue; but he had the power of publicity, and he pioneered the tactics of reckless accusation and sensationalism that were harnessed by his imitators in the 1950s—his successors at HUAC, the many state-level "little HUACs," the U.S. Senate Internal Security Subcommittee (the SISS), initially headed by Patrick McCarran, and the Senate Committee on Government Operations, chaired by Joseph McCarthy.

Three Brooklyn professors testified before the Dies Committee in 1938, describing the college, in the now-familiar metaphor, as a "hotbed of communism." But BHE chair Ordway Tead responded that "the political views of the members of our faculties are naturally diverse"; indeed, differences of opinion on campus "are a wholesome sign of vitality" and provide students "with a useful cross-section of the divergence of views in the community at large." Tead expressed confidence "that the allegations made before the Dies committee are, like the famous premature report of Mark Twain's death, 'grossly exaggerated.'"[67]

Tead's statement was a celebrated, if short-lived, defense of academic freedom. He was a prominent book editor (being on the BHE was a part-time, volunteer job), and his instincts were liberal. Under his leadership, the BHE had enacted new bylaws democratizing the administration of the public colleges by, among other things, giving professors the authority to hire new faculty, to make curricular decisions, and to elect their own department chairs.[68] But Tead could not hold the line a few years later, when the Rapp-Coudert investigation got under way. The BHE was to promise Rapp-Coudert its "full cooperation" and order all municipal college faculty to help the committee achieve its goals.[69] By the time Tead was interviewed for the Columbia Oral History Project in 1964, he failed to mention his earlier liberalism and defended the BHE's anti-communist purges in the 1940s and '50s.[70]

By the late '30s, Congress also was catching up with the states' passion for loyalty oaths. The 1939 Hatch Act, whose main purpose was to bar U.S. government employees from working on political campaigns, also disqualified from federal jobs all individuals who belonged to organizations that they knew advocated "the overthrow of our constitutional form of government by

Teachers Union march, 1945. Legislative representative Rose Russell in the first row; president Sam Wallach to her right. (Courtesy of United Federation of Teachers, UFT Photographs Archive, Tamiment Library, New York University; photograph by Henry Cordes)

force or violence." The next year, a Hatch Act amendment specified that "an affidavit shall be considered *prima facie* evidence" that the person swearing does not advocate, and is not a member of a group that advocates, violent revolution. The Civil Service Commission implemented the amendment by requiring a non-communist affidavit from all employees.[71]

Ironically, the Supreme Court ruled in 1943 that schoolchildren could not be forced to pledge allegiance to the flag in violation of their conscientious beliefs. In the Court's most celebrated explanation of both the danger and inefficacy of forced rituals of loyalty, Justice Robert Jackson wrote that "compulsory unification of opinion achieves only the unanimity of the graveyard."[72] Jehovah's Witness children were the pledge refusers in this famous case, but neither its logic nor its rhetoric were much use, given the political climate just a few years later, to adults objecting to loyalty oaths as conditions of employment.

The culmination of anti-communist action at the federal level came in 1940 with the Smith Act, making it a crime to advocate "the duty, necessity, desirability, or propriety" of overthrowing the government of the United States or any state by force or violence or to organize, to attempt to organize, to be a member of, or to be "affiliated" with any group with such an aim.

This was America's first peacetime law criminalizing the expression of anti-government ideas since the Alien and Sedition Acts of 1798, passed during a time of hysteria over the French Revolution.[73] (The Espionage and Sedition Acts of 1917 and 1918, which severely punished dissent, were wartime measures.) The Smith Act broadly embraced the concept of guilt by association, a departure from the usual assumption under American law that guilt is personal and cannot be inferred simply from a person's membership in disapproved organizations. Guilt by association was to prove a devastating tool of repression in the 1950s.

The same year that Congress passed the Smith Act (1940), the New York legislature charged its Rapp-Coudert Committee, initially created to investigate education financing, to look into subversion in the schools. The catalyst was CCNY's appointment of the British philosopher, mathematician, atheist, and free-love advocate Bertrand Russell to its faculty. New York City's Episcopal bishop, William Manning, sparked the drive to undo the appointment by publishing an open letter in the *New York Sun* quoting Russell's writings on free love, adultery, and "temporary childless marriage" for university students. The Catholic hierarchy and the *Journal American*, the city's Hearst paper, soon joined the chorus, while the Brooklyn diocese's *Tablet* called for an investigation of the BHE and hoped that the appointment would "awaken some of the citizens of this city to the dangers presented by the city colleges."[74] Mayor Fiorello LaGuardia wrote to Ordway Tead, "Why is it that we always select someone with a boil on his neck or blister on his fanny?"[75]

Few issues "caused a greater clamor" in New York than the hiring of Bertrand Russell, writes Lawrence Chamberlain. "Sentiment was by no means unanimous, but the opposition, much more vocal and intense, made the stronger showing."[76] On March 22, 1940, the state senate officially protested Russell's appointment. A few minutes later, Senator John Dunnigan introduced the amendment that diverted the Rapp-Coudert Committee into a sweeping investigation of "un-American and subversive organizations" in New York City schools. Among its many "whereas" clauses, Dunnigan's amendment took aim at the BHE by asserting that the city's educational administrators had sponsored subversion, adhered to "so-called liberal theories and philosophies," and thus attempted to instill "ungodly and un-American traditions . . . in the hearts and minds of the children."[77] The amendment did not define "subversive," and its coupling with "un-American" suggested that Dunnigan, like ideological watchdogs before and since, had in mind much more than acts of sabotage or perversion of the education process. A broader house-cleaning, aimed at left-wing beliefs, was in order. The legislature quickly approved Dunnigan's amendment.

Meanwhile, a Brooklyn woman, Jean Kay, filed suit as a city taxpayer against the BHE, seeking a court order to block the British philosopher's appointment. Her attorney's brief excoriated Russell as "lecherous, libidinous, lustful, venerous, erotomaniac, aphrodisiac, irreverent, narrow-minded, untruthful, and bereft of moral fiber."[78] He added that Russell approved of homosexuality and that his views on marriage and sex would harm Mrs. Kay's daughter (even though she did not attend City College, which only admitted males at this point in history).[79] But the legal irregularities of the case and the lawyer's rhetorical overkill did not stop Judge John McGeehan from granting the requested injunction on the ground that Russell was an immoral person whose views could lead impressionable students to violate state laws against fornication. McGeehan's opinion quoted passages from Russell's books, then declared that although the BHE had "sole and exclusive power to select the faculty of City College," it could not use that power to encourage conduct "tending to a violation of the penal law." Even if Russell did not promote his immoral doctrines in class, McGeehan said, his appointment nevertheless violated "a perfectly obvious canon of pedagogy, namely, that the personality of the teacher has more to do with forming a student's opinion than many syllogisms." Russell was "the more dangerous" because of his outstanding abilities.[80]

McGeehan assured readers that he would not dream of interfering with "'valid' academic freedom" but that academic freedom "does not mean academic license. It is the freedom to do good and not to teach Evil." And just in case his diatribe against Russell would not hold up legally, McGeehan also noted that the man was a foreigner and had not taken a civil service exam.[81]

Although McGeehan's ruling made a shambles of state education law, he was not wrong, in 1940, to ignore the First Amendment as a legal bar to government interference in the hiring of professors. Academic freedom had been in the air at least since the AAUP's 1915 "Declaration of Principles" and was to be a frequent rallying cry of those who opposed the Rapp-Coudert Committee, but it was as yet far from a viable legal concept. Indeed, the Supreme Court was still taking baby steps in its overall approach to the First Amendment. It had been barely 20 years since it applied the amendment's protection of free speech—not very strenuously—to criminal prosecutions and barely 16 since it had said that the amendment limited the acts of not just the federal government but also the states.[82] In 1939, the Court ruled that government officials could not prohibit labor organizers from holding a rally on a city street.[83] It would be a while yet before the courts' understanding of the First Amendment extended to decisions by public employers, including public universities.

Russell's supporters, confident that McGeehan's ruling would be overturned, awaited the BHE's appeal, but Mayor LaGuardia struck the appropriation for Russell's salary from the city budget and told the Corporation Counsel not to appeal. Russell enlisted the ACLU to help him intervene in the case, but McGeehan denied their motion. Two private attorneys then volunteered to represent the BHE, which had voted to pursue an appeal, but the courts said the board had no authority to engage private counsel.[84]

Professors, universities, and public intellectuals across the country were understandably alarmed by the fact that one taxpayer, one crusading attorney, and a bigoted judge could summarily undo an academic hiring decision. The prospect of such a regime stirred even the *New York Times* to comment that "a blow has been struck at the security and intellectual independence of every faculty member in every public college and university in the United States."[85] The poet Allen Ginsberg, years later, had a less lofty summary of the incident:

> Einstein alive was mocked for his heavenly politics,
> Bertrand Russell driven from New York for getting laid.[86]

The AAUP did not respond very forcefully to the Bertrand Russell fiasco, but it did, in collaboration with the Association of American Colleges, issue a new 1940 "Statement of Principles" reiterating that "institutions of higher education are conducted for the common good," which "depends upon the free search for truth and its free exposition." The core of the statement, as in 1915, was a three-part protection for academic freedom: research, teaching, and extramural speech. But now, the AAUP was even more careful than in 1915 to qualify each of the parts. Thus, teachers' "full freedom" in research and writing is "subject to the adequate performance of their other academic duties." In the classroom, they "are entitled to freedom" but "they should be careful not to introduce into their teaching controversial matter, which has no relation to their subject." And as to off-campus activity, professors

> should be free from institutional censorship or discipline, but their special position in the community imposes special obligations. As scholars and educational officers, they should remember that the public might judge their profession and their institution by their utterances. Hence they should at all times be accurate, should exercise appropriate restraint, should show respect for the opinions of others, and should make every effort to indicate that they are not speaking for the institution.[87]

This equivocal language probably reflected a desire to protect the academy by discouraging teachers from provoking angry reactions or running afoul of loyalty laws. But the AAUP's posture, especially as to "controversial matter" in the classroom and "appropriate restraint" in extramural activities, signaled an excessive caution that left professors vulnerable in the next two decades. It was not until 1970, after the heresy hunts of the 1950s had abated and after the Supreme Court had identified academic freedom as "a special concern of the First Amendment," that the AAUP explained in a set of "Interpretive Comments" that the intent of the 1940 statement was not meant "to discourage what is 'controversial,'" because "controversy is at the heart of free academic inquiry."[88]

3

Rapp-Coudert

The Investigation Begins

The Teachers Union was quick to respond to the 1940 law creating the
Rapp-Coudert Committee and directing it to investigate subversion in the
schools. It organized "Friends of the Free Public Schools" and collected more
than $150,000 for a campaign against the pending probe. Bella Dodd set up
booths at state and county fairs, procured free time on radio programs, and
organized "Save Our Schools" community clubs.[1] Ordway Tead, chair of the
Board of Higher Education, co-sponsored an April 1940 rally to protest "current attacks on public education."[2]

But although many liberals like Tead opposed the subcommittee, headed
by State Senator Frederic Coudert, that had been established to run the investigation, by August 1940 it had opened an office and invited concerned citizens to come forward with information. Coudert, the city's only Republican
state senator and a partner in an international corporate law firm, delegated
the details to the subcommittee's chief attorney, Paul Windels. Windels was a
respected moderate who had served as the city's Corporation Counsel under
Mayor LaGuardia, and his presence reassured the New York Times, which
commented, "if further evidence were needed" that the subcommittee "does
not propose a witch hunt, it was provided by the appointment of Paul Windels. . . . If there are subversive activities in the schools, he will find them, but
we can trust him not to invent them."[3]

The Times's optimism was misplaced. Windels began the investigation by
subpoenaing the TU's 6,000-strong membership list. The tactic suggested an
attempt to break the union: in this atmosphere, exposure, interrogation, and
harassment were foreseeable consequences of disclosing members' names. At
the same time, Windels began to subpoena suspects for private questioning,
without the rudiments of due process: the right to have an attorney present, to see the evidence against them, or even to review a transcript. Without
transcripts, witnesses could not correct stenographic errors, and they would
be at considerable disadvantage at the public hearings, not knowing whether

Windels or his associate attorneys were quoting out of context from documents that only they possessed.[4] And despite Windels's claim, on the opening day of public hearings, that he did not intend a witch hunt, the Coudert subcommittee was investigating political beliefs and associations. Windels honed techniques that came to define Red hunting in the late 1940s and early '50s: equating communist beliefs with subversion, conducting inquisitions behind closed doors, and using secret informants of sometimes dubious credibility to expose and stigmatize the people they named as present or former Communist Party members.

Early in the fall of 1940, the subcommittee happened upon an ex-communist professor at Brooklyn College who had recently gone public with articles and letters to the editor criticizing the Party's rigidity, secrecy, and obeisance to Moscow. Bernard Grebanier was a popular English teacher whose Shakespeare courses attracted hundreds of students every year. He had joined the Party in 1935, as he told Windels in private testimony, out of concern over the menace of fascism. But by the end of 1938, he was convinced that whatever the CP said "was a pretext" for supporting the USSR.[5] He now hated Stalinism but apparently did not foresee that he would be used by the subcommittee to attack fellow teachers. As he told the *New Leader* newspaper in late November 1940, just days before he became a public informer, "I have every possible desire to see the Communist Party exposed out of existence as an agent of totalitarianism. But I am not convinced that an investigating committee can do much good to offset the harm involved in making Stalinist martyrs."[6]

Grebanier began by reluctantly naming five Brooklyn College colleagues as CP members in private testimony in October 1940; they were, he said, "the only ones I can speak of with any certainty."[7] A month later, however, after repeating, "I appear with the greatest reluctance," he added a sixth person, and in another private interview in January 1941 he named 23 more.[8] Those named were subpoenaed for interrogations at which a subcommittee member, usually Coudert, would appear briefly; then Windels or an attorney on his staff would be the only questioner present. By the time public hearings began in December 1940, 25 people had refused to cooperate in the private interviews, pending judicial resolution of legal challenges to the procedure.

Frederic Ewen was one of the original five named by Grebanier and, like him, was a popular teacher of literature at Brooklyn College. One of 11 children of an immigrant family from Austria, Ewen had arrived in the United States at age 12, graduated from City College, earned master's and doctorate degrees from Columbia, and started teaching at CCNY in 1923. He moved to Brooklyn College in 1930 and soon was deeply involved in anti-fascist and labor politics—a leader of the college's Association of Instructors, Tutors, and Fellows and later of its TU chapter and a prolific lecturer at the campus English Club, American Student Union, and peace meetings during the period of the Nazi-Soviet Pact.[9] Ewen's FBI files detail his numerous speeches and writings in the 1930s–1950s, noting which communist-leaning organization or journal was the sponsor. The Rapp-Coudert Committee's copious notes indicate that he participated in one May Day parade wearing his cap and gown—garb that did not, however, distinguish him from many academics who marched under the banner of the College Teachers Union.[10]

Grebanier also named his colleague Harry Slochower, a nationally recognized specialist in German literature. Slochower had a PhD from Columbia, had won a Guggenheim fellowship to study in Europe, was listed in "Who's Who of German Scholars," and had been honored at a testimonial dinner given by the American Society for Race Tolerance in 1937, to which Governor Herbert Lehman and Senator Robert Wagner, among others, had sent letters of congratulation.[11] Slochower considered himself a "a philosophical Marxist," wrote for the communist-led journals *New Masses* and *Science & Society*, and was listed as a signer of the 1938 *New Masses* "Statement by American Progressives" in support of the Moscow purge trials, although when he finally testified before Rapp-Coudert, he claimed not to recall having signed.[12]

Slochower, like several others, would falsely deny that he had ever joined the CP, though he later told an interviewer that he had wanted to be thought a member in the 1930s because "they worked like devils" to stop Nazism: "I felt menaced by Hitler and I wanted to be in the vanguard." But he insisted that "by temperament he could not join the Party because he was too much of an individualist to follow a prescribed dogma."[13] After the Nazi-Soviet Pact, he became disillusioned and criticized the Party, which then, true to form, denounced him as a Trotskyist.[14]

Howard Selsam was a third Brooklyn radical named by Grebanier. An assistant professor of philosophy with a PhD from Columbia and three years of experience teaching in Beirut, Selsam made no secret of his Marxist creed but was scrupulous about not forcing it on students. He later recalled what many students told his chairman: "while I made my position clear, I was eminently fair and objective in dealing with theirs."[15] He was to resign in 1941, but not before swearing, in private testimony, that he had never been a member of the CP. Selsam afterward directed the Jefferson School of Social Science, which became a refuge for radical professors.[16]

On December 2, 1940, Windels began public hearings at the Foley Square courthouse in Manhattan. About 100 people awaited admission to the room, which, Bella Dodd complained, was already "packed with friends of the prosecution." TU attorney William Mulligan wanted to cross-examine witnesses but was ruled out of order and was ejected when he tried to make a legal argument. As Senator Coudert explained, the hearings had a "simple, limited objective": to hear the evidence collected by committee staff; there would be no opportunity to question it.[17]

Windels began the hearings by promising "to proceed with complete objectivity," to "refrain scrupulously from presenting gossip, rumor, or hearsay," and to respect free speech, even if used "to advocate political doctrines or social theories which are abhorrent to the vast majority of our people."[18] His assurances satisfied the *New York Herald Tribune* that the hearings would not threaten "true academic freedom" but only "cause concern to those who have abused the trust which the community has reposed in them for the education of its youth."[19] But Windels in the same opening speech attacked communism and communist teachers, who, he said, were under orders to indoctrinate students and thus "help prepare the ground for the day when the proletariat shall rise and seize the government."[20] That the investigation was fundamentally about political beliefs became obvious the next day, as Windels questioned TU president Charles Hendley, who appeared in response to the committee's subpoena but would not produce the union's membership list. "Is it your view of the function of the union that it should engage in the class struggle?" Windels asked Hendley. "We should do all we can to eliminate the class struggle," Hendley replied.[21]

Ex-communist witness Bernard Grebanier's testimony was the highlight of the first two days. He told the committee that in 1927 he was asked to teach at the Brooklyn branch of City College, which subsequently became Brooklyn College; he had been there ever since. In 1935, Howard Selsam recruited him into the Communist Party. He was greatly disturbed by the menace of fascism in Europe, and both "the political situation and the local situation seemed to crystallize around a group of people"—the liberal contingent on campus, in contrast to those who simply "thought of their work as jobs." His CP unit, one of two or three at the college, was highly patriotic: "We were out-democrating the Democrat[ic] Party. . . . It would be wrong to picture any deep plotting involved" in discussions at unit meetings.[22]

Grebanier was gradually disillusioned. Initially, unit members "insisted that the Communist Party was an American party," not beholden to Stalin. But, he said, "I began to perceive, as I thought over the activities of the Party, that everything was oriented in accordance with what was approved in Moscow." So, "in the spring of 1939 I decided I would get out no matter what it meant." He sent Ewen a resignation letter explaining that he had finally resolved to stop being "an intellectual prostitute." The response he received charged him with "Trotskyite ideas," which made him "a counter-revolutionary enemy of the working class"; his punishment was "expulsion from the party and isolation from the revolutionary and progressive movement." Grebanier wrote in reply, "To be 'expelled' after one has resigned is a piece of felicitous humor which only you seem likely to miss," but, "expelled or dismissed, it is a pleasure to be disassociated from a movement that finds the building of a 'democratic front' best achieved through an alliance with Hitler."[23]

Windels asked Grebanier to name the others in his Party unit. "I think, since you seem to have the information, you ought not to ask me such a question," Grebanier pleaded; but he had already named names in private and surely knew that Windels would insist he do so publicly. In addition to Selsam, Ewen, Slochower, and two others he had identified in private testimony—English instructors Murray Young and David McKelvey White—Grebanier now also named Henry Klein, a former tutor in history; Maurice Ogur, a tutor in chemistry; and Millicent Ellis, a former biology instructor and Selsam's wife.[24] Windels introduced documents that he said bolstered Grebanier's accusations, among them an announcement for a course, "Introduction to Philosophy: A Marxist Interpretation," to be taught by Selsam in 1939 at the Workers School, and a pamphlet issued by the college's Karl Marx Society, advertising a lecture by Ewen: "A Marxist Looks at Literature."[25] Windels essayed no distinction between Marxism and CP membership.

Selsam, Ellis, Ewen, Young, Ogur, and Klein spoke to reporters and indignantly denied Grebanier's charges. Selsam called them "preposterous"; Klein, "a downright lie," which showed "the extent to which emotionally disturbed individuals will falsify in order to gain some temporary notoriety for themselves." Ewen said Grebanier bore him a grudge because their joint plan for a book on English literature had disintegrated; Grebanier had then "appropriated" the plan.[26] But the professors did not at this point repeat their denials before the committee. They had already refused to cooperate in the private interviews and, aided by TU lawyers, were challenging the whole Rapp-Coudert procedure in court.

Their boss, Harry Gideonse, took the witness stand on December 4. He accused "an organized minority" of communists at Brooklyn College of using threats and intimidation to control the student body. To disrupt the new in-class student elections, the young rebels had called "an unauthorized so-called peace demonstration"; they blew whistles, ran into classrooms, and posted notices "to deter" other undergraduates from going to class by urging him them not to "'scab on peace,' and similar slogans." The next week,

Gideonse said, after his administration had suspended two campus groups for disrupting classes and holding the unauthorized demonstration, protesters jammed his office phone lines, picketed his home wearing gas masks, and sent intimidating telegrams, including one "which announced a death" and "had a quite startling effect" on his wife, "who was somewhat new to this particular-seeming aspect of public life." The final words of the telegram were that academic freedom had died.[27]

Gideonse urged the subcommittee to find "evidence that would stand up in a court of justice," which he could use to get rid of communist professors. This meant "not just statements of party memberships," since he understood state law to prohibit firing people for their political associations. What he needed was "evidence that teachers abuse their trust and are responsible for, let us say, activities of the sort that you happen to be interested in, and if there is evident misrepresentation of their activity, and things of that sort," it might, "together with other evidence," amount to "abuse of their professional trust and warrant discharge."[28]

The public hearings were front-page news, with huge daily banner headlines in the *Brooklyn Eagle* and only somewhat more restrained reportage in other city papers. The Hearst *Journal American* outdid the *Eagle*, boasting that it had exposed "a far-flung Red network" among teachers in a series of articles months before. A special "final night extra" in its December 3 issue shouted "demand ouster of red teachers," with pictures of Selsam, Grebanier, Ewen, and Klein underneath.[29]

On Brooklyn College's Flatbush campus, students had a range of reactions to the unfolding drama. Some told Grebanier, "we're with you, Professor"; other, "left-wing units," according to the *Eagle*, called him a "stool pigeon," circulated pamphlets, and held rallies.[30] Mostly, another paper reported breathlessly, the students were perturbed, reacting to press reports "like a fighter to a staggered body blow." The bad publicity, they said, "damns them wherever they go." And "although none of the students who gathered in little groups in the corridors of the college buildings at Bedford Avenue and Avenue H, Brooklyn, doubted the truth of Professor Grebanier's statement, almost all were quick to put in a good word for the faculty members named." Ewen, Slochower, and the others "were generally recognized as among the ablest teachers at the college."[31] "These men don't manipulate facts in their classes," one senior said; "they don't distort anything. If political discussions are necessary to the proper understanding of the subjects they teach, they give both sides of the picture." Another thought Grebanier's position "entirely unjustified" because "the men whom he accuses are unquestionably the most brilliant people in school. If the college loses them as a result of this, the loss will be irreparable."[32] *Vanguard* agreed, in purple prose: an editorial above the masthead warned that "free higher education is imperiled" and that "the Judases will meet with fulsome retribution in their own repentant anguish."[33]

After four days, Windels suspended the public hearings, pending resolution of a bundle of lawsuits. One, by the TU, challenged Windels's subpoena of its membership list; a countersuit sought a contempt order against Charles Hendley, who refused to produce it. The TU was also challenging the subcommittee's closed-door interviews, with their conspicuous lack of due process, on behalf of 25 professors and staff who refused to participate. Windels countered by seeking contempt judgments against five of the 25: Selsam, Ewen, Slochower, Ogur, and Young. And a suit by taxpayers was demanding the immediate dismissal of the same recalcitrant professors.[34]

For the rest of December 1940, students, teachers, community activists, and union leaders organized and agitated in opposition to the investigation. A rally drew about 5,000 people in "defense of free public education," according to the TU paper, *Teacher News*, including representatives of 25 trade unions and assorted parent-teacher associations. Among the speakers was one of the ACLU's star cooperating attorneys, Osmond Fraenkel, who told the assembled throng that recent free-speech-friendly court decisions had protected criminal defendants; now those precedents must be applied to people haled before legislative committees.[35]

But the hearings were evidently having their effect. The *Brooklyn Eagle* reported that "a wave of resignations" from the TU had followed Windels's subpoena for the membership list and that hundreds of former members had applied to join the rival Teachers Guild and other associations. But it relied only on reports from the rival groups, and the TU responded that there had been no mass desertion.[36]

No Relief in the Courts

Three related lawsuits came before Judge Benedict Dineen in December 1940: the Brooklyn College professors' challenge to the Coudert subcommittee's private interview process, Paul Windels's contempt case against five of them, and the taxpayer suit seeking their immediate dismissal. Selsam, Ewen, Slochower, Ogur, and Young each submitted an affidavit denying any past or present CP affiliation.[37] Slochower's affidavit averred that he was not really a political person and detailed at length his scholarly accomplishments.[38] The display of erudition did not impress Dineen, who held the five professors in contempt of the subcommittee and ordered them to "purge" themselves by forthwith "testifying in private before Senator Coudert or any other duly designated member."[39] The judge had already dismissed the taxpayers' suit as procedurally improper, although he lauded its goal—to relieve taxpayers from subsidizing professors "who may be attempting to tear down and destroy our American way of life."[40]

A different judge, John Carew, meanwhile rejected the TU's challenge to the subpoena for its membership list and held Charles Hendley in contempt for failing to produce it. In late January 1941, the New York Court of Appeals affirmed those rulings.[41] The privacy of associational membership, particularly when the association is controversial and under political attack, was not yet a recognized legal principle, and the judges were unmoved by *amicus curiae* briefs from several labor unions arguing that the demand for membership lists "was a clear violation" of the Constitution and contravened "the public policy of the State."[42] Given the legal firepower, political stakes, and media attention focused on the case, one might have expected an exacting legal analysis, but the Court of Appeals' decision was cursory: since the investigating committee was duly created and the subpoena was duly issued, there was no legal problem with demanding the names. And the fact that only one legislator—Coudert—was present when Hendley initially appeared and refused to produce the list was also no impediment, since the resolution creating the committee authorized public or private hearings before just one member.[43]

The Coudert subcommittee hailed the Court of Appeals ruling, but its decision to go after a list of rank-and-file union members alienated many of the anti-communist liberals who otherwise supported its work.[44] The TU called the ruling "a dangerous precedent to the whole labor movement" because of the "discrimination, reprisals or publicity which might result from surrender of the lists."[45]

It would be another 17 years before the Supreme Court recognized the danger to free expression and association when controversial groups are forced by hostile state agencies to disclose membership lists. In that 1958 case, it was the Alabama branch of the NAACP that was being persecuted at the height of white racist resistance to the civil rights movement. Justice John Harlan, writing for the Court, explained that "compelled disclosure of affiliation" with groups that advocate unpopular causes can be an effective means of intimidation and repression: "inviolability of privacy in group association may in many circumstances be indispensable to preservation of freedom of association, particularly where a group espouses dissident beliefs."[46]

Windels's legal victories cost him respect among liberals, but he did not alter his tactics. In February 1941, he subpoenaed the College Teachers Union's list of about 1,000 members. The *New York Times* meanwhile reported that a subcommittee investigator had inspected Brooklyn College records "to see whether teachers who have been called before the committee had shown any favoritism to left-wing students."[47] Windels was searching, but he did not produce any evidence of improper conduct.

With the Brooklyn professors' legal options exhausted, they now faced a dilemma. Bella Dodd in her memoir was cagey about what happened next. The TU, she said, "instructed those teachers who were not Party members to appear before the Committee and to tell the truth. But there were hundreds for whom the truth might mean dismissal, and these we decided to protect." For these communist or ex-communist teachers and professors, there were various choices, none of them appetizing. Some of them, Dodd says, "were instructed not to answer questions and to take a possible contempt citation. Some were instructed to resign from their jobs, because we feared the Committee would publicize the facts about their international connections. If the teachers told the truth, they might involve other Party contacts."[48] Dodd was less ambiguous when she testified before the Senate Internal Security Subcommittee in 1952 and clearly said that teachers who were CP members were told to lie under oath.[49]

Most of the professors were not hard-line communists who thought that any interest of the Party, or the fight against capitalist oppression, justified any act, no matter how distasteful or illegal. But despite the morally dubious and legally risky nature of the strategy, they could rationalize perjury on a variety of grounds: resistance to an illegitimate and dangerous political inquisition; well-founded fear that admitting past or present CP membership would mean being forced to "name names" of former comrades; and simple desire to keep the jobs they loved and keep bread on their families' tables. As Stephen Leberstein writes, it was an "impossible dilemma of betrayal on the one hand or certain firing on the other."[50] A lawyer for a professor charged by the University of Washington justified the tactic several years later by arguing that since the investigating committee "was not using legal methods, . . . once in a while you have to fight fire with fire": "I did advise him that he didn't have to tell the truth under those circumstances."[51] But the lies took their toll: not only did they "hasten the demise" of City College activism (in Leberstein's words), but, as the biographer of Alex Novikoff, a brilliant scientist and one of the Brooklyn College communists, writes, although Novikoff believed he was forced into perjury "by an 'illegal' proceeding, he felt a loss of pride and a sense of compromised principles."[52]

The City College Purge

Despite Ordway Tead's co-sponsorship of an early protest rally, the BHE did not hold out for very long against Rapp-Coudert. Even before the start of the public hearings, the board voted to cooperate, and on December 6, 1940, it held a special meeting that, in the none too subtle words of the CP's *Daily Worker*, "in effect gave way" to the demands of the American Legion and other super-patriot groups "for dismissal of teachers whom stool-pigeons chose to call 'Communists.'" The board targeted 21 professors who had refused to cooperate with Windels's private interviews. More than 100 protesting students "crowded in the lobby of the Board meeting room, but all they were permitted to do was send in their protests in written form."[53]

Several days later, the city's chief lawyer, William Chanler, responded to a query from Tead, advising that, yes, professors could be forced to cooperate with the subcommittee, on pain of dismissal if they refused.[54] Just before Christmas, arguing before Judge Dineen for dismissal of the taxpayers' lawsuit that sought the immediate firing of the targeted professors, Chanler revealed that the BHE had now appointed a committee to look into cases of "conduct unbecoming" against those who had refused to cooperate. "We are cleaning house; no need for the courts to interfere," Chanler was essentially saying. Arguing unsuccessfully against Chanler, the lawyer for the taxpayer plaintiffs charged ominously that "the tentacles of this octopus of communism is crushing to death" the youth of the city colleges.[55]

The BHE increased its pressure. In January 1941, it directed all employees "to give such testimony and other information" as the subcommittee requested. In March, it promised to fire any member of a "Communist, Fascist or Nazi group" or "any group which advocates, advises, teaches or practices subversive doctrines or activities." In April, it announced that in addition to the prohibited advocacy of "subversion by force or unlawful means," other grounds for firing would be "participation in activities disruptive of the educational system."[56]

The Coudert subcommittee thus won its tug-of-war with the BHE, but in the end, the purge was not as extensive as it might have been. At Brooklyn College, Grebanier was the targeted professors' only accuser, and because two witnesses were required for perjury to be proved in court, the BHE decided not to charge them with either lying or communism. At City College, it was a different story. Windels's private interviews yielded four ex-communists who were willing to inform; numerous others denied Party membership or, as in the case of Morris Schappes, tailored their testimony so as not to implicate colleagues.

Schappes was a 33-year-old English tutor whose job had been saved five years before by a campuswide support movement and an accommodating BHE.[57] Testifying on March 6, 1941, he readily acknowledged his CP membership from 1934 to the winter of 1939–40, when he resigned because the demands of Party activism left him insufficient time to pursue scholarship that might help him advance beyond his tiny $2,400-per-year tutor's salary. Schappes said there were only three other communists on campus in the late 1930s—one man who was now a Party organizer, one who had died in the Spanish Civil War, and a third who had also gone to Spain and was reported missing. After these three were gone, he edited the communist paper on campus, the *Teacher-Worker*, alone.

The testimony was not credible, even apart from the four ex-communist witnesses who were waiting in the wings, and Windels made his skepticism obvious. "You've not named anybody who could be adversely affected by your testimony, is that right?" he asked. Schappes replied, "There is not anyone else." Windels quipped, "That is quite a coincidence."[58] Schappes's subsequent prosecution on four counts of perjury was the harshest penalty suffered by an ex-communist professor as a result of Rapp-Coudert. Within weeks of his testimony, Schappes was imprisoned in Manhattan's Tombs jail. He was convicted and served 13 months in prison.[59]

Bella Dodd wrote that initial Party instructions had been for Schappes to "refuse to answer questions and take a contempt citation and loss of job"; but then instructions changed: he should admit he was a communist and say that there were only three others (now either dead or gone from the college) and that he had written the campus paper by himself.[60] If she is correct, the Party had no more sense than Schappes in predicting the consequences of such dubious testimony. But Dodd does not give Schappes credit for making his own moral choice: he had decided that, as between perjury and "cooperating with repressive forces" that would subject former comrades "to all sorts of harassment and persecution," the latter was the more grievous sin. Lawyers for besieged radicals, he said, had not yet come up with the Fifth Amendment as a basis for refusing to answer.[61]

The subcommittee's main witness from City College was ex-communist history instructor William Canning, who testified on March 6 just after Schappes. Canning said there had been 40–50 communists on the faculty or staff over the past few years, including a cluster in the registrar's office; he identified 34 by name. Schappes must have been "confused" when he said there had been only four communists at City College, Windels teased. "He just dropped one decimal, and made it four, is that it?" Canning agreed.[62]

Canning painted a dire picture of attempted communist indoctrination in the classroom. But his only example was a professor who thought he had succeeded in planting Marxist ideas after one student complained that he used such terms as "proletariat" and "dialectical materialism" too often. Schappes and others chastised the hapless colleague for his clumsiness: the proper way to indoctrinate was much more subtle—introducing class struggle as a way to understand the history of the 1870 Paris Commune, for example. By contrast, Canning explained, "the bourgeois historian" might regard the Commune "as a more elaborate and complex movement."

The colloquy highlighted the slippery nature of the theory of "indoctrination" on which the Rapp-Coudert investigation hinged. Every history teacher makes an effort to analyze, interpret, and understand the events being studied. A Marxist interpretation, like a "bourgeois" interpretation, may provide useful insights. Although there is undoubtedly a line between propagandizing and genuine teaching, Windels's charge of indoctrination at this point in the proceedings came close to a demand that teachers simply avoid discussing class struggle, analyzing capitalism, or exploring myriad other subjects from a critical perspective.

Canning continued his testimony the next day (March 7, 1941), naming 20 more people currently or recently at CCNY as communists. Four other ex-communists testified the following week, three of them from City College.[63] They largely corroborated Canning's testimony, thereby providing the ammunition that the BHE needed to conclude that the dozens of professors who, over the next few months, denied CP membership were lying and to start proceedings to fire them.

CCNY's acting president, Harry Wright, announced meanwhile that no "confirmed" communist could be "a satisfactory or effective member of the teaching staff" because "they make use of any issue upon which they can lay their hands, . . . issues which are not theirs by right." By way of example, he mentioned "peace issues, . . . issues of liberalism of one type or another."[64] Wright failed to explain why the CP was not entitled to press causes such as peace or civil rights. Indeed, whatever the Party's ulterior motives and myriad failings, it championed causes such as racial equality well before mainstream liberals embraced them.

The CCNY purge was now under way. Thirty-three teachers or staff, almost all from City College, were charged, suspended, and fired in the spring of 1941 for falsely denying CP membership in testimony before the Rapp-Coudert Committee. Among them was Philip Foner, one of four left-wing brothers, all at City College, and a rising academic star. The BHE charged him with being a communist, obstructing the Coudert subcommittee by lying about it, and trying to indoctrinate students. The third charge was dropped early in the proceedings, since there was no evidence to support it. Columbia historian Allan Nevins, who had advised Foner on his PhD, testified that he was an excellent scholar who had never introduced "subversive material" into his work.[65] None of this was relevant to the trial committee, which found Foner guilty of lying before Rapp-Coudert based not so much on the testimony of Canning, whose memory was blurry, but on that of two of the other witnesses, who said they had seen him at Party meetings.

Samuel Woolf, a member of Foner's trial committee, wrote a separate opinion agreeing that he should be fired despite his talents and the fact that he "kept his political leanings apart from his work." As "a non-indoctrinating communist," Foner "was not a threat to the college," Woolf said, but his lying, "either through shame in his beliefs or to save his job, [made him] as unfitted to remain a teacher as the informers who spoke to save theirs." Woolf was thus "as repelled by" the prosecution witnesses' motives for informing as he was by Foner's "motives for concealing."[66] His foreshadowing of the moral swamp that was to engulf ex-communist witnesses in the 1950s shocked the Rapp-Coudert Committee, which expressed "grave doubt as to whether a person [such as Woolf] who expresses such views in an official capacity is fit to hold public office."[67]

Foner continued to write prolifically after his firing. As one admirer summarized, he "tirelessly documented the lives of workers, African Americans, and political radicals,"[68] thus offering an alternative to the view of American history as a triumphalist march of progress. In 1947, while co-managing a publishing house, he wrote the first of what eventually became a ten-volume *History of the Labor Movement in the United States*. He went on to publish books on African American history and on social-reform leaders from Helen Keller to Mother Jones.[69] Shut out from academia for a quarter century, Foner "nonetheless helped lay the basis for the explosion of scholarship in labor and black history" in the 1980s and '90s.[70] In 1967, he was hired by Lincoln University, where he taught until he retired. All this time, the FBI watched him and reported on his family, his travels, and communist-tinged social events held at his country home.[71]

Morris Schappes, although not able to return to academia for many years, also pursued a scholarly life after his conviction and incarceration for perjury. Schappes had grown up in an anarchist-atheist household on Manhattan's Lower East Side, but in prison he began a study of Jewish history and culture that engrossed him for the rest of his life. After his release, he edited the left-wing magazine *Jewish Currents* for four decades and wrote, among many other essays, one titled "Shylock and Anti-Semitism."[72]

The Brooklyn professors, having lost their court fight, testified before the Coudert subcommittee in 1941. Frederic Ewen swore he had never joined the CP or gone to a Party meeting, though he acknowledged reading the *Daily Worker* every few weeks and attending a 1938 meeting sponsored by the Friends of the Soviet Union—a fellow traveler, in other words. Windels asked, "Have you ever heard of the word cell?"[73]

"It is a biological term," said Ewen.

"It has something to do with the Communist Party?"

"I don't know. . . ."

"Have you any knowledge of Communist activity in Brooklyn College?"

"Yes," Ewen said, citing periodicals and pamphlets.

"Have you ever discussed communism with Professor Grebanier?"

"We discussed labor problems." But their friendship cooled after their plans for a jointly authored anthology of English literature ran aground and Grebanier "appropriated the outline," "went to work on the book himself," and got it published with another collaborator.

Harry Slochower, once forced to testify, also told the subcommittee that he had never been a Party member; he was to repeat the denial to Gideonse and members of his Brooklyn College promotion committee later in the 1940s. An exchange of letters with his colleague John Whyte sheds light on how he may have rationalized his denials. On June 29, 1941, he reported to Whyte on a talk with Lauson Stone of the BHE, which was wrestling with the question of how to deal with the professors named by Grebanier. The "general drift," Slochower wrote, was that "they don't regard me as being, or having been part of any 'inner circle,' but at most of having been a philosophic Marxist, with perhaps 'some little tie-up.' Hence, he urged me not to involve myself in any way which might expose me to the charge of perjury."[74]

Whyte replied, "From what I know of Stone and other influential members on the Board, they will try to save as many members on the staffs as possible, but they will be powerless to save those that commit perjury. . . . I can only repeat what I have said to you before, namely, that your chance of being 'saved,' saved for your own future in the profession is, in the vernacular, to 'come clean.'" Then Whyte added, "One can't philosophize membership in a party away by saying that one wasn't really or essentially a communist, since one did not religiously follow the line. That may salve one's conscience, but it won't convince the judges or the jury or the public."[75]

Slochower did not follow this advice. In his July 1941 private testimony, according to a BHE investigator, he "depicted himself as an anticommunist, a scholar and a liberal; an intellectually independent person," and he "inquired why [the] committee felt it was so important whether he was ever an actual

CP member." The questioner "replied it was important to him since his denial would not preserve his good features if other witnesses put him in the party." At this point, Slochower "suggested that the technical act of membership in the CP should not be given any weight if the person involved became a member by accident and has a good record otherwise."[76] He was right, and he was pleading to continue in a profession in which he had already achieved gratifying renown, but when it became clear that none of this meant anything to the committee, he began a pattern of denials that would come back to haunt him.

The Academic-Freedom Debate

Lawrence Chamberlain, later the dean of Columbia's undergraduate college and a scholar hardly sympathetic to communism, concluded that because the Rapp-Coudert investigation was "tarnished by none of the hypocrisy or the buffoonery of its two predecessors" (New York's Lusk and McNaboe committees), its "many shortcomings" were "particularly disquieting. . . . It proceeded from challengeable assumptions, employed procedures that produced unnecessary personal hardship and mental anxiety, and established precedents which weakened traditional principles of civil liberties and academic freedom." The basic problem, Chamberlain said, was that "to argue that a Communist has already lost his freedom of choice and is, accordingly, unable to participate in the quest for truth is to state a thesis that may or may not be true depending upon the individual concerned." More than a million people had joined and left the Party since its founding; "such an unstable membership" undermined the argument that a person who joined had "lost his freedom." If the number of ex-communists so far outweighed the number of current Party members, then "the traditional principle of the free market" was still "the most effective instrument for counteracting communism" in academia.[77]

As for the BHE, Chamberlain—with a large dose of understatement—found its response "not reassuring." The board "was evidently more intent on sloughing off an embarrassing problem than of thinking it through." It timorously accepted the Coudert subcommittee's attack on the TU and its view of subversive activity. The TU's activities may have been annoying, but "most of the objectives which the union was working for were reasonable or at least understandable. Better pay, expanded facilities, greater retirement benefits, and so forth, are not subversive goals."[78]

In the end, more than 500 professors, teachers, staff, and students were interrogated by Rapp-Coudert. Thirty-three were fired or resigned while their cases were pending. An unknown number of others—estimates put the toll at slightly more than 50—were untenured and did not have their contracts renewed, or resigned rather than go through a process of suspension and dismissal whose result was probably a foregone conclusion.[79]

But the larger impact was on the academy. Howard Selsam recalled that most of his colleagues were "fearful even to be seen speaking to one who had been subpoenaed"; the real problem was "not of the loss to themselves or our society of the victims of witch hunts in the academic world"; it was "the effect of such purgations on those who remain[ed]—timidity, servility, seclusion, pre-censored and self-censored teaching and research."[80] The *New Republic* magazine described Rapp-Coudert in similar terms: although it was "too late in the 20th century to be naïve about either the objectives or the tactics of the communists," the drive against those named at committee hearings was far from disinterested; one of its purposes was "to terrorize liberal teachers of every persuasion, in public and private institutions alike."[81] The use of informers, the surveillance of campus activities, the questioning of hundreds of faculty members about their teaching, scholarship, reading habits, and political beliefs threatened all three prongs of academic freedom that the AAUP had identified in 1915. The Rapp-Coudert investigation made it dangerous for scholars of history, literature, sociology, science, or religion to write or teach about Marxism, socialism, the Soviet Union, revolution, and indeed social change of any kind. The subcommittee's questions delved into all these areas. Defenders of the investigation argued that only indoctrination was forbidden, not legitimate scholarship, but the distinction is murky, especially when the investigators have political agendas. The scholarship of a Marxist such as Philip Foner, who was pioneering a radical reinterpretation of history, was, to those who were on the other side of the ideological divide, subversion and heresy. Although it was to be another decade before any Supreme Court justice mentioned academic freedom in a Court decision, the Rapp-Coudert investigation put the issue on the front burner of American politics.

By 1942, Rapp-Coudert's fireworks were petering out. Hitler's invasion of the Soviet Union in June 1941 put a violent end to the Nazi-Soviet Pact and transformed Russia into America's likely ally. Once the United States entered the war in December 1941, there was no longer a political advantage in churning up panic about communism. But the issues raised by Rapp-Coudert over the meaning of academic freedom would resurface when the subcommittee's heirs emerged with new energy after the war.

PART II

Teachers and Free Speech

4

The Board of Education and the Feinberg Law

Postwar Purges

In March 1946, British prime minister Winston Churchill delivered his famous "iron curtain" speech in Fulton, Missouri. Churchill warned that an aggressive, totalitarian Soviet Union already controlled eastern Europe and that communist "fifth columns" in Italy, France, and other Western democracies "constitute[d] a growing challenge and peril to Christian civilization." He urged military preparedness—not appeasement.[1] The post–World War II Cold War had begun.

In New York City that year, Mayor William O'Dwyer filled a slot on the Board of Education from a list submitted by the ardently anti-communist head of the New York archdiocese, Francis Cardinal Spellman. O'Dwyer's choice, the lawyer George Timone, had been linked with anti-Semitic and fascist groups in the late 1930s.[2] The Teachers Union, the Teachers Guild, the NAACP, and many others protested that Timone had no educational credentials and that (in the words of one critic) his selection was "a staggering blow" to "our free, liberal educational system."[3] The *New York Post* questioned the speed and secrecy of the appointment.[4]

Timone was to spearhead the coming Red hunt in New York City. His first major concern, however, was defending the Catholic Church against attacks from the *Nation* magazine, which published a series of articles in 1948 describing some of the Church's reactionary social doctrines and its support of European fascism. William Jansen, who became schools superintendent in 1946, acquiesced in Timone's demand that the magazine be banned from school libraries, and the Board of Superintendents backed him up.[5]

The Board of Higher Education, though it did not have a George Timone, was also not about to return to the defense of academic freedom that its chair, Ordway Tead, had articulated in the prewar years when he responded to an attack from the House Un-American Activities Committee by explaining that diversity of political views among professors is a boon, not a threat, to education. Certainly, the BHE did not rein in Brooklyn College's president,

Harry Gideonse, despite a complaint to Tead from the TU in 1946, charging Gideonse with nine instances of abuse of power. Gideonse penned a 16-page reply refuting each charge and accusing the TU of trying to retaliate for his aggression in battling campus radicals.[6]

Gideonse was equally combative in response to a 1948 decision by Commissioner of Education Francis Spaulding that affirmed a ruling by his assistant commissioner exonerating a City College instructor whom the BHE had suspended after he was accused at the Rapp-Coudert hearings of being a communist. The instructor, Francis Thompson, had denied the charges, and the matter was left in limbo while he served in Army Intelligence during the war. In December 1946, Thompson having returned to New York, the BHE fired him. The assistant commissioner ruled the firing unlawful because even if the evidence had proved Thompson was a CP member (which it had not), the Party was legal—it was regularly on the ballot in New York State—and there was no claim that he had advocated subversion. The ruling distressed local officials, including the BHE, which asked Commissioner Spaulding to reopen the case on the ground that its charge of CP membership was actually intended to cover not only official affiliation "but all who espoused communist doctrines." The Board of Education, which controlled the lower schools, made the argument even more sharply in an *amicus* brief: "it is not alone *membership* in the Communist Party that is incompatible with the obligations of public school teachers"; it is beliefs.[7]

Although Spaulding gave the city what it wanted—his ruling backed off from the view that Party membership was not in itself grounds for dismissal—he refused to reopen the case because the evidence was simply insufficient to support the BHE's charge against Thompson. Gideonse was furious: he told 1,500 freshmen assembled in the Brooklyn College gymnasium that Spaulding had ignored evidence of Thompson's perjury, and he attacked the commissioner for "amend[ing] the Bill of Rights to say that, whereas all other citizens will be punished for perjury, totalitarianism will be granted a special exemption."[8]

BHE member Ira Hirschmann was "amazed and shocked" at Gideonse's intemperate blast against the head of the state education system and his use of the freshman class "as a sounding board for his own personal political views." Hirschmann asked Tead to open an inquiry into Gideonse's conduct. Gideonse shot back that college presidents also enjoy academic freedom, and "their remarks are not submitted to individual board members for approval."[9]

On the national stage, the Democratic Party was eager not to be outshone by Republicans in anti-communist ardor. President Harry Truman's March 1947 executive order, creating a sweeping program of loyalty investigations for federal employees, was the critical step in inaugurating the prolonged and virulent national Red hunt. The program was to command the energies of thousands of investigators and bureaucrats in the coming years. Truman's loyalty boards, housed in every federal agency, used anonymous informers, refused to allow the accused to confront their accusers or to see the evidence against them, and inquired into their reading choices, their taste in art, their political and social activities, and their beliefs in anti-fascist, anti-poverty, and civil rights causes. His executive order directed the Justice Department to create a list of subversive organizations—the "Attorney General's List"— that was to become the national reference point for guilt by association.[10] Membership in any group on the list created a presumption of unfitness and disloyalty. Congress's enactment of the Taft-Hartley Act in 1947, meanwhile, drove left-wingers out of leadership positions in organized labor by requiring a non-communist affidavit from every official whose union was covered by collective bargaining law.

State legislative committees began new Red hunts. Washington's Canwell Committee, named after its head, freshman state representative Albert Canwell, led the way in 1947 with an investigation of the Washington Pension Union, an advocacy group. The next year, it targeted the University of Washington; dozens of professors were investigated, and the administration, instead of resisting on grounds of academic freedom, set a precedent by eventually firing three of them, one for being uncooperative and two for being communists.

The two acknowledged communist professors were Joseph Butterworth, an expert on medieval English literature, and Herbert Phillips, a philosophy teacher who frankly told his classes at the start of each semester that he was a Marxist "and that this fact should be kept in mind in appraising his personal views and opinions."[11] Phillips and Butterworth refused to answer Canwell's questions about their political associations on constitutional grounds, but others who were nowhere near the CP also refused to cooperate. Three witnesses were ex-communists who testified about themselves but would not name others. A sixth, psychology professor Ralph Gundlach, refused to testify but privately told the university that he had never been a CP member. Some who had been communists, such as anthropology professor Melville Jacobs, insisted that the Party did not compromise their independence. Jacobs said he had "often been in sharp disagreement" with the Party line on matters of science.[12]

In this first major post-war challenge to academia's ability to choose its own faculty, University of Washington president Raymond Allen quickly acquiesced. He praised the committee for helping the university address

Florence Bean James, co-founder of the Seattle Repertory Playhouse, confronting the Canwell Committee after a witness accused James and her husband of being communists. (Courtesy of *Seattle Post-Intelligencer* Collection, Museum of History and Industry)

accusations of "communistic or atheistic teachings on the campus"[13] and believed that by purging communists on the theory that they could not be competent teachers, he would be able to protect the university against further political intervention. Events in Washington set the pattern for legislative investigations, followed by university purges, nationwide.

Charges were brought against six Washington professors. At this point, Phillips and Butterworth acknowledged CP membership. A majority of a faculty "trial committee," finding that Phillips was one of the best teachers in his department, that both were good and honest scholars, and that neither religiously followed the Party line, recommended against firing them. For Gundlach, however, who continued to resist the inquisition, a majority recommended dismissal, concluding that his advocacy of anti-lynching laws, price controls, and fair employment practices showed that he supported the CP program. Allen agreed to fire Gundlach but rejected the recommendation to keep Butterworth and Phillips; in early 1949, the university fired all three. The three former Party members who had refused to name names were required to sign an oath abjuring any connection with the Party and were put on two years' probation, during which time "participation in any communist or communist front activities" would be grounds for dismissal.[14]

Gundlach, Phillips, and Butterworth never again found academic jobs. Gundlach was convicted of contempt for refusing to cooperate with the Canwell Committee, served 30 days in jail, and worked as a clinical psychologist for the rest of his career. Phillips eventually became a laborer. Butterworth wrote to all 2,000 members of the Modern Language Association seeking work, without success, and eventually went on public assistance.[15]

The events in Washington dramatized the academic-freedom issue: should long-tenured, outstanding professors be fired simply for being communists? In a much-discussed exchange in the *New York Times Magazine*, the civil libertarian philosopher Alexander Meiklejohn debated the question with the NYU professor, former communist, and now fervent anti-communist Sidney Hook. Hook said yes, because all communists were mental slaves of Moscow. Meiklejohn responded that CP members are free to leave; their minds are not controlled by a foreign power. By automatically disqualifying them, college administrators were "attributing to their victims their own intellectual sins"—that is, "advancing one set of ideas and banning another."[16]

It was a debate that continued throughout the 1950s and '60s. Although the AAUP in 1947 and '48 had opposed excluding communists from academia, it did little to advance this stand in the decade to come; and the American Association of Universities (AAU), representing the nation's top academic institutions, took the opposite view. By 1953, when the AAU officially adopted a statement rationalizing its blanket opposition to allowing any communist to teach, this was already the established policy at most universities.[17]

In the Washington case, there had been no evidence that the punished professors misbehaved, apart from resisting the Canwell Committee. But the university followed a pattern familiar from the days of Rapp-Coudert: rapidly caving in to pressures from a legislative committee. Whether or not the acquiescence was politically necessary became a sharply debated question as events unfolded in nearby California. (Canwell lost when he ran for state senate in 1948.)

In January 1949, California senator Jack Tenney, chairman of that state's "little HUAC," introduced 17 bills aimed at subversion, including test oaths for doctors, lawyers, and professors. "The lawyers and doctors protested at once," as one author recounts, "with a vigor that put an end to this nonsense as regarded their own professions. But a kind of palsy apparently overcame Robert Gordon Sproul," president of the University of California.[18] Sproul proposed, and the state university's Board of Regents quickly approved, a loyalty oath for all faculty, requiring them to abjure belief in forceful overthrow of the government or membership in any organization with such a view. Unlike the affirmative loyalty oath prescribed by the California Constitution, this negative oath, requiring a denial of membership in the Communist Party, triggered faculty outrage. UC's Academic Senate rejected it with only one dissenting vote, and about 300 professors refused to sign. By 1950, protest was still vigorous enough to sustain another vote of opposition at Berkeley's Greek Theater, with about 8,000 students cheering the professors on. Eighteen professors who were fired for refusing to sign the oath eventually prevailed in court, but meanwhile, legislative investigations, collaboration by the university in FBI and police probes, and the pressures of interrogation and dismissal either drove out most dissenters or persuaded them to abandon their objections.[19]

The professors' battle became moot once California created an antisubversive oath for all employees, not just academics. This "Levering oath" remained on the books until 1967, when California's high court, relying on the U.S. Supreme Court's *Keyishian* decision, invalidated its anti-subversive section. The court left in place the affirmative part of the Levering oath, which requires that public workers swear to defend the state and nation "against all enemies, foreign and domestic."[20]

The California oath controversy was notable for the number of professors who initially resisted. Although the *New York Times* faulted them for their "stubborn" objection to a ritual to which "no good citizen could possibly object," it also betrayed ambivalence, regretting "the noonday madness" of the anti-communist crusade and urging that "what is essential is that after this ceremony has been performed, the teacher be left free to teach according to his conscience."[21]

In retrospect, Sproul's panicked reaction to Senator Tenney's assault was probably unnecessary. The state legislature soon replaced Tenney as chair of its un-American activities committee and tabled his bills. But by this time, writes the journalist Carey McWilliams, Sproul and the regents "were caught in the meshes of their own intrigue" and "felt compelled to defend the test oath on principle."[22]

Congress also revived heresy-hunting committees after World War II. The most notorious was HUAC, whose sensational 1947 "Hollywood Ten" hearings quickly resulted in a blacklist that drove suspected communists out of jobs in movies, radio, and television.[23] HUAC went on to attract even more stupendous headlines when one of its members, Richard Nixon, steered a confrontation between the ex-communist espionage courier Whittaker Chambers and the Roosevelt administration bureaucrat Alger Hiss toward a perjury conviction for Hiss after he denied having passed documents to Chambers or having known him after a certain date. As the 1950s began, other federal and state bodies, most notably the Senate Internal Security Subcommittee (SISS), headed by Pat McCarran, and the Permanent Subcommittee on Investigations of the Senate Government Operations Committee, headed by Joseph McCarthy, competed for publicity and new suspects.

In New York, inquisitors used three devices to pick up where the Rapp-Coudert Committee had left off: the state's 1949 Feinberg Law; the Board of Education's separate program of investigations and dismissals; and section 903 of the city charter, which prohibited city employees from asserting the Fifth Amendment right to remain silent in the course of any official investigation. But the Rapp-Coudert experience was also a spur to the lawyers representing the Teachers Union and to individual teachers as they began to articulate the legal arguments for academic freedom.

The Teachers Union and the Feinberg Law

New York's first anti-subversive law, passed in 1917, made "the utterance of any treasonable or seditious words or the doing of any treasonable or seditious act" grounds for dismissal from employment in the public schools. In 1939, the state broadened the ban to cover anyone employed in the civil service and made it grounds for discharge that a person advocated "the overthrow of government by force, violence, or any unlawful means" or published material or joined any group with such an aim.[24] Once the Cold War began, the state legislature decided that these two laws were not enough, because neither one mandated administrative machinery to investigate the beliefs and associations of each employee.

So in March 1949, the legislature hurriedly passed a third law, without the benefit of public hearings and while the state Education Department was preparing materials to oppose it.[25] Named after its sponsor, state senator Benjamin Feinberg, the new law covered all public workers, but teachers were a special concern because, as the legislature said in a lengthy preamble, there was "common report that members of subversive groups, and particularly of the communist party and certain of its affiliated organizations," had infiltrated classrooms; as a result, "subversive propaganda" might be "disseminated among children of tender years." Worse, "such dissemination of propaganda may be and frequently is sufficiently subtle to escape detection."[26]

Rather than conclude from this difficulty of discerning subversive propaganda that radical teachers did not in fact try to indoctrinate students, the Feinberg Law assumed the opposite: absence of evidence was proof of danger. The legislature therefore determined that "in order to protect the children," the earlier anti-subversive laws must be "rigorously enforced." There followed a series of amendments to the state education and civil service laws, plus a new education law section directing the regents to create a process for investigating teachers and firing those found to be disloyal. Among other things, the regents would create a list of subversive organizations, "membership in which shall constitute *prima facie* evidence of disqualification for appointment or retention." With a nod to the U.S. Attorney General's List, which by this time contained almost 200 organizations, the law authorized the regents to "utilize any similar listings or designations" prepared by any federal agency.[27]

Opposition to Feinberg's bill did materialize in the brief period between its introduction and passage. The ACLU, the American Labor Party, the National Lawyers Guild, the New York State CIO, the Teachers Union, and the United Parents Association were among the objectors—"the usual suspects," one might say, at a historical moment when the American left was becoming isolated from liberal allies. But the *New York Times*, hardly a radical publication, also opposed the bill: its editorial "Blunderbuss at Albany" protested "the untenable and illiberal theory of 'guilt by association'" that was at its core.[28] Even the zealously anti-communist Teachers Guild was "shocked at the speed" with which Governor Thomas Dewey signed the bill and complained that its "loosely worded" text "undermines our basic tenure law" and "gives unprecedented power to the Board of Regents" to "stigmatize an organization as subversive and deprive hundreds of teachers of their jobs" after "a mere perfunctory hearing or inquiry."[29]

The Teachers Union, which had been ejected from the American Federation of Teachers in the wake of the Rapp-Coudert hearings and was now Local 555 of the CIO's United Public Workers, immediately began to organize opposition to the law's implementation. TU chronicler Celia Zitron writes that hundreds of members stood at street corners "with petitions and postcards addressed to Governor Dewey; others spoke from sound trucks at street meetings."[30] A coalition that included the American Jewish Congress, the AAUP, and the New York State Baptist Convention urged the regents to hold hearings on the law's merits, but the board said no purpose would be served by doing so, as the law was already on the books. In April, it created a committee, in the words of the *Times*, to "devise means to implement provisions of the Feinberg Law that require[] the board to purge the school system of teachers with subversive leanings."[31] "Leanings" was the operative term, for although the law focused on organizational membership, the investigations it required would delve into people's reading preferences, social activities, rallies attended, petitions signed, and beliefs on current political issues.

The Feinberg Law was scheduled to go into effect on July 1, 1949. But the committee that the Board of Regents had appointed to recommend procedures to carry it out was sharply divided. Should an oath or questionnaire be required? How should suspect teachers be tried? The June meeting of the board produced no forward action except an announcement (on July 6) that it had identified five organizations as subversive; they would be given hearings—all on one day—before the list was made final in September.[32] The brevity of the projected "hearings" was just one indication that the groups would have little real chance to overturn the board's listings.[33]

The regents issued rules for implementing the Feinberg Law. Each school district was to appoint one or more officials to report on the loyalty of every teacher. The authorities were either to dismiss or to prefer charges against any teacher within 90 days of an adverse report. Evidence of membership in an organization before it was listed by the regents as subversive would create a presumption that the teacher remained enrolled, in the absence of a showing that the teacher had terminated the membership "in good faith." Each school district would report annually to the Department of Education on the measures taken to enforce the rules and on the number of employees found innocent or guilty of disloyalty.[34]

After publishing the rules, Commissioner of Education Spaulding distributed a memo elaborating on the evidence to be considered in loyalty investigations. "The writing of articles, the distribution of pamphlets, the endorsement of speeches made or articles written or acts performed by others, all may constitute subversive activity," Spaulding wrote. There was no need to show that such activity took place in the classroom, for "treasonable or subversive activities or statements outside the school are as much a basis for dismissal as are similar activities in school."[35]

But, as if acknowledging the implications of the investigatory apparatus he was constructing, Spaulding added a caveat. "Good teachers are likely to raise many questions and make many suggestions about possible improvements in the American form of government" that "cannot in any just sense be construed as subversive"; moreover, teachers should not feel inhibited from taking "full advantage of their own privileges as citizens" to speak out on political issues; they should even feel free to "enter into discussions . . . about forms of government different from our own."[36] These assurances may have enabled Spaulding and his staff to persuade themselves that they were protecting free speech, but the distinction between subversive and legitimate criticism of government is muddy and was not likely to undo the inhibiting effect of the system of surveillance he was putting into place. As Lawrence Chamberlain observed, the memorandum gave "no guidance concerning the nature of articles, speeches, or activities which would be regarded as objectionable."[37]

The Board of Regents responded to the widespread consternation among teachers and civil libertarians with assurances about fair hearings on charges of subversion and rights of appeal contained in the education and civil service laws. Once teachers were deemed disloyal, they could appeal to the commissioner of education or go straight to court.[38] But in either case, teachers accused of belonging to a designated group could not challenge the designation; they could only try to persuade the authorities either that they were not, and never had been, members or that if they had been, they had fully renounced their past beliefs. Whatever fair procedures the regents or the commissioner of education seemed to promise, the presumption of guilt from membership would be hard to rebut, especially since the informers who provided the evidence could not be cross-examined; indeed, their identities were usually not revealed.

"We will challenge this law in the courts," TU president Abraham Lederman and legislative representative Rose Russell (a former French teacher and Bella Dodd's successor) assured the membership; "we will stop this heresy hunt" and "take every other available step to have it written off the books, as were the Lusk Laws and the Alien and Sedition Laws which disgraced two earlier periods of anti-democratic hysteria."[39] Before school opened in September 1949, the union announced that it was ready to sue and had signed up parents, teachers, and citizen-taxpayers as plaintiffs.

The Communist Party got to court first, filing suit in Albany and obtaining a temporary injunction that halted publication of the regents' list and ordered them to "show cause" why they should not be restrained from enforcing the Feinberg Law. A hearing was scheduled for September 23 before Judge Harry Schirick. But Board of Education president Maximilian Moss said the injunction applied only to the state; local boards could still move against suspected subversives.[40] And this is exactly what New York City did: on September 13, the same day the CP obtained its injunction, Superintendent Jansen directed school officials to send him lists of all employees who had been cleared as well as those whose loyalty was suspect.[41] The BHE adopted a lower profile, although it did announce a possible plan to conduct loyalty screens on some 7,500 students who were preparing for teaching careers. Ordway Tead explained that although City, Brooklyn, Queens, and Hunter College students already had to take a loyalty oath, there was up to this point "no check on political beliefs."[42]

Events all over the country echoed what was happening in New York. The AAUP was swamped with complaints of academic-freedom violations.

Teachers from eight colleges alleged that they were dismissed because they had supported 1948 Progressive Party presidential candidate Henry Wallace. For the most part, they did not have tenure; their contracts were simply not renewed, and in some cases the college presidents asserted it was for "lack of competence" or some other non-political reason. Among the cashiered scholars was Yale Russian studies professor John Marsalka, who had organized the Wallace campaign in Connecticut and had also invited the Russian composer Dmitri Shostakovich to campus; Yale had canceled Shostakovich's appearance. Some administrators were awaiting the outcome of the AAUP's three-to-six-month investigative process before taking action against suspected communists on their campuses, for even though the organization, now with 35,000 members, had no direct power over the colleges, it could put them on its "censured" list, which at least might diminish their prestige and their ability to attract faculty.[43]

Even at this difficult moment for academic freedom, the higher-education establishment sometimes showed it could resist. In June 1949, HUAC wrote to about 70 colleges and to boards of education in every state, requesting lists of both assigned and supplemental texts, in order to "give the committee a start on finding out whether communist propaganda had gotten into schoolbooks."[44] College officials were nearly unanimous in their opposition. Wellesley's president attacked HUAC's request as a symptom of "the fear which permeates our modern age," and Vassar's responded by inviting the committee to inspect the college library's 260,000 volumes. The BHE's Ordway Tead denounced the request as "educationally ominous."[45] Faced with massive resistance, HUAC backed off, but not before the Brooklyn, Queens, and City College presidents all said they would comply. (Hunter was not on HUAC's list.) Harry Gideonse reportedly sent a list of 161 books to the committee.[46]

The First Amendment in the 1940s

The attorneys challenging the Feinberg Law relied on Supreme Court cases from the 1930s and '40s that had recognized the First Amendment rights of such beleaguered groups as labor organizers, Jehovah's Witnesses, and socialists. Although these cases did not address academic freedom, the important point was that the Court had moved a long way since its post–World War I decisions allowing prison sentences of up to 20 years for people who protested U.S. foreign policy. There were now solid constitutional arguments for striking down the Feinberg Law.

Three cases in the mid-1920s paved the way. The first affirmed the conviction of a communist organizer under New York's criminal anarchy law, but at least the Court was willing to measure repressive state laws, not just federal ones, against the demands of the First Amendment.[47] Because states and localities were so active in passing repressive legislation, the decision was a watershed—a dramatic assertion of the supremacy of the federal Constitution and, to states' rights advocates, an intrusion on their sovereignty. The second case also affirmed a conviction (for "criminal syndicalism"), but it occasioned a concurrence by Louis Brandeis that became one of the most celebrated flights of First Amendment oratory in our national literature. Brandeis urged that the "clear and present danger" test, invented in 1919 by Justice Oliver Wendell Holmes in the Court's first major free-speech case, be given real bite, not simply recited as a vague formula to ban any speech that posed a remote risk to the national interest. "Those who won our independence," Brandeis wrote, "believed that freedom to think as you will and to speak as you think are means indispensable to the discovery and spread of political truth" and that "the fitting remedy for evil counsels is good ones," not enforced silence.[48]

A third case from the 1920s broke the Court's pattern by actually overturning a guilty verdict. The defendant was a Wobbly (a member of the Industrial Workers of the World), and the sole basis of his conviction for criminal syndicalism was the organization's constitution, which proclaimed that "the working class and the employing class have nothing in common," that "there can be no peace so long as hunger and want are found among millions of working people," and that class struggle would continue until workers "take possession of the earth and the machinery of production." The Court overturned the conviction on due process grounds (the Kansas law was "arbitrary and unreasonable"), rather than applying the First Amendment, but clearly the justices were disturbed by the idea that revolutionary rhetoric alone could condemn a person to jail.[49]

By the mid-1930s, the anti-Bolshevik panic that possessed America after the Russian Revolution had receded; there were also new Supreme Court justices. President Herbert Hoover had appointed the eminent lawyer and former New York governor Charles Evans Hughes as chief justice in 1930. (Hughes had been on the Court from 1910 to 1916 but had resigned to run for president.) Hoover appointed Benjamin Cardozo, a celebrated scholar and judge from New York, in 1932. Five years later, Franklin Roosevelt was able to begin repopulating the Court: he appointed Hugo Black in 1937, Stanley Reed in 1938, William Douglas and Felix Frankfurter in 1939, Frank Murphy in 1940, Robert Jackson in 1941, and Wiley Rutledge in 1943. Although Cardozo and Murphy had relatively short stays, and Reed did not leave a large imprint, Black, Douglas, Frankfurter, and Jackson were to dominate the

Court for the next two decades with their sometimes vicious quarrels and their debates about constitutional law.[50]

Black was the eighth child of a rural Alabama shopkeeper and attended law school at the University of Alabama when it had only two professors. He joined the Ku Klux Klan to further his political ambitions, left when he no longer needed the affiliation, became a powerful senator and New Deal supporter, and skirted the issue of his past Klan membership when asked about it in the Senate after his nomination to the Court.[51] He was to be an uncompromising defender of the First Amendment, though as he aged, he came to hate the political upheavals of the 1960s and yielded to a shrill conservative impulse, angrily dissenting, for example, in the landmark case that gave public school students the right to wear black armbands to express their opposition to the Vietnam War.[52]

William Douglas was to be the Court's other great First Amendment champion. He had grown up poor in the Pacific Northwest, raised by a single mother after his itinerant-preacher father died. He worked as a janitor to pay his way through college, excelled academically, taught law at Columbia and Yale, and while still in his 30s became a member of the Securities and Exchange Commission, where he "parlayed that low-profile post into the high-profile chairmanship by barnstorming for the job and intimating that he had an offer to be dean of Yale Law School."[53]

Felix Frankfurter also grew up poor, on Manhattan's Lower East Side, after arriving with his family from Austria in 1894 at the age of 12. He attended that haven for Jewish immigrants, City College, then excelled at Harvard Law School. After a stint at a corporate law firm and a series of government jobs, he was appointed to the Harvard faculty; from this perch, he joined civil liberties struggles, including the ultimately unsuccessful fight to save the lives of the Italian anarchists Nicola Sacco and Bartolomeo Vanzetti, who were executed in Massachusetts for robbery-murder after a trial that featured virtually no proof of their involvement in the crime but copious evidence of their violent political beliefs. Frankfurter's activism "generated fear and paranoia among conservatives" when the Senate considered his nomination to the Court,[54] but they need not have worried. Reacting in part to the pro-business judicial activism of the previous decades, in which the justices had invalidated social-reform laws based on the presumed inviolability of property rights, Frankfurter became the Court's most fervent—and longwinded—apostle of judicial restraint. Douglas once complained that his lectures at the Court's conferences lasted 50 minutes—exactly as long as the typical law school class—and in 1954 Douglas wrote to Frankfurter (ccing the other justices) that his "insolent" refusal to answer a question was

"OYEZ, OYEZ, THE HONORABLE SUPREME COURT OF THE UNITED STATES—"
FEBRUARY 9. 1944

Cartoonist Daniel Fitzpatrick on the infighting among Supreme Court justices.
(Reprinted with permission of the *St. Louis Post-Dispatch*, copyright 1944)

"a degradation of the Conference and its deliberations."[55] Frankfurter's practice of judicial restraint meant that he would rarely disapprove even extreme
repressive measures; but he was not consistent and departed from his professed passivity when the spirit moved him.

Robert Jackson began as an upstate New York country lawyer, often arguing his cases in makeshift courtrooms. While working for the U.S. Justice
Department, Jackson endeared himself to President Roosevelt by strenuously supporting his ill-fated "court-packing plan" to increase the number of
Supreme Court justices so that there would be a majority in support of New
Deal legislation. At a political moment when many FDR loyalists thought
the plan a grave mistake, Jackson's support, as one scholar noted, provided
him entrée into "Roosevelt's inner circle."[56] From there it was only a few steps

to Jackson's appointment as attorney general, then to the Court, and then, without resigning as a justice, to be chief prosecutor of Nazi war criminals at Nuremburg. Although he shared much of Frankfurter's philosophy of judicial passivity and thus often provided a swing vote for the Court's approval of repressive laws, Jackson was also a brilliantly eloquent defender of free speech.

The Court's first important First Amendment case of the 1930s was decided before any of these four titans had been appointed. In 1931, the justices struck down a California law that banned public display of a red flag as a sign of "opposition to organized government," an "invitation or stimulus to anarchistic action," or an "aid to propaganda that is of a seditious character." Chief Justice Hughes's opinion for the Court was hardly a radical change in ideology; it only invalidated the law insofar as it criminalized display of the flag as a symbol of peaceful protest. States may punish speech that incites violence and threatens overthrow of existing government, Hughes wrote; California could still ban "anarchistic" or "seditious" expressions.[57] Hughes did not recognize the extreme vagueness and subjectivity of a law that banned any "stimulus" to anarchy or "aid" to seditious propaganda. Nevertheless, this modest case was the first "in the history of the Court in which there was an explicit victory for free speech."[58]

The Court was more expansive in 1937 when it overturned a criminal syndicalism conviction from Oregon. Dirk DeJonge had spoken at a public CP meeting, called to protest "illegal raids on workers' halls and homes" and the shooting of striking longshoremen by police. There was no evidence that anything violent was said or any revolutionary literature distributed; the prosecutor relied on communist writings that had been published elsewhere. Hughes wrote an opinion reaffirming that states may punish "an attempted substitution of force and violence in the place of peaceful political action in order to effect revolutionary changes in government" but warning, "none of our decisions goes to the length of sustaining such a curtailment of the right of free speech and assembly as the Oregon statute demands in its present application." The very idea of republican government "implies a right on the part of its citizens to meet peaceably for consultation in respect to public affairs and to petition for a redress of grievances."[59]

A year later, Harlan Fiske Stone, who had been on the Court since 1925 but whom FDR was soon to promote to chief justice, began forging a "strict scrutiny" test for judicial review of government restrictions on speech. In perhaps the most famous footnote in Supreme Court history, Stone wrote that although in most cases judges should defer to the political process, "there may be narrower scope" for judicial restraint when a law seems to clash with "a specific prohibition of the Constitution, such as those of the first ten amendments." Furthermore, when "discrete and insular minorities" are targeted, "more searching judicial inquiry" may be required.[60] This was a direct challenge to Frankfurter's theory of judicial restraint, at least where free speech or other civil liberties are at stake. The justices "divided bitterly" over the issue, one scholar writes: Black, Douglas, Murphy, and Rutledge supported Stone's theory of a "preferred position" for First Amendment rights; Frankfurter, and usually Jackson, disagreed.[61]

The Court applied Stone's "more searching judicial inquiry" the next year (1939) in a case that pitted labor organizers against Frank Hague, mayor of Jersey City, New Jersey. Hague had orchestrated the passage of an ordinance that forbade the leasing of any hall, without a permit from the police chief, for any public meeting at which a speaker "shall advocate obstruction of the Government of the United States or a State, or a change of government by other than lawful means." The plaintiffs said the city had denied them the right to hold lawful meetings and had run out of town "persons they considered undesirable because of their labor organization activities." The Court struck down Hague's ordinance without further addressing the alleged communist sympathies of the organizers.[62]

The Court's march toward expanded First Amendment rights continued during World War II. Although a majority opinion by Frankfurter initially upheld a school board's punishment of Jehovah's Witness children for refusing, on grounds of religious conscience, to salute the flag, the decision was overruled three years later: Jackson now wrote for the Court, in soaring prose, that "if there is any fixed star in our constitutional constellation, it is that no official, high or petty, can prescribe what shall be orthodox in politics, nationalism, religion, or other matters of opinion or force citizens to confess by word or act their faith therein."[63]

The same year (1943), Justice Frank Murphy, who as mayor of Detroit and then governor of Michigan had proved himself a humanitarian liberal, assembled a narrow majority to reverse the Justice Department's revocation of citizenship, granted 12 years earlier, to an active communist. The petitioner's beliefs, Murphy said, neither conflicted with the basic requirements for citizenship nor exceeded "the area of allowable thought" under the Constitution: not only the First Amendment but Article V, providing for amendments that change the structure of the government, "refute the idea that attachment to any particular provision or provisions is essential, or that one who advocates radical changes is necessarily not attached to the Constitution."[64]

Harlan Fiske Stone, joined by Frankfurter and by Herbert Hoover appointee Owen Roberts, dissented in the citizenship case because he thought that the petitioner's devotion to the CP undermined his loyalty to America. Frankfurter oozed contempt in a memo that called Murphy's draft opinion a "gossamer web of evasion and word-juggling and casuistry"; in a note to Murphy, he sarcastically suggested adding "that Uncle Joe Stalin was at least a spiritual co-author with Jefferson of the Virginia Statute for Religious Freedom." Eight years later, he quipped to Stanley Reed, "Today you would no more eat Murphy's tripe than you would be seen naked at Dupont Circle at high noon."[65]

In 1946, the Court gave its first response to the anti-communist pressures that had been building since the late 1930s and that exploded once the Cold War began. It struck down a law that prohibited salary payments to three federal employees because of their radical politics. Black wrote the decision, with a compelling narrative of the events leading up to the law: HUAC investigations in the late '30s, culminating in a 1943 speech by Martin Dies attacking 39 federal employees by name as "'irresponsible, unrepresentative, crackpot, radical bureaucrats' and affiliates of 'communist front organizations'"; among them were Robert Lovett, Goodwin Watson, and William Dodd, Jr. An amendment was accordingly added to an appropriation bill, forbidding salary payments for all 39. This precipitated a lengthy debate: some members of Congress were ready to pass the bill based on Dies's accusations, "while others referred to such action as 'legislative lynching,' smacking 'of the procedure in the French Chamber of Deputies during in Reign of Terror.'" The resolution that eventually passed created a subcommittee to examine the evidence, which consisted largely of reports by HUAC and the FBI, "the latter being treated as too confidential to be made public." The subcommittee found Watson, Dodd, and Lovett guilty of subversion by virtue of their "views and philosophies as expressed in various statements and writings." After more debate, the law depriving the three of further compensation passed the House. The Senate voted 69–0 against it, but the House was insistent, and finally the Senate acquiesced.[66]

The Supreme Court in *United States v. Lovett* ruled that the law was an unconstitutional bill of attainder—a law that targets specific individuals or groups for punishment without benefit of trial. Black's opinion relied on a nearly century-old decision striking down a Civil War–era loyalty oath in Missouri. That oath had contained 30 separate tests, including a promise that the affiant had never manifested "adherence to the cause" of the country's enemies or a "desire" for their triumph and had never been a "member of, or connected with, any order, society, or organization inimical to the government of the United States." Clergy was among the professions covered; a priest was convicted for preaching without having taken the oath. The Court in *Cummings v. Missouri* denounced the oath because it subverted the presumption of innocence, altered the rules of evidence, and required individuals to prove their innocence "only in one way—by an inquisition, in the form of an expurgatory oath, into the consciences of the parties."[67]

As in the Missouri case, Black said the law targeting Lovett and two others "clearly accomplishes the punishment of named individuals without a judicial trial." The fact that the punishment consisted of denying them salaries made it "no less galling or effective" than a criminal conviction. In either case, basic principles of due process, such as representation by counsel, were required before a person is punished by the state.[68]

Only seven justices participated in *Lovett*: Jackson was off trying war crimes at Nuremburg; Stone had died two months earlier and not yet been replaced by Truman's friend Fred Vinson, the affable but ineffective chief who was to attempt, without success, to unite the quarreling justices. Frankfurter and Reed joined in the judgment but disagreed with Black's reasoning: they would not have reached the constitutional issue but would have turned intellectual somersaults to interpret the law narrowly so that it did not forbid payments for services already rendered.[69]

The *Lovett* case did not turn out to be a precursor of the Supreme Court's response to the flood of repressive laws, investigations, and administrative actions that soon followed. The facts were too singular for it to serve as a broad precedent. But the problem ran deeper. Despite the free-speech-friendly decisions of the 1930s and early '40s, most of the justices were still not comfortable with revolutionary exhortations or "subversive" ideas. When the Cold War came, they were as vulnerable to anti-communist panic as the rest of American society.

5

Insubordination and "Conduct Unbecoming"

Early Victories

The Supreme Court's First Amendment decisions in the 1930s and '40s gave encouragement to the Teachers Union in its challenge to the Feinberg Law. The TU's attorneys filed suit in Brooklyn, with union president Abe Lederman as the lead plaintiff and dozens of others joining, among them parents, parent-teacher associations, a social worker, the head of a religious group, teachers, taxpayers, and other unions.[1] This diversity made a political point, but the trial judge, Murray Hearn, soon ruled that only the taxpayers faced sufficient harm from the law's enforcement (based on costs the state would incur) to entitle them to sue. Although Judge Hearn thought the teachers also had standing and, given the chilling effect of the law, should not have to wait until it actually went into effect to bring a legal challenge, he was bound by a Supreme Court case that had held the opposite.[2] Some of the taxpayers were also teachers, though; among them was Irving Adler, a math teacher, dedicated communist, and leader in the union's efforts to reform the curriculum. Adler eventually gave his name to the case. He had little interest in the legal strategy; he simply considered the lawsuit one among many means for pushing back against the oncoming purge.[3]

The Communist Party had already filed its challenge to the Feinberg Law in the state capital of Albany, and a third suit, also in Albany, was initiated by state senator Fred Morritt on behalf of four teachers, a principal, and a former member of the Board of Education. The principal in question was Abraham Lefkowitz, head of the Teachers Guild and a bitter foe of the TU. Lefkowitz and Morritt no doubt wanted to show the courts that patriotic liberals, unthreatened directly by the Feinberg Law, were nevertheless worried about its repressive effect. But the trial judge in Albany, Harry Schirick, consolidated Morritt's case with the suit brought by the CP, thereby muddying the political point.

The consolidated challenges to the Feinberg Law attracted several friend-of-the-court briefs at the trial court level. (Such *amicus curiae* briefs are usually only filed on appeal.) Among the *amici* supporting the CP's case were the American Jewish Congress, the National Lawyers Guild, the American Labor Party, the International Fur and Leather Workers Union, and the National Association of Teachers of Social Studies. The ACLU was conspicuously missing, though it did put in an appearance once the case went up on appeal. Supporting the law as *amicus* was the American Legion.[4]

The case moved quickly, and on November 28, 1949, Judge Schirick in Albany handed down his ruling. Schirick found numerous constitutional problems with the Feinberg Law. It was a bill of attainder because it amounted to a legislative finding of guilt without trial. It violated due process because it was unduly vague—"a dragnet which may enmesh anyone who agitates for a change of government." It unconstitutionally failed to provide for a hearing before the regents decided whether an organization was subversive, then made their finding "*prima facie* evidence" of a teacher's disqualification, without any "proof of illegal purpose or act"; this was "'guilt by association' with a vengeance."[5]

Underlying these findings was Schirick's understanding of the right-privilege distinction in constitutional law. The state, defending the Feinberg Law, had relied on Justice Oliver Wendell Holmes, Jr.'s hoary epigram from 1892 ("the petitioner may have a constitutional right to talk politics, but he has no constitutional right to be a policeman").[6] Holmes's catchy phrase was to haunt public-employee cases in the 1950s, but Judge Schirick interpreted it narrowly. Words must "be read in their context," he said, and Holmes's statement should not be applied beyond the facts in the policeman's case:

> To do otherwise would do violence to the long struggle for the preservation of constitutional liberties with which the name of Mr. Justice Holmes was so long and so closely linked. The issue is not whether there is a constitutional right to teach, but whether the ground asserted for denying this right or privilege, whatever it is, is one which is protected by the Constitution against legislative encroachment.[7]

A New York judge in 1949 thus rejected the notion that conditions on employment, no matter how onerous, do not raise constitutional problems. It would take many years before this doctrine of "unconstitutional conditions" was firmly grounded in the law. But even putting aside Holmes's glib and simplistic epigram, most courts in the 1950s would assume that purging the nation's school systems of communist teachers was a reasonable condition of employment. Schirick did not, and he explained why. He was not "oblivious to the practices of international communism," he said, "which have met with such universal and well-merited contempt among free men." But it would be "small service, indeed, to our democracy" to emulate "the tactics of communism" and thereby destroy political freedom.[8]

Two weeks later, on December 14, 1949, Judge Hearn in Brooklyn reached the same result. Like Schirick, he emphasized the "preferred place" that the Supreme Court over the previous 20 years had accorded the First Amendment. Especially in schools, "the atmosphere must be one which encourages able independent men [sic] to enter the teaching profession" and, once there, to help students think for themselves.[9]

As it turned out, Hearn and Schirick were ahead of their time—or, more precisely, behind it: that is, they relied on Supreme Court precedents that were increasingly ignored as the Red hunt intensified. In March 1950, the appellate division of the New York courts made short work of their studious opinions. The law was not a bill of attainder, the appellate division said, because it did not specifically condemn communists without trial; the Party was only named in the preamble. As for the First Amendment, "one does not have a constitutional right to be a public employee except upon compliance with reasonable conditions." The judges relied on Supreme Court decisions from the World War I era and on that old warhorse, Justice Holmes's one-liner about the policeman.[10]

The Board of Education Cannot Wait

Judges Harry Schirick and Murray Hearn had temporarily stopped the New York State Board of Regents from implementing the Feinberg Law, but the city Board of Education did not want to wait. A partial explanation for its impatience was the pressure brought to bear by a subcommittee of the House of Representatives, which had come to town in the fall of 1948 to investigate the Teachers Union. The owners of a private school of radio electronics, embroiled in a union battle with their teachers, had asked the committee to come.

The TU was not particularly interested in organizing the teachers at these private trade schools; it had enough other challenges on its plate.[11] But poor working conditions had spurred the teachers to seek the union's help, and it had negotiated contracts with several of the schools. In June 1948, a TU organizer wrote to the Radio Electronics School in Manhattan that "an overwhelming majority" of its instructors had joined the union, and enclosed a proposed contract for its "consideration."[12]

The school's directors thought their employees were quite happy without a union. They refused to negotiate; there was a teacher walkout, followed by a school closing, followed by picketing, at which point the directors wrote to the House committee chair, Fred Hartley (coauthor of the Taft-Hartley Act), to complain that the TU "is generally recognized" as communist controlled and that the picketing was accompanied by "threats, coercion, and intimidation" of the faculty and student body; moreover, because the teachers were content with their working conditions, the TU's efforts were designed to undermine the students' patriotism "through control of their instructors and the dissemination of subversive propaganda."[13]

This was the first attack on the TU by a committee of the U.S. Congress, and Rose Russell, the union's legislative representative, lost no time in accusing the committee of "heresy hunting."[14] Indeed, the TU's communist link was the focus of the hearings. Board of Education superintendent William Jansen and board president Andrew Clauson both testified that they would not allow "a proven member of the Communist Party" to teach in any of the city's 750 schools. But they had no evidence, beyond rumors, that any communist teachers were employed.[15]

George Timone, who testified next, gave a report on the TU, its "consistent espousal of communist causes," and its recommendations of class readings published by "organizations described by the Department of Justice as communistic"—that is, organizations on the Attorney General's List. These included such pamphlets as "Religion Today," published by the Council of American-Soviet Friendship, and "Unequal Justice," published by the American Committee for Protection of the Foreign Born. Timone had prepared his report at the committee's request.[16]

History teacher Sam Wallach, former president of the TU, was called to testify but refused to answer questions about his political beliefs, his alleged communist affiliations, and the alleged communist domination of the union. As he told the politicians, he had taught his students "a deep devotion to our American and democratic way of life"; they had studied the Bill of Rights and understood that it "meant that your beliefs, your religion, your opinions were sacred to you." He could not now disillusion the kids by collaborating in a political inquisition.[17]

Rose Russell also testified, defending the union against the "slanders" of other witnesses, crediting "its militancy" with improving the conditions of teachers and students, and countering Timone's selective citations from TU publications with examples of materials from other, completely non-suspect groups that it had also recommended. Responding to testimony from the Teachers Guild's Abraham Lefkowitz that TU members were "innocent dupes," Russell quipped that they were "neither dupes nor dopes": no organization in the city was as democratically run as the TU, and its members "should not be maligned" by suggestions that they were "being taken in by some nefarious thing they cannot fathom."[18]

"Don't you know that you placed your job in jeopardy?" a reporter asked Sam Wallach after the hearing. "Those guys in there placed the Constitution in jeopardy" was Wallach's reply.[19] He did not lose his job over this, but the next year, Jansen began calling in suspect teachers for questioning. Apparently, given the pressure from the committee and, on his own board, from Timone, Jansen's passive approach of waiting to receive evidence of CP membership among teachers would no longer do.

The 1948 hearings were not Timone's first assault on the Teachers Union. The year before, at the urging of the Catholic War Veterans, he had introduced a resolution to ban the use of school buildings for meetings by the Communist Party, the American Youth for Democracy, or any other group that the superintendent had "reason to believe" was communist or fascist, fostered "racial or religious intolerance," or was a "front" for any such organization. After heated debate, the board rejected the proposal; city councilman Michael Quill, speaking in opposition, remarked, "some here profess to be experts on communism, but they are more familiar with alcoholism."[20] A lawsuit challenging the vote was dismissed on the ground that the CP, despite "widespread public aversion," had the right to function as a political party and the board had discretion to decide who gets to use school property.[21]

The First Teacher Investigations

Even before the Hartley committee probe, William Jansen and others in city school management targeted one activist teacher in a dispute that sharply focused the issue of academic freedom. In February 1948, Louis Jaffe, a social studies teacher and handball coach at Tilden High School in Brooklyn, published an article, "Challenges to Academic Freedom," in the *Bulletin* of the Association of Teachers of Social Studies (the ATSS). Among other things, it criticized the city school system. Jansen wrote to Jaffe, "I have just read the ATSS Bulletin. If you have not made other plans for Friday morning, Feb. 13, I should like you to drop in about 10 o'clock in order to discuss your article with you." It was an oddly disingenuous way of summoning a teacher for a dressing down; Jaffe dutifully "dropped in" and listened to Jansen's critique.[22]

A month later, the chairman of Jaffe's department at Tilden observed two of his classes and, although he found them "fair" and "satisfactory," took issue with his discussion of Cold War topics involving the veto power at the United Nations and peaceful coexistence in the atomic age. Jaffe responded that his lessons were balanced and that the chairman was displeased only because

Jaffe had not slanted them in a jingoist pro-U.S. direction. There the matter probably would have rested had not Tilden's principal, Abraham Lefkowitz, intervened. Lefkowitz, the fiercely anti-communist head of the Teachers Guild, was still smarting from his loss of control of the Teachers Union in 1935. He wrote to Jaffe that this was not an issue of academic freedom: "No point of view has ever been outlawed at Tilden. But academic freedom can't be used by you or another teacher at Tilden to overemphasize a point of view contrary to that of America and the United Nations to favor the Soviet Union and her satellites, without a protest or a recorded warning from a loyal Head of Department or anyone who witnessed it."[23]

Despite the circumlocutions, a "point of view" obviously *was* being disapproved at Tilden—"a point of view contrary to that of America and the United Nations"—though Jaffe continued to insist that his lessons were fair, and a committee of assistant superintendents, after reviewing the dispute, found in his favor. They nevertheless transferred him to Erasmus Hall High School because of a "strained teacher-supervisor relationship."[24]

Despite Jaffe's exoneration, the superintendents were not finished with him. In December 1948, they questioned him further, now about his political beliefs and activities outside class. Among the questions were, "Do you believe there is freedom in the Soviet Union?" and "Do you believe Stalin is an enemy of the U.S.?" Jaffe, who chaired a union committee on education, had presented criticisms two years before of the treatment of U.S.-USSR relations in the American history syllabus; at that less politically fraught moment, the Board of Superintendents made several changes that he recommended.[25] Now the city's top education officers, through their pointed questions, were discouraging any departure from American political orthodoxy.

Under pressure from Timone and the Hartley committee, Jansen began additional investigations in late 1948. At first, they did not follow any coherent plan. TU president Abe Lederman was called in; Jansen wanted to know if he had ever collected funds for the Communist Party. Staten Island elementary school teacher Minnie Gutride was summoned from her classroom in December and ordered to the principal's office, where an assistant superintendent and the board's law officer questioned her about alleged communist meetings in 1940 and '41 and threatened her "with hints of legal action and charges of insubordination if she refused to answer then and there."[26] In a letter to Jansen, Gutride protested the "complete disregard" for due process and called it "highly unfair and improper to call a teacher out of class and subject her to this type of questioning without any warning or prior notice or opportunity to consult with anyone for advice as to her legal rights." Gutride, who was suffering from cancer, committed suicide two days later.[27]

Whether or not Gutride's suicide and the subsequent bad publicity gave Jansen second thoughts, there were no further publicized incidents until the following April (1949), when Jansen summoned seven teachers for questioning: all were TU officers and therefore responsible for criticizing Jansen and the board on many issues, from racism in textbooks to deplorable conditions in inner-city schools. The seven were Latin teacher and TU secretary Celia Zitron, English teacher and editor of the union's paper Isadore Rubin, TU president Abe Lederman, science teacher Mark Friedlander, math teacher Abraham Feingold, Harlem activist and elementary school teacher Alice Citron, and once again, Louis Jaffe. All refused to answer questions about their political beliefs and affiliations. An eighth suspect, David Friedman, had been interviewed in January 1949 and again in March. He was also a TU activist and the chairman of a junior high school English department; informers had placed him at CP meetings. Like the others, Friedman had refused to answer Jansen's questions about his politics.

The New York Police Department's BOSSI unit (Bureau of Special Services and Information) was a fertile source of information on these eight teachers. Memos in the city's archives have "P.D." notations indicating that the teachers were being watched and their colleagues questioned about their political sympathies.[28] Louis Jaffe, according to one memo, had admitted at a departmental meeting in 1933 or '34 that he was a communist. "P.D. records" indicated that Isadore Rubin was part of the CP's Flatbush Club; an informant said that in 1945 he had given a talk to the club on Soviet trade unions and was introduced as a member. Celia Zitron was identified by another informant as having attended numerous Party meetings in 1934–36; two ex-communist witnesses had the "general impression" that she was "high up in party and real brains behind TU." Alice Citron was, according to "P.D. records (very recently made available to us)," an "active member" of the Party; moreover, she had the same address as Isidor Begun, an "exposed communist," and was "generally believed" to have lived with him "as if man and wife." Thus, "it looks as if we could make out quite a good case for conduct unbecoming a teacher on the grounds of having been Begun's mistress."[29] No matter how sleazy the tactics, the files grew.

Jansen's intensification of his anti-communist program in 1949 coincided with a radical escalation of Cold War tensions. Mao Tse-tung's communists took power in China, and the USSR tested its first atomic bomb. In New York, a dramatic show trial of 11 Communist Party leaders under the Smith Act dominated headlines for the first nine months of the year. To counter American saber rattling, the CP, doggedly loyal to Soviet interests, made peace a major focus of its energy. A Conference for World Peace at New

York's Waldorf Astoria in March brought together communists, liberals, fellow travelers, and cultural celebrities such as Arthur Miller and Aaron Copland. Peace was the main theme of the 1949 May Day parade, which, according to the CP's *Daily Worker*, vastly outnumbered a "loyalty" march staged by "warmongers."[30] The TU meanwhile organized postcard campaigns: Jansen's files in the Municipal Archives contain hundreds of cards protesting his assaults on teachers, including about a dozen referring to Louis Jaffe and his efforts to promote peace. One card reminded Jansen of Governor Al Smith's praise for teachers' "right to freedom of thought and just criticism of existing institutions" in signing the repeal of the Lusk laws in 1923.[31]

Jansen's April 1949 interviews of Zitron, Jaffe, and five other targeted teachers were crammed into one day and were accordingly brief. Once they refused to answer his questions about politics and Party memberships, Jansen could charge them with insubordination and conduct unbecoming a teacher. David Friedman, interviewed earlier, was the only one actually charged with communism. Thus, with the exception of Friedman, the Board of Education's disciplinary procedures did not focus, as did the Feinberg Law, on whether an individual was a CP member but on whether she or he cooperated with the interrogation. Disobedience, not subversive beliefs, became the offense.

All eight were suspended without pay in May 1950. The year's delay was likely due to the Feinberg Law litigation; it was only after the decisions of Judges Schirick and Hearn were overturned on appeal that the Board of Education went forward against its first eight targets. But the board, and the city lawyers, continued to argue that their proceedings against the rebel teachers were independent of, or at least supplementary to, the demands of the Feinberg Law.

The board continued throughout the early 1950s to charge teachers with insubordination and conduct unbecoming for refusing to answer questions, rather than substantively charging them with CP membership or subversive activity. It thereby circumvented even the minimal due process provisions of the Feinberg Law, which at least allowed teachers a hearing at which they could try to rebut allegations of CP membership or the presumption of unfitness flowing from it. Rose Russell noted the irony that "the notorious Feinberg Law" offered teachers "more safeguards than the superintendent of schools is ready to grant them; safeguards against arbitrary rulings, against whims and caprice." To "subvert the fair play and tenure provisions of the education law," she said, Jansen and the city attorneys "devised a trick": Jansen asked questions that he knew many teachers would "deny he has a right to ask, and on that basis, without having to bring charges, without having to bring his witnesses, or lay his testimony on the line where people can see it, he is ready to destroy careers."[32]

Parents, teachers, and community groups protested the first eight suspensions with letters, meetings, and testimonial dinners. Of the 55 teachers in Alice Citron's Harlem school, 48 wrote to Jansen that Citron had "worked tirelessly in behalf of the children": "we who have worked with her are not concerned with her political or extracurricular affiliation. . . . We are deeply concerned over her value as a teacher of merit who has worked untiringly with love and devotion, with personal sacrifice in the community where she is serving." A parade of Harlem mothers testified to the same effect during Citron's trial.[33]

The presidents of the four city colleges barred the suspended teachers from speaking on their campuses. The Queens College student council and three other campus groups had invited Celia Zitron; they refused to revoke the invitation, and several hundred people "stood outdoors in the rain to hear her."[34] The college then suspended the charters of the student groups; President John Theobald put 21 students on probation for defying the ban and announced, "Any future violations of this sort will result in immediate dismissal."[35]

At the same time that the Board of Education was gearing up for administrative trials of the eight suspended teachers, it was escalating its attack on the Teachers Union. Early in the spring of 1950, George Timone introduced a resolution that barred the union from representing teachers before the board or negotiating with the board on any issue.[36]

A union campaign elicited dozens of petitions opposing the Timone resolution, from teachers, parents, other unions, and civil rights groups. The anti-TU forces were equally impassioned. More than 100 people spoke at a public meeting in April 1950, many of whom waited for over six hours for their turn.[37] Rose Russell was in fighting form, charging that it was "not an accident that, behind the smokescreen of alleged communist domination, this attack on the Teachers Union comes at the moment when the Mayor's budget provides for no salary increases, but threatens larger classes, elimination of positions, heavier workloads, and continued seasonal unemployment for hundreds of substitutes." Russell challenged any organization to match the TU's "34-year history of championship of better schools"—for "improvement of plant, equipment, building, and recreational facilities; enrichment of curriculum; elimination of discrimination; safeguarding of academic freedom." The "so-called 'dossier' on the Teachers Union, peddled by Mr. Timone and his inveterate chorus from the American Legion, Catholic War Veterans and allied groups," was "replete with irrelevancies, innuendos, half-truths,

The first eight teachers fired by the Board of Education. *From left*: Alice Citron, Abraham Feingold, David Friedman, Celia Zitron, Abraham Lederman, Mark Friedlander, Isadore Rubin, Louis Jaffe. (Thanks to Irving Adler for all but one of the identifications.) (Courtesy of United Federation of Teachers, UFT Photographs Archive, Tamiment Library, New York University)

and downright lies." For example, "Mr. Timone delights in recalling that 700 teachers left the Teachers Union in 1935 to form the Teachers Guild. He omits to add that 1,200 remained, to build the Teachers Union into an organization which then for the first time grew to more than 6,000 in three years."[38]

If Russell was not entirely candid about the extent of communist leadership in the TU, she nevertheless had a point about the Board of Education's motives. Communist domination gave the board an excuse for blacklisting an organization that had been an annoyance for the past two decades. The union's adherence to the CP line did not prevent it from wholeheartedly advocating for teachers, parents, and children.[39]

The Board of Education postponed a final vote on the Timone resolution to June 1950, when it passed with only one dissent.[40] It was a devastating blow, but remarkably, the TU survived for another 14 years. Just two weeks after the resolution passed, the union sent all board members except Timone copies of its just-published report on the pervasive racism in textbooks used in the city schools, many of them authored by board officials. Among the numerous examples was a text contending that slavery was "a happy life" because it meant that slaves had "no cares except to do their work well"; another book, written by Superintendent Jansen, asserted that "the native people of Africa, who belong to the Negro race, are very backward."[41]

The TU had been complaining about such statements in textbooks since the 1930s, pointing out their deadly effect on the morale of African American students. The board stubbornly resisted change. One scholar comments, "Although it is hardly a revelation that resistance to desegregation fueled the McCarthyism of conservatives, especially in the South after the *Brown v. Board of Education* decision, it is far less commonly understood in regards to anticommunism in northern, cosmopolitan cities such as New York."[42]

The union continued to publish materials on African American history, and to fight for school integration, until it disbanded in 1964, but the Timone resolution, as one scholar notes, "marked the beginning of a protracted and costly battle" for survival.[43] In 1952, Commissioner of Education James Allen dismissed a TU appeal from the board's refusal to allow it to use school buildings, even though the union was never given an opportunity to be heard. Allen said the board had discretion to refuse a request when "the sentiment of the community is divided." In this case, the American Legion, the Catholic War Veterans, and the VFW participated as *amici curiae* praising the board's ruling; Osmond Fraenkel, one of the relatively few liberals who continued to defend the free-speech rights of communists, filed a brief on the other side on behalf of the New York Civil Liberties Union.[44] Fraenkel had "a reputation for integrity and legal craftsmanship,"[45] according to the *New York Times*; this made him an important figure in legitimizing the arguments of the TU and others who could be dismissed by the mainstream press as defenders of free speech only when their own interests were at stake.

First Casualties

The administrative trial of the eight suspended teachers began in September 1950. It was not a propitious moment for those who were suspected of communist sympathies. The first six months of 1950 were filled with sensational revelations about atomic espionage and accusations against American communists, culminating in the arrest of Julius and Ethel Rosenberg in July. The Korean War began in June. The Board of Education's trial examiner, Theodore Kiendl, took advantage of the situation by orchestrating a joint trial of the eight to begin not with Alice Citron's case, as was initially anticipated, her name being first alphabetically, but with David Friedman's, the only one of the eight actually accused of CP membership. The prosecution, led by New

York City Corporation Counsel Michael Castaldi, was thus able to spend the first week of the trial presenting witnesses who explicated in detail the revolutionary tenets of international communism. The most prolific of them, Louis Budenz, had been managing editor of the *Daily Worker*, was now a convert to Catholicism, and had served as a paid informant to the FBI, a star witness before Washington State's Canwell Committee, and a prosecution witness at the Smith Act trial of CP leaders the previous year. The defense attorneys objected and demanded separate trials, to no avail.[46]

The proceedings began with an inflammatory opening speech by city lawyer John McGrath, proclaiming that "ten nations of the western world have already been engulfed by the communist menace" and "the blood of our sons is being shed in a foreign land [Korea]."[47] There followed eight days of testimony from Budenz and other ex-communist witnesses on the history and ideology of communism, replete with citations to Marxist and Leninist texts and personal recollections of experiences going back 20 years, none of them connected to the defendants.

But Kiendl would not permit the testimony of Professor Thomas Emerson of Yale Law School and other experts on academic freedom. Not relevant, he said, rejecting defense lawyer Nathan Witt's argument that "the relationship between academic freedom and inquiries of teachers as to their political beliefs, opinions, and affiliations" was at the heart of the case.[48]

On day 12 of the trials, the TU's Rose Russell, not a lawyer but a gifted advocate, cross-examined Jansen:

RUSSELL: Did you learn or receive any information to the effect that Mr. Friedman advocated the violent overthrow of the government?

JANSEN: No. . . .

RUSSELL: Did you learn from Mr. Friedman's supervisors that Mr. Friedman had ever uttered any treasonable words?

JANSEN: I did not.

RUSSELL: Did you learn from Mr. Friedman's supervisors that Mr. Friedman had ever uttered any seditious words?

JANSEN: I did not. . . .

RUSSELL: Did you receive such information from any other source?

JANSEN: In the classroom—I did not.

RUSSELL: From any other source?

JANSEN: I did not.

RUSSELL: Did you learn from Mr. Friedman's supervisors that Mr. Friedman had ever used his position to inculcate the communist doctrine into pupils in the public schools?

JANSEN: I did not.

RUSSELL: Did you learn or receive information that Mr. Friedman had ever used his position to inculcate the communist doctrine into his pupils from any other source?

JANSEN: I did not. . . .

It was classic cross-examination: Russell knew that the answers would be negative. Trial examiner Kiendl stopped her: "It does seem to me that you are trying to disprove something which is not being charged." Russell reminded him that prosecutor McGrath had made just these charges in his opening statement. But he had not proved any of it, Kiendl replied; the only issue was whether Friedman was a CP member and whether the CP advocated violent overthrow of the government.[49]

The eight teachers were duly convicted—that is, Kiendl submitted his findings and recommendations to the Board of Education, which officially fired them in February 1951. Several months later, the TU newspaper *New York Teacher* commented, in a story headlined "1950–51: Year of Disaster for Our Schools," that the board had faced "documented fraud in school contracts, rat-infested school buildings, leaky crumbling roofs, filthy toilet facilities, bulging classrooms, children without classrooms, [and] double and triple shifts," yet its, and Jansen's, "only concern was the non-existent problem of 'subversive' teachers."[50]

Meanwhile, Jansen was prosecuting eight more teachers for insubordination and conduct unbecoming. This group included Mildred Flacks, an elementary school teacher and activist in Brooklyn's poor, minority Bedford-Stuyvesant neighborhood, and Irving Adler, already a plaintiff in the suit against the Feinberg Law. On December 6, 1951, the board also officially resolved that no CP member could continue in employment and that past membership would be evidence of present membership unless the teacher showed it had been "terminated in good faith."[51] The best way to demonstrate good faith was to identify others who might have been in the Party, attended a Marxist study group, marched in a May Day parade, or otherwise manifested leftist tendencies. "Naming names" thus became a standard interview question.

The board resolution of December 1951 gave official sanction to what was already going on, but it went further than the Feinberg Law or the Truman loyalty program, which merely established, at least in theory, rebuttable presumptions that communist affiliation made one unfit for employment. The board's policy was pure guilt by association, leaving no room for argument that one's membership was brief, innocent, or free of any revolutionary intent. The TU challenged the policy as part of an appeal by the second group of eight teachers, who were suspended without pay in January 1952; their case came to be known as *Adler II*.

The lawyers in *Adler II* had two other important arguments: that the board had no business asking about the teachers' politics in the first place and that even if it did, the procedures it used were illegitimate because they violated the Feinberg Law. But neither the commissioner of education nor the state courts were listening. By this point, the Supreme Court had upheld the federal loyalty program (in April 1951), a loyalty oath imposed by the City of Los Angeles (in June 1951), and, finally, the Feinberg Law (in March 1952).[52] There was little chance that in the face of these precedents, the teachers could persuade the New York courts that the board's investigations were unlawful.

In July 1951, Jansen turned the interview process over to Saul Moskoff of the Corporation Counsel's office. Moskoff was eager and conscientious: he had once spent months at the police academy studying the intricacies of pinball machines so that he could represent the city effectively in its campaign to ban them.[53] Moskoff, his chief investigator, John Dunne, and a detective from the police department's BOSSI unit began a thorough combing of the files for more teachers to question.[54]

Moskoff conducted hundreds of interviews at what TU chronicler Celia Zitron describes as "an old, depressing building" near Board of Education headquarters at 110 Livingston Street in Brooklyn.[55] The interviews, the subsequent disciplinary proceedings, appeals to the commissioner of education and to the courts, and eventually, demands that ex-communist teachers "name names" of former comrades or lose their jobs went on for most of the 1950s. Eventually, more than 1,000 employees were interrogated; more than 200 resigned rather than go through the process and face the distasteful choice of either being purged or "telling all" and, most likely, being forced to inform on others. Thirty-three were officially fired.[56] One newspaper commented that "the rather remarkable total" of resignations and voluntary retirements "is considered by school authorities to be a tribute to one clever, indefatigable man—Saul Moskoff—and to his methods."[57]

In addition to teachers' past or present CP membership, Moskoff's questioning covered "books they had read, people they knew, whether they had contributed to the cause of Republican Spain or the support of Spanish refugees after the victory of Franco, whether they had ever enrolled in the American Labor Party or signed nominating petitions for minority parties."[58] One of their anonymous accusers was the ex-communist informer Harvey Matusow, whom Moskoff hired as an advisor in 1952. Matusow's memory was vague even when he was not deliberately fabricating, as his subsequent

Cartoonist Bernard Kassoy's view of the New York Board of Education investigations; from *New York Teacher*. (Courtesy of the Kassoy family)

memoir, *False Witness*, explained. Moskoff pursued one teacher based on Matusow's "recollection" that she was a communist, even though he did not remember her name or what she taught.[59]

Moskoff was deeply invested in the politics of anti-communism. His interviews often began with a prescribed script: "Are you now a member of the Communist Party? Were you ever a member of the Communist Party? Have you ever made any financial contribution to the support of the Communist Party? Have you attended any meetings, lectures, conferences, or schools sponsored by the Communist Party?" If the teacher admitted membership, there were further questions as to "when he joined, when he left, why he left, to which unit he belonged, who recruited him, where his unit met, and the names of other teachers, if any, in the unit."[60] But Moskoff would depart from the script when inspired or provoked. The interviews thus included hot debates between Moskoff and his upset, frightened, and indignant targets. The debates were philosophical and theological: Moskoff and nearly all the teachers he interrogated were Jewish, and some cited religious roots for their objections to the procedure and particularly to informing.

In Moskoff's interrogation of high school science teacher Maurice Kurzman, for example, Kurzman takes the offensive, calling the process "an attempt to impose thought control upon our school system"—part of "a widespread witch hunt against all progressive and liberal elements in our country." Then he gets personal: the investigation, he tells Moskoff, "is a conspiracy against American values, and you are part of it." Furthermore, "it is no accident that most of the teachers who have been called before this inquisition have been of the Jewish faith. In all great periods of oppression it is the Jewish people who have been persecuted by these inquisitions." Moskoff's response is unlikely to lower the temperature: "Are you Jewish, Mr. Kurzman?" he asks, "because I doubt your Jewishness." Kurzman replies, "I feel strongly about the role which you are playing here, because among all honest people the role of procurer or informer is considered the vilest and very basest. Among all Jews this type of activity is considered the most depraved, the most anti-Jewish conduct in the book."

"You had better study the Talmud," Moskoff retorts. Kurzman responds,

I have studied the Talmud. You are following the same pattern which is becoming so popular now wherein the enemies of the people use willing and compliant Jews to do their hatchet work for them. . . . There were some Jewish policemen in the Warsaw ghetto who sought to save themselves from the Nazis by acting as informers and betraying their fellow countrymen. They found out too late that they, too, were sucked into the abyss which they sought to prepare for others.[61]

6

The Vinson Court

Judicial Passivity

Fred Vinson, the new chief justice, arrived at the Supreme Court in June 1946, just three weeks after it had decided in *United States v. Lovett* that a law firing specifically named federal employees was unconstitutional.[1] The facts of the *Lovett* case were unusual, but the ruling at least suggested that the justices were willing to overturn a law passed by Congress if its anti-communist enthusiasms got out of hand.

The early Vinson Court showed promise of similar liberalism in 1948 when it ruled that the Constitution prohibits courts from enforcing racially restrictive covenants—private agreements not to sell property to African Americans.[2] Two years later, it paved the way for *Brown v. Board of Education* by striking down racial segregation in graduate schools and in railroad dining cars.[3] But when it came to political inquisitions, the Vinson Court was decidedly less assertive. Although eventually it invalidated a few of the more egregious anti-communist initiatives, it did nothing effective to limit the heresy hunt, and it made a wreck of the First Amendment jurisprudence that the Court had built under its previous chiefs, Charles Evans Hughes and Harlan Fiske Stone.

In part, the Court's lamentable performance was a function of chance. Liberal justices Frank Murphy and Wiley Rutledge died in 1949, enabling President Truman to appoint his old friend, Indiana senator Sherman Minton, and his Texan attorney general, Tom Clark, to the vacant slots. Both were national security oriented and weak on civil liberties; Clark, like Vinson one of the president's poker buddies,[4] had been managing the Attorney General's List of subversive organizations for the past two years. Whereas Murphy and Rutledge had formed a pro-civil-liberties bloc with Justices Black, Douglas, and Stone, Minton and Clark gave a solid majority to the Court's conservative wing, which proceeded, as Harvard law professor Morton Horwitz writes, to uphold "virtually every repressive governmental measure justified in the name of national security."[5]

Of the other Vinson Court justices, FDR appointee Stanley Reed was "a cosmopolitan, soft-spoken Kentucky aristocrat," a connoisseur of race horses and good bourbon,[6] who left little imprint on the Court; Harold Burton of Ohio, appointed in 1945, was considered "the most liberal" of Truman's four appointments,[7] but that is not saying much, given that Vinson, Minton, and Clark were the other three. As for Felix Frankfurter, he taxed his colleagues' patience with long disquisitions on the importance of judicial deference to the other branches of government and often wrote long concurring opinions to explain why he was upholding various civil liberties violations even though he personally disapproved of them. Frankfurter made exceptions to judicial restraint, however, when it came to issues about which he felt particularly passionate, such as academic freedom. Robert Jackson also wrote lengthy and ambiguous concurrences that did nothing tangible to stop the political repression engulfing America.

The first sign of Vinson Court passivity came two years after *Lovett*, when the justices refused to review the contempt-of-Congress convictions of two people who had refused to cooperate with HUAC, now no longer chaired by Martin Dies but by New Jersey congressman J. Parnell Thomas, with active assistance from fledgling California congressman Richard Nixon. Leon Josephson's case was the first. He was the older brother of Barney Josephson, proprietor of Café Society, New York's first interracial nightclub outside Harlem, where some of the most brilliant musicians of the time, among them Billie Holiday and Lena Horne, performed. Café Society's racially progressive politics did not endear it to the FBI's J. Edgar Hoover and others who equated racial integration with communism.[8] Josephson, an ex-communist, was the club's lawyer and also represented the International Workers Order, a large mutual-aid and insurance society that was soon to be listed by the attorney general as a communist front.

Believing Josephson to be implicated in passport fraud, HUAC subpoenaed him in February 1947. Josephson resisted questioning; the Second Circuit Court of Appeals affirmed his conviction for contempt of Congress. The court explained that even if HUAC's questions about peaceful dissent would have violated the First Amendment, at least some questions it might have asked— about the violent overthrow of the government, for example—would have been legitimate. Since Josephson had refused to testify at all, the court reasoned, "he cannot now claim that the authorizing statute is invalid merely because it did not furnish him with criteria that were sufficiently definite to permit him to determine the pertinency of some question that might never have been asked."[9]

Judge Charles Clark dissented, arguing that congressional committees "cannot undertake a completely unlimited inquisition in the area protected by the First Amendment." The term "un-American" in the House resolution authorizing HUAC was completely undefined, giving the committee unbridled power to go after "all varieties of organizations," among them the National Catholic Welfare Conference, the Farmer-Labor Party, and publications including *Time* magazine.[10]

Clark's dissent in *Josephson* pungently chronicled the excesses of congressional inquisitions, but it did not persuade the Supreme Court to review the case or the U.S. Court of Appeals for the District of Columbia Circuit to reach a different result in the next First Amendment challenge to HUAC. During the Spanish Civil War, Dr. Edward Barsky had joined with other physicians to supply ambulances and medicines for the Loyalist forces. After Franco's victory, Barsky organized the Joint Anti-Fascist Refugee Committee (JAFRC) to aid both prisoners in Spain and exiles living in refugee camps in Vichy France and North Africa. From 1942 to 1946, JAFRC worked under license from the U.S. War Relief Control Board,[11] but after the war, HUAC began to investigate its progressive politics. In its very first post-war subpoena in December 1945, HUAC ordered JAFRC to produce all "books, ledger sheets, bank statements, documents, and records" that disclosed the identities of its 30,000 or so contributors and of the refugees who had received its aid in the two past years. Some of them were in hiding inside fascist Spain.[12]

Each of JAFRC's 17 board members was called before HUAC and refused to surrender the records. All were convicted of contempt of Congress in March 1946, almost a year before HUAC went after Leon Josephson or the Hollywood Ten.[13] But the court proceedings took longer, and by the time the case was on appeal, *Josephson* had already been decided. Rejecting the defendants' argument that the HUAC investigation was unconstitutional, the D.C. Circuit reasoned that they "were not asked to state their political opinions. They were asked to account for funds." The D.C. Circuit judges did acknowledge that HUAC might have probed the defendants' politics and that "swirling currents of public emotion in both directions" made the case "difficult and delicate." Although admittedly the JAFRC directors posed no imminent danger, the court said "it would be sheer folly" for the government "to refrain from inquiry into potential threats to its existence or security until danger was clear and present."[14]

The judges in *Barsky*, as in *Josephson*, thus abandoned the "clear and present danger" standard that the Supreme Court had begun to apply seriously in the 1930s to limit the government's power to interfere with First Amendment rights. And as in *Josephson*, there was a dissent: Judge Henry Edgerton argued that HUAC's *modus operandi*—"uncovering and stigmatizing" unpopular views, thereby exposing people to "insult, ostracism, and lasting loss of employment"—was a powerful deterrent to free speech.[15] Edgerton's ability to see past the perceived urgencies of the time eventually earned him the gratitude of the Washington, D.C., affiliate of the ACLU, which created the Henry W. Edgerton Civil Liberties Award in his honor. But in 1948, he was unable to sway the Supreme Court, which, as in *Josephson*, declined to review the convictions of the JAFRC officers.[16]

Without any word of caution from the Supreme Court since the *Lovett* case in 1946, all branches and levels of government were by 1949 fully engaged in exposing and rooting out suspected communists. January 1949 saw the opening of the nine-month criminal trial of 11 CP leaders for conspiracy to advocate the overthrow of the government, in violation of the 1940 Smith Act. HUAC was busy with numerous investigations. In February 1950, Senator Joseph McCarthy stupefied the country with the first of his many reckless charges that the federal government—in this instance, the State Department—was filled with treasonous communists employed in high places.

Loyalty Oaths for Labor

In May 1950, the Vinson Court took its first plunge into the legal morass created by the new loyalty apparatus. The case involved section 9(h) of the 1947 Taft-Hartley Act, which required affidavits abjuring communist associations or beliefs from all officers in unions that wanted the protections of federal labor law.[17] Congress had passed Taft-Hartley over Truman's veto, but as attorney Victor Rabinowitz, who represented a union of telegraph and radio operators in challenging the oath, recalled, Truman's solicitor general argued enthusiastically in defense of the law: "If he was representing a president who wanted the law repealed, he certainly gave no sign of it."[18]

Rabinowitz knew that his chances were slim, not only because of the tense political atmosphere but because Justices Murphy, Rutledge, and Douglas were all absent from the oral argument. "I well remember that appalling summer of 1949," Rabinowitz later wrote: "Justice Murphy died of a heart attack in July. Justice Rutledge had a stroke and died in August. And then, late in September, Justice Douglas had a horseback-riding accident at Goose Creek in Washington and was unable to take his place on the bench when it convened in October. Three sure votes lost, in two short months." The oral argument was grim: "The hostility in the courtroom was palpable. I knew that disaster was inevitable."[19]

Rabinowitz attacked section 9(h) as a violation of the First Amendment, as unconstitutionally vague, and as an unconstitutional bill of attainder—the reason the Court had struck down Civil War loyalty oaths a century before. But the Court in *American Communications Association v. Douds* swept aside his arguments. Chief Justice Vinson wrote the opinion, although only Reed and Burton joined in all of its reasoning. Frankfurter and Jackson concurred in the basic result. This first major Supreme Court encounter with the test oaths, blacklisting, and guilt by association that came to define the Red hunt of the 1950s was thus decided by a fractured majority of five justices, but it was cited ceaselessly in the years to come as signaling the Court's approval of nearly any anti-subversive measure.

Vinson's opinion in *Douds* primarily justified the Taft-Hartley oath as a means of preventing strikes. Congress had evidence "that communists and others proscribed by the statute had infiltrated union organizations not to support and further trade union objectives, including the advocacy of change by democratic methods, but to make them a device by which commerce and industry might be disrupted when the dictates of political policy required such action."[20] In simpler terms, Congress thought communists would organize strikes not just to achieve better pay and working conditions but to disrupt the economy sufficiently to prepare for revolution.

But these were speculative perils, hardly enough to meet the "clear and present danger" test that applies when government invades free speech. Vinson's answer was to interpret "clear and present danger" so loosely that it became meaningless. "A rigid test requiring a showing of imminent danger to the security of the Nation is an absurdity," he said. He acknowledged that "the breadth" of the Taft-Hartley oath "would raise additional questions" if read literally "to include all persons who might, under any conceivable circumstances," hold revolutionary ideas. So he interpreted the language narrowly to cover only those "persons and organizations who believe in violent overthrow of the Government as it presently exists under the Constitution as an objective, not merely a prophecy." Then he assumed that any CP member fell in the latter category.[21]

Vinson may have thought that by limiting the scope of 9(h), he was keeping the heresy hunt within bounds. What he failed to realize—or ignored—was that the distinction between an "objective" and a "prophecy" is difficult to make in the most deliberative of circumstances. It is rarely made by loyalty boards, FBI investigators, or prosecutors in politically uncertain times. And the oath itself made no such distinction: it barred anyone who was a member of, or "affiliated" with, the Communist Party.

Justice Frankfurter agreed that section 9(h), as written, was too broad and vague, but unlike Vinson, he did not think the Court could simply interpret the oath's language to make it narrower. His concurring opinion was full of insight into the dangers of test oaths. To ask a person to disavow belief in revolution "trenches on those aspects of individual freedom which we rightly regard as the most cherished aspects of Western civilization." Frankfurter thus was willing to be a judicial activist on the subject of test oaths. Why then, did he vote with the majority to uphold section 9(h)? Psychoanalysts can debate the point, but the justice's explanation was that the "offensive provisions" of the oath left its valid portion unaffected; he only wanted the language focusing on belief to be deleted.[22]

A great writer of essays in the form of opinions and a gifted coiner of ringing phrases, Robert Jackson was "a lone wolf on the Court," as William O. Douglas wrote in his memoirs, with "no close friend except Frankfurter" and an unfulfilled ambition to be chief justice that "truly poisoned his career."[23] Jackson's concurring opinion in *Douds* recognized that the effects of the Taft-Hartley oath were neither minor nor indirect: "No one likes to be compelled to exonerate himself from connections he has never acquired." If the law required union officers "to forswear membership in the Republican Party, the Democratic Party or the Socialist Party," Jackson wrote, "I suppose all agree that it would be unconstitutional." But the CP-USA was different: behind its "political party facade, the Communist Party is a conspiratorial and revolutionary junta." He did not forgive the CP's flip-flop after Hitler broke his pact with Stalin and invaded the USSR and the Party line switched from avid efforts to retard any U.S. aid to the allies to unconscionable demands "that American soldiers, whose equipment they had delayed and sabotaged, be sacrificed in a premature second front to spare Russia."[24]

Jackson's passionate anti-communism thus warped his reasoning, for it did not follow from the sins of the Party leadership in 1941 that any CP member in 1950 should be deprived of First Amendment rights. But because he found the oath so troubling, and its chill on free speech far more serious than Vinson did, Jackson did not want the *Douds* decision to be used as precedent for suppressing political opinions; hence, he limited his concurrence to the evils of communism—"without which," he said, "I should regard this Act as unconstitutional." After all, "our own Government originated in revolution. . . . That circumstances sometimes justify it is not Communist doctrine but an old American belief."[25]

Jackson thus aimed to exclude communists from First Amendment protection. But he was deeply ambivalent about the result. When the justices first discussed the case after oral argument, he had voted to strike down the non-communist oath.[26] His papers in the Library of Congress leave no clue as to why he changed his mind. Even his admirer, Harvard professor Arthur Schlesinger, Jr., who wrote to Jackson diplomatically praising his "masterly opinion," wondered whether his "contention that 'every member of the Communist Party is an agent to execute the Communist program' is factually true." Jackson replied that, certainly in some circumstances, "a distinction should be drawn between a potential agent and an actual agent," but he did not think such a distinction was called for in *Douds*. "That is one of the difficulties from confining attention closely to the concrete situation while the profession will apply the opinion more generally," he lamented.[27]

Hugo Black's approach was simpler: the First Amendment had the "express purpose" of barring Congress from abridging expression or belief. Black offered a historical lesson on the test oath:

> It was one of the major devices used against the Huguenots in France, and against "heretics" during the Spanish Inquisition. It helped English rulers identify and outlaw Catholics, Quakers, Baptists, and Congregationalists— groups considered dangerous for political as well as religious reasons. And wherever the test oath was in vogue, spies and informers found rewards far more tempting than truth. . . . Whether religious, political, or both, test oaths are implacable foes of free thought.[28]

Black was right to invoke history. The creators of the American government made a decision to ban test oaths, at least religious ones: Article VI of the Constitution requires executive, legislative, and judicial officers, both state and federal, to be "bound by Oath or Affirmation" to support the Constitution but adds that "no religious Test shall ever be required as a Qualification to any Office or public Trust under the United States." Objectors during the 1950s argued that Article VI invalidates all test oaths, not just strictly "religious" ones. (They did not consider a simple oath to support the Constitution as a "test.")

At least one of the Constitution's framers agreed. Alexander Hamilton denounced all test oaths, arguing that it would be an obvious infringement of the Constitution if, "instead of the mode of indictment and trial by jury," the legislature were simply to declare "that every citizen who did not swear he had never adhered to the King of Great Britain, should incur all the penalties which our treason laws prescribe."[29] But America could not resist such oaths: George Washington used them during the Revolution; North and South used them during the Civil War. Inquisitions into political belief during Abraham Lincoln's administration prefigured the range of abuses that flourished a century later: freelance compilers of blacklists, informers of dubious credibility, anonymous sources, innuendo, guilt by association. A historian of American loyalty oaths notes that neither security nor the cause of independence was "rendered a whit stronger by all the oaths taken and refused"; nevertheless, by the end of the Civil War, oaths had become a convenient way to strip those who were unwilling or unable to swear past and present fealty to the winning side of their property, their civil rights, and even their ability to buy food or marry.[30]

Ironically, it was the enthusiasm for test oaths that eventually led to the collapse of loyalty programs after the Supreme Court's 1967 decision in *Keyishian v. Board of Regents*. Oaths greatly expand the pool of people affected—that is, they drag into the administrative net people who otherwise might not even notice the existence of a loyalty program. If the faculty at the State University of New York at Buffalo had not been forced to sign an oath disclaiming CP membership, then Harry Keyishian and his fellow plaintiffs would probably never have brought their legal challenge to the Feinberg Law.

The Odd Twins: *Bailey* and *JAFRC*

The Vinson Court's next brush with anti-subversive machinery encompassed many more people than the Taft-Hartley oath had. President Truman's executive order requiring loyalty investigations of all federal workers had been in effect for about a year when Dorothy Bailey, a personnel trainer with the Civil Service Commission, learned that her regional loyalty board had "received information" that she was or had been a member of the Communist Party, the American League for Peace and Democracy, and the Washington Committee for Democratic Action, all organizations on the Attorney General's List. Bailey was fired after a hearing in which she never learned the source of the accusations and vigorously denied them. She admitted she had once been a member of the American League and, when a student at Bryn Mawr in 1932, had attended one communist meeting "in connection with a seminar study of the platforms of the various parties." She submitted 70 supporting affidavits, and four witnesses testified to her character, including job supervisors and a Methodist minister who was "dumbfounded" by the accusation of disloyalty.[31]

The Court of Appeals for the D.C. Circuit acknowledged that Bailey's case was "undoubtedly appealing": she "was not given a trial in any sense of the word, and she does not know who informed upon her." But since she was not in the "classified service" at the time of her firing, she was not entitled to a hearing, and even if she had been, there was no violation of due process or the First Amendment. The "clear and present danger" test was irrelevant because "no one denies Miss Bailey the right to any political activity or affiliation she may choose"; she was simply denied a government job. Given the tense world situation, the judges said, it was for the president to decide that "only those whose loyalty is beyond suspicion should be employed by this Government."[32]

As in the *Barsky* case, Judge Edgerton dissented. He disputed the majority's cavalier approach both to the First Amendment and to the government's unfair procedures for depriving people of their livelihoods. He pointed to the types of questions asked of employees at loyalty hearings: "What books do you read?"; "Do you think that Russian Communism is likely to succeed?"; "How do you explain the fact that you have Paul Robeson record[s] in your home?"; "Do you ever entertain Negroes in your home?" And he argued that even the executive order creating the loyalty program did not allow firings based on anonymous sources with no opportunity to rebut the evidence or to cross-examine.[33]

The Vinson Court agreed to consider Bailey's appeal. It was, as one of the law clerks observed, the flip side of another case that was already pending, brought by organizations challenging the Attorney General's List. One case was about the fate of organizations; *Bailey* was about the fate of individuals.[34] Oral argument was heard in October 1950. The treatment of tens of thousands of federal workers—and by extension, thousands more in state loyalty programs—was riding on the result. But the Korean War had begun the previous June, and anti-communism had reached epidemic heights. On April 30, 1951, the D.C. Circuit's decision in *Bailey v. Richardson* was affirmed by an equally divided vote of the justices, with no explanation of reasons. Minton, Burton, Reed, and Vinson voted to affirm Bailey's treatment; Jackson, Douglas, Frankfurter, and Black voted to reverse.[35] Clark, the former attorney general, did not participate. Affirmance without a written opinion was standard in 4–4 cases, but as one critic observed, the practice of appointing attorneys general to the Court "makes the four to four decision a constant obstacle in the way of clarification."[36]

The same day as *Bailey*, the justices imposed their first, albeit modest, limit on the mounting repression, and although its decision in this case had little practical effect, it was at least evidence that the Vinson Court would not be completely supine. Truman's order establishing the federal loyalty program directed the attorney general, "after appropriate investigation and determination," to compile a list of "totalitarian, fascist, communist, or subversive" organizations. By the time of oral argument, JAFRC, the lead plaintiff in the lawsuit challenging the Justice Department's method for compiling the Attorney General's List, had already been decimated by the jailing of its entire board and its staff director for refusing to disclose to HUAC their contributors and recipients of aid. Now, with its co-plaintiffs, the National Council of American-Soviet Friendship and the International Workers Order

(IWO), JAFRC was contesting its designation as a "communist" organization. The IWO, a fraternal benefit society, primarily provided life insurance to its 185,000 members. The National Council of American-Soviet Friendship was an educational and cultural group that denied "any totalitarian, fascist, communist, subversive, or otherwise violent or unlawful purpose."[37]

Although technically a part of the federal loyalty program, the Attorney General's List was also used by state and local loyalty boards, by private corporations, by universities, and by freelance compilers of blacklists. Being listed had a predictably devastating effect on organizations' membership and contributions. Meeting places became difficult to find; fund-raising was crippled. The Internal Revenue Service revoked the tax-exempt status of eight organizations based on the list; New York's insurance commissioner began proceedings to dissolve the IWO.[38] Yet the Justice Department offered no due process and gave organizations no chance to contest the listings.

The government lawyers were so sure of the attorney general's unbridled power to compile the list that they did not even contest the plaintiffs' claims that they were not communist organizations. A federal district court had nevertheless dismissed the lawsuit. On these facts, and for reasons elaborated in five separate opinions, a majority of the Supreme Court found the attorney general's procedures unlawful, reversed the lower court order dismissing the case, and sent it back for further proceedings.

There was much contention at the Court, and many draft opinions were exchanged. Jackson wrote at one point that he had received Douglas's draft and that, "lest the similarity of our results create some impression that I am sympathetic with his reasons, I desire expressly to disassociate myself from his opinion." He was incensed by Douglas's attack on the Justice Department: "As judges," Jackson said, "it would suffice if we find that a good faith mistake in an unsettled and debatable field has been made as to the procedural safeguards necessary to a conclusive finding of disloyalty"; it did not "seem necessary also to join the Communist campaign to smear our own Government by accusing this measure of being 'totalitarian' in trend, of borrowing 'totalitarian' techniques."[39]

In the end, Harold Burton wrote the "opinion for the Court," but only Douglas joined in its reasoning. Burton essayed no view on the constitutionality of the loyalty program, simply ruling that the procedures ascribed to the Justice Department, which it did not deny, were "patently arbitrary." Burton was careful to note, "Nothing we have said purports to adjudicate the truth of petitioners' allegations that they are not in fact communistic." Whether the attorney general could "reasonably find them to be so" would have to "await determination by the District Court."[40]

Justice Burton's choice of a narrow ground to strike down the attorney general's procedure—rather than, for example, ruling that guilt by association is unacceptable as a means of uncovering subversives—left ample room for further Justice Department maneuvering. But as Douglas later noted, if Burton had decided the constitutional issues, he "would have been with the dissenters."[41]

Frankfurter, despite his philosophy of judicial passivity, did not think the Court could ignore the constitutional issue of due process. The "heart of the matter," he wrote in a concurring opinion, was that "democracy implies respect for the elementary rights of men, however suspect or unworthy; a democratic government must therefore practice fairness," and fairness, embodied in the Constitution's due process clause, "can rarely be obtained by secret, one-sided determination of facts decisive of rights."[42] Frankfurter received a congratulatory note on his concurrence from none other than Frederic Coudert. Due process of law is "one of our fundamentals," Coudert wrote, apparently forgetting the denial by his own subcommittee of such basic safeguards as the right to confront and cross-examine witnesses. Never, he said, was an expression of the principle "more needed than in our time."[43]

The oddity of the Supreme Court's performance on April 30, 1951—striking down the shoddy procedures that produced the Attorney General's List but approving the use of that list to fire an employee—did not go unremarked. Douglas chose pungent language to express his outrage: "The critical evidence may be the word of an unknown witness who is 'a paragon of veracity, a knave, or the village idiot.' . . . The accused has no opportunity to show that the witness lied or was prejudiced or venal." And although the determination of disloyalty turned on "association with or membership in an organization found to be 'subversive,'" the accused was "not allowed to prove that the charge against the organization is false." This technique of guilt by association is "one of the most odious institutions of history. Guilt under our system of government is personal. When we make guilt vicarious we borrow from systems alien to ours and ape our enemies."[44]

Hugo Black's concurrence in *JAFRC* was equally indignant. "In the present climate of public opinion," he said, the attorney general's "much publicized findings, regardless of their truth or falsity, are the practical equivalents of confiscation and death sentences for any blacklisted organization not possessing extraordinary financial, political or religious prestige and influence." Yet the government not only defended the power "to pronounce such deadly edicts"; it argued that the condemned organizations had "no standing to seek redress in the courts." Black warned that at a historical moment when "prejudice, hate and fear" were rampant, "it may be futile to suggest that the cause of internal security would be fostered, not hurt, by faithful adherence to our constitutional guarantees of individual liberty."[45]

For years after the *JAFRC* decision, the Justice Department erected roadblocks to any reconsideration of its listings and evaded further court challenges.[46] It was a good lesson in *realpolitik*: the decision had no practical effect in limiting the purge. But at least it stood as a rebuke to the government and, in that sense, helped to build, albeit slowly, public and judicial awareness of the excesses of the anti-communist crusade.

Crime and Oaths Revisited

By mid-June 1951, the Vinson Court had approved a political test oath for labor leaders (in *Douds*). It had affirmed the firing of a government worker on evidence that she could not see or contest (in *Bailey*). It had chastised the government, requiring at least somewhat more judicious procedures before branding an organization as subversive (in *JAFRC*). But the Court had not yet addressed the most direct sort of political repression: criminal prosecution for holding and teaching revolutionary ideas.

The 11 defendants in *Dennis v. United States* were officers of the U.S. Communist Party. They had been convicted, after a tumultuous nine-month trial, of violating the 1940 Smith Act by conspiring to advocate the forceful overthrow of the government at some undisclosed future time. All but one were sentenced to five years in prison and a $10,000 fine. The evidence consisted largely of writings by Marx, Lenin, and Stalin, supplemented by historical facts about the American CP: Popular Front–style democratic participation in the late 1930s, culminating in dissolution of the Party and its replacement by the Communist Political Association, then an abrupt change after World War II when the United States and the USSR were no longer allies. Fred Vinson wrote the opinion for the Court affirming the convictions. As he had in *Douds* the year before, Vinson applied such a weak and murky version of the "clear and present danger" test as to make it meaningless.

Vinson began by rejecting the argument that the Smith Act was unconstitutional because it did not require the government to show that the defendants actually intended to overthrow the government. He acknowledged that the Court had poured meaning into "clear and present danger" in the early '40s, in cases involving labor leaders, Jehovah's Witnesses, and occasionally even communists. But, as in *Douds*, he thought it "obvious" that the test "cannot mean that before the Government may act, it must wait until the putsch is about to be executed, the plans have been laid and the signal is awaited." Following the lead of Judge Learned Hand at the court of appeals stage of the case, Vinson substituted a balancing test: "the gravity of the 'evil,' discounted by its improbability, justifies such invasion of free speech as is necessary to avoid the danger." From here, it was an easy step to affirm the convictions: "The mere fact that from the period 1945 to 1948 petitioners' activities did not result in an attempt to overthrow the Government by force and violence is of course no answer to the fact that there was a group that was ready to make the attempt."[47]

Justices Burton, Reed, and Minton joined Vinson's opinion; that made four out of the eight who voted in *Dennis*. (Clark recused himself; as attorney general, he had initiated the prosecution.) Black and Douglas, of course, dissented. That left Frankfurter and Jackson, and as in *Douds*, they had all sorts of reservations but failed to act on them.

Frankfurter's concurrence was characteristically long, convoluted, and insistent on the limited role of courts, especially in hot political cases: "Courts are not representative bodies. . . . History teaches that the independence of the judiciary is jeopardized when courts become embroiled in the passions of the day." But whether from a need to assert his liberal sympathies or to leave a trail of breadcrumbs for the future, when the political climate might be less fraught, he closed with a long quotation from the Cold War scholar George Kennan, attacking the "emotional stresses and temptations" engendered by fear of communism and the danger that Americans would become "rather like the representatives of that very power we are trying to combat: intolerant, secretive, suspicious, cruel, and terrified of internal dissension because we have lost our own belief in ourselves and in the power of our ideals."[48]

As for Justice Jackson, one might have hoped that his passion for free speech would prevail over his hatred of communism, but like Frankfurter, he opted for judicial passivity. Deciding whether the Smith Act unconstitutionally punished speech that created no clear and present danger, he said, would require the Court to "appraise imponderables, including international and national phenomena which baffle the best informed foreign offices and our most experienced politicians." It is a fair enough point, but Jackson went on to "appraise such imponderables" anyway. He said the "clear and present danger" test was inappropriate because it would mean that "Communist plotting is protected during its period of incubation; its preliminary stages of organization and preparation are immune from the law; the Government can move only after imminent action is manifest, when it would, of course, be too late."[49]

The Black and Douglas dissents in *Dennis* required no such appraisal of imponderables. Douglas acknowledged that "the teaching of methods of

terror and other seditious conduct" could be prohibited. But all these defendants did was teach Marxism-Leninism—an insufficient basis for sending
them to jail. Communism was not a clear and present danger in the United
States; in fact, it had been "so thoroughly exposed in this country that it has
been crippled as a political force." True, "in days of trouble and confusion,
when bread lines were long, when the unemployed walked the streets, when
people were starving, the advocates of a short-cut by revolution might have
a chance to gain adherents." But those conditions were long gone. Communists now were "miserable merchants of unwanted ideas."[50]

Black had a simpler approach. The First Amendment said Congress shall
make no law "abridging the freedom of speech." The Smith Act was precisely
such a law. It was "a virulent form of prior censorship." Public opinion, "being
what it now is," would generate little protest against jailing the CP leaders,
but "there is hope that in calmer times, when present pressures, passions and
fears subside, this or some later Court will restore the First Amendment liberties to the high preferred place where they belong in a free society."[51]

Dennis is often considered the defining First Amendment case of the
Cold War era. Vinson's opinion eviscerated the "clear and present danger"
standard and deeply compromised free speech. The biggest impact was not
on the already floundering CP; it was on the many thousands of individuals who were subject to loyalty programs, to blacklisting, and to legislative
inquisitions.[52] And if there was any question, after the Court's tortured decision in *Douds* and its silent affirmance of the firing of Dorothy Bailey, that
loyalty purges could go forward unimpeded, it was answered on the same
day as *Dennis*, in a case again involving that familiar ritual, the test oath.

Los Angeles mandated such an oath in 1948 to implement a loyalty program that the state legislature had put into place seven years before. The 1948
ordinance required all city employees to swear that they had not within the
past five years, and would not while employed by the city, advocate the forceful overthrow of the government or belong to an organization with such an
aim. In a separate affidavit, employees had to disclose any past membership
in the Communist Party or the Communist Political Association, with dates
and durations. Fifteen employees refused both the oath and the affidavit; two
more signed the oath but balked at the affidavit. They all lost their jobs, and
with the help of three of California's leading left-wing lawyers and *amicus*
support from the local ACLU, they filed suit to challenge the oath and, with
it, the city's entire loyalty program.

When the Vinson Court first discussed the case, a majority, including
Jackson, voted to strike down the oath; Douglas drafted an opinion calling it
an unconstitutional bill of attainder. But Jackson could not accept the bill of

attainder argument: being fired, he thought, was not a form of punishment. Frankfurter agreed: "Needless to say I am dead against the basis of Bill's opinion," he wrote to Jackson. "But I have some other things to say about the case. And since you said you would go the other way 'unless somebody gave you a better reason' for adhering to the way you voted at Conference, I hope you will wait and see what I have to say before you make up your mind."[53] Frankfurter drafted a partial dissent that justified the oath as "relevant to effective and dependable government, and to the confidence of the electorate in its government," although acknowledging that "this kind of inquiry into political affiliation may in the long run do more harm than good." Jackson drafted a separate dissent that noted his lack of faith "in compulsory self-disclosures to detect really disloyal persons" but said that just "because the method is more naïve than effective does not mean that the Constitution prevents a city from trying it."[54]

With the two wavering wordsmiths now leaning again toward judicial deference, Douglas had lost his majority. Eventually, Justice Clark wrote the opinion in *Garner v. Board of Public Works*, proclaiming that a municipal employer is free to ask its employees questions "that may prove relevant to their fitness and suitability." Fair enough, but what matters *are* relevant to fitness and suitability? According to Clark, "past loyalty may have a reasonable relationship to present and future trust." The test oath and accompanying investigations were "reasonable," Clark said, citing a Supreme Court decision just a few months earlier that had approved an oath that the state of Maryland required of candidates for political office.[55]

Having said all this, Clark nevertheless read a limit into the Los Angeles oath. He trusted that the city, and the California courts, would not interpret the oath "as affecting adversely those persons who during their affiliation with a proscribed organization were innocent of its purpose, or those who severed their relations with any such organization when its character became apparent." Clark thus assumed that specific knowledge, or *scienter*, was "implicit in each clause of the oath."[56] This notion that oaths and loyalty programs are constitutional if they only punish those who "knowingly" support a group's revolutionary aims was to become a defining feature of the Vinson Court, but it did nothing to diminish the effects of the loyalty purges.

The reasons were eminently practical. For one thing, whether or not past or present political associations were "unknowing," they still had to be disclosed. The Court majority seemed oblivious to the real-world impact of such disclosure, given the fierce anti-communism of the time. It was equally oblivious to the effect of a program that forces people to forswear beliefs and investigates their thoughts to discern whether membership was "knowing."

Such investigation inevitably touches on petitions signed, books read, and donations made to progressive causes. And even if, as the justices assumed, the process would function fairly to sift out "knowing" from "unknowing" membership—an assumption belied by the *Bailey* case as well as any realistic assessment of the decision-making process in loyalty programs—there remained the same basic problem the Court had identified in the Civil War-era cases: test oaths turn due process upside down because anyone who does not sign is assumed guilty and punished without evidence or trial. If Justices Clark and his brethren thought they were protecting innocent employees and restricting the zeal of loyalty investigators by imposing the *scienter* rule, it was an unrealistic hope.

Frankfurter, despite his frequent invocation of judicial restraint, was sufficiently sensitive to the danger of test oaths that he dissented in part. The city's oath was not limited to "knowing" membership, he said, and would thus "operate as a real deterrent to people contemplating even innocent associations. . . . All but the hardiest may well hesitate to join organizations if they know that by such a proscription they will be permanently disqualified from public employment. These are considerations that cut deep into the traditions of our people."[57] Burton agreed with him, though on narrower, technical grounds.[58] Black and Douglas, of course, dissented.

The *scienter* limitation on test oaths in the *Garner* case had little practical impact, but at least it suggested that even in 1951, the Vinson Court would not acquiesce in just any procedure concocted by loyalty officers. This incremental process of limiting the worst aspects of the Red Scare while refusing to wade into the political maelstrom and try to stop it was typical of the Vinson Court and of many later decisions by the Warren Court as well. Judges are always aware of the limits of their power—they are "the least dangerous branch" of government, as Alexander Hamilton famously pointed out, because they have the power neither of the sword nor of the purse.[59] Yet in our system, they are a critical check on the excesses of majority rule, a role that the swing justices, Frankfurter and Jackson, continued to resist.

Irving Adler and the Feinberg Law

It was not surprising, given the Vinson Court's early responses to the Red hunt, that New York State's high court in late 1950 affirmed the ruling of its appellate division that the trial judges Murray Hearn and Harry Schirick had been mistaken when they struck down the Feinberg Law. The unanimous decision by the New York Court of Appeals was not elaborate. It began on the common note of judicial restraint: "We may not, of course, substitute our judgment for that of the Legislature as to the wisdom or expediency of the legislation." And although it acknowledged that not every disqualification for public employment would be constitutional, it found the Feinberg Law reasonable because it dealt with "the vital field of education." There followed the same fluid application of "clear and present danger" that the Supreme Court had used in *Douds* to uphold a test oath and was soon to reprise in *Dennis* to send CP leaders to jail, only this time in the context of education: deference to the legislature's findings that communists had "infiltrated" the schools, so that "subversive propaganda can be disseminated among children of tender years." The plaintiffs' arguments about vagueness and bill of attainder were disposed of with equal dispatch, and with many citations to *Douds*.[60]

The New York high court emphasized that the Feinberg Law made membership in a listed group merely *"prima facie* evidence of disqualification." Once a teacher introduced evidence to contest the charge, the presumption disappeared; the authorities would then have the burden of proving disloyalty.[61] But suspect teachers could not actually do much by way of rebuttal: they might claim that they were falsely accused of membership, but they could not contest the organization's listing—a point that Justice Douglas drove home in his eventual dissent in *Adler v. Board of Education*.

By the time the Supreme Court agreed to review the Feinberg Law case, the Communist Party had dropped out as a plaintiff. The trial court in the Teachers Union suit—the only one of the three challenges that survived— had found that of the 40-odd plaintiffs, only eight taxpayers had standing to sue. In the first round of voting, the justices were 6–2 in favor of affirmance, with Frankfurter in the middle, insisting that with only taxpayers as plaintiffs, there was not a sufficient showing of any harm from the law to create a live controversy.[62] As for the four taxpayer-plaintiffs who were also teachers—Irving Adler, Martha Spencer, and George and Mark Friedlander— Frankfurter pointed out that the papers filed by their lawyers were short on specifics; they had not disclosed whether these four were CP members, advocated government overthrow, uttered seditious words, or had any plans to do so.[63]

Frankfurter's argument that the case was premature did not stop the train wreck. By January 3, 1952, when *Adler* was argued in the Supreme Court, it was a foregone conclusion that the plaintiffs would fail. The *Garner* decision seven months before had rejected a constitutional challenge to Los Angeles's loyalty program, noting that it was reasonable for employers to look into the character and background of their workers. As in *Garner*, the Supreme Court majority in *Adler* was to emphasize that only "knowing" membership in a listed organization could be punished.

Osmond Fraenkel argued for the plaintiffs. Frankfurter had many questions about their "standing"—should not the Court wait until somebody was actually fired or otherwise mistreated? Teachers are "sensitive people," he said; probably thousands of them, in their youth, "thought the Holy Grail was just around the corner" and embraced doctrines or organizations they later abandoned. Jackson interjected that city teachers must be more sensitive than the country ones where he went to school: "They were the most watched of anyone in the community: they can't dance, can't smoke, can't cuss like the rest of us."[64] Whether this was just cornpone or an argument in favor of the government was difficult to tell, but Fraenkel insisted that the case was ripe for review even though there was as yet no direct evidence that the Feinberg Law had caused anybody to be fired. The law created "a miasma of fear and intimidation," he said, which "has a terroristic effect upon the teachers."[65] Two weeks later, he wrote to the Court reiterating that the law was causing present harm, and he enclosed, to prove his point, a copy of Superintendent Jansen's "Order on Teacher-Loyalty Reports," which referenced the regents' July 15, 1949, rules implementing the Feinberg Law and required reports on all employees.[66]

This did not persuade Frankfurter, who wrote in his *Adler* dissent that the Feinberg enforcement scheme was "still an unfinished blueprint": "We are asked to adjudicate claims against its constitutionality before the scheme has been put into operation."[67] Six of his brethren swept aside these arguments in a March 3, 1952, opinion by Sherman Minton, the most anti-civil-liberties of the justices,[68] upholding the law.

Minton did not beat around the bush. Emphasizing the right-privilege distinction encapsulated half a century earlier by Justice Holmes in his famous comment that a person may have a right to talk politics but no right to be a policeman, Minton said that although the First Amendment assures that everybody may "assemble, speak, think and believe as they will," people cannot expect to work in the school system "on their own terms." Teachers work "in a sensitive area in a schoolroom," where they shape young minds. "One's associates, past and present, as well as one's conduct, may properly be considered in determining fitness and loyalty." Minton assumed that the Communist Party was a serious enough threat to justify firing any "knowing" member. Besides, the New York courts had interpreted the Feinberg Law to make membership in a listed organization merely "*prima facie*" evidence of unsuitability for employment, so there was no due process problem.[69]

The opinion at least had the virtue of candor; there was, as one contemporary critic observed, "no mealy-mouthed set of insignificant qualifications, no pretense of doing less than is being done. Guilt by association? Justice Minton sees nothing wrong with showing personal disqualification by checking the views of associates, and he says so. Free speech for teachers? Justice Minton thinks that if they want free speech so badly, they should get other jobs." There was "not even a conventional bow" to academic freedom. According to Minton, "if he doesn't like it here, let him go back where he came from."[70]

As in *Douds* and *Dennis*, Hugo Black's dissent was more in the nature of a political warning: "This is another of those rapidly multiplying legislative enactments which make it dangerous—this time for schoolteachers—to think or say anything except what a transient majority happen to approve at the moment."[71] Douglas was more expansive: he detailed the perils of loyalty programs that turn on "a principle repugnant to our society—guilt by association." A teacher is disqualified because of membership in an organization "found to be 'subversive.'" And the finding of "subversive" character is "made in a proceeding to which the teacher is not a party and in which it is not clear that she may even be heard." True, Douglas said, "she may have a hearing when charges of disloyalty are leveled against her. But in that hearing the finding as to the 'subversive' character of the organization apparently may not be reopened." Instead, "the mere fact of membership in the organization raises a *prima facie* case of her own guilt." And to rebut this presumption of guilt—to determine whether her membership was "innocent" or her former membership was genuinely abandoned—the loyalty patrols must scrutinize all of her associations and views.[72]

Douglas now introduced a new term into the Supreme Court's lexicon. The law, he said, would be "certain to raise havoc with academic freedom." Teachers would "tend to shrink from any association that stirs controversy." The school system would be turned "into a spying project" where "the principals become detectives; the students, the parents, the community become informers. Ears are cocked for tell-tale signs of disloyalty." What, for example, "was the significance of the reference of the art teacher to socialism? Why was the history teacher so openly hostile to Franco Spain? Who heard overtones of revolution in the English teacher's discussion of *The Grapes of Wrath*?" "Where suspicion fills the air and holds scholars in line for fear of their jobs, there can be no exercise of the free intellect," Douglas said. In language that William Brennan was to echo 15 years later in *Keyishian*, Douglas warned, "A pall is cast over the classrooms." This did not mean "that the classroom may become a Communist cell." But "the guilt of the teacher should turn on overt acts. So long as she is a law abiding citizen, so long as her performance within the public school system meets professional standards, her private life, her political philosophy, her social creed should not be the cause of reprisals against her."[73]

Reactions to *Adler* were as varied and vociferous as the passions that inspired the Feinberg Law. One admirer wrote wistfully to Black, "Were the late Justices Rutledge and Murphy still on the Supreme Court, we would not have had this decision." It was "saddening to think that the six members who give us this thoroughly bad precedent" included all four Truman appointees—Truman, "who espouses civil rights as no other president in history!" On the opposite end of the spectrum, an angry missive from Missouri chastised Black for defending "subversive teaching" and blamed him for "giving Godless Russia everything she wanted up to half the world. Without your recognition [*sic*] and money Stalin could never have enslaved his own people. . . . You and your 'tax, spend, elect' boys have given us a doped prosperity that must always be at war. Our boys are daying [*sic*] today because you gave Russia Manchuria and China."[74]

Other responses were more restrained. There were many congratulatory editorials, such as the *New York World-Telegram*'s, which cheered the Court for putting "into plain words exactly what most loyal American parents and taxpayers have long felt." The *New York Times* was more skeptical: although it insisted that communists should not teach in the public schools, it called guilt by association a method "that arouses our gravest doubts. . . . It would seem wiser and more in keeping with the American spirit to judge teachers on the basis of their conduct in the classroom, rather than on the basis of fringe organizations to which they may or may not have belonged in the past." Lauding Douglas's "eloquent dissent," the *Times* warned against a "system of scholastic espionage or intellectual terrorism worthy of a police state."[75] But it did not explain how it thought communist teachers should be rooted out, except by the very methods it was condemning, and in this it resembled much of the liberal anti-communist establishment, uncomfortable with the crudity, recklessness, and use of sleazy professional informers that characterized the Red hunt and rationalizing that somehow more polite procedures or less demagogic rhetoric would make it all right.

Although Douglas's *Adler* dissent remained a minority view on the Supreme Court until the mid-1960s, he had made the case for academic freedom as a critical part of the First Amendment. Eleven months later, the Court for the first time in the Cold War era struck down a state loyalty program that included a test oath for public employees, including state college faculty. This Oklahoma oath was problematic even by the legal standards of the time, for it forced employees to swear that they were not, and for the preceding five years had not been, members of any organization on the Attorney General's List, regardless of whether they knew of the group's allegedly unlawful aims. Clark, writing for a unanimous Court, based the decision on

THE VINSON COURT >> 123

this lack of a "*scienter*" requirement, but Frankfurter wrote a fervent concurrence that turned on academic freedom.

Frankfurter said the Oklahoma oath threatened "that free play of the spirit which all teachers ought especially to cultivate and practice." Democracy depends on "disciplined and responsible" public opinion, which is unlikely to exist unless teachers can do their jobs. That is, public opinion "can be disciplined and responsible only if habits of open-mindedness and of critical inquiry are acquired in the formative years of our citizens." Frankfurter then unleashed a religious metaphor: "To regard teachers—in our entire educational system, from the primary grades to the university—as the priests of our democracy is not to indulge in hyperbole. It is the special task of teachers to foster those habits of open-mindedness and critical inquiry which alone make for responsible citizens." And teachers "cannot carry out their noble task if the conditions for the practice of a responsible and critical mind are denied to them."[76] It was a flicker of libertarian sentiment in an otherwise ghastly Supreme Court year, but Frankfurter's passion for academic freedom was to gain converts among the justices after Fred Vinson's death and the appointment of Earl Warren to head the Supreme Court.

PART III

The Purge Comes to Higher Education

7

The McCarran Committee and the City Colleges

Trouble in Brooklyn

Harry Gideonse saw "old problems resurfacing" at Brooklyn College after World War II.[1] As in the late 1930s, Gideonse thought "a determined ideological minority" was using college facilities for nefarious ends. In the spring of 1949, the student Karl Marx Society invited Henry Winston, the Communist Party's organizational secretary, to speak. Winston was one of the 11 Party leaders then on trial for conspiring to advocate the overthrow of the government. Just as Gideonse's administration had, ten years before, barred CP general secretary Earl Browder from campus, so now it told the Karl Marx Society that even an off-campus meeting would violate the "spirit" of the college's policy banning speakers who were charged with crime.[2]

The students said it was unconstitutional for Gideonse to impose "arbitrary rules" that denied them the right to hear speakers of their choice. They held their meeting with Winston; the administration suspended the society and three of its officers for the rest of the school year. A protest meeting precipitated two more suspensions. Thomas Coulton's history of Brooklyn College snidely describes the meeting: "a noisy gathering . . . , held without prior authorization"; "a sorry-looking group" that met "to hear each other's speeches." The student council voted to walk out in protest of the new suspensions; the administration warned that it would strictly enforce regulations "prohibiting the unauthorized leaving of classrooms."[3]

And so the battle escalated. About 200 students, representing ten clubs, walked out and held an off-campus demonstration. The college retaliated by suspending more clubs, including the Harriet Tubman Society, the Young Progressives of America, the Philosophy Club, and Hillel.[4]

The turmoil subsided as the semester ended, but the next spring (1950), Gideonse resumed his war with the campus newspaper, *Vanguard*. In April, *Vanguard* learned that the administration had vetoed the reappointment of a popular history professor as department chair; the professor had been critical of Gideonse. *Vanguard* reported, against the recommendation of its faculty advisor, that Gideonse had blocked the appointment; the advisor resigned, ostensibly in a dispute over the paper's insistence on naming as editors three students who were not "eligible." Absence of an advisor automatically suspended a student publication, but the staff raised enough money to publish an independent if short-lived journal called *Draugnav* (*Vanguard* spelled backward); it distributed more than 5,000 copies outside the college gates. The administration responded by ousting the staff from its office, suspending five editors, and putting 50 other student journalists on probation. It followed with a new rule for campus publications: there must be "simultaneous presentation through editorials of multiple student opinion on controversial issues," meaning that opposing views must receive the same layout and equal space.[5]

When classes resumed in the fall of 1950, *Vanguard* was reinstated; its sports editor, William Taylor, was elected editor in chief. A student group, the Labor Youth League, denounced as "imperialist" the American role in Korea, where war had erupted the previous June. The administration suspended the league on the ground that its political position was inconsistent with its charter. *Vanguard's* first fall issue protested the suspension; it followed the equal-viewpoints rule but also published a separate article supporting the league.[6] Gideonse saw in the paper's position "the manipulative hand of the Communists."[7]

"We were all rankling at the restrictive intrusion into our freedom of expression," a *Vanguard* staffer recalled. She wrote an editorial protesting the equal-viewpoints rule; the student council president wrote the opposing piece, which "exceeded the allotted word count by a lot, so I cut it to fit. And that was it! The next day we were history, locked out and accused of censoring opinions that conflicted with ours."[8]

Vanguard's charter was revoked in early October 1950 for alleged violation of the equal-viewpoints rule. The administration created a new student newspaper, the *Kingsman* (Brooklyn is officially Kings County), while *Vanguard's* editors began their own weekly, *Campus News*. It was sponsored by nine student groups, including the Committee on Racial Equality, the Eugene Debs Society, the Socialist Club, the Young Democrats, and the Young Zionists. But the venture lasted only six weeks: the administration notified the sponsoring organizations that their charters did not include publishing newspapers. The furor continued, with demonstrations, speeches, and folk songs.[9]

The drama may have been healthy student rebellion, but the consequences were serious. Gideonse told *Vanguard* editor in chief Taylor that a reprimand would be entered in his permanent record, the reason being Taylor's statement to the press that the dissolution of the paper was an attempt

Staff of the *Brooklyn College Vanguard*, locked out of its offices, 1950. (Courtesy of the *Vanguard* alumni group)

to "squelch the expression of any student opinion which does not agree with that of the administration." Gideonse said, "I hate to ruin anyone's career, but in your case, I'm prepared to make an exception." Fifteen years later, the FBI performed a background check preparatory to Taylor's nomination as staff director of the U.S. Civil Rights Commission; Gideonse told the investigators there had been a "remarkable similarity" between *Vanguard* editorials and "communist literature," and another administrator condemned Taylor for membership on the student council, which, he said, had "espoused liberal causes such as the rights of the Negro in the South."[10]

The ACLU's Academic Freedom Committee investigated the *Vanguard* controversy and in April 1951 submitted a report to the Board of Higher Education. The committee concluded that, yes, there had been a technical violation of the administration's equal-viewpoints rule, but there had been no bad faith: the "thoughts expressed by the writers were preserved," and it was "difficult to see evidence of intent to distort or weaken the opposing point of view." It was therefore unfair to revoke *Vanguard*'s charter; "we regard it as inevitable," the committee wrote, "that the *Vanguard* staff should feel itself the victim of serious injustice." Furthermore, and contrary to Gideonse's claim that *Vanguard* was communist dominated, the paper's editorials had mocked the Labor Youth League's clumsy propaganda and had predicted

that "the only clear and present threat" from the league and other communist groups was "the same old double-talk they've been spouting for years."
Thus, said the ACLU, Gideonse's charge that *Vanguard* had communist leanings was "not supported by adequate proof, and loosely indict[ed] a large
number of students in contradiction to American principles of establishing
personal guilt."[11]

The ACLU concluded on a conciliatory note, recognizing that the *Vanguard* affair was "only part of a generally tense situation" at the college and
hoping that the report would "lead to constructive, remedial action," so that
"one of the chief colleges of this country may again effectively foster . . . a free
and responsible student newspaper."[12] But as Jacob Fischel, the author of a
PhD dissertation on Gideonse, dryly notes, the president "did not accept the
report benignly." In a "sharply worded letter" to BHE chair Ordway Tead, he
accused the ACLU committee of bias because its chairperson was a Brooklyn College professor (although he had not participated in the investigation). "Once having convinced himself" that the committee members were
not objective, Fischel writes, "the Calvinist" in Gideonse "arose to meet their
challenge": with an "acerbic tongue," he attacked their integrity, denied the
existence of tensions on campus, and denied that he had influenced the decision to kill *Vanguard*.[13]

In 2001, in what the *New York Times* called "a gesture of both contrition
and pride,"[14] Brooklyn College invited William Taylor to speak at commencement and gave him an honorary degree. Taylor, who had attended Yale Law
School, worked with Thurgood Marshall on school desegregation cases, and
dedicated his career to civil rights advocacy, took the opportunity to praise
the ongoing mission of the college in educating poor and minority youth.[15]
The *Times* report on the event recalled the "tumultuous" Cold War tensions
at Brooklyn College: "Some called the college the little red schoolhouse
because of the number of faculty members and students believed to be communist sympathizers." Gideonse "had been brought in to upgrade the college
and repair its reputation. But he also banned anyone with ideas he considered radical from speaking or performing on campus."[16]

"He was brought in to repaint the schoolhouse," said the law professor
Alan Dershowitz, a 1959 graduate who also received an honorary degree that
day.[17]

Five years after Brooklyn College honored Taylor, it apologized to *Vanguard*. In April 2006, a plaque honoring the paper was installed on Boylan
Hall, the building that had housed its office. On the occasion, one of the
paper's aging veterans ruminated on "what Harry Gideonse did for us"—
"the bonds created by the adversity we faced together. We were no longer

colleagues but buddies, trenchmates. I believe relationships which might have developed under normal circumstances were strengthened immensely by the battle we fought. Many of these relationships have lasted to this day." The *Vanguard* community, another alum recalled, "was where we extracted the most pleasure and kicks from the ideas factory that Brooklyn College was for us."[18]

The McCarran Committee

Despite political pressures and campus rows, the Board of Higher Education did not engage in the same hunt for suspect professors that Board of Education superintendent William Jansen and his aide Saul Moskoff were pursuing against elementary and high school teachers in the years 1950–52. The Board of Education continued to interrogate and fire teachers for insubordination and "conduct unbecoming" and had won *Adler I*, the Teachers Union's challenge to the Feinberg Law.[19] By the fall of 1952, *Adler II*, the lawsuit contesting board procedures that denied suspects the minimal due process of the Feinberg Law, was pending before Commissioner of Education Lewis Wilson. While he was considering the case, Wilson ordered a stay of both Saul Moskoff's interviews and the administrative trials needed to effect formal dismissals.

It was in this already charged atmosphere that the Internal Security Subcommittee of the U.S. Senate Judiciary Committee—the SISS—came to New York City in September 1952 to investigate subversion in the city's public colleges and schools. The SISS, created in 1951, was headed by Pat McCarran, a politician described by one scholar as "a fanatical anti-communist who believed that only a handful of the world leaders were alert to the Red Menace—Franco, Chiang Kai Shek, and the Pope, in particular."[20] Why did the SISS choose to descend on New York? The TU believed that George Timone, now head of the Board of Education's law committee and incensed at Commissioner Wilson's stay of the Moskoff interviews, had urged the subcommittee to come—to use its power to generate publicity and its status as an arm of the federal government to pressure Wilson into lifting his stay.[21] But the SISS was also busy competing with HUAC and other congressional committees interested in investigating education, and it was determined to press the BHE into more aggressive action. Its chief counsel, Robert Morris, had been a staffer on the 1940–41 Rapp-Coudert Committee, whose efforts at a full-throttle anti-communist purge had been frustrated by the absence of a second witness against suspected professors at some of the city colleges, primarily Brooklyn.[22] Now that Bella Dodd, the CP's talented legislative representative, had left the Party, she might identify other ex-communists who, in turn, might become second witnesses against Frederic Ewen, Harry Slochower, and others who had denied communist affiliation once they had lost their appeals and been forced to testify before Rapp-Coudert.

The SISS hearings, chaired by Senator Homer Ferguson and organized by Morris, began on September 8, 1952, with Ferguson's opening statement assuring listeners that the subcommittee had no intention of interfering in local education; its inquiry was limited to "considerations affecting national security," which, however, naturally included "subversion in our educational process."[23] Bella Dodd, the first witness, gave emotional testimony about the CP, the Teachers Union, her early idealism, and her rude awakening to Party intrigue. Dodd said there were about 750 communist teachers in the New York metropolitan area in 1944, when she left the TU to become a full-time communist functionary; some worked at private schools and colleges, but most were in the public system.[24]

Within the TU, she said, communists on the executive board had fought "the socialists, the Lovestoneites, and the other splinter groups" to gain power. The communists won, "then pushed the union to support the Party line on political questions." But on issues closer to home, in particular, the Party's alleged pressure on its teacher-members to inject communism into their classrooms, Dodd had nothing to contribute beyond the fact that the Party's theory of education was "progressive." This was far from the damning evidence that subcommittee counsel Robert Morris wanted. He persisted the next day, but Dodd still had little to offer. The Party "always was very active in having youth committees," she said, and the youth committees sometimes "brought up certain questions of what was going on in the schools," but "I had nothing to do with that."[25]

George Timone testified next. Referencing Dodd's estimate of 750 communist teachers in the city, with perhaps 500 of those in public schools, he announced that it was "500 too many"; but at the same time, he said, "there are 38,000 teachers in our public-school system. So that, percentagewise, we must not let the impression go out that any substantial percentage of our teachers ever belonged to the Communist Party or were ever in the Teachers Union, for that matter." Timone assured the subcommittee that the Board of Education was vigilantly pursuing communist teachers. It had been interrogating suspects for several years; when they admitted past CP membership but said they had resigned and when their "subsequent conduct and activity ha[d] not been inconsistent with that resignation, we have accepted it." Counsel Morris sought to clarify: was it the board's position that if an ex-communist teacher "cooperates completely with you, even to the extent of making known details of that person's activity in the Communist Party, that there is no disciplinary action against such a person?" Every case was judged individually, Timone replied.[26] He did not quite say that "making known the details" included informing on others, but that was the thrust of Morris's question. And in fact, Timone, Moskoff, and company did consider naming names the *sine qua non* of a sincere break with communism.

Timone made clear his frustration over Commissioner Wilson's stay of the Board of Education purges: it had "brought comparatively to a standstill our efforts in weeding out communists and subversives from our school system." He hoped that even if the commissioner did not decide the matter quickly, he would lift his stay. Certainly, the SISS hoped for the same thing. In dismissing Timone, Senator Ferguson piously reiterated that the subcommittee did not want to interfere with local education. "Far from interfering, we think you help our efforts," Timone replied.[27]

With these assurances from Timone, the SISS now turned its attention to the less inquisitorial Board of Higher Education. True, the BHE had passed a resolution at the start of the SISS hearings promising its "full cooperation" and urging all professors to "assist the committee,"[28] but Morris and company wanted more. To pressure Tead and the board, the SISS now subpoenaed professors on whom it had gathered information, and like Red-hunting committees before and afterward, it began with private sessions that resembled the Catholic confessional. As one historian writes, the committee would "redeem penitent sinners" in private, then arrange for a public display of the "conversion."[29] But not all "sinners" were penitent. On September 24, 1952, public hearings resumed with ten uncooperative witnesses, among them Vera Shlakman of Queens College and Frederic Ewen and Harry Slochower of Brooklyn.

This was a first for Shlakman: unlike Ewen and Slochower, she had not been called by the Rapp-Coudert Committee in 1940–41. Shlakman without doubt was a leftist; indeed, she had grown up in an anarchist-socialist household in Montreal, where Emma Goldman would stay when she was in town.[30] But as a colleague and former student wrote, Shlakman "was scrupulously impartial and leaned over backwards not to indoctrinate her students."[31] Another student remembered her "sitting on the desk, her legs crossed, posing some problem based on the day's reading and drawing students into a discussion."[32]

Subcommittee counsel Morris questioned Shlakman. After establishing that she had been at Queens for 14 years and was a vice president of the TU, he asked if she had ever been a Party member. Her reply—or rather, her explanation of her intent not to reply—was less bombastic and seemingly less well rehearsed than many responses of protesting witnesses both before and after her. "Mr. Morris, I find it extraordinarily difficult to face my students," she began and then lost the thread, mentioning "the rule of free inquiry necessary to the preservation of self-government": "I am getting involved in this sentence, but what I am getting at is, that the question is such as to destroy the rule of free inquiry, and therefore to impair self-government."[33]

This was essentially a First Amendment objection; the problem was that the courts had been rejecting free-speech challenges to loyalty investigations for the past five years, and anyone who relied on the First Amendment would face prison for contempt of Congress. What was left to Shlakman was the Fifth Amendment, which bars the government from forcing people to testify against themselves. In common shorthand, this was the "self-incrimination" clause, and anyone invoking it in the early 1950s was almost universally considered a "Fifth Amendment communist." But Shlakman had little choice: she cited the Fifth Amendment as well as the First in justifying her refusal to answer questions about past or present political affiliations and beliefs.

Investigating committees like the SISS loved to repeat the questions they knew would not be answered. Again, Shlakman was asked about membership; again she refused to answer. Had she ever attended a "Communist caucus meeting" at the union; again she refused. Did she think a CP member "can be a college teacher?" "I think that any teacher must be judged on the basis of her performance and scholarship; . . . that if a teacher follows professional standards in the classrooms and is a scholar, he is entitled to teach."[34]

After Shlakman's testimony, she wrote to colleagues that she had assumed the questioning would concern the union and the performance of her "professional duties," but the committee asked "only two trivial questions" about the union and none about her scholarship or teaching. They were interested in her political associations and beliefs—a fact Shlakman surely knew in advance; but whatever the rhetorical liberties she took in her letter, she described a familiar dilemma: "Let there be no mistake about the situation in which the entire academic community now finds itself. It must either grovel and accept the standards of orthodoxy prescribed by the McCarrans and McCarthys, and those who have capitulated to them, or it must resist." She urged defiance, reminding colleagues that "sharp and immediate protests from many educational leaders" had halted HUAC's attempt in 1949 "to pry into textbooks, that these protests were widely applauded, and that such capitulations as occurred were deplored by staffs and students."[35]

Citing the Fifth Amendment did not necessarily mean Shlakman was a CP member or even held communist beliefs. People active on the left could be prosecuted for perjury in denying membership if an ex-communist witness

Queens College economics professor
Vera Shlakman. (Photo courtesy of Vera
Shlakman and Ellen Holahan)

or FBI informer testified that they had appeared at a Party meeting, participated in an organization thought to be a communist front, signed a nominating petition for a CP candidate, or written for a Party-dominated magazine. Whether informers were sincere (if not always accurate) like Bella Dodd or opportunist and amoral like Harvey Matusow made little difference.

By invoking the Fifth Amendment, Shlakman avoided a criminal prosecution for contempt of Congress, but she did not avoid losing her job. Section 903 of the city charter provided that an employee's job would "terminate, and such office or employment shall be vacant," if the person pleaded the Fifth Amendment in response to questions from a court or investigating committee about "the property, government, or affairs of the city . . . or the official conduct of any officer or employee." It was not clear initially that the city would use section 903 to fire tenured professors summarily, but the Corporation Counsel's office advised the BHE that it could do so.[36]

Section 903 had been enacted in 1936 in the wake of New York judge Samuel Seabury's celebrated investigation into corruption during the administration of Mayor Jimmy Walker.[37] The refusal of police officers and others complicit in the scandal to testify, on Fifth Amendment grounds, inspired the passage of the historically understandable but constitutionally dubious charter provision. Enacted to address "tin-box grafters,"[38] not people resisting questions about their politics, section 903 was about to be enlisted against professors.

The day after Shlakman's testimony, September 25, 1952, the SISS heard ex-communist Brooklyn College biology professor Harry Albaum. His fellow biologist Alex Novikoff had recruited him to join the Party in 1938.[39] Now he was about to become an informer.

Albaum showed none of the ambivalence about aiding the purge or naming names that his colleague Bernard Grebanier had expressed to the Rapp-Coudert Committee 12 years before. Portraying himself in the 1930s as an innocent young dupe, Albaum testified that he was a reluctant Party member who tried to avoid meetings and dues, refused to collect petition signatures or sell the *Sunday Worker*, and was told, when some time after the Nazi-Soviet Pact he summoned the courage to leave, "Brother, you don't get out of this thing, you don't resign. All that can happen is you are expelled."[40]

Albaum helped the SISS shore up its theory of communist indoctrination. "There was an emphasis that one ought to at every opportunity try to present the principles of Marxism" in class. This was not easy in courses such as biology, and many teachers would not do it even if the opportunity arose. But, Albaum said, "some people—I remember one man who took great pride in showing how he could introduce the principles of Marxism into his particular area." Senator Ferguson wanted an example; Albaum could not remember.

Ferguson: "But he did tell you how he was able to slant, and I use the word advisedly, along the communistic line?"

Albaum agreed but emphasized that "by and large, many of these people made no attempt of this kind."

Albaum said he had falsely denied CP membership before the Rapp-Coudert Committee. Bella Dodd, who had orchestrated the TU's strategy, told him, "If you are asked the $64 question,[41] say that you are not."

Ferguson: "In other words, if you were asked whether you were a member of the Communist Party, you were advised to say that you were not . . . even though you were?" Albaum agreed.

Ferguson: "Now, did you know whether or not you were free or not free to follow that advice?"

Albaum: "Well, the impression I got at the time was . . . that you have got nothing to really worry about unless two people involve you. Since the only one that had involved me, presumably, . . . was Professor Grebanier, . . . that I really had nothing to fear and wasn't taking much of a risk and, therefore, you plead that you are not."

Ferguson: "In other words, you were advised that if the committee did not have two witnesses, and you were not telling the truth, that you could get away with it?" Albaum again assented. "I was trying to protect my own skin. I didn't want to lose my job. . . . I felt very uncomfortable and guilty about it, but this was a time when jobs were scarce and I knew that any other statement that I would make, I would lose my job."

The testimony was explosive. It confirmed what Bella Dodd had said to the SISS in more muted terms and what Hunter philosophy professor Jerauld McGill admitted in executive session the day before.[42] Two years later, McGill told a BHE committee trying charges against him that he had felt "morally forced" to lie because his conscience "would not permit him to reveal the names and activities of his associates in the communist unit at Hunter College." The BHE thought it a pitiful excuse, and even if credible, "that kind of 'conscience' cannot be entrusted with teaching philosophy at Hunter College."[43]

Brooklyn College was in turmoil after Albaum's testimony. The *Kingsman* and the administration began a campaign to present the college in a more positive light. The *Brooklyn Eagle* reported approvingly that a *Kingsman* editorial had asserted no communist could be a qualified teacher. Three days later, the *Eagle* congratulated *Kingsman* editor in chief Estelle Siegel for "shatter[ing] the spurious notion of pseudo liberals and outright Moscow followers that Commies are denied freedom when the Government deems them unacceptable in the school system."[44]

The *Eagle* followed with a series of eight articles by students designed to refute the college's reputation as a hotbed of communism. One article described ROTC and the bravery of young officers in training. Another praised apolitical activities such as the Booster Squad, with its "snappy black and white uniforms," and "Hi-Hites and Toppers," a social club for "tall beauties at least 5 feet 7 inches in height." The last article in the series reported that Brooklyn in just 20 years had become "the largest undergraduate liberal arts institution in the world," with 26,000 students "thirsting for knowledge but of limited finances, who have made the most of their taxpayer-financed education."[45]

The *Eagle* was not the only journalistic enterprise to wave the flag. The Hearst-owned *Journal American* praised Estelle Siegel's anti-communist editorial, while the *Herald Tribune* used loaded language in its news coverage to damn protesters, noting that despite "shouts from various organizations denouncing 'witch hunts,'" the "almost-to-be-expected rallies, demonstrations, and protests did not come off. . . . Some students appeared at the subcommittee hearings and the same faces were among a straggly group of 75 students who paraded around the building where the Board of Higher Education met."[46]

A few days after the testimony of Shlakman and Albaum, Commissioner Wilson announced his decision rejecting the challenge by the second group of non-cooperating city schoolteachers to the policies and interrogations that led to their firings. There was nothing in the Feinberg Law that precluded the

Board of Education from "independently establishing" its own list of subversive organizations or its own loyalty procedures, Wilson ruled.[47] He surely felt pressured by the SISS hearings, but it was also clear by this point that the Supreme Court was not going to disapprove anti-subversive investigations and firings.

The state courts eventually agreed with Wilson, explaining that despite a prohibition in the civil service law against questioning employees about their political beliefs and associations, asking about CP membership was not forbidden because the law "did not envision" a political group dedicated to "the overthrow of democratic government, by force and violence if necessary, and, incidentally, the destruction of all parties except itself." In any event, the teachers were terminated for insubordination, not communist beliefs.[48] The teachers' lawyers asked New York's high court to consider a further appeal, but the court denied the request.

Gideonse's Revenge

Frederic Ewen and Harry Slochower had been on President Gideonse's list of likely perjurers ever since they denied CP membership before the Rapp-Coudert Committee, and even though Gideonse acknowledged that they were first-rate scholars and teachers, he was aching to fire them. In the decade since, he could not proceed because the BHE followed the "two witness" rule in cases of suspected perjury, and nobody had yet surfaced to back up ex-communist witness Bernard Grebanier's testimony that Ewen, Slochower, and about a dozen others at Brooklyn College were or had been communists.

But Gideonse did in those years operate his own confessional. He would question suspect professors, and if he believed they were sincere in renouncing communism, he would protect them.[49] He later told the SISS of one ex-communist professor who had repented and was now "a reliable member of the staff." Gideonse was gratified: "There is more joy in heaven over one sinner than over 99 of the righteous."[50]

Slochower was up for promotion to associate professor in 1946; he had the support of his department and the relevant academic committees, but Gideonse disapproved. At a long meeting, the president questioned Slochower about his recent book, *No Voice Is Wholly Lost: Writers and Thinkers in War and Peace*. According to Slochower, Gideonse granted that the book "as a whole showed a sense for critical values, individual freedom and opposition to totalitarian conformity," but "he then shifted the discussion to what he admitted were 'minor points,' but which were important to certain groups who were looking for a change of heart." Gideonse "feared that were he to promote me, he would be attacked by certain newspapers: that what I therefore needed was to write something that would show that I am as much 'against' as I 'appeared' to have been 'for'; otherwise he could see scary headlines in two or three publications." Slochower resisted the demand, telling Gideonse, "For me to go in for political harangues would be falling out of character." Gideonse then proposed that "we wait and see whether in your new projected study on the literary myth you will show that you have changed. I replied that this book will take me another five years to write; that in any case it would have no more, and probably less, to do with politics than my *No Voice is Wholly Lost*."[51]

Afterward, Slochower wrote to Gideonse summarizing the meeting. He wanted to make a record so that he could appeal his promotion denial to the BHE. Gideonse had faulted his book for criticizing fascism but not communism, he wrote: "You added that in the future if I showed a 'change of heart,' you would consider endorsing my promotion." Slochower asked Gideonse to verify that this was an accurate account. Gideonse's reply was cagey. He did not deny the letter's accuracy but refused to verify it: "I fail to see how a letter could possibly clarify a matter which hours of personal conversation have still left opaque. . . . The City of New York does not require the president to prove a case against the members of the faculty who are not promoted."[52] Slochower lost his appeal, despite attesting, in a 1947 letter to a faculty committee, "I have not been and am not a member of the Communist or of any other political party."[53] Slochower finally got his promotion in 1951, but the issue of his pro-communist past was not dead: the SISS's arrival in New York in September 1952 gave Gideonse hope that he could finally fire him.

Slochower chose a compromise for his SISS testimony: what had come to be called the "diminished Fifth." Unlike Vera Shlakman or Frederic Ewen, he did not refuse to answer political questions: he avowed that he had not been a CP member for the past 11 years. As to 1940–41, however, he invoked his Fifth Amendment right. Possibly he thought that his response for all but a short period a decade past would show his willingness to cooperate; if so, it was not a successful strategy. The inference that he must have been a CP member in 1940–41 and therefore lied to the Rapp-Coudert Committee (and in a state court affidavit) was almost inescapable.

Thirty years after Slochower's SISS testimony, he remembered it in a jovial light: "I had a ball" with the subcommittee; "I played cat and mouse with them."[54] But the transcript does not read as if Slochower were having fun or getting the better of his questioners. He began plaintively, noting that a pending promotion to full professor might be derailed by his subpoena: "The very mention of this type of thing, you are aware of it, Senator, is enough to indict one. You have only to be accused, then you are guilty. First comes the verdict and then comes the trial."[55]

"That has been a very fine speech," Senator Ferguson replied. "In other words, you are criticizing this committee for trying to look into the question of the internal security of the United States of America?"

Slochower was conciliatory: "No, sir."

Robert Morris homed in on the Rapp-Coudert hearings. "Were you at that time a member of the Communist Party?"

Slochower said he wanted to answer "with a literary allusion."

Morris: "Well, it calls for a yes or no answer, unless you want to invoke some kind of privilege."

Slochower: "This is a very serious matter and I think you ought to allow me a little leeway. I beg your indulgence."

Ferguson: "Are you going to answer the question?"

Slochower: "I am going to answer, in my way. . . . Chances are that Senator Ferguson and the others are acquainted with a famous novel called *The Trial.*"

"Has that anything to do with your answer?" Ferguson wanted to know.

"It has a lot," Slochower said. "In that novel there is a character who is accused by somebody of something—he did not know what it was, and for the rest of his life is investigated and reinvestigated until the end, when they starved him to death. . . . Since 1940, 12 years, this question has been asked again and again, . . . and I have had 12 years of the utmost difficulty in trying to live down the accusation that was made."

The literary analogy was not very apt. Joseph K. in *The Trial* did not know what he was accused of; Harry Slochower knew very well. Ferguson wanted to know if he had ever answered the question.

Slochower: "Yes; I did answer it."

Ferguson: "Go ahead and answer it now."

Slochower continued not to: "I want you to understand the difficulty of facing the prospect of answering this question for the rest of your life. Is it original sin? Once somebody has accused you, you are guilty for the rest of your life?"

Morris: "What is your answer?"

Slochower: "I am not a member of the Communist Party."

Morris: "That is not the question. Were you at the time you are referring to, when you state some charge was made against you, were you at that time a member of the Communist Party?"

Slochower refused to answer. "I hope that the time is coming when the higher courts are going to declare that a question of this sort is in violation of those traditions of America which I have learned to cherish," in particular the First Amendment guarantee of free speech. Ferguson, as expected, would not recognize the First Amendment. Slochower next argued the subcommittee's lack of jurisdiction over local education. Again, Ferguson ruled against him.

"In that case I am left with only one answer," Slochower said. "I have to invoke the Fifth Amendment with regard to the question of whether I had been a member of the Communist Party in the years 1940 or 1941. . . . However, I want to add I am not implying I am guilty. I understand that the Fifth Amendment has been put into the Constitution for the purpose of protecting the innocent. I am availing myself of that privilege."

Morris pushed for a show of repentance: had Slochower "done anything in the last 10 or 12 years that would indicate" opposition to communism? Slochower asserted his political innocence: "My field is not politics. My field is philosophy, literature, art, and now it is the myth."

Did Slochower believe that "freedom of thought" existed in Russia? He replied, "Russia and the whole East has never known economic, social, political, and intellectual freedom. They never had an American Revolution and never a French Revolution. Absence of a middle class prevented all of those wonderful things."

Slochower, like Shlakman and a third recalcitrant witness, psychology professor Bernard Riess of Hunter College, was suspended without pay within days of his SISS testimony. The BHE scheduled a meeting for October 6, 1952, to decide whether to fire the three.[56] Slochower wrote to Ordway Tead requesting a hearing before the board took final action, in order to present "the particular features in my case, . . . my standing and record in the larger cultural community." Dismissal, he said, "would destroy a whole lifetime of preparation for a vocation which has had my exclusive devotion and love and is the only vocation I am fitted for."[57]

Slochower got no formal hearing, but the board allowed each of the three to speak briefly. Slochower once again pleaded his professional accomplishments. Shlakman, by contrast, chose to address the larger issue of the BHE's "capitulation" to pressure from the SISS. She pointed the rhetorical finger at Ordway Tead, who, she said, had "written and spoken of democracy." What would he think of an employer "who permits employees to learn from the press that they had been suspended without pay" (as was the case with Riess and Slochower)? If the board were truly "interested in the welfare of higher education, it could now strike a blow in defense of the integrity of the teaching profession," but to do so, it "would have to assert its independence of highly questionable outside political pressure by refusing to accept the dictation of the McCarran Subcommittee and by revoking the suspensions so hastily imposed."[58]

The TU, student groups, and the three professors pleaded for hearings rather than summary termination. What was the huge hurry? TU legislative representative Rose Russell asked. "Were they doing anything harmful in the classroom that you had to get rid of them" in mid-semester? A Queens student bemoaned the "suddenness with which these teachers were suspended"; there was only one class where Shlakman had even been able to say goodbye. Tead acknowledged that the three had good records but explained this was irrelevant in view of section 903.[59]

More professors were fired summarily in the fall of 1952 after refusing to answer the SISS's questions. Among them were three remarkable women: Henrietta Friedman, for 25 years a professor of Greek and Latin at Hunter College; Sarah Riedman, a biology professor at Brooklyn College; and the physicist Melba Phillips, also of Brooklyn. Phillips's biography was particularly impressive: from modest beginnings on an Indiana farm and a spotty undergraduate education, she became one of J. Robert Oppenheimer's first doctoral students at the University of California–Berkeley; her research with Oppenheimer in the 1930s led to discovery of the "Oppenheimer-Phillips effect," an explanation for the behavior of deuterium, or heavy hydrogen, atoms. "It's considered one of the classics of early nuclear physics," a student from Phillips's days at Brooklyn later said—and added, "She was a spectacular teacher."[60] Phillips also lost a part-time job at the Columbia University Radiation Laboratory after her SISS testimony. She was unemployed for several years, during which she wrote textbooks, and although she had a notable career thereafter, she never returned to groundbreaking research.[61]

Harry Slochower wrote an emotional farewell to students. "I was sacrificed to a formula, rigidly and mechanically applied," he said, referring to section 903. "Yet behind the formula stand sinister powers busily exploiting the apathy or delirium of the hour." Gideonse and the BHE "acted like Eliot's 'hollow men,' like the robots and Mr. Zeros of expressionistic drama, or like Charlie Chaplin's 'Modern Times.'" Slochower explained that he could not testify about the period before 1940–41 because if he had admitted even being around the CP in those days, he would have been asked to name others who attended meetings. "I could have saved my job" by naming names, he said, but in the end, "I could not contribute toward wrecking the lives of people who may be innocent and decent."[62] In later years, this became his sole explanation: anything other than a principled refusal to name names "would have been psychic suicide," even though he had just become a father, at age 50, and briefly considered saving his job to take care of his daughter.[63]

Frederic Ewen had less explaining to do. He also invoked the Fifth Amendment before the SISS but was not fired; he had resigned from

Brooklyn College the day before his September 1952 testimony. At age 53 a wildly popular teacher and the prolific author of books on Heine, Schiller, Viennese music, and 18th-century English literature, among other subjects, Ewen received piles of letters bemoaning his departure. He had combined true learning with teaching talent, one former student wrote: "But for your courses in literature my knowledge of books would be far more meager than it is. Writers like Balzac, Aragon, Gissing and Howells would be completely unknown to me." Another ex-student wrote from Hampton, Virginia:

> Even in this out-of-the-way place we are daily discussing how we can go about redeeming the world from fascism, from that demonic pair, McCarthy and McCarran, and all their slimy host of informers and chicken-hearted penitents. I think of you often, . . . your own scholarship and inspired teaching. To see the relationships, the human values, without getting bogged down in formalism and pedantry, to activate the student with respect to the societal issues—that, I feel, is teaching literature—and you did that with consummate skill.[64]

People supporting the purge might have considered this teaching style—engaging literature with "societal issues"—to be indoctrination; others would have argued it is exactly what education should be. Either way, Ewen's classes were exciting. Another former student recalled her good fortune: "I was actually able to find your courses open to me at registration time. They were so popular, and for good reason. I remember the packed room: students sitting on radiators and floors. . . . Whether it was 18th century English literature, the contemporary novel, etc., literature suddenly became alive, real, and related to our lives. . . . When the hour was finished, we resented the intrusion of the bell."[65]

The *Kingsman* published Ewen's farewell:

> Technically, I am retiring from my teaching post on a small pension. Actually I have been driven from the field of my life's activity by the shameless persecution of freedom of thought and speech now disgracing our country. . . . It is a bitter thing to break with friends and associations lasting through so many years; to leave the field of activity for which I prepared myself so arduously—to leave all these at a time when my usefulness is far from ended. But I am sure it is more important to understand the meaning of my retirement. If there is anything at all to be left to freedom of education, now is the time to rally to its defense.[66]

8

"The Laughing-Stock of Europe"

More Turmoil in Queens and Kings

Vera Shlakman testified before the Senate Internal Security Subcommittee on a Monday in late September 1952. The next day, as her colleague Oscar Shaftel recalled, "the students called a protest meeting. I spoke there and got a subpoena on Thursday." There was an "original euphoria; you carried the flag and people rallied round." Shaftel was "ordered to show up at the judicial building downtown on Columbus Day," but, he said, "they ran out of time before I had to testify. So I continued teaching into the next semester with this ax hanging over my head."[1]

Shaftel had been a rebel ever since his days as editor of a student newspaper at the Brooklyn branch of CCNY, when he was suspended for defending a columnist's joke that administrators found in bad taste.[2] He graduated in 1931, earned a combined PhD at Harvard in English, aesthetics, and Greek and Latin classics, and started teaching at Queens in 1937. His served in Army Intelligence during World War II, despite reports by an informant that on campus Shaftel had "made a point of cultivating the underprivileged"; thus, the informant "certainly would not recommend" him "for any position of confidence within our Armed Forces." A War Department report similarly surmised that Shaftel was a communist or "or at least a fellow-traveler" because he chaired "a known communist-dominated union" and his "activities and interests" paralleled those of the Party; but it acknowledged that he might simply be "extremely liberal-minded." Another informant said Shaftel had "a good reputation in the community"—"there isn't a finer fellow as far as temperament and disposition are concerned"—and "emphatically stated" that he had "never been active in any type of subversive activity."[3] In 1948, Shaftel organized a group to support Henry Wallace for president. By 1952, he was 40, married, and the father of two children.[4]

Shaftel finally testified on February 9 and 10, 1953, when the SISS resumed its hearings in Washington, D.C. Before he went, he urged his colleagues to make a statement of opposition to the committee: "It would certainly be encouraging to me and certainly useful in furthering the ideals of academic freedom." The English Department formed a committee to discuss the request but did not act.[5]

An editorial in the student newspaper, *Crown*, protested Shaftel's subpoena. He was a "well-loved, respected, and stimulating teacher" who "strongly encourages his classes to disagree" with his ideas. Class discussions were "always provocative because he forces his students to think. But he never tells them *what* to think."[6] Harry Keyishian, a *Crown* editor when this piece was written, had taken Shaftel's course in literary criticism the previous year and remembered his warning students who had written term papers about Marxist theory: "I hope you're not doing it to please me. That's not what I'm here to teach you."[7]

Senator William Jenner, an outspoken fan of his colleague Joseph McCarthy, presided at the SISS's February 1953 hearings. The room was "jammed with spectators and newsmen."[8] When Shaftel's turn came, he objected to the "$64 question" about CP membership on the basis of the First Amendment and the subcommittee's lack of authority to supervise local education, as well as his Fifth Amendment right "not to bear witness against myself." But as with Vera Shlakman, Bernard Riess, and Harry Slochower the previous fall, the SISS accepted only the Fifth Amendment justification for refusing to answer its questions.

Shaftel later explained, "They asked if you were a communist. If you said no, and they had different information, that was perjury. If you said yes, they said, 'name everyone that you know, all your friends.' If you forgot any, that was perjury."[9] He was not exaggerating—Morris Schappes had served 13 months in prison for perjury after telling the Rapp-Coudert Committee that there were only four communists at City College in the late 1930s.[10]

But if Shaftel resisted questioning about his politics, he had plenty of other things to tell the subcommittee. Its entire enterprise was "making our colleges the laughing-stock of Europe." He was "sick at heart at the obscene spectacle of college presidents falling all over themselves, like Keystone cops, in haste to fire teachers who have taken a principled stand" and at the sight of "teachers huddling separately in fear, hoping maybe a McCarran or a McCarthy or a Velde committee may overlook the bad thing they once said about fascism, or the time they chose to teach *The Grapes of Wrath* in class."[11]

The result was predictable. Queens College president John Theobald suspended Shaftel on February 18, 1953, pending the BHE's final decision, to be made at a meeting in March. Shaftel distributed an impassioned statement in preparation for the BHE. He accused board members of abandoning their "sacred function of protecting the road to knowledge." He warned that

Professor Oscar Shaftel at Queens College in 1947.
(Photo courtesy of Ann Shaftel)

if they expected students "to listen respectfully, without a snicker," at their commencement speeches, then they should think about the example they were setting by acquiescing in the spectacle of "innuendo and false witness-bearing." Shaftel's final thrust was a quote from John Milton's "Lycidas." He picked lines pungent in their imagery of "blind mouths," "hungry sheep," and "foul contagion" spreading across the land.[12]

The BHE followed the pattern it had set with Shlakman, Riess, and Slo-chower the previous fall. It said that Shaftel had essentially fired himself because section 903 of the city charter made an employee's job "vacant" if he refused, on Fifth Amendment grounds, to answer questions regarding the affairs of the city or the "official conduct" of its employees. Since section 903 made termination automatic, they reasoned, no due process hearing was needed—no consideration of individual factors or situations, even for ten-ured professors. With respect to elementary and high school teachers called by the SISS, the Board of Education and Superintendent Jansen had already applied section 903 in the identical way.

It was a harsh penalty for people who had been competent, even out-standing teachers, some of them for 20 years or more. It also forced them to relinquish their Fifth Amendment right as a condition of keeping their jobs—a practice that the city's lawyers thought constitutional in view of the Supreme Court's recent decisions approving various Red-purge techniques, including *Adler v. Board of Education* a year before.

But the Teachers Union was determined to challenge section 903, and Harold Cammer, a prominent labor lawyer and one of the union's regu-lar counsel, had already filed a case in state court on behalf of Shlakman,

Slochower, and Riess. He brought a companion case for eight public school teachers. Still a third group, six in all, including Oscar Shaftel, was represented by Osmond Fraenkel, who entered into a stipulation with the city to be mutually bound by the result of the two litigated cases.[13]

Cammer's suit did not fare well. A state court judge outdid the SISS's rhetoric in ruling that, far from being "arbitrary and capricious," the city had merely fulfilled its duty "to safeguard the children from being debauched mentally and morally." The resisting teachers had put on a "false show of indignation"; they were "apparent enemies of the nation, . . . falsely claiming to be immune to questions that go to the roots of their honesty and loyalty" and refusing to say "whether they belong to a group generally regarded as godless, disloyal, destructive and dishonest." The city was fully justified in "cleansing" its school system "of such foulness and danger," and in any case, under section 903, the teachers were "their own executioners."[14]

After this bristling loss, Harry Slochower decided to seek separate counsel. He hired Ephraim London, a First Amendment expert who had just won a remarkable Supreme Court victory—striking down a part of New York State's film censorship scheme that denied exhibition licenses to movies deemed "sacrilegious." Cardinal Francis Spellman had pressured the state to revoke the license for Italian neorealist director Roberto Rossellini's film *The Miracle*; Spellman and the Catholic groups that pressed for the ban charged the film with not only sacrilege but atheism and communism.[15] Slochower had heard about London's victory and was impressed. He later remembered London as "the most marvelous attorney," who had a "vision" of how to win the case and took it on a contingency-fee basis.[16] London and Cammer went forward with their respective appeals.

The state's intermediate court was less ideological but no more sympathetic to the fired professors and teachers than the lower court had been: in brisk, cursory opinions, it affirmed that the city's use of section 903 was proper. There were, however, two dissenters, who insisted that the teachers were not city employees within the meaning of section 903; instead, they were employees of the two education boards, which were public corporations separate from city government. This hardly meant that the boards were without power to deal with subversion (under the Feinberg Law, for example), but the dissenters thought that section 903, with its summary punishment, "should not be enlarged by implication" beyond its fair meaning.[17] It was a credible argument but one that skirted the more basic problem with section 903: its denial of a constitutional right as a condition of keeping one's job.

The atmosphere at Queens College was demoralizing. Shaftel remembered that some faculty expressed regret at the summary nature of the firings, but in general, there was a "loss of nerve": most colleagues, "if they said hello, they looked around to see who was reporting. It was not nice. I was already known as one of the leaders of the left. I spoke all the time at student meetings. It was not as if they had suddenly discovered a carrier of a disease. But after being fired, there was really no movement of support." He appealed to the AAUP; it investigated but did not act. "A couple of us from New York made a presentation at the next meeting of the AAUP and tried to get some help from the leadership, but nothing happened."[18]

In January 1954, Harry Keyishian wrote a farewell editorial for the *Crown*. He praised "the genuine closeness and interest" in students "displayed by the faculty here at Queens": classmates who were now in graduate school "frequently remarked that they find nothing like it at the schools they are attending." On the other hand, he wrote, "we have felt the effects of the general nationwide 'scare' on campus, to the extent of having teachers fired from our faculty." Although academic freedom "has become something of a hack phrase these days, that doesn't lessen the importance of the concept. It's really very simple: a teacher's fitness or unfitness should be judged on the basis of his ability to teach."[19]

The SISS Winds Down

The Senate Internal Security Subcommittee continued to question uncooperative witnesses through the winter and spring of 1953. Three more Brooklyn professors were forced to repeat their Fifth Amendment objections as subcommittee counsel Robert Morris asked them the same questions about communist affiliation, and the senators debated them on politics, educational philosophy, and patriotism.

Joseph Bressler, a 27-year veteran of Brooklyn's health and physical education faculty, testified the same day as Shaftel. He acknowledged that he had been active in the Teachers Union. He did not know what Morris meant by asking whether he had "signed petitions in defense of communist schools" (Morris evidently had such a petition in his possession), but he acknowledged signing one on behalf of the Jefferson School. Morris noted for the record "that the Jefferson School is on the Attorney General's subversive list."[20]

Two weeks later, the SISS questioned Brooklyn College English instructor Murray Young. Like the school's tennis coach, Elton Gustafson (who testified before Bressler), Young had been named as a communist by Bernard Grebanier at the Rapp-Coudert hearings a decade earlier.[21] One senator debated him about his "duties under the American Constitution": did

Professor Young think he was fulfilling them by refusing to give information that "might help this committee and help the Congress to ferret out the communist plan to dominate the education process in America?" Young replied that it was the subcommittee that was destroying academic freedom. "Do you think it would hurt freedom of thought and speech for you to tell us the truth as to whether or not you have been or are a member of the Communist Party and whether or not you have been meeting or have met with communists?"[22] And so the argument continued.

Senator Olin Johnston: "Is it your opinion that you should be allowed to practice here as a teacher the communistic program?"

Young: "I am an English teacher. I teach subjects that are set for me and the courses that are set for me."

Johnston: "You come in contact with the students, do you not?"

Young: "It would be difficult to teach without doing that."

Johnston: "And doing that, you have them looking up to you in a way, do they not?"

"Insofar as I am a good teacher, I certainly hope they look up and respect me."

"And you would have a large influence over them, would you not?"

"I am afraid I cannot say. I suppose every teacher hopes that by helping students to understand something about the nature of the world, something about the great literature of the past, that he does influence you."

Harry Gideonse, testifying a few weeks later, told the subcommittee that automatic dismissal under section 903 was convenient because firing a teacher otherwise, under the state tenure law, "requires that there have to be specific charges, trial committees, and so on." But he was not altogether happy with this outcome: it had "the appearance of acting on a technicality" and left out the real reason for ousting the rebels: their communist affiliations and perjury at the Rapp-Coudert hearings a decade before. So, "in the interests of making it plausible that the college administration, and behind it the Board, were acting on grounds that were not just superficial little technical pretenses," he had prepared a statement explaining why using section 903 to fire Harry Slochower the previous fall had been justified.[23]

"These cases do not involve issues of academic freedom or freedom of thought," Gideonse's statement averred. Twelve years ago, Slochower had sworn before Rapp-Coudert that he was not a CP member. If he—or Frederic Ewen—had repeated the denial under oath, "they could foresee that testimony now available to the Senate subcommittee would make charges of perjury unavoidable." (Although the statute of limitations barred a criminal prosecution for perjury, the BHE could fire them for it, since it now had two witnesses against them.) Ewen and Slochower pleaded the Fifth Amendment before the SISS, "with a smokescreen of language designed to make their action appear as a defense of freedom and democracy rather than a carefully planned avoidance of perjury charges."

Gideonse acknowledged that Slochower was "a good scholar" and "an effective teacher." But he had continued to lie about CP affiliation when the faculty was considering his promotion. Then he was called by the SISS:

> He came in to get advice from me, and I told him, "I don't see that you have a problem. You have told the faculty committee and you have told me that you were not and never have been. . . . All you have to do is go and tell that committee just exactly what you have told us and what we have in writing from you." His reply to me was, "If I do that, they will prove perjury on me." That gives you a picture of the kind of morale that we are dealing with. These are not issues that are worthy of being considered by anyone who is really professionally interested in academic freedom. This is the academic gutter.

The dilemma that Slochower and others had faced at the time of Rapp-Coudert—not wanting to cooperate in a witch hunt, certainly not wanting to inform, and hoping to keep their jobs—did not mitigate their crime in Gideonse's view.

Gideonse clearly did not believe that academic freedom protected communists, but he was also not comfortable with the more fanatic wing of the Red-hunting establishment. He described a visit to Brooklyn College by HUAC chair Parnell Thomas, who had refused to participate in a radio discussion of "who and what is un-American" and, when pressed, replied that "he didn't care about the Bill of Rights." Gideonse considered Thomas an embarrassment and HUAC "amateurish, ignorant, and lacking in the qualities that would make its work fruitful." While "the fringes grow and are increasingly irresponsible, it is time to strengthen the center," he said. Gideonse's goal was thus a nicer, more rational purge. He did not perceive—or else would not acknowledge—that in the field of heresy hunting, it is difficult to avoid unseemly allies.

The SISS ended its investigation in June 1953 with Joseph Cavallaro, who had recently replaced Ordway Tead as BHE chair. An admirer of Senator McCarthy,[24] Cavallaro assured the committee that the BHE was now dealing harshly with recalcitrant witnesses and had initiated a process that would replicate what Saul Moskoff had been doing at the Board of Education. Senator Jenner was mollified but made the SISS's expectations explicit: to date, he said, 14 city college professors had invoked "their privilege against incrimination" in public hearings; others had done so in executive session, "and the subcommittee has evidence that still others have been, at least, members of the Communist Party." Rapp-Coudert, "using procedures basically similar to those used by this committee, was successful in causing an appreciable number of these communists to be removed from the school system early in the 1940s," yet, from the fall of 1942 until the SISS took up the cause, "virtually no action was taken by the New York City authorities."[25]

Cavallaro reassured Jenner. The BHE had not only fired the 14 professors but had begun investigating all 3,503 teachers who were employed at the day and evening sessions of the four city colleges. He had asked the city for funds to hire staff to assist a lawyer who would interrogate anyone considered suspicious.[26] The lawyer was Michael Castaldi, an expert in loyalty investigations who had successfully argued *Adler v. Board of Education* in the Supreme Court.

Cavallaro defended the BHE against charges of previous negligence. The board had adopted "several resolutions" during the days of Rapp-Coudert, asserting the unfitness of communist teachers and commanding all employees to cooperate. He laboriously introduced each resolution into the SISS hearing record. One senator said, "I assume from what you have just said you have no fears this committee is trying to stifle academic freedom?" Cavallaro did not; he then read at length from Judge John McGeehan's 1940 decision voiding Bertrand Russell's appointment to City College and defining academic freedom as "the freedom to do good and not to teach evil."[27]

Cavallaro's papers document the BHE's effort to duplicate the Jansen/ Moskoff process of investigation. Sources included the FBI and the city police department's BOSSI unit. By March 1954, Cavallaro could write to Jenner that the BHE's "Special Investigating Unit" had "perfected its working machinery."[28] That machinery, according to a concerned letter to Cavallaro from board member Ruth Shoup, included discourtesy, "threats of subpoenas, and coercion." The danger, Shoup said, was that such methods could "enlist sympathy for people who in no way deserve it." She noted that the situation at the colleges was "explosive."[29] Ordway Tead, now having resigned himself to the heresy hunt, also wrote a concerned letter, to the chair of the BHE's "903 Committee": "If it seems to you and the committee members that it is imperative to authorize a further six months of expenditure for '903,' I am willing to give my affirmative vote. But I feel strongly that the Board should receive at its first meeting this fall a clear and explicit statement of just exactly what has been done in recent months and what remains to be done which requires the service of special counsel." Tead was concerned that the investigation "may well prove to be unfruitful as well as disturbing and dis-ruptive with our faculties."[30]

But Tead was out of power, and the hunt went on. In late 1956, the BHE still had charges pending against 13 people,[31] among them Queens College English instructor Dudley Straus, who refused to answer the "$64 question" as to CP membership at any time before 1953. At Straus's 1955 BHE trial for insubordination and conduct unbecoming, attorney Victor Rabinowitz asked President Theobald whether he had used the services of the by-now-notori-ous perjurer Harvey Matusow to identify professors with past communist affiliations. According to Matusow, Theobald had been "extremely intense and determined upon cleansing his school of all 'non-American' ideas": "I would talk to him about how the communist teachers worked. It was all bullshit, but he wanted to hear it."[32] Theobald denied having consulted Matu-sow, except for asking him to be an "intermediary" in a "private matter."[33] Straus, who was fired, was a "great teacher," according to a former student who many years later organized an exhibit at Queens College to document the events.[34]

Slochower v. Board of Higher Education

Attorneys Ephraim London and Harold Cammer took their case against section 903 to New York's Court of Appeals. The ACLU was conspicuously absent from the litigation; the only *amicus curiae* brief was from the Public Education Association, a group of teachers, parents, and community activ-ists that had opposed the Feinberg Law in 1949. But the association took a cautious approach: its only argument was that teachers were not city employ-ees within the meaning of section 903; otherwise, it agreed that CP mem-bers were automatically unqualified to teach because, "so far as appears from the known evidence," joining the Party "involves a surrender of freedom of opinion."[35]

In April 1954, New York's high court upheld the use of section 903 to dis-miss Shlakman, Slochower, and the others. It relied on the Supreme Court's *Adler* decision for the proposition that teachers "have no right to work in the school system on their own terms." Justice Holmes's old canard that a person may have a constitutional right to talk politics but not to be a policeman was trotted out to prove the point. The judges ignored the real question: how far can government go in demanding the relinquishment of constitutional rights as a condition of employment? The court found no conflict between section 903 and portions of the state education law that protected tenured teachers against firing without good cause and only after a hearing.[36]

Judge Charles Desmond dissented, but he did not address this issue of unconstitutional conditions. Desmond agreed that "communism in the United States is a conspiracy against our Government, and that participation in such a conspiracy is entirely inconsistent with the loyalty required from a schoolteacher." But he thought section 903 inapplicable because, first, the teachers were not "employees" of the city and, second, the SISS was "not authorized to conduct an inquiry into the property, affairs and government of the city or the official conduct of its officers and employees"[37]—the prerequisite for section 903 to apply.

The teachers' next step was the Supreme Court, but only Ephraim London, representing Slochower, had raised the due process protections of the U.S. Constitution as a bar to the application of section 903. That is, Cammer had not raised a "federal question" that would trigger Supreme Court review. Both London and Cammer filed motions with the Court of Appeals to amend its judgment to specify that questions under the federal Constitution "were presented and passed upon," but the court granted only London's motion.[38] Although both Cammer and London then sought Supreme Court review, only London got it.

When *Slochower v. Board of Higher Education* arrived at the Court in 1955, Earl Warren had been chief justice for fewer than two years. His predecessor Fred Vinson had died of a heart attack in September 1953. William Douglas wrote to his colleague Hugo Black at the time, "I wish Eisenhower would make you Chief Justice. It would be the smartest thing he could do politically and the best possible appointment on the merits. But I do not think he's smart enough to do it." Douglas did not know that the president had already promised Warren, the governor of California, the next vacancy on the Court, probably in return for actively campaigning for Eisenhower during the 1952 election.[39] Whether or not Eisenhower was smarter than Douglas thought, he later lamented that appointing "that S.O.B. Earl Warren" was the "biggest damn-fool mistake I ever made." The reason, in large part, was "those Communist cases—all of them," Warren reported that Eisenhower later told him.[40]

Warren's first big initiative was the Court's unanimous 1954 decision in *Brown v. Board of Education*, striking down racial segregation in public schools, but in 1955, the Warren Court had not yet addressed the loyalty programs, oaths, and legislative investigations that now pervaded the American scene. This was still dangerous political territory, even though the demagoguery of Senator McCarthy had been exposed at the televised Army-McCarthy hearings in April 1954, and McCarthy had been censured by the Senate eight months later. On April 2, 1956—just a week before it decided *Slochower*—the

Warren Court took a step toward slowing the loyalty juggernaut when it invalidated Pennsylvania's anti-sedition law on the ground that the federal Smith Act occupied the field when it came to defining and punishing subversion.[41] If this was not quite the "dramatic return to libertarian values" that one historian claims,[42] at least it was notable for indicating that there might now be a majority to build on the few modest limits that the Vinson Court had imposed on loyalty programs.

Despite the significance of the issue raised in *Slochower*—whether employees could be fired, without any semblance of due process, for refusing to relinquish their Fifth Amendment rights—the only friend-of-the-court brief to the Supreme Court came from Osmond Fraenkel and Emanuel Redfield on behalf of the New York Civil Liberties Union. After oral argument in October 1955, the justices discussed the old right-privilege distinction: Frankfurter, although opining that "Holmes cover[ed] it all in [the] policeman case," nevertheless acknowledged that "to fire a person in 1950 because he does not say in 1940 that he was or was not a member of the Party is unreasonable." But Frankfurter, along with Eisenhower appointee John Harlan, wanted to postpone deciding the case, and Justices Reed, Burton, and Minton, all Vinson Court holdovers, voted to affirm, finding no due process violation in Slochower's firing.[43]

The justices conferenced the case again in March 1956. Now, former attorney general and hard-line Cold Warrior Tom Clark voted to reverse the New York courts, but on the relatively narrow ground that the BHE deprived Slochower of basic due process by firing him summarily.[44] Clark wanted to avoid a broader ruling on the issue of unconstitutional conditions. With five votes to reverse—Clark, Warren, Frankfurter, Douglas, and Black—and needing to hold onto Clark's vote, Warren assigned him to write the majority opinion.

Clark's decision in *Slochower v. Board of Higher Education* firmly rejected the simplistic Holmes principle that any condition on public employment was constitutional. To say that nobody has a right to a government job, Clark explained, "is only to say that he must comply with reasonable, lawful, and nondiscriminatory terms"—which meant that employers and courts, in deciding what is reasonable, must weigh "the State's interest in the loyalty of those in its service with the traditional safeguards of individual rights." In this case, the city's use of section 903 as an automatic basis for discharging a tenured professor, without any hearing or other inquiry into "the subject matter of the questions, remoteness of the period to which they are directed, or justification for exercise of the privilege," was so arbitrary as to violate due process.[45]

But Clark did not ignore the Fifth Amendment. Part of the reason Slochower's firing was unreasonable was that, contrary to the popular view, invoking the Fifth Amendment is not equivalent to admitting guilt. "We condemn the practice of imputing a sinister meaning to the exercise of a person's constitutional right under the Fifth Amendment," he said. "The privilege against self-incrimination would be reduced to a hollow mockery if its exercise could be taken as equivalent either to a confession of guilt or a conclusive presumption of perjury." Because the BHE had "seized upon [Slochower's] claim of privilege" and "converted it through the use of §903 into a conclusive presumption of guilt," his firing "falls of its own weight as wholly without support." Clark ended, however, by noting that the city had "broad powers in the selection and discharge of its employees, and it may be that proper inquiry would show Slochower's continued employment to be inconsistent with a real interest of the State."[46]

Black and Douglas appended a brief note in *Slochower*, that they "adhere[d] to the views" expressed in their dissents in *Adler v. Board of Education* and *Garner v. Board of Public Works*—that is, they objected to Clark's thinly veiled suggestion that the city could fire Slochower for his politics as long as it gave him due process. Reed, Burton, Minton, and Harlan dissented, with Harlan arguing that a teacher's refusal to answer questions "jeopardizes the confidence that the public should have in its school system"[47]—an argument that was to prevail two years later when Harlan assembled a majority to undo much of the reasoning of *Slochower*.[48]

The *Slochower* decision incensed those who had long excoriated "Fifth Amendment communists." Joseph McCarthy, censured by the Senate but not yet silent, called it "a new low in judicial irresponsibility," and SISS's new chair, segregationist James Eastland, speaking of "just one pro-communist decision after another," concluded that there was "some secret, but very powerful, Communist or pro-communist influence" at work on the Court.[49] Sidney Hook, chair of the Philosophy Department at NYU and a vociferous proponent of the teacher purges, blasted the decision as "one of the most intellectually confused" ever handed down by the Court. Hook cited the AAUP—"than whom there is no more jealous watchdog of the rights of teachers"—which had said that invoking the Fifth Amendment "is sufficiently compromising to justify inquiry into a teacher's good faith. How much graver," Hook urged, "is the moral significance, where evidence such as exists in the Slochower case is at hand." The evidence, according to Hook, consisted not only of five witnesses who could place Slochower at CP meetings but also of Slochower's Party membership book; Hook identified it with the number 689.[50] Hook did not say how he learned this detail—the FBI, Gideonse, and the BHE are all possibilities.

The BHE's Michael Castaldi, on loan from the Corporation Counsel's office, had been preparing his case against Slochower in anticipation of an adverse Supreme Court decision. A week before the oral argument in *Slochower*, the BHE decided that if the Court ordered Slochower reinstated, new charges "would be immediately served," and Gideonse "would forthwith suspend him" again from Brooklyn College.[51] Two months after the argument but still before the decision, Castaldi submitted three proposed charges against Slochower, for lying in 1940, 1941, and 1947.[52]

The day after the decision was announced, TU attorney Harold Cammer called Castaldi to urge that Vera Shlakman and four other professors he represented, who had been fired under section 903 but whose cases the Supreme Court had declined to review, "be given the benefit of the Supreme Court ruling." Castaldi refused. Gustave Rosenberg, who chaired the BHE's "903 Committee," thought that at the very least the other six professors who had been fired in 1953 and who were covered by the stipulation that the city had signed, giving them the same relief as Slochower and Shlakman, would now be entitled to reinstatement.[53] Ultimately, the city not only refused relief to the Shlakman group but backed out of the stipulation as well.

Within hours after the Supreme Court decision, Gideonse announced that Slochower would be momentarily reinstated and then immediately suspended on charges of conduct unbecoming a professor.[54] The BHE scheduled a preliminary hearing for January 5, 1957. Slochower, with London by his side, refused to answer questions about Party membership before 1945 on the ground that they were not relevant to any legitimate inquiry.[55] On February 26, the day before his administrative trial was to begin, Slochower resigned. Castaldi could hardly contain his glee but also his disappointment at not being able to present his carefully assembled evidence. "At the zero hour," he told the press, "Slochower has 'thrown in the towel,' so to speak. And this notwithstanding his previous statements in the press, television, and radio that he was looking forward to his day in court." The reason, Castaldi said, "is not difficult to understand." The BHE had five witnesses, plus "documentary evidence," that Slochower lied when denying CP membership. "In fact, we were prepared to prove that Slochower was in the Communist Party under the Party name of 'FLINT' and that his Party membership book was No. 689." In view of this "proof of Slochower's perjuries," Castaldi felt "duty bound" to suggest that the BHE refer the case "to the appropriate authorities for their consideration and disposition."[56] Nothing came of this threat of criminal prosecution, but Slochower's academic career was over.

Did Castaldi have "documentary evidence"? His trial preparation notes mention "Dues Stamp Book 689" and indicate that the testimony about it came from Bernard Grebanier, Slochower's first accuser, or possibly another ex-communist informer, who told Castaldi that the book was "kept by member . . . spring 38—Party—new Book—at Slocher's [*sic*]—given by Gustafson."[57] If this informer intended to testify that he saw Slochower's dues book, he would have needed a very good memory to recall the number; but a cryptic reference in Castaldi's notes to "G's affidavit & notebk"[58] suggests that Grebanier, already anticipating his departure from the Party, may have kept notes on the other members, including the numbers of their dues books. In any event, the evidence was overwhelming: Slochower's original lies to the Rapp-Coudert Committee explained his refusal now to testify about CP membership. His old colleague John Whyte probably had it right when he suggested that Slochower had rationalized away his membership "by saying that one wasn't really or essentially a communist, since one did not religiously follow the line."[59]

Slochower's explanation for "throwing in the towel" was characteristically evasive, yet it had a measure of truth. "The present issue involves only myself," he said, whereas his original refusal to answer the SISS's questions was "to vindicate a basic principle, namely, that it is good Americanism to stand by the Constitution." He still "loved to teach and lecture" but had already moved on: "I find my present work—the practice of psychoanalysis and psychotherapy—even more satisfying."[60] However genuine this protestation, it was characteristic of a man who combined brilliant intellect with a strong capacity for rationalization. It would not be the first time that an important Supreme Court decision vindicated the rights of a flawed human being.

Despite the disappointing outcome for Slochower, the decision that bears his name had a bracing impact on constitutional law.[61] But it did no good for Vera Shlakman and the other non-cooperators. Neither the Supreme Court nor the New York Court of Appeals was willing to apply the ruling to them, on the ground that their lawyers had not raised the due process argument initially. And the city wriggled out of its stipulation to apply the final result to the six teachers who had not filed appeals; its argument was that the stipulation was only binding if the outcomes in *Shlakman* and *Slochower* were the same. Since Slochower had won and Shlakman had not, there was no uniform result. Osmond Fraenkel went back to court for an order forcing the BHE to apply the Supreme Court's ruling in *Slochower* to the others, but he lost.[62]

Instead of appealing this decision, Fraenkel now simply submitted his clients' claims for back pay to the BHE. When that was denied, he began a new suit, but with no better luck. The New York Court of Appeals dismissed it on the technical ground that a lawsuit to recover salary must be brought under a different section of the state legal code than Fraenkel had used.

Judge Desmond, dissenting, was aghast: "every consideration of justice and fair play" suggested that the New York courts should "vindicat[e] plaintiffs' rights as already declared by the United States Supreme Court. No statute or controlling precedent stands in the way. Yet this court rejects their suit on the most narrow of procedural grounds."[63] The New York courts were not yet ready to apply equity, or constitutional law, to "Fifth Amendment communists," and it took the BHE another generation to do so.

No Ivory Tower

Justice Stanley Reed, dissenting in *Slochower*, cited the Association of American Universities' 1953 statement that membership in the Communist Party "extinguishes the right to a university position." The statement had been signed by the presidents of 37 of the country's most prestigious universities, even though some had reservations.[64] The AAU justified its stand on two grounds: first, the vague and ambiguous one that all professors must be "diligent and loyal in citizenship" and, second, that they must be independent thinkers, which "renders impossible adherence to such a regime as that of Russia and its satellites."[65] With this sweeping generalization, the nation's leading university presidents, supposedly champions of an unintimidated and unfettered academy, capitulated to a system of surveillance, informers, and inquisitions that later generations of administrators have admitted was dangerously misguided.

The AAUP, champion of academic freedom, did not do much better. Its 1947 position that "individual culpability," not guilt by association, should be the standard for dismissal had no effect, for the organization did not try to enforce it.[66] More than one historian attributes the group's "completely ineffectual" performance in part to "a disastrous failure of internal leadership and management."[67] Ellen Schrecker, whose study of the purge in academia is aptly named *No Ivory Tower*, is less harsh, wondering whether anti-communist hysteria at the time was "so powerful that no organization, not even one that claimed to protect the status and ideals of the academic profession, could prevent the rest of the academy from collaborating with McCarthyism."[68]

There were only a few exceptions to university collaboration in the Cold War heresy hunt. Robert Maynard Hutchins, president of the University of Chicago, had announced his commitment to academic freedom in 1935 when he responded to an Illinois legislative committee that had been convened to investigate charges that students were assigned to read *The Communist Manifesto* and to critique the capitalist system. Hutchins replied that "free inquiry is indispensable to the good life, that universities exist for the sake of such inquiry, [and] that without it they cease to be universities." He refused demands that he fire an English professor accused of communist sympathies, and the legislative investigation fizzled.[69]

Hutchins had not changed his stand 14 years later when Illinois was considering anti-subversive legislation similar to the Feinberg Law. Testifying before the state senate, he explained that at Chicago, faculty were guaranteed "complete academic freedom" and that whether they had communist sympathies was none of the university's business. He would not exclude communist students from higher education either, for "if we did, how would they ever learn better?" Hutchins condemned the then-recent decision by the University of Washington to fire three professors and declined to say whether he agreed with President Truman's statement that all CP members are "traitors." "Am I required to?" was his reply.[70]

Hutchins had vocal support from students. The investigation collapsed, and the bill never passed.

Sarah Lawrence College, just north of New York City, was another outpost of resistance. In 1951, when the local American Legion attacked the college and sent a delegation to its president, Harold Taylor, demanding the dismissal of three suspect professors, the board of trustees "responded by ignoring the Legion's charges and, instead, releasing a statement on academic freedom."[71] Four years later, Taylor and the trustees stood behind an ex-communist professor who refused to name names before the SISS; the trustees voted to give him a sabbatical if he were sent to jail for contempt of Congress.[72]

What would have happened had the academic establishment followed the examples of Robert Maynard Hutchins and Harold Taylor? Could some of the damage to students, faculties, and independent education—not to mention the hundreds of individuals who lost their jobs—have been averted if the universities, or even just the AAUP, had taken a more defiant stand? One can only speculate, but a chronicler of Sarah Lawrence's response to congressional pressures concludes that it was only through such acts of defiance "that the predatory threats of McCarthyism were thwarted."[73] Similarly, Schrecker writes that had universities defied the heresy hunters, "they might have succeeded"; Hutchins's experience suggests "that support for the anti-communist crusade was superficial and that resistance to it entailed far fewer risks than people imagined. By refusing to take those risks, the majority of the nation's college professors must share some of the responsibility for the repression that followed."[74]

The perennial fear of reduced funding in part explains the academy's collective failure of nerve. The AAU's 1953 statement made this consideration explicit. "The universities owe their existence to legislative acts and public charters," the administrators wrote. "The state university is supported by public funds. The privately sustained university is benefited by tax exemptions." Both forms of support "carry with them public obligations." When legislative bodies "scrutinize these benefits and privileges," it is "clearly the duty of the universities and their members to cooperate in official inquiries directed to those ends."[75]

In this disquisition on the obligations of institutions that receive government aid, the AAU adopted the right-privilege distinction in stark form. Are there any limits to the power of legislative funders to impose conditions or to drive out disapproved professors? What about museums and libraries that receive government funds? Should they acquiesce in legislators' demands to remove books or works of art? These questions are ever recurring: they were fiercely debated more than 30 years later when the National Endowment for the Arts responded with fear and trembling to the outrage of some legislators over "indecent" or "blasphemous" works whose creators had received federal grants. "Not with the taxpayers' money" was the constant refrain. But it was never clear whether a defiant, articulate response from the arts establishment, rather than the diplomatic silence it largely chose, would have dissipated the threat.[76]

The "failure to protect academic freedom eroded the academy's moral integrity," Schrecker concludes.

> For almost a decade until the civil rights movement and the Vietnam War inspired a new wave of activism, there was no real challenge to political orthodoxy on the nation's campuses. The academy's enforcement of McCarthyism had silenced an entire generation of radical intellectuals and snuffed out all meaningful opposition to the official version of the Cold War. When, by the late fifties, the hearings and dismissals tapered off, it was not because they encountered resistance but because they were no longer necessary. All was quiet on the academic front.[77]

Of course, it was not only university administrators who acquiesced in the anti-communist fervor; the Vinson Court in the early '50s failed to protect civil liberties and adopted virulent anti-communist rhetoric even while claiming to defer political decisions to the elected branches of government. It approved the jailing of communist leaders, it upheld test oaths for public employees and labor union officers, and it approved the Feinberg Law's apparatus for investigating the beliefs and affiliations of teachers and firing those deemed disloyal. The Warren Court essentially continued this pattern in its 1956 *Slochower* decision: although it invalidated the peremptory discharge of a tenured professor without any individual consideration of circumstances, it implied that with a little due process, he could be fired for unacceptable beliefs. It was only with a series of Supreme Court decisions the following year, and in particular with its ruling on behalf of Marxist scholar Paul Sweezy in his battle with the attorney general of New Hampshire, that the Court took a large, substantive step toward curbing heresy hunts. *Sweezy v. New Hampshire* would also be the first case in which a Supreme Court majority embraced academic freedom.

9

The Moral Dilemma: Naming Names

"Informers Wanted—Must Be Able to Teach"

Harry Slochower justified his refusal to answer the Senate Internal Security Subcommittee's questions in 1952 by saying that he did not want to become an informer. If this was not exactly consistent with what his boss, Harry Gideonse, said Slochower told him—that he was afraid of perjury charges— it is understandable that Slochower would publicly choose the more high-minded rationale. By 1952, the moral dilemma of forced informing was causing anguish and bitterness nationwide. It had become the defining ritual of anti-communist investigations.

The dilemma was memorably dramatized by the actor Larry Parks, questioned by HUAC in 1951. Parks, who had been a Communist Party member in the early 1940s, gave what one commentator aptly called "the most excruciating" testimony ever given before HUAC; he pleaded, "Don't present me with the choice of either being in contempt of this Committee and going to jail or forcing me to really crawl through the mud to be an informer."[1] The congressmen were not moved, and Parks named names.

Despite its drama, Parks's objection to informing was too broad. Bearing witness to crime or other wrongdoing is sometimes the more ethical path, as film director Elia Kazan demonstrated in *On the Waterfront*, an apologia for his own naming of names before HUAC. The film's hero, incarnated by a brooding Marlon Brando, violates the rules of his tribe but serves a higher good by testifying against murderous gangsters. Ex-communist informers, however, were not bringing murderers to justice; they were causing serious trouble for people who, for the most part, had committed no worse sins than enthusiasm for radical social change and naïveté about the evils of Stalinism.

In 1952, the playwright Lillian Hellman received a subpoena from HUAC and wrote an open letter in reply, offering to talk about her own political past but refusing to "bring bad trouble" on old acquaintances whom she thought innocent of disloyalty or subversion. "To hurt innocent people whom I knew many years ago in order to save myself is, to me, inhuman and indecent and dishonorable," Hellman wrote; "I cannot and will not cut my conscience to fit this year's fashions."[2] Her letter soon became famous as a crisp statement of the moral issue involved. Like fellow playwright Arthur Miller, who took the same position a few years later, Hellman risked imprisonment for contempt of Congress. Both avoided that fate,[3] but what if one did not have the stature of a Lillian Hellman or Arthur Miller? To keep one's job and support one's family were powerful incentives to give investigating committees, the FBI, and their counterparts on boards of education what they wanted, especially if one could rationalize, as Kazan and many others did, that the Red hunters already had the names, that communists were not worth sacrificing one's livelihood to defend, or, as the more fervid anti-communists such as the self-dramatizing Whittaker Chambers asserted, that the informer was a "patriot, prophet, and moral hero."[4]

Informing was problematic for reasons beyond those so trenchantly stated by Hellman. First, even when a board of education or investigating committee already had the names, providing confirmation of what might only be the muddy recollection of an opportunistic or frankly delusional informer would indeed harm people who had not committed any crime.

Then there was the sense of betrayal when witnesses, to save themselves, named former (and sometimes current) friends. The biologists Harry Albaum and Alex Novikoff had been colleagues and close friends at Brooklyn College in the 1930s and '40s, but in 1952, Albaum, under pressure from Gideonse, confirmed to the SISS that Novikoff had been in the Party. Novikoff, confronted with the same dilemma the following year, resisted the subcommittee's imprecations and those of his employers at the University of Vermont: he refused to name names. "I would rather have lived through this period than have to live with myself if I did what Harry did," he wrote to a friend.[5]

Finally, informing meant participating in a debasing ritual premised on a Manichean myth of good and evil. The ritual was not, as Victor Navasky points out in his book *Naming Names*, "a quest for evidence; it was a test of character."[6] One journalist called forced informing a "glorification of betrayal," a "sadistic attempt to break men intellectually and spiritually and leave them drained of all self-respect and self-esteem."[7]

For those who were willing to answer questions about their own political past but refused to name others, there were practical choices to be made. Legally, the question was whether to cite the First or Fifth Amendment, or some other legal or ethical constraint, in justifying one's refusal. By the early 1950s, the First Amendment would not stand as a legal defense; one risked criminal prosecution for contempt of the investigating committee. The Fifth

Amendment was safer legally, but it often meant loss of employment and it also had the odor, in the public mind, of guilt.

In New York, Board of Education inquisitor Saul Moskoff pressured, bullied, and cajoled teachers who confessed former communist sympathies to name names, but he did not yet have the authority to force them. His February 1954 colloquy with Harry Adler, a teacher of radio electronics, was typical. Moskoff got Adler to acknowledge that if CP members actually "engaged in subversive activities," it would be "unwise and improper."[8]

"Now, that being so," Moskoff said, "you must be aware of the obligation that is placed upon Dr. Jansen to determine whether or not there are any such people in our school system." Adler understood the implication: "You mean that I am obligated to—?"

"No, no," Moskoff interrupted, but "do you recognize that as a teacher in the employ of the Board of Education it is your job not to place any obstacles in his path in performing his duties?"

Adler: "I am wondering what you mean by 'obstacles.'"

Moskoff now was explicit: in refusing to name names, Adler was "serv[ing] the purposes of the Communist Party" by helping it "to keep secret and unknown its present members": "By withholding the information you are making it impossible or extremely difficult for Dr. Jansen to ascertain the facts."

"In clear conscience, I couldn't do that," Adler responded.

Moskoff was frustrated by the impasse. As early as March 1954, he complained to the Corporation Counsel's office that "certain members" of the board were "reluctant to prefer charges" against teachers who refused to name names.[9] Five months later, perturbed that Superintendent William Jansen had not acted on his recommendation to bring charges against teachers who "flatly refused" to inform on others, Moskoff wrote to George Timone, who headed the board's Law Committee, seeking advice. He described a number of people, identified only by initials, who had refused to inform and noted that some of them had falsely denied communist affiliations in their job applications and could be prosecuted on that basis too.[10]

Moskoff and Timone were allies by this point against the more circumspect Jansen. The previous year, Moskoff had asked Timone to secure a job at a Bronx parochial school for the wife of a police detective, with whom, he said, "we have been on exceedingly good terms" and who "has cooperated to a large extent with us in our program."[11] It was an indication both of their mutual trust and of Timone's clout with the Catholic hierarchy.

Jansen resisted the pressure. In September 1954, he issued a statement to the board rebutting Moskoff's charges and clarifying the issue of false denials of communist affiliation on application forms. If it were board policy to dismiss every employee who had lied in answer to the question, that would be one thing, Jansen wrote. "However, this has not been the policy. . . . The circumstances surrounding the making of the false affidavit are taken into consideration. In the case of former communists among teachers, immunity has been given if they name names," but this did not mean that informing should be mandatory or that teachers who refused to inform should be punished with a false-affidavit charge.[12]

Moskoff shot back that Jansen "took lightly the making of a false statement." He criticized the superintendent for reinterviewing some teachers without telling him and for "expressing concern" over the sheer number of teachers who were being pursued.[13] Moskoff urged adherence to the policy proposed in a recent *World-Telegram and Sun* editorial, which argued that if a teacher had "otherwise proven" his break with communism, he should not be forced to name names "as further proof of his patriotism," but that the board would be justified in requiring "extra proof" from teachers who had "a long record of affiliation with the left-wing Teachers Union or with recognized front organizations."[14]

Newspapers got word of the dispute. Responding to one front-page article, TU president Abe Lederman and legislative director Rose Russell wrote an alert to "All Teacher Interest Committees" urging that although people might differ "about the general policy of the recent inquiries, they must all view with abhorrence any attempt to force teachers into becoming informers" and thereby "to impose wholesale degradation on the profession."[15]

In late February 1955, the Board of Education held a public hearing on a proposal generated by Timone that would require teachers to inform. It was not an exercise in sober debate. A representative of the Queens County American Legion thought it "surprising we should be here today debating whether the Board should perform its manifest duty," but said, "unfortunately, the humpty-dumpty upside-down proletariat have promulgated a doctrine in this country that communists and ex-communists have rights superior to those of other Americans." A rabbi from the American Jewish League Against Communism thought a forced-informer policy necessary because "the sea of red is slowly surrounding America." Although crediting the board with being "one of the brighter spots in this picture," the rabbi complained, "The tempo is so slow that we still aren't catching up with the brand new devices of communist propaganda. We are beset by hesitancies, complexes and paralyses," and "our own superintendent of schools, however sincere, is unfortunately not leading our battle as he should be but must be dragged in the right direction."[16]

It got nastier. Rose Russell said that all the spying and particularly the use of disreputable informers whom even the board's administrative trial judges found worthless had made the school system into a "cesspool." A man from the Catholic War Veterans responded that the only "cesspool" was the one "attempting to destroy the New York City school system and every free institution in America"—the Communist Party. Charles Hendley, former TU president, wondered "from what source comes this demand for more names. Apparently somebody thinks the market for red herrings is just unlimited." But he predicted there would be "a break in the market" and that the "aspiring politicians" in the Corporation Counsel's office and Department of Education would not reap the political rewards for which they were hoping.[17]

There was a shorter hearing on March 17, 1955; this time, board president Charles Silver allowed only one speaker in opposition: TU lawyer Harold Cammer, who protested that a forced-informer policy would make New York the only city in the United States where the test of fitness to teach is willingness to name names. But the vote for the policy was 7–1, the sole dissenter being the board's newest member, Cecile Ruth Sands; she thought that "conscientious scruples against naming others should be respected."[18] The new policy authorized Jansen and his agents to require employees who admit past communist sympathies to "disclose any relevant information" about others in the school system "who may be, or may have been, members of the Communist Party."[19] "Informers Wanted—Must Be Able to Teach" was the headline in the British *Manchester Guardian*, reporting on the vote.[20]

"This Type of Inquisition Has No Place in the School System"

The staunchly anti-communist Americans for Democratic Action denounced the new resolution, as did the New York Board of Rabbis, an umbrella group with more than 700 members, which sent a telegram to President Silver citing "the long and honored ethical tradition of Judaism" which "denies the informer a share even in the world to come."[21] The Council of the Catholic Diocese of New York also protested, and the *New York Times* editorialized that while, of course, "adherence to communist doctrine" should be "an automatic disqualification for teaching," nevertheless coerced informing is "morally wrong."[22]

Four months after enactment of the forced-informer policy, Commissioner of Education Lewis Wilson signaled his disapproval. The case involved four teachers who had been dismissed for the usual insubordination and conduct unbecoming in refusing to cooperate with Moskoff; one of them had based his refusal on a fear that answering questions about his politics would lead to a demand that he name others. Wilson upheld the firings but noted in passing, "In my opinion, a board of education is without power" to require teachers to inform.[23] The city's chief lawyer, Peter Campbell Brown, dismissed this warning as a mere aside and advised the board to go ahead and enforce the new policy.[24] His opinion persuaded the board to authorize (in essence, direct) Jansen in late August 1955 to suspend five employees who had talked with Moskoff about their own past communist involvement but had refused to name others—unless they changed their minds.

These five protesters, like the overwhelming majority of targeted teachers, were Jewish.[25] Samuel Cohen, a 20-year veteran of the school system, had risen through the ranks to become principal of a Brooklyn elementary school. Harry Adler, the radio electronics teacher, had also taught for 20 years, with time out for military service. Julius Nash and Irving Mauer were experienced science teachers in tough inner-city schools; both were World War II veterans, and both had joined the Party after the war because of financial hardship. Nash had been a substitute teacher since 1933; he received his permanent license in 1941, but when he returned to teaching after the war, as he told Moskoff, "my entrance salary was $1,500 per year. I didn't get any prior service credit, I was married, my wife was pregnant, we had a baby in 1946, and my financial situation was such that—I went to a party once and somebody made a speech and I just joined. Well, I thought at the time that that was the answer to the problem."[26] Minerva Feinstein had been a clerk for nearly 20 years at the same Brooklyn school where Cohen was principal; later, three-quarters of the staff at the school signed a letter to Jansen expressing shock that he had suspended a "person of the caliber of our clerk."[27] Mauer and Nash also had lavish praise from their supervisors for dedication and for effectiveness in engaging the interest and affection of their underprivileged students in Harlem and the Bronx.

Moskoff had interviewed each of the five before enactment of the inform-or-else policy. Nash told him at their first encounter, "I don't want to be an informer. I think it is against lots of principles going back to Jesus Christ. Nobody likes or praises Judas for being an informer." Moskoff argued, "You are making it well-nigh impossible" for Jansen to do his job; Nash explained, "I am willing to talk about myself—I admit my indiscretions; I joined in a fit of depression, and because of working hard and improving my economic conditions, I left the Party, and I disagree with their philosophy today." Moskoff offered a final inducement: Nash was one of those who had falsely denied CP affiliation in a job application. "If you can demonstrate in some conclusive manner that you have left the party, then that might be taken into consideration in determining what should be done about your false statement." Nash repeated, "I cannot be an informer."[28]

Mauer, who had likewise denied his communist past on job forms, pressed the religious point in his second interview with Moskoff, after the board had enacted the forced-informer policy. Both a prominent rabbi and his own father had warned him against informing. His father did so on the first night of Passover, no less. "He used the word 'moser.' I didn't know what the word meant; he said: 'informer,' and he pointed out to me what a reprehensible thing this would be to do, and that an informer was not to be buried in hallowed ground." Moskoff did not overlook a chance to discuss Jewish law and asked whether Mauer knew that it violates the Talmud to lie under oath. Moskoff then reminded him that Jansen must report to the board any evidence of falsity in job applications but that naming names might impress the board and mitigate his punishment.[29]

Mildred Grossman, a teacher of bookkeeping who had been suspended in 1954 on the usual charges of insubordination and conduct unbecoming, was incensed by Moskoff's role in the unsavory business that was now convulsing the Jewish community. In April 1955, she wrote a "Dear Friend" letter to the synagogue in Queens where Moskoff was an officer, describing his "main role as chief inquisitor"—that is, "to force teachers to become informers." The Jewish people, she wrote, "have always condemned those who resort to the vile practice of betraying others to save their own skins. Is it not even more reprehensible to be paid to procure informers?"[30] Grossman listed the New York Board of Rabbis, the American Jewish Congress, and the Metropolitan Council of B'nai B'rith as among the groups opposing the forced-informer policy, and she enclosed a copy of the Board of Rabbis' resolution.

Moskoff reacted with fury. He wrote to Grossman that her "poison pen diatribe" had failed to accomplish its "evil purpose to create dissension in the Jewish community": "My telephone has been busy over the weekend with calls from members of my congregation expressing their indignation over your vile, filthy and malicious venom." The next day he wrote again. He had spoken with someone at the Board of Rabbis, who told him that although the organization had sent a telegram denouncing the forced-informer policy, it had never "officially" adopted the resolution that Grossman had enclosed with her letter. According to Moskoff, this made the resolution "spurious." He demanded that she promptly retract "this gross misstatement of fact" and threatened, "Your refusal to correct what appears to be a deliberate misrepresentation . . . will require further action on my part."[31]

Attorney Leonard Boudin responded on Grossman's behalf: "I do not understand your reference to a misrepresentation and your request for a retraction. The resolution referred to was in fact adopted by the executive committee and is set forth in full at page 12 of the appellants' brief filed on

March 25, 1955 with the Commissioner of Education."[32] This ended the matter. Moskoff's threat did nothing to enhance the reputation he hoped to gain as a benevolent inquisitor.

With the suspensions of Mauer, Nash, Adler, Cohen, and Feinstein imminent in late August 1955 because of their refusal to inform, attorney Victor Rabinowitz (Boudin's partner) rushed an application for a stay to the new education commissioner, James Allen. He filed on behalf of Harry Adler and others "similarly situated." On September 7, Allen issued a temporary stay of "all acts and proceedings" that related to Adler's refusal to inform, pending the final disposition of the case. The Board of Education took the position that this applied only to Adler, so Rabinowitz had to hurry back to Albany to seek stays for Nash, Mauer, and Feinstein. (Cohen was separately represented by attorney David Ashe, who did the same.) Rabinowitz notified Jansen on September 9, a Friday, that Commissioner Allen would consider his motions the following Monday. Rather than awaiting the commissioner's decision, Jansen rushed to suspend Nash, Mauer, Feinstein, and Cohen. His September 9 memo to the board gave three reasons: the Feinberg Law, "which places the burden of proof on a teacher to prove complete separation from the Communist Party and Communist activities"; "refusal to name other teachers who were members of the Communist Party"; and, as to Mauer, Nash, and Cohen, false affidavits in applications for employment.[33]

Commissioner Allen ordered the additional stays on September 12, but Jansen and the board flouted them. (Jansen later suspended Adler as well.) Their theory was that the charges of falsity on job applications and of suspected communism under the Feinberg Law were not covered by the stays. They were technically right with respect to the false affidavits, but as to the Feinberg Law, their reasoning was circular—that is, since the board viewed naming names as the only sure way to prove "complete separation from the Communist Party and Communist activities," its charge of violating the Feinberg Law simply duplicated its charge of violating the forced-informer policy. But whatever the niceties of the legal arguments, the reality was that the five who had refused to name names were suspended without pay for the indefinite future.

In August 1956, Commissioner Allen invalidated the forced-informer policy. His decision reaffirmed his predecessor's view that the Board of Education was without power to coerce teachers to inform, but he said the problem "is a much deeper one" than simply the question of legal authority. Allen had canvassed educators and reported that "there is near unanimity" that "the indiscriminate use of this type of interrogation immediately engenders an atmosphere of suspicion and uneasiness in the schools and colleges. . . . No one knows when the finger of suspicion may be pointed at him." A school system that "sets one teacher against another in this manner is not conducive toward the strength and cohesion which needs to exist in order to instill character into the student body." In short, "this type of inquisition has no place in the school system."[34]

The union was jubilant. Rose Russell and Victor Rabinowitz called for immediate reinstatement of the five, in time for the new school year. Adler's high school had not been able to replace him, Russell pointed out, though it had advertised all year; and Mauer's loss as a science teacher "in an all-Negro and Puerto Rican junior high school has been attested to by all his supervisors."[35] But the city would not budge: it announced that it would appeal the commissioner's ruling to the courts and meanwhile would go forward against the five on its other charges—violation of the Feinberg Law and (as to Nash, Mauer, and Cohen) falsifying job applications.

Moskoff in particular resented the commissioner's decision invalidating the forced-informer policy. In early 1958, a state investigator asked him about former English teacher Dorothy Bloch, one of the second group of eight who had been fired for insubordination and conduct unbecoming. She had now applied for a psychologist's license. Moskoff wrote Jansen, "I informed the investigator I would be unable to provide him with information concerning Mrs. Bloch's background since I interpreted the decision by Commissioner Allen, prohibiting dissemination of information by teachers with respect to other Communists, as also applicable to me."[36] This was so silly—Allen's decision obviously did not prohibit voluntary disclosure of information—that either Moskoff was posturing or he was so blinded by his zeal that he could not think straight. By this time, a judge had affirmed the commissioner's ruling, and a few months after Moskoff's fit of pique, the appellate division of the state court unanimously affirmed.[37]

At this point, opponents of the forced-informer policy again endeavored to persuade the city to call it quits. The New York Times editorialized that coerced informing is "morally repulsive" and "fatal to the morale of any teaching body"; New York Post columnist Murray Kempton wrote sardonically that in the early 1950s, when perilously substandard school conditions prevailed, the board nevertheless "found nothing endangering the schools but communist teachers." By 1955, it "was running low in suspects"; "as a means of increasing the crop," it decided to require informing. When the board announced its decision to appeal again, this time to the state's highest court, the Post called it "vindictive" and "municipal McCarthyism." The board was more interested in "saving its own face" than in "decency and justice," and its victims "were paying an outrageous price for a repudiated era of hysteria."[38]

The case at the New York Court of Appeals (the state's highest court) was closely watched. The American Jewish Congress, the Public Education Association, the National Lawyers Guild, and the Teachers Guild—no friend of radical teachers—filed *amicus* briefs denouncing the forced-informer policy. Osmond Fraenkel appeared in a companion case for a Hunter College professor, Charles Hughes, who had been fired for both alleged communism and refusing to cooperate with a Board of Higher Education inquiry; Hughes had won the right to a new trial in state court on the issue of communist affiliation but had been fired again, this time for refusing to name names.[39]

The Court of Appeals decision, in May 1959, did not wax eloquent, as Commissioner Allen had, about the poisonous atmosphere engendered by forced informing. Instead, the judges simply deferred to the commissioner's judgment that "the desirable objective of ridding the school system of Communists would not be served by the method of inquiry pursued by the [Board of Education] and that such method of inquiry would do more harm than good." But they did note that naming names is hardly the only means of fighting subversion: "If the enforcement of our laws were to depend upon informers alone, as the Board appears to contend is the fact as to the Feinberg Law, we would live in a chaotic state. Those charged with the duty of enforcement know this and so resort to other traditional methods for obtaining the desired information," such as background investigations. "It is also noteworthy that no other school board, of the several hundred existing in the State of New York, has found it necessary to compel teachers to inform on their fellow faculty members."[40]

An Exercise in Vengeance

Its legal options now exhausted (there was no "federal question" on which it might seek Supreme Court review), the Board of Education still balked at reinstating the five. The TU mounted another campaign; the *Post* continued its critique; even Eleanor Roosevelt mentioned the issue in her newspaper column: "These teachers have legally won their point," she wrote, "and should be returned to their teaching positions."[41]

In November 1959, the *Post* noted that it had now been 106 days since the Court of Appeals decision, and still the board had not acted.[42] Victor Rabinowitz returned to court seeking an order to reinstate the five. The city requested a stay of the suit and a month later announced that it would drop the charges based on alleged violations of the Feinberg Law, would accordingly reinstate Adler and Feinstein, but would proceed against Nash, Mauer, and Cohen for false statements on job applications. The board "apparently forgave" other ex-communist teachers who had lied on applications, the *Post* editorialized, "but what the board won't forgive is that these three wouldn't involve others. How much longer will this exercise in vengeance continue?"[43]

The board's response, a month later, was to prosecute four more employees on false-statement charges. It had long known about their denials of previous communist affiliation. Charging them now was an attempt to undercut the argument that Nash, Mauer, and Cohen were really being pursued for refusing to inform, not for lying years before on application forms.

The convoluted process of hearings before a "trial examiner" on the false-statement charges moved lugubriously forward. By June 1961, the examiner had submitted his recommendations to the Board of Education. The *Post* took the occasion to comment on "our disintegrating school structures" as well as the legal limbo in which Mauer, Nash, and Cohen had been living for the past six years: "Is the Board waiting for some final reassurance that Senator McCarthy will not return?"[44] The *Times* likewise reported that a group of "distinguished religious and civic leaders" were asking the board "to remember 'mercy as well as justice'"; it explained that the case involved teachers who, "after more than five years, continue to be suspended without pay, ostensibly for false statements made in their applications many years ago but actually because they refused to turn informers against other teachers." It was "high time for the board to call off a persecution that, in the name of human decency, ought to be recognized as being immoral, in addition to having long since become senseless."[45]

No decision on the false-statement cases had been made by September 1961, when a new Board of Education took office; the state legislature had removed the previous one for multiple acts of neglect, mismanagement, and corruption.[46] The new board decided to hear reargument; a year later, it disgorged a voluminous opinion that bestowed markedly disparate treatment on the six teachers charged with falsely denying their communist leanings on application forms. (A seventh teacher had resigned shortly after she was charged.)

Samuel Cohen, the Brooklyn principal, was forgiven and reinstated with partial back pay, because he had demonstrated "forthrightness of character and a strong sense of moral responsibility"—that is, he had sufficiently expressed repentance for his communist past. Three others suspended in January 1960 for falsity were reinstated with the same partial back pay. Only Nash and Mauer were fired: the board found no reason for mercy because it viewed some of their answers to Moskoff as evasive. Nash, for example, had taken a break during his interview to consult with his advisor before acknowledging that the Communist Party was "sinister and evil"; Mauer had also taken breaks (at Moskoff's invitation) and was insufficiently forthcoming in recognizing the perils of communism.[47]

Rabinowitz, Boudin, and lawyers representing the teachers who had been reinstated but without full back pay appealed to the commissioner of education, arguing both that the board's distinctions among the different teachers made no sense and that Nash and Mauer were still being punished for refusing to inform. Commissioner Allen rejected their appeal and, in a retreat from his 1956 ruling that invalidated the forced-informer policy, adopted the city's argument that when an ex-communist teacher "cooperates with the board to the fullest, including the naming of names, he thereby gives strong evidence of his actually having severed his connection with the party"; moreover, he "helps to eradicate, as far as he can, the evil to which he has succumbed in the past." So, although the teacher "cannot be required to name names, his voluntary action in so doing does set him apart," like a criminal who turns state's evidence and who is therefore entitled to "a remission of punishment."[48] It was a sadly circular justification for accomplishing indirectly the same result as the forced-informer policy.

Rabinowitz and Boudin returned to court, arguing again that the board was really punishing Nash and Mauer for refusing to name names; indeed, the city's lawyers admitted that "informers as a class may be given preferential treatment over non-informers."[49] They said the board's rationale for firing Nash and Mauer—that their testimony lacked candor—was "a mere makeweight": the transcripts instead showed frightened individuals "caught in a situation where they knew their teaching careers might be at stake if they failed to inform, yet bound by conscience not to name names."[50] This was true, yet there had been a measure of defiance in Nash and Mauer's approach to the whole sordid business that Moskoff noticed, as did the trial examiner. Unlike some of their colleagues, they just did not have it in them to make a sufficiently lavish expression of remorse. The lawyers got nowhere in the county court. It was not until 1973 that Mauer and Nash, along with 31 other teachers dismissed during the Red hunt, won any compensation for their years in the educational wilderness.

Why did the New York City Board of Education go beyond the usual panoply of heresy-hunting techniques to make forced informing a condition of employment, and why did it stick to the policy so stubbornly despite repeated defeats in the courts? As the Court of Appeals pointed out, no other school system in the state went this far. But New York City was where the radical TU, with its agenda of educational reform and racial equality, was strongest and where communists, although proportionally a tiny fraction of the teaching ranks, had been most vigorous. Left-right antagonisms, stoked in part by an anti-Semitism that was sometimes but not always indirect,[51] fueled the city's extreme and mean-spirited policy.

The religious aspect made the battle over forced informing particularly traumatic. The Talmudic interchanges with Moskoff were a consequence of the overwhelmingly Jewish character of teacher radicalism in New York. Their numbers in turn were a function of both a Jewish tradition of social-justice activism and societal discrimination that limited the access of educated Jews to other professions. For the inquisitors, it undermined suspicions of anti-Semitism to have Jews conducting the prosecutions, and for passionate anti-communists such as Moskoff, it was equally important to show that far from all Jews were subversives. His debates with Adler, Nash, and Mauer over informing—and on a more cosmic level, his earlier barbed exchange with Maurice Kurzman over Jewish collaboration in the Shoah (see chapter 5)—dramatized the intensity of the battle.

Ultimately, the forced-informer policy backfired. Religious and political leaders who had no sympathy for leftism or even liberalism were repulsed at a basic human level. In that sense, like Senator McCarthy's vindictive performance at the 1954 Army-McCarthy hearings, mandatory naming of names in New York City helped turn public opinion against the entire anti-communist purge.

PART IV

The Supreme Court and Academic Freedom

10

Red Monday and Beyond

"An Intellectual Strait Jacket"

The Supreme Court took cautious steps in the mid-1950s toward dismantling loyalty programs. In 1955, it overturned the federal Loyalty Review Board's blacklisting of a Yale professor of medicine who had been a consultant to the Public Health Service, but it ruled on technical grounds and avoided the constitutional question of whether loyalty boards could use evidence from secret informants, evidence that the employee could not see and therefore try to discredit or rebut. The justices had left that question hanging since their deadlock over Dorothy Bailey's firing from her federal job four years before.[1] Justice William O. Douglas wanted a broader ruling: the professor had been "condemned by faceless informers" who, for all the loyalty board knew, might be "psychopaths or venal people"; cross-examining one's accuser was "essential if the American ideal of due process is to remain a vital force in our public life."[2]

In June 1956, two months after the Court's *Slochower* ruling, it reversed another loyalty-program dismissal without deciding whether firing someone based on alleged membership in an organization on the Attorney General's List violated the right to freedom of association.[3] As Douglas later wrote, although the Court reached the right result in these cases, it "never made the resounding declaration of human rights that was sorely needed."[4]

The first whiff of major change came in May 1957, in two cases that invalidated decisions by state bar committees denying admission to the practice of law on the basis of previous Communist Party membership. One involved Rudolph Schware, who had joined the Party during his last year of high school and quit in 1940, disgusted by the Hitler-Stalin Pact; he freely answered the committee's questions. The other bar hopeful was Raphael Konigsberg, who had refused to answer questions about his political past. In both cases, the Court found violations of due process and rejected the guilt-by-association rationale that had been critical to Vinson Court decisions upholding loyalty programs. Hugo Black, writing for the majority in

Schware, pointed out that the CP "was a lawful political party with candidates on the ballot in most States" when Schware was a member. His political faith "may have been unorthodox," but "mere unorthodoxy" does not negate "good moral character," the standard for bar admission.[5] This was exactly what opponents of the Red hunt had long been saying, and although the Warren Court's path through the thicket of loyalty programs for the next decade was hardly smooth or straight, the *Schware* decision marked a notable setback for enforcers of political conformity.

In early June 1957, the Court waded deeper into the turbulent waters. Union leader Clinton Jencks had been criminally convicted for filing a false Taft-Hartley affidavit. A new justice, William Brennan, wrote for the majority that the trial judge had violated Jencks's due process rights when he refused to order the government to disclose reports by FBI informants who had testified at trial, among them the perjurer Harvey Matusow.[6] The *Jencks* decision was the first sign that Brennan, whom President Eisenhower had appointed because he needed a Democrat and a Catholic from the Northeast to shore up his reelection chances,[7] would turn out to be a judicial strategist whose ability to forge Supreme Court majorities would ultimately dismantle much of the legal scaffolding of loyalty programs.

Even though *Jencks* turned on a point of criminal procedure, it had major implications for the use of secret evidence in political cases—a point not lost on Tom Clark, who had urged at the Court's conference that it would be a "big mistake to open up FBI records on the showing here," and whose anger "only grew as his warnings went unheeded."[8] Clark's dissent charged that intelligence agencies might as well "close up shop, for the Court has opened their files to the criminal and thus afforded him a Roman holiday for rummaging through confidential information as well as vital national secrets."[9]

Clark's rhetoric provided ammunition for what Brennan's biographers call "the still-potent Red Scare powder keg." The public reaction to *Jencks* "was swift and overwhelmingly negative. Within a day, members of Congress introduced eleven different bills aimed at thwarting it."[10] The justices, including Brennan, were distressed by the reaction,[11] but it did not deter them from issuing four more rulings, on June 17, 1957, that rejected major pillars of the anti-communist purge. The impact was so striking that the date became known as "Red Monday."

One of the four decisions reversed the Loyalty Review Board's dismissal of a China expert from the State Department, even after he had been cleared five times by departmental loyalty boards. A second case, *Yates v. United States*, shrank the Court's previously broad interpretation of the Smith Act in the 1951 *Dennis* decision by requiring evidence of incitement, rather than just abstract teaching, before a person could be jailed for advocating revolution.[12] *Yates* sparked a heated reaction from FBI director J. Edgar Hoover, who saw that it would make further prosecutions of communist leaders nearly impossible. Fearing just such a ruling, Hoover had instituted his illegal program of surveillance and dirty tricks, COINTELPRO, almost a year earlier, when the Court agreed to review the convictions in *Yates*.[13]

The other two Red Monday rulings dealt with open-ended loyalty investigations. In one, the Court reversed the contempt conviction of labor organizer John Watkins, who had cooperatively answered HUAC's questions about his own political past and even agreed to name people he knew to be current CP members but refused to name others who were no longer in the Party. Chief Justice Warren wrote for the Court that because the extent of HUAC's authorization was unclear and because there is no congressional power to "expose for sake of exposure," Watkins was justified in refusing to answer.[14] Early drafts of his opinion had strong First Amendment language, but Justice Frankfurter, fearing political repercussions, pushed Warren to remove it: "As a matter of prudence," he wrote, "the stiffer our condemnation of action by Congress the less provocative should be the expression of it."[15]

The fourth of the Red Monday cases involved the Marxist scholar Paul Sweezy, convicted of contempt for refusing to answer a few of the many questions posed by New Hampshire Attorney General Louis Wyman, acting as a one-man investigating committee. Sweezy was not shy about his political views, but he balked at providing information about people who had been active in the Progressive Party, including his wife; and although he assured Wyman that he had not, in a guest lecture at the state university, advocated the violent overthrow of the government, he refused to reply to some specific queries—for example, did he tell the students that "socialism was inevitable in this country?" Did he "advocate Marxism?"[16]

When the case arrived at the Supreme Court, Warren's law clerk was dubious. He reasoned that Sweezy's answers conceded the government's right to ask about his lectures, and the professor could not pick and choose where the questioning should stop. Furthermore, the attorney general's inquiry was polite, not a "public circus"; it lacked the "flamboyant abuses of power" found in the "McCarthy approach."[17] Warren rejected the advice. He circulated a draft opinion that used the same logic as the *Watkins* case: the extent of the attorney general's authorization was unclear; hence, Sweezy's right to due process was violated. But Warren now added a new forensic ingredient: academic freedom. Echoing Douglas's dissent in *Adler v. Board of Education* ("a pall is cast over the classrooms") and Frankfurter's paean to the "priests of our democracy" in *Wieman* (the Oklahoma loyalty oath case), Warren wrote that "the essentiality of freedom in the community of American universities is almost self-evident," because of "the vital role in a democracy that is played by those who guide and train our youth." Then, as if directly addressing the nationwide teacher purges, Warren chose a vivid metaphor: "To impose any strait jacket upon the intellectual leaders in our colleges and universities would imperil the future of our Nation. Scholarship cannot flourish in an atmosphere of suspicion and distrust. Teachers and students must always remain free to inquire, to study and to evaluate, to gain new maturity and understanding; otherwise, our civilization will stagnate and die."[18]

This powerful rhetoric bolstered those who had been opposing loyalty investigations for years on academic-freedom grounds; it validated what the Frederic Ewens, Irving Adlers, and scores of others had been saying. But really, one might wonder why forcing Paul Sweezy to describe his lectures would have infringed his academic freedom. Certainly, any student, including one moonlighting as a journalist, could have published the contents. It was the "atmosphere of suspicion and distrust," the questioner's effort to wrestle a complex subject—socialism—into simplistic accusations, and the chilling effect of government investigation that threatened teachers' and students' freedom "to inquire, to study and to evaluate, to gain new maturity and understanding."

All the while that *Sweezy* was under consideration, Felix Frankfurter had been compiling files on academic freedom. He was particularly interested in a situation in South Africa, where the legislature was threatening to reduce "non-European" (read: non-white) university students to second-class status, thereby interfering with the faculty's governance of the school.[19] As Warren was preparing his opinion, Frankfurter reminded the chief of his pedigree: "A quarter century of my life was lived as a university teacher. . . . Both before I came to the Harvard Law School and since coming here, the problem of the relation of universities to the state has been a chief concern of mine."[20] Ultimately, Frankfurter (joined by John Harlan) wrote a separate concurrence in *Sweezy* that turned on academic freedom rather than merely treating it as a "plus" factor in a due process case, as Warren had.

Frankfurter's concurring opinion found the state's vaguely framed national security justification for its questions "grossly inadequate" when "weighed against the grave harm resulting from governmental intrusion into the intellectual life of a university." Free inquiry is essential to the "pursuit of understanding," especially "in the groping endeavors of what are called the social sciences." He bolstered his argument by quoting the recent "poignant plea" of South African scholars, which identified "four essential freedoms of a university—to determine for itself on academic grounds who may teach, what may be taught, how it shall be taught, and who may be admitted to study."[21] It was one of the ironies of the case that while the four liberal activist justices (Warren, Black, Douglas, and Brennan) rested the ruling on due process, the Court's two conservative champions of judicial restraint would have recognized a full-fledged right to academic freedom in order to frustrate a political branch of state government.[22]

Frankfurter's opinion in *Sweezy* did not distinguish between the unfettered inquiry of individual scholars and the "four essential freedoms" of the university—for him, it was all part of the same enterprise. But taken out of context, as Frankfurter's line about the four freedoms often was in the years after *Sweezy*, it seemed to elevate the interests of the institution over those of the scholars who do the crucial intellectual work. Frankfurter's vision of academic freedom thus failed to account for situations in which university administrations themselves, rather than outside government investigators, seek to squelch non-conforming professors.

Legal scholar Harry Kalven later illuminated the likely reason that the Supreme Court's four liberals did not vote for a straightforward academic-freedom ruling in *Sweezy*. Frankfurter and Harlan were fair-weather allies when it came to free speech, and in this case, they concurred in the result because the questions concerned Sweezy's academic Marxism and the activities of the Progressive Party; as Frankfurter said, if Attorney General Wyman's questions had directly implicated the CP, it would have been a different story.[23] Kalven thought that Warren, Brennan, Black, and Douglas were "unwilling to make such a concession"; they were "not ready to give up altogether on the First Amendment possibilities even in the Communist cases." Their strategy was thus "to protect the witness by means of procedural safeguards, while saving the First Amendment challenge for some later day."[24]

Whether or not the two dissenting justices in *Sweezy* (Tom Clark and Harold Burton) understood this at the time, they protested Warren's "elaborate treatment" of academic freedom. Clark wrote tartly, "Since the conclusion of the majority is not predicated on First Amendment questions, I see no necessity for discussing them."[25] It was a fair point and helped stoke many of the outraged responses to *Sweezy*, *Watkins*, and other recent cases from a still vociferous Red-hunting constituency. SISS chair James Eastland proposed a constitutional amendment requiring justices to be reconfirmed every four years, and Senator William Jenner, after a scathing attack on the Court, introduced a bill to remove its jurisdiction over a broad swath of loyalty and subversion cases.[26]

If loyalty enthusiasts were livid about Red Monday, their opponents were ecstatic. Radical journalist I. F. Stone exulted that *Watkins* and *Sweezy* vindicated the few circuit court judges, such as Henry Edgerton and Charles Clark, who had objected to the jailing of non-cooperating HUAC witnesses a decade before. Edgerton, he reminded readers, "was the lone dissenter" when the courts sent the Hollywood Ten, the directors of the Joint Anti-Fascist Refugee Committee, and others to jail for contempt of Congress. June 17, 1957, Stone proclaimed, "will go down in the history books as the day on which the Supreme Court irreparably crippled the witch hunt."[27]

Stone was overly optimistic. The year after Red Monday, by a 5–4 vote, the Court approved loyalty dismissals of a teacher in Pennsylvania and a subway conductor in New York. Justice Harlan, writing for the majority in the New York case, made the circular argument that the firing was legitimate because even though the conductor had pled the Fifth Amendment just as Harry Slochower had, he was not fired for invoking his constitutional privilege but "for creating a doubt as to his trustworthiness and reliability by refusing to answer the question."[28]

Frankfurter and Harlan had switched sides between the 1957 and '58 cases. One scholar opines, "The justices were acutely aware of the attacks against their decisions, and they were willing to make concessions when they felt that danger had become too threatening."[29]

One Step Forward, One Step Back

1958 was not entirely a year of retrenchment for the Court. The same day as the Pennsylvania and New York decisions, Justice Brennan displayed his talent in assembling majorities by striking down a California law that mandated a disclaimer test oath as a condition of receiving a tax exemption. Brennan said that requiring taxpayers to prove their loyalty turns due process upside down: ordinarily, it is the state that must prove wrongdoing, and especially so when free thought is in question: "The man who knows that he must bring forth proof and persuade another of the lawfulness of his conduct necessarily must steer far wider of the unlawful zone than if the State must bear these burdens."[30] The reasoning was convoluted, but Brennan had pinpointed a primary problem with oaths—their shift in the burden of proof. He also midwifed the concept of an unconstitutional "chilling effect" on speech when laws are not precisely drawn. As censorship laws are almost by definition not precisely drawn, the Court was to have many future opportunities to note that uncertain meanings lead citizens to "steer far wider of the unlawful zone." Brennan himself reused the phrase nine years later in his *Keyishian* decision.

Brennan's biographers say that "there was little to suggest at the time" that his opinion in the tax-exemption case "would become a building block in the rights revolution that lay ahead."[31] The opinion itself was cautious and took pains to acknowledge precedents such as *Garner* (upholding Los Angeles's test oath for city employees) and *Douds* (upholding the Taft-Hartley oath). In these cases, Brennan said disingenuously, the oaths did not punish political speech but simply vindicated governmental concerns about efficiency or safety. Brennan carefully distinguished *Adler*, too, because there, teachers "could only be dismissed after a hearing at which the official pressing the charges sustained his burden of proof by a fair preponderance of the evidence."[32] The distinctions were not persuasive, but they were needed because in 1958 there was not a majority prepared to overrule the precedents supporting loyalty programs.

It was very much one step forward and one step back. In June 1959, a five-justice majority decided the question that Warren, Black, Brennan, and Douglas had avoided in ruling that the New Hampshire attorney general's questions to Paul Sweezy violated his due process rights. Now, the Court upheld the contempt conviction of Lloyd Barenblatt, a Vassar professor who had refused to answer HUAC's questions about CP activity when he had been a graduate student at the University of Michigan. Harlan wrote in his opinion for the Court that even though academic freedom is "essential to the well-being of the Nation," this "does not mean that the Congress is precluded from interrogating a witness merely because he is a teacher."[33] Harry Kalven ruefully commented that the Warren-Black-Brennan-Douglas strategy of "marking time with procedural protections until some later day backfires. The 'later day' arrives too soon, and the four find themselves in dissent where they now openly rest their objections on the First Amendment grounds they had so carefully eschewed in *Sweezy*."[34] As Douglas later observed, HUAC's authorization for its questioning of Barenblatt—to investigate "the extent, character and objects of un-American propaganda activities"—was exactly the same as it had been when it questioned John Watkins, but somehow now it was sufficient: "What had been six to one for Watkins became five to four against Barenblatt" and two other recalcitrant HUAC witnesses who lost their cases in 1961.[35]

Political backlash, and criticism from one organization in particular, drove the Court's retreat in *Barenblatt*. In 1959, Peter Campbell Brown, who had unsuccessfully defended New York City's forced-informer policy through the courts, teamed up with New Hampshire Attorney General Louis Wyman, still smarting from his loss in *Sweezy*, to persuade a committee of the American Bar Association to recommend legislation that would override recent Supreme Court decisions that "weaken[ed]" internal security.[36] This threatening critique from so august an institution as the nation's major professional lawyers' association could not have escaped the notice of President Eisenhower's newest appointment to the Court, Justice Potter Stewart, or of Harlan and Frankfurter, who switched sides between *Watkins* and *Barenblatt*.[37]

Stewart was an Ohio federal judge who saw himself as non-ideological—"trying to be a good lawyer, looking at every case," not "some great big philosopher king."[38] J. Edgar Hoover, distressed over the liberal leanings of Warren and Brennan, had pushed for Stewart's appointment after FBI agents told him that the judge had frequently praised the agency.[39] Stewart—who was to go down in history as the justice who wrote of pornography that although he could not define it, "I know it when I see it"—had already emerged "as the key swing vote" in loyalty cases.[40] His support was critical in another case, decided the same day as *Barenblatt*, that further undermined the hopes raised by Red Monday two years before.

Again, a witness had resisted questions posed by New Hampshire Attorney General Wyman in his role as a one-person investigating committee. This time it was a demand for information about employees, invited speakers, and guests at the summer camp of the leftist World Fellowship. Neither the principles of associational privacy, recently established in a case involving the state of Alabama's demands for the NAACP's membership list,[41] nor the due process limits on the investigation of Professor Sweezy worked to persuade more than the usual quartet of Warren, Brennan, Black, and Douglas to invalidate Wyman's demand. Tom Clark wrote for the majority that although guilt by association "remains a thoroughly discredited doctrine," this should not stop a legislative investigation "undertaken in the interest of self-preservation." Rights of associational privacy, "however real" in the circumstances of the NAACP case, were "here tenuous, at best." And, said Clark, "the academic and political freedoms discussed in *Sweezy* are not present here in the same degree, since World Fellowship is neither a university nor a political party."[42] Clark had added the softening phrase, "in the same degree," at Stewart's behest; Stewart was ambivalent about the case and pointed out that "political and perhaps also academic freedom can be at least to some extent involved even when it is not a university or a political party that is being investigated." He had suggested other changes to smooth the hard edges of Clark's draft, as had Harlan.[43] Both of their votes were necessary to Clark's 5–4 majority in the case.

The difference between non-violent civil rights protesters (in the NAACP case) and presumably underhanded revolutionaries at the World Fellowship drove Clark's decision in the New Hampshire summer-camp case, just as the hot political reaction to the Court's 1957 decisions culminating in Red

Monday contributed to the Court's retrenchment. Justices do not fail to notice when Congress starts considering bills to remove them or to shrink their jurisdiction. Frankfurter was probably the most sensitive in this regard: he wrote to Brennan during deliberations in the summer-camp case that political factors, including "the vast appropriations that the Congress votes each year to Edgar Hoover," persuaded him not to question the legitimacy of New Hampshire's investigation.[44]

In the long term, the retrenchment was temporary. In 1960, Stewart wrote an opinion for a 5–4 majority invalidating an Arkansas law that required all publicly employed teachers to disclose every organization to which they had belonged or contributed within the past five years. The law was an attempt primarily to smoke out civil rights supporters. Stewart wrote that free association is "closely allied to freedom of speech" and that "the vigilant protection of constitutional freedoms is nowhere more vital than in the community of American schools."[45]

The Court Tackles Test Oaths

Although the Supreme Court had outlawed two test oaths of loyalty after the Civil War,[46] they kept resurfacing, especially in times of political uncertainty. In the 1930s, with radicalism growing in response to the Great Depression and the rise of fascism, state legislatures created new oaths. By 1936, 21 states and the District of Columbia required public school teachers to sign them.[47] After a hiatus during World War II, demands for ritual abjurations of subversive associations resumed. In 1947, Congress passed the Taft-Hartley law, extending non-communist oaths from federal employees to labor unions. In 1949, 15 states enacted new oaths for public employees.[48]

Once the Supreme Court approved Los Angeles's test oath for municipal workers in 1951,[49] more states and localities exacted similar pledges. By 1956, 42 states and more than 2,000 county or city governments had created new oaths for their employees. Some states demanded them as well from private school teachers, pharmacists, barbers, insurance or piano vendors, lawyers, voters, wrestlers and boxers, junk sellers, and applicants for unemployment benefits, tax exemptions, public housing, or fishing licenses. Texas banned any book in the public schools unless the author filed an oath disclaiming communism; in the case of authors who were no longer living, such as Aristotle or Shakespeare, the publisher had to file an oath on the author's behalf.[50]

A story recounted by Roger Revelle, founder of the University of California at San Diego, nicely demonstrated the obnoxiousness of these oaths by recounting the following anecdote. During the controversy over California's test oath for professors, General "Howling Mad" (Holland M.) Smith was asked by "a couple of the good ladies of La Jolla . . . why those professors aren't willing to say they aren't communists. And General Smith said, 'Madam, if somebody asked you to take an oath that you were not a prostitute, what would you do?'"[51]

In 1959, virtually the entire academic establishment opposed a provision of the previous year's National Defense Education Act that required every student receiving a federal fellowship or loan to swear an oath disclaiming any belief in, or membership in an organization that believed in, the overthrow of the government by illegal or unconstitutional methods. The oath had been part of earlier Cold War laws to beef up science and defense-oriented education; but it was now almost the end of the '50s, and college administrators increasingly resented being singled out, as if the very people the country was relying on to win the science race with the Soviet Union were automatically suspected of disloyalty. Harvard, Yale, Princeton, and 29 other colleges withdrew from the NDEA program in protest. Senator and soon-to-be presidential candidate John F. Kennedy co-sponsored legislation to repeal the oath, arguing that it contravened the law's purpose—to give all qualified students access to higher education—and that "it is distasteful, humiliating, and unworkable to those who must administer it."[52] Although the repeal was a compromise—it substituted a provision making it a crime for any member of a "Communist organization" to apply for or attempt to use NDEA or National Science Foundation funds—it illustrated how potent resistance from universities could be.[53]

In Florida in late 1959, high school teacher David Cramp was called to the principal's office and told to sign a state-mandated oath swearing that he was not a member of the Communist Party, did not believe in the forcible overthrow of the government, was not a member of any group with such beliefs, and had not—and would not in the future—lend his "aid, support, advice, counsel or influence" to the Party. Cramp had been teaching for nine years; now he was told "that some of the original pledges were mislaid" and he would have to sign another one. But, as he wrote to the ACLU, "I never signed the first one and I told them I wouldn't sign this one. . . . I am not nor never have been a communist and I probably won't ever become one but I feel it is a violation of my rights as a citizen of the United States to have to so state in order to hold my job." Cramp added that he was married, with three children, and thus did not relish losing his job, but, he said, "I feel that I must take this stand."[54]

Cramp's letter landed on the desk of ACLU cooperating attorney Tobias Simon. He interviewed Cramp and by late December had a draft lawsuit ready to be reviewed by the ACLU's legal counsel, Edward Ennis, in New York. Simon told Ennis that Cramp was "a most delightfully amazing fellow" who "just intuitively believes that the requirement is wrong."[55] The lawsuit averred that Cramp was "a loyal American" who had no fear of perjury if he signed the oath but that it violated the First Amendment, the constitutional ban on bills of attainder, and various sections of the Florida Constitution.

Simon had good reason to file the case quickly: the school board was scheduled to meet on February 8, 1960, to consider firing Cramp. The state trial judge denied his request for an injunction to put the discharge on hold pending the outcome of the case, and by January 27, Simon was asking the chief justice of the Florida Supreme Court for relief, again to no avail. In March, the trial judge ruled against him, and in November 1960, the Florida Supreme Court affirmed, in an opinion notable for its hostility to Cramp's dilemma. The court relied on Justice Harlan's recent use of a loose First Amendment balancing test that favored vaguely defined interests in national security in upholding the power of HUAC to question Professor Lloyd Barenblatt about his past politics; it also trotted out the old right-privilege distinction in ruling that the oath did not interfere with Cramp's right to speak freely; it merely meant that "when one speaks out to advocate the violent overthrow of the government, . . . he cannot simultaneously work for and draw compensation from the government he seeks to overthrow."[56]

Simon's appeal to the Supreme Court was a broad attack on the chilling effect of test oaths, and it pushed hard on the theme of academic freedom. He quoted Felix Frankfurter's encomium to teachers as "priests of our democracy" in the Oklahoma oath case of 1952. Florida's oath bore "no reasonable relationship" to job qualifications, Simon wrote; in fact, the opposite was true—by executing the oath, "an affiant pledges himself to so fetter his mind that he thereby takes a large step in destroying his own qualifications as a teacher."[57]

When Simon set out for Washington, D.C., in October 1961 to argue the case, his co-counsel jokingly wrote to the director of the local ACLU, "Since it is our first appearance before the U.S. Supreme Court, we expect that you will call out the color guard and have Justice Warren and Bobby Kennedy meet Toby when he lands in Washington. . . . It is assumed, of course, that you will show him the ropes; but don't suggest to him that you will argue the case for him if you value your life."[58]

It was not clear what the Supreme Court would do with the Florida oath. The four justices likely to strike it down would need a fifth vote, but their brethren had spent the past three years, for the most part, backing off from the 1957 Red Monday decisions that had set some limits on loyalty purges.

At their conference on October 23, 1961, six justices voted to strike down the Florida oath because it was so spectacularly vague and broad. Justice Clark said that vagueness was the "vice here—one could be subjected to prosecution for just about anything." Justices Harlan and Whittaker would have dismissed the case because they thought the Florida Supreme Court's decision was based on state law rather than federal; Frankfurter was inclined to agree.[59] But eventually, everybody went along with the majority opinion, written by Potter Stewart.

Stewart's December 11, 1961, opinion in *Cramp v. Board of Public Instruction* took aim at Florida's open-ended pledge not to lend "aid, support, advice, counsel or influence to the Communist Party." CP candidates had "in the not too distant past" appeared on the ballot in many state and local elections, he pointed out; could anyone who had voted for such a candidate "safely subscribe" to the oath? Indeed, "could a lawyer who had ever represented the Communist Party or its members swear with either confidence or honesty that he had never knowingly lent his 'counsel' to the Party? Could a journalist who had defended the constitutional rights of the Communist Party conscientiously swear that he had never lent the Party his 'support'?" In a draft of the opinion, Stewart had also included "a judge who had ever decided a lawsuit" in favor of the Party, but this was ultimately deleted.[60]

The "very absurdity" of these examples, Stewart said, "brings into focus the extraordinary ambiguity of the statutory language. . . . With such vagaries in mind," the oath might well "weigh most heavily upon those whose conscientious scruples were the most sensitive." Although a perjury prosecution against journalists, lawyers, or ordinary voters might seem "fanciful," it would be "blinking reality not to acknowledge that there are some among us always ready to affix a Communist label upon those whose ideas they violently oppose." Florida's oath violated the rule against laws that are "so vague that men of common intelligence must necessarily guess at" their meaning. All the more dangerous was this "vice of unconstitutional vagueness" where the law in question affects individual freedoms: "A man may the less be required to act at his peril here, because the free dissemination of ideas may be the loser." Black and Douglas appended a terse concurrence, reminding readers of their series of dissents in previous loyalty cases. The Court should have ruled on broader First Amendment grounds, they said, and outlawed test oaths entirely.[61]

The outcome was anti-climatic for David Cramp. The case went back to the Florida high court, which ruled that because the U.S. Supreme Court had only struck down the "aid, support, advice, counsel or influence" portion of the oath, Cramp must promptly swear to the rest: that he did not believe in the overthrow of the government by force or violence and that he was not a member of any organization teaching such a doctrine.[62] ACLU legal director Mel Wulf wrote Simon asking if he intended further litigation, although the prospects were admittedly "bleak"; Simon's reply chastised "'Half Empty' Melvin": "Down in these here parts, we regard the *Cramp* case as a major victory; one which warms the cockles of the heart. It has put the lie to the rumor that we are a bunch of losers, and judges, lawyers, friends, enemies, etc. give grudging respect to us as we walk down the streets." Simon acknowledged that the Supreme Court chose "a very narrow ground," but he did not think it fair to ask Cramp to continue litigating. He had been "financially hardpressed" since he lost his job. "He has now signed the oath as amended . . . , and an effort is under way to secure the return of his teaching position."[63]

"By Precept and Example"

In Washington State, another oath challenge had been percolating for years. A 1931 law required all teachers and professors to swear not only to support the constitutions and laws of the United States and the state of Washington but, "by precept and example," to "promote respect for the flag and institutions" of the state and nation, "reverence for law and order," and "undivided allegiance to the government of the United States." The vague terms were not just empty rituals: in addition to loss of employment, anyone who a prosecutor and jury thought had violated these promises would be found guilty of perjury and face up to 15 years in prison.[64]

In 1955, the legislature added a second oath, requiring every public employee and job applicant to state "whether or not he or she knowingly is a member of the communist party or other subversive organization, or is a subversive person."[65] A false statement, here too, was punishable by up to 15 years in prison, and anyone who failed to sign would be fired. At the University of Washington, still smarting from the firing of three professors under pressure from the Canwell Committee in 1949, litigation to challenge these two oaths followed a circuitous path.

Two professors represented by the local ACLU filed suit to challenge the 1955 law. Howard Nostrand was an emeritus professor of Romance language and literature with 42 years' tenure; Max Savelle was a historian specializing in American colonial history and had been on the faculty since 1947. They won an injunction from a state judge, who found the oath unconstitutional, but the Washington Supreme Court reversed, in a decision rife with quotations from the Canwell Committee and the state's governor about the "evil menace of expanding communism" and "the strategic geographical position of the state of Washington."[66]

The Supreme Court vacated the decision and sent the case back to the Washington courts to decide whether a teacher who refused the oath could be fired without a hearing. The Washington Supreme Court finessed that question by ruling that although the 1955 law did not provide for a hearing, as tenured professors, Nostrand and Savelle would be entitled to one before being fired. Since there were no untenured teachers in the case, this disposed of the due process problem for the time being. An appeal to the Supreme Court was dismissed "for want of a substantial federal question," whereupon the injunction that had prevented enforcement of the 1955 anti-subversive oath was dissolved.[67]

In May 1962, the Washington Board of Regents set October 1 as the deadline for signing both the 1955 oath and the earlier pledge to "promote respect for the flag and institutions" of government and "reverence for law and order." The University of Washington chapter of the AAUP was now sufficiently aroused to join the local ACLU in preparing another suit, this time on behalf of 64 plaintiffs, a logistical challenge that, in the words of two local chroniclers, "occasioned much bitter wrangling over legal strategy and who should serve as counsel."[68] Ultimately, Ken MacDonald, a longtime ACLU activist, and Arval Morris, a young law professor known to students as "Arval the Marvel,"[69] joined forces to challenge both oaths. The 64 plaintiffs, they hoped, were varied enough to guard against the procedural frustrations that had bedeviled Nostrand and Savelle for the previous seven years. The plaintiff group included untenured as well as tenured professors, foreigners for whom an oath of allegiance to the United States was problematic, Quakers who could not sign for religious reasons, a non-teaching meteorologist, an assistant editor at the university press, a detailer in the cyclotron department, four students, and two secretary-typists.

The first-named plaintiff, Lawrence Baggett, was a prominent mathematician. Giovanni Costigan, an Englishman, was a historian, a lecturer of legendary skills, and an outspoken opponent of America's escalating war in Vietnam. Melvin Rader, who had successfully fought the Canwell Committee's accusations, taught philosophy and included *The Communist Manifesto* among his assigned readings. Zygmunt Birnbaum, a Polish-born math professor, regularly attended international meetings that included communist scholars; he said he could not sign the 1955 oath and continue these activities.[70]

Other plaintiffs faced similar dilemmas: a nuclear physicist felt he could not continue to communicate with scholars from communist nations if he signed the two oaths. A professor of geography and member of the university's Far Eastern and Russian Institute was "responsible for aiding, advising and teaching scholars throughout the world, including communist academicians from the Soviet Union and Communist China." A history professor could not sign the "precept and example" oath without injecting "historically incorrect doctrines into his teaching."[71]

Baggett v. Bullitt was filed in federal court in June 1962 and assigned to a three-judge court to consider the constitutional issues. The judges granted a temporary injunction, held pre-trial hearings, and got the opposing lawyers to agree to the underlying facts. In February 1963, the court handed down its decision, rejecting all of Morris and MacDonald's well-honed constitutional claims. "We are not concerned with the effectiveness or the wisdom of loyalty oaths," the judges began, striking a Frankfurter-like note of judicial restraint. "We perceive the truth of the remark of Justice Black: 'I am certain that loyalty to the United States can never be secured by the endless proliferation of "loyalty" oaths; loyalty must arise spontaneously from the hearts of people who love their country and respect their government.'" But "questions of wisdom and effectiveness are matters of legislative and not judicial concern."[72] It was a strangely deferential approach, for even the Vinson Supreme Court had applied a balancing test to weigh constitutional rights against the government's asserted interests in national security.

The Washington federal judges viewed the plaintiffs' academic-freedom argument as an exercise in élitism—a claim that scholars "stand in a category apart." Although they made passing reference to "the essentiality of the preservation of universities as centers of thought, research and teaching," they adopted the argument that had been made by purge enthusiasts since at least the late 1940s: freedom of inquiry "is not possible for an individual who is fettered" by membership in a subversive group; such a person is "bound by a rigid adherence to an ideology governed by the political expediencies of its revolutionary purpose."[73]

The vagueness of the two oaths gave the judges the hardest time, but here too they found a way to avoid deciding. They admitted that it was difficult to know what was meant by requiring teachers to swear to "promote, by precept and example," the flag, the institutions of government, and "reverence for law and order." But the Washington Supreme Court should have a chance to elucidate these terms; its interpretation might "avoid the constitutional issue, or show it in clearer perspective, or resolve it."[74] Once again, a procedural hurdle threatened to frustrate the case.

The injunction remained in effect while MacDonald and Morris made their way to the U.S. Supreme Court. The justices "noted probable jurisdiction," and *Baggett v. Bullitt* was scheduled for oral argument in March 1964.

11

The Road to *Keyishian*

Buffalo, 1964

In Buffalo, New York, attorney Richard Lipsitz was closely watching the *Baggett v. Bullitt* case. A few professors at the Buffalo branch of the State University of New York (SUNY) had contacted him in January 1964 after learning that all faculty must sign the "Feinberg certificate," a disclaimer of CP affiliation that the SUNY Board of Trustees had made a condition of employment in 1956. This was four years after the Supreme Court had upheld the Feinberg Law in *Adler v. Board of Education* and three years after the legislature had extended the law to universities.[1]

The Feinberg certificate required employees to acknowledge that they had read the state's rules implementing the Feinberg Law and that these rules were terms of their employment. The rules, composed in 1949, included a memo from the commissioner of education identifying the "writing of articles, the distribution of pamphlets, [and] the endorsement of speeches made or articles written or acts performed by others" as ways that teachers might manifest subversive beliefs. The certificate required employees to deny that they were members of the Communist Party or, if they ever had been, to state that they had disclosed this fact to the SUNY president.[2]

No doubt the Feinberg certificate was a response to the bureaucratic burden of conducting loyalty investigations on thousands of employees. But like all disclaimer oaths, it affected many more individuals than the relatively few who might realistically fear retaliation for radical beliefs or associations. It thus greatly expanded the pool of potential plaintiffs—people with standing to sue if they were punished for refusing to sign.

The University of Buffalo, founded in 1846, was a private institution when the SUNY trustees created the Feinberg certificate. In 1962, as part of Governor Nelson Rockefeller's ambitious plan to upgrade the state college system, the private university became SUNY-Buffalo, a prestigious centerpiece of New York's higher-education empire. Soon every employee would be confronted with what was essentially a test oath.

The faculty was up in arms. Samuel Capen, Buffalo's president from 1922 to 1950, had been a solid defender of academic freedom. Scholars must be "free to investigate any subject, no matter how much it may be hedged about by taboos," he had said in a celebrated speech, and he had written that "the only people who can make a university are the professors. But a faculty of cowed professors can only make a rabbit hutch."[3] The Capen tradition contributed to the university's decision in 1953 to refrain—but just barely—from firing philosophy professor William Parry, an ex-communist who had offered to tell HUAC about his own past but refused to name names: instead, Parry was stripped of his tenure and placed on annual contracts for the next three years.[4] By 1962, the university had recovered sufficiently to challenge—with success—a court order that barred the communist scholar Herbert Aptheker from speaking on campus.[5]

The Buffalo AAUP chapter met on December 10, 1963, with about 300 faculty in attendance. Most were outraged by the required certificate; they asked the chapter's Academic Freedom and Tenure Committee to study their legal options. The administration agreed to postpone the deadline for signing until the end of January, and a team of law professors began to do research. SUNY-Buffalo president Clifford Furnas circulated a letter arguing that the certificate was not really a loyalty oath because it did not have to be sworn.[6]

The AAUP chapter leaders were eager to appear conciliatory. After the *Buffalo Evening News* mistakenly reported that the group had voted not to comply with the certificate, the executive committee vehemently denied it and sent a letter to both local and national news outlets emphasizing the AAUP's "fruitful and harmonious relation" with the administration and confirming that the chapter did not recommend non-compliance.[7]

Early in January 1964, the law professors submitted the results of their research. They concluded that since the Supreme Court had upheld the government's power to inquire into "the subversive associations" of its employees, there was little hope for a successful challenge to the certificate or the Feinberg Law.[8] In retrospect, of course, the law professors were shortsighted, but at the time, their analysis was reasonable. True, the Supreme Court had made some encouraging noises in the direction of limiting the Red hunt and supporting academic freedom, but it still cited *Adler* approvingly when doing so. And *Cramp*, the most recent decision on point, was narrowly limited to the extremely vague language of one portion of Florida's oath, while apparently finding no fault with the disclaimer of CP membership. If anything, *Cramp* suggested that there were still only four votes, not five, on the Court for any broader dismantling of loyalty apparatus.

The Academic Freedom and Tenure Committee incorporated these conclusions into a report to be discussed at the next AAUP chapter meeting.

But, seeing the handwriting on the wall, a small group of professors—among them Harry Keyishian and three of his English Department colleagues, George Hochfield, Ralph Maud, and George Starbuck—had already contacted Richard Lipsitz and his partner, Herald Fahringer. Lipsitz headed the local ACLU chapter and was familiar with anti-communist investigations, having represented union leaders before HUAC and other committees.[9] At a meeting on January 21, Lipsitz told the assembled teachers that he thought the law and the certificate were "constitutionally vulnerable," but he needed "some money for . . . expenses and some very modest attorney's fees." Hochfield thought that the prospect of even small fees may have deterred some of the protesters but added that professors are "not especially brave"; most are "essentially careerist" and "do not think about the university." Ultimately, only five people would refuse to sign and sue to challenge the Feinberg Law.[10]

At a bitterly contentious January 24 meeting, the AAUP chapter passed three resolutions: one disapproving the Feinberg certificate, a second resolving to protest to the SUNY trustees, and a third urging that SUNY not fire non-signers without hearings and other rudiments of due process.[11] But the chapter did not vote to recommend non-compliance, a decision that powerfully undermined the resisters' momentum. Equally troubling, as philosophy instructor and later plaintiff Newton Garver said, was that "there were close to 300 people who felt really humiliated by this but went ahead and signed."[12]

The first direct confrontation came not over the certificate but over a similar pledge required on a state civil service form. Derived from New York's 1939 anti-subversive law, the form asked employees whether they had "ever advised or taught," or been members of any group that taught, that the government should be overthrown "by violence or any unlawful means."[13] George Starbuck, already a celebrated poet who had started work as an acquisitions specialist at the university library the previous September, refused to answer the question.

Starbuck had spent the previous year on a prestigious Guggenheim fellowship at the American Academy of Arts and Letters in Rome. He had studied with Archibald MacLeish and Robert Lowell at Harvard, where he and two other students, Sylvia Plath and Anne Sexton, had "formed a sort of rump road show Algonquin Round Table. In their case, it was at the Ritz [in Boston], where they would sometimes drink and talk away the afternoon after class." (This led to a love affair between Starbuck and Sexton.)[14] In 1960, Starbuck won the Yale Younger Poets Prize for his first book, *Bone Thoughts*. With his Guggenheim fellowship ending in August 1963, Starbuck wrote to Oscar Silverman, formerly English Department chair and now director of university libraries, whom he knew from earlier visits to Buffalo, to inquire whether a position might be available on short notice. Silverman found him the library job.[15]

Starbuck was not confronted with the civil service questionnaire until late October 1963. He found the question about political beliefs both vague and obnoxious. "I prefer not to answer," he wrote on the form, "at least until the pertinence and necessity of such a question are properly explained to me."[16] By December, SUNY had begun the process of firing him. In January, he wrote to a colleague who had fortuitously offered him a position in the University of Iowa's creative writing program:

> The answer is yes. It couldn't have come in a better season. I'm being a U. of Buffalo librarian, teaching one modern lit course, finding unexpectedly good bright odd people on the faculty, enjoying the place, and in fact getting enthusiastic enough about it to have joined a few others in a fight against one of them damn loyalty oaths which I had thought, in my innocence, to have died out with McCarthy. Result: I'll most likely be out of a job by July, if not by February 1. At best I'll probably be involved in a long litigation to regain my job. A year or two subbing for Justice [presumably the poet Donald Justice] at Iowa while fighting for justice in New York would be perfect.

And so, Starbuck went on, "though I would have preferred to avoid it, and would have taken a different job if I had known of the oath requirement, I'm enjoying the battle here. There are good lawyers pitching in, and there happens to be a good constitutional case to be made." The Feinberg Law "has only been tested and upheld in lower school cases, and . . . Oh hell, I've been delivering this lecture in detail ten times a day. . . . I'm no revolutionary and never was a joiner; I've signed the damn things for the Army, . . . but I'm just not going to sign one more sweeping general promise about what I will forbid myself to think, discuss or condone."[17]

Starbuck's situation was urgent by the end of January 1964; administrators were about to fire him unless he completed the questionnaire. He retained Lipsitz, who rushed a complaint into federal court, alleging breach of contract and violation of Starbuck's First Amendment and due process rights. Judge John Henderson—a "charming guy," according to Lipsitz, but very conservative[18]—drew the case and entered a temporary injunction to keep Starbuck in his job pending an evidentiary hearing. Lipsitz, meanwhile, had been corresponding with Charles Morgan, Jr., at the national office of the AAUP about legal strategies and hurdles. On March 24, Starbuck wrote to Morgan requesting help in paying court costs and thanking him for "heartening" advice that he contrasted with his colleagues' "sympathy of the sick-room variety," as if he and the others fighting the oath "were all terminal cases of quixotism." Starbuck continued in his inimitable style:

> I still try to explain that martyrdom isn't in question—that there's a real case at law to be made, with a sporting chance of winning—but they've had it explained to them by the authorities: the Law is the Law; and they smile indulgently at my pose of modesty. They know the stake and faggots are being prepared for me: after all, what lesser danger could have deterred them from joining me? Therefore, aside from any question of money, it's a welcome reassurance to know that a skeptical outside investigation has reached the conclusion that the fight is worth betting on at the odds.[19]

Morgan, soon to become a crusading civil rights lawyer, was at the AAUP for only a brief time but had a key role in seeing that the national office donated needed funds to the case that eventually became *Keyishian v. Board of Regents.* As SUNY administrators in Albany argued with the holdouts in the spring of 1964, Keyishian, Maud, and Hochfield also wrote to Morgan seeking help. Keyishian vividly remembers the day he arrived in Lipsitz's office with the AAUP's check that meant Lipsitz would take his case.[20]

Keyishian had been an English instructor at Buffalo since 1961 on a series of one-year contracts; he had not yet finished his PhD dissertation. He was attracted to Buffalo by English Department chair Albert Cook, who brought "amazing people" to the school, among them poets.[21] Although he viewed resistance as an opportunity to challenge the entire loyalty apparatus that had driven wonderful professors from Queens College a decade before, still his decision was not easy. His Armenian-immigrant parents were distressed by the hint of disloyalty; his father wrote a "heartbreaking" letter, Keyishian later recalled, saying he hoped "I wouldn't do anything to harm this country that gave him so much."[22]

Ralph Maud and George Hochfield, untenured professors of English, were, like Keyishian, risking their jobs when they resisted the Feinberg certificate. Maud, an Englishman from Cornwall and a poetry expert, had been at Buffalo since the fall of 1958, after a PhD at Harvard and a stint at the University of Utah. A rising academic star, he was attracted to Buffalo by its unique collection of Dylan Thomas materials. The English Department was wonderful in those days, he said—a place of "gentleman scholars."[23] Maud was an iconoclast, "a dear and loony friend," Keyishian recalled admiringly, who would "do any radical thing"; Maud later joked that he was married to a "wonderful Trotskyist Jewess" who would not let him sign the oath, on pain

SUNY-Buffalo English instructor
Harry Keyishian with his T. S.
Eliot dartboard. (Photo courtesy
of Harry Keyishian)

of withdrawing marital privileges.[24] He explained to SUNY administrative officer J. Lawrence Murray, who was the point man in Albany for dealing with the protesters, that the certificate was "a demoralizing invasion of a person's privacy"; he would neither answer it nor affirm that he understood and accepted the regents' convoluted and "unduly vague" anti-subversion rules.[25] But Maud was also not eager to change jobs. While doing his own legal research and consulting outside experts, he also tried to negotiate for modified wording or a personal exemption.

George Hochfield, a specialist in transcendentalism, had come to Buffalo with the rank of associate professor in 1963, having left Ohio State after a free-speech uproar resulting from the president's decision to ban left-wing speakers from campus. At a meeting, about a third of the Ohio State faculty had voted to censure the president; after the vote, life became "intolerable" for the dissenters. "We were not harassed or threatened," Hochfield later recalled, "but we found ourselves in such an unfriendly place [Columbus, Ohio] that people began to leave." For Hochfield, the experience of "being rolled over" by a university administration on a free-speech issue "made me determined that I would never let it happen again."[26]

A World War II veteran, Hochfield had attended the University of California after the war (first UCLA, then Berkeley). In 1949, the year that California faculty rebelled *en masse* against that state's test oath, Hochfield, supported by the GI Bill and "in love with the idea of Europe," went to France. He returned to Berkeley in 1950 for a master's degree, then took a teaching

SUNY-Buffalo English professor
George Hochfield, 1960s. (Photo
courtesy of George Hochfield)

job at Penn State. He finished his PhD dissertation (a literary study of Henry
Adams) and moved to Ohio State in 1957.[27]

Like Keyishian and Starbuck, Hochfield did not just want a personal
exemption; he wanted to "get the certificate thrown out entirely." It was a
"test of conformity for entry into the teaching profession"; hence, academic
freedom was the issue.[28]

Philosopher and Quaker Newton Garver, the only non-English-teacher
among the five plaintiffs, was already "a campus celebrity," according to Keyishian, a "charismatic guy"[29] known for his pacifist principles. Garver had
studied philosophy at Oxford, then taught for two years at an Arab school in
Lebanon. He had served a year in prison for draft resistance during World
War II; although he acknowledged that there might sometimes be justifications for war, he thought civilization also needed people "who will refrain
and who will be an example of just saying, 'I won't join in the violence.'" In
1962, he was spokesman for a group that demonstrated in Buffalo against the
U.S. government's brinksmanship during the Cuban missile crisis; as a result,
he said, "we got harassment for weeks afterward: somebody put an ad in the
newspaper saying, 'Russian sable for sale; other furnishings—must leave
town immediately.' Someone called the house nearly every night between 12
and 1, saying, 'We're gonna kill you.'" His wife, Anneliese, responded gamely:
"You've called several times; why don't you come over and do it?"[30]

For Garver, the Feinberg certificate violated the Quakers' rule of "plain
speaking" and their corresponding injunction to avoid "flattery, judicial
oaths, slogans, jargon, abstractions [and] hollow formalities."[31] He signed
only after crossing out the non-communist disclaimer, hoping the change
would be acceptable, or unnoticed. He was not out to set a precedent; he

SUNY-Buffalo philosophy instructor Newton Garver with his young twins. (Photo by Anneliese, courtesy of Newton Garver)

simply needed an exemption on grounds of conscience. "My wife was extraordinarily sympathetic," Garver recalled, even though she was not a Quaker at the time. "She could have been really angry," but "she grew up in Germany, under Hitler, and she was in Germany after the war for a number of years under the communists, so she didn't have a high respect for authority as such."[32]

There followed months of indecision—neither the university nor SUNY officials in Albany wanted a suit by a religious objector—but J. Lawrence Murray was not making concessions, apart from approving a modification in the certificate to reflect that the commissioner of education's memo detailing the various activities that might constitute subversion was not technically a part of the Feinberg Law rules.[33]

Was it coincidence that four of the five who risked their jobs to challenge the Feinberg Law were members of the English Department? Although no scholarly field has a monopoly on principled risk-taking, George Hochfield thought the "liberal atmosphere" in the department gave moral support to the dissenters, and besides, he pointed out, English professors care about free speech.[34] Ellen Schrecker suggests that "literary scholars were overrepresented among the disenchanted academics of the 1960s" in part because of their "training in criticism and their cultural (perhaps even high-cultural) disdain for ordinary bourgeois values."[35]

Philosophy Department chair Rollo Handy struggled with his conscience but ultimately signed the certificate, then wrote to administrators urging them to resist: "Everyone concerned, I think, wants to make SUNY one of the finest universities in the world. To do so, we cannot rest content with statements on academic freedom, no matter how fine, which are not backed up by appropriate action when that freedom is threatened."[36] Handy got nowhere; the university fired Starbuck, refused to renew Keyishian's contract for the next academic year, and threatened to start proceedings against Maud and Hochfield.

In this discouraging atmosphere, Ralph Maud was oddly sure of victory. He had an instinct that the courts would not permit the firing of competent scholars untainted by past or present communism, simply for an act of conscience. In January 1964, he wrote that the certificate would "very likely be declared unconstitutional" and that "this Feinberg inquisition is a demoralizing thing, calculated to turn men against their fellows."[37] He also wrote to the Emergency Civil Liberties Committee (ECLC), a small, left-wing alternative to the larger but more conservative ACLU, opining that the case was "impossible to lose" and asking for help. The ECLC forwarded his letter to attorney Leonard Boudin, certainly not one to avoid a challenge. But Boudin warned Maud, "The case you present cannot, in my view, be described as 'impossible to lose.' On the contrary, it is far closer to *Beilan*, *Lerner* and *Adler* than it is to *Speiser*."[38] (*Beilan* and *Lerner* were the 1958 Supreme Court cases upholding loyalty inquisitions against teachers and subway employees, respectively; *Speiser* was the case striking down a loyalty oath required as a condition of property-tax exemption.)[39]

But the five rebels remained hopeful. Starbuck, who had also been doing his homework, wrote to Lipsitz that the Supreme Court in *Adler* was simply deferring to the state legislature's judgment that "children of tender years" might be harmed by subversive teachers, but higher education is different: it works by "free and fearless discussion. . . . Academic freedom in such a system is not a professional privilege; it is a political duty." It was only after the *Adler* decision that the state extended the Feinberg Law to universities and SUNY invented the oath. To claim that all this was sanctioned by *Adler* "is to claim much more than the courts might reasonably allow."[40]

In April 1964, Judge Henderson wrote a preliminary decision in Starbuck's case that essentially approved the civil service questionnaire.[41] Lipsitz decided to withdraw the case before the judge had a chance to render a final adverse ruling. He would then join Starbuck with Keyishian, Hochfield, Maud, and Garver in a new lawsuit.

Ralph Maud (*left*) and Gregory Corso (*right*) at the SUNY-Buffalo Student Book Shop, 1965. In the center: Meirion Maud, held by Edward Bukowski. (Photograph courtesy of Ralph Maud)

Positions hardened in March and April as the plaintiffs-to-be continued to wrestle with SUNY administrators in Albany. After a meeting with J. Lawrence Murray, Ralph Maud wrote to advise him, "I have had the good fortune to get my two books reviewed, favorably, on the front page of the *Times Literary Supplement*"; he reiterated, "It would be an ugly and wasteful violation of the Feinberg Act to dismiss teachers who are not subversive. . . . What we have at the moment is a situation in which the university is making a fool of itself pretending to enforce a law against subversives by means of a fake certificate which asks everybody to say they are not."[42]

Further raising the political temperature in the spring of 1964, HUAC arrived in Buffalo accompanied by the usual headlines; it heard testimony from FBI informants and subpoenaed suspected communists, including three from SUNY. President Furnas reiterated the administration's decade-old policy of suspending any professor who refused to cooperate with legislative investigations, pending a hearing at which the resister would have to "demonstrate that he is qualified to continue as a member of the faculty." But this was 1964, not 1952, and elsewhere in the country activists were ridiculing the old Red-hunting committee. Even Furnas, while demanding cooperation, simultaneously proclaimed the university's commitment to academic freedom, which, he said, meant "the exclusion of governmental intervention in the intellectual life of a university."[43]

The student senate, meanwhile, appropriated funds for anti-HUAC picket signs, and Joan Baez, in town for a concert, urged resistance. "Buffalo was not used to such carryings-on," Keyishian recalled. "Between the noise of the pickets, the uncooperativeness of the witnesses, the editorial opposition of the *Courier Express* [the more liberal of the city's two dailies], and the failure of the city council to approve a resolution welcoming them to Buffalo, the committee had a rather rough time and left town ahead of schedule."[44]

But six people were fired as a result of the hearings, among them English instructor Paul Sporn, who had signed the Feinberg certificate while appending a statement that he thought it a "threat to academic freedom" and was now accused of lying because an informant testified that he had been told Sporn was a Party member and that Sporn's landlady "reported what seemed to her to be political meetings at his home." The university suspended Sporn in June for refusing to answer HUAC's questions, and although administrators acknowledged that the evidence was weak and despite protests from the English Department, they fired him the following fall.[45]

"To Steer Far Wider of the Unlawful Zone"

While events unfolded at Buffalo, attorneys Ken MacDonald and Arval Morris were filing their briefs to the Supreme Court in *Baggett v. Bullitt*, the case challenging Washington State's two loyalty oaths. They emphasized the chilling effect of the oaths, especially the earlier one requiring teachers to promise by "precept and example" to "promote respect for the flag" and "reverence for law and order." They cited facts and figures showing the damage to academic freedom from loyalty programs: a study by sociologists at Columbia University had found that since the Cold War began, 46% of the teachers surveyed (historians, economists, and others in the social sciences) felt apprehensive about their freedom to teach, write, and speak out on public issues—54% if only younger teachers without tenure were considered—and that this apprehension put a "noticeable damper" on their activities and opinions. Some professors "toned down their writings"; some avoided controversial subjects in class.[46] About 500 teachers at public schools and universities had lost their jobs between 1948 and 1958, mostly for refusing to answer questions or to execute loyalty oaths.[47]

The lawyers also argued that recent Supreme Court decisions such as the *Cramp* loyalty oath case had rejected the rigid right-privilege distinction on which Justice Minton had relied to uphold the Feinberg Law in *Adler*.

Furthermore, they said, *Adler* was decided before the Supreme Court rec-ognized the constitutional right to freedom of association (in the 1958 Ala-bama case condemning the state's demand for NAACP membership lists). As for test oaths, MacDonald and Morris offered analogies: Washington could clearly not require that all employees "execute oaths that either they are, or are not, Jews, Catholics or Protestants" or "that either they are, or are not, members of the Republican or Democratic parties."[48]

The justices discussed *Baggett* at their April 6, 1964, conference. Brennan, Douglas, Black, Warren, and the newest justice, Arthur Goldberg (appointed by President Kennedy in 1962) voted to strike down both oaths. Warren opined that they were "too broad and too vague" and that the right to a hear-ing "means nothing, because explanation of reasons gets you nowhere." Clark protested: "I thought we'd passed on loyalty oaths. This case is premature." Harlan agreed. Stewart wondered if they "might not better vacate with inten-tion to retain jurisdiction," and Byron White, another Kennedy appointee, said he could "go either way."[49] Again, the professors were in danger of delay, but this time there were five votes to reach the merits of the case. Ultimately, Stewart and White went along with the majority, and Warren assigned White to write the opinion.

White, a Rhodes scholar and an all-American football player in his youth, was not an exponent of expansive First Amendment rights. As in *Cramp* three years before, Chief Justice Warren had chosen the least libertarian of the justices who voted in the majority to write the opinion for the Court. And as in *Cramp*, the Supreme Court ruling in *Baggett* did not squarely attack anti-subversive programs; instead, it used the malleable doctrine of vague-ness to invalidate the two Washington oaths without reaching the broader, and more politically treacherous, questions that MacDonald and Morris had raised about academic freedom. Nevertheless, *Baggett v. Bullitt*, announced on June 1, 1964, was a broader decision than *Cramp*, and it gave a great boost to Richard Lipsitz and his quintet of Buffalo rebels.

White said that Washington's 1955 anti-subversive oath suffered from "similar infirmities" as those that doomed Florida's oath in *Cramp*. "A teacher must swear that he is not a subversive person" and does not advocate "the commission of any act intended to overthrow or alter, or to assist the over-throw or alteration, of the constitutional form of government by revolu-tion, force or violence." What a person might reasonably conclude from this verbiage was that any aid to the Communist Party or one of its members could make you a "subversive person." Hence, "the questions put by the Court in *Cramp* may with equal force be asked here": What about endorse-ment or support of communist candidates for office? What about a lawyer who represents the Party or its members, or a journalist who defends their rights, or "anyone who supports any cause which is likewise supported by Communists?"

The "aiding and abetting" sections of the law were even vaguer. "A person is subversive not only if he himself commits the specified acts, but if he abets or advises another in aiding a third person to commit an act which will assist yet a fourth person in the overthrow or alteration of constitutional government." Although the Washington Supreme Court had read "knowledge" into the law, what, exactly, was it "that the Washington professor must 'know'?" Would it be subversive, for example, to "participate in international conventions of mathematicians and exchange views with scholars from Communist countries?"[50] The questions may have seemed far-fetched, but they demonstrated the wisdom of MacDonald and Morris's strategy of having many plaintiffs who could give examples of the chilling effect of test oaths.

After this, it was a simple matter for Justice White to dispose of Washington's 1931 "precept and example" oath. A teacher "who refused to salute the flag or advocated refusal because of religious beliefs" might well be thought to have broken the promise not to disrespect the flag. Indeed, "even criticism of the design or color scheme of the state flag or unfavorable comparison of it with that of a sister State or foreign country could be deemed disrespectful." The law's reference to "institutions" was even more enigmatic. This wildly vague oath could stop a professor "from criticizing his state judicial system or the Supreme Court or the institution of judicial review" or from "advocating the abolition, for example, of the Civil Rights Commission, the House Committee on Un-American Activities, or foreign aid."[51]

White concluded his *Baggett* opinion with now-familiar language about the perils of vague laws in "sensitive areas of basic First Amendment freedoms." Uncertain meanings "require the oath-taker teachers and public servants to 'steer far wider of the unlawful zone'" than if the boundaries are "clearly marked." People "with a conscientious regard for what they solemnly swear or affirm" would have to confine their activities "to that which is unquestionably safe. Free speech may not be so inhibited."[52]

Tom Clark's dissent in *Baggett*, which Harlan joined, was particularly indignant at the majority's invalidation of the 1955 oath, which was no different from myriad others that targeted advocacy of revolution, including some that the Court had approved. Clark thought it "strange" that White found unconstitutionally vague language that the Court had considered perfectly fine in a 1951 case from Maryland. Other states had copied the Maryland law, he said, "primarily because of our approval of it." Furthermore, it was "absurd" to think that professors might violate this oath by teaching history or any other subject "to a class in which a Communist Party member might sit": "to so interpret the language of the Act is to extract more sunbeams from cucumbers than did Gulliver's mad scientist."[53] As for the 1931 oath, Clark and Harlan thought the Court should not have invalidated it but instead sent the case to the state courts for a definitive interpretation.

Clark was right about the implications of *Baggett*. Washington's 1955 oath was considerably narrower than the one the Court had struck down in *Cramp*. If this typical anti-subversive oath was unconstitutional, what was left of all the state and federal loyalty programs that used very similar language?

Keyishian, Round One

Two days after *Baggett v. Bullitt* was announced, Charles Morgan informed Keyishian, Maud, and Starbuck that the AAUP Academic Freedom Fund would support their case.[54] The amounts were small even by 1964 standards—$1,200 for Starbuck and $1,000 each for Maud and Keyishian—and although the AAUP later granted additional amounts for appeals, Lipsitz was to donate much of his time for the next three years.

Hochfield and Garver were still undecided about being plaintiffs. Garver was looking for a solution short of litigation and thought administrators in Albany "were considering making an exception in my case on religious grounds."[55] He wrote a long letter to SUNY vice president Murray on June 8: "I have tried very hard not to be willful or disobedient nor to put myself in opposition. . . . If I had wished to challenge you and the authority behind the certificate, I should have refused to sign anything at all. Instead I reluctantly executed as much of the certificate as I could in good conscience execute." But to sign the oath in full would mean "participating in a kind of ritual, and hence going beyond the plain way of speaking Jesus recommended." He had "naturally been under considerable temptation to capitulate on this point," but "articulation of the principles involved has helped to make them clear, and it seems rather silly to have commitments at all if one neglects to follow them when they have clear application."[56]

Another SUNY officer, David Price, tried to break Garver's resolve. An evangelical Christian, Price engaged Garver in religious debate and told him that the Feinberg certificate actually fostered academic freedom by helping the university ward off political attacks.[57] Garver wrote a conciliatory reply but on the main issue did not budge. The disclaimer "still seems a species of 'vain protestation.' . . . It also still seems a sort of ritual act, and hence out of harmony with the ways of Friends, who eschew ritual even in religion." He said he would seek advice from the American Friends Service Committee (the AFSC) and from Quakers at their upcoming meeting in July.[58]

On July 8, Lipsitz filed *Keyishian et al. v. Board of Regents* in federal court, with both Hochfield and Garver as plaintiffs. Price did not give up. He wrote to Garver that his own "personal relationship with Jesus Christ as Savior and Lord . . . neither compels nor permits me to refuse compliance with the Feinberg Law"; on the contrary, communism should be disclaimed because it is "openly inimical to the Christian faith." Several weeks later, he told a Quaker group that came to Albany to present their yearly meeting's endorsement of Garver's stand that "two or three" of his co-plaintiffs were "unsavory characters."[59] Garver was not swayed by this effort at divide-and-conquer: "I didn't think of any of them as unsavory even though none of them had the motivation I had."[60]

Price's strategy was soon replaced by a more respectful tone. A new SUNY chancellor, Samuel Gould, was to take office in September, and Rollo Handy wrote to him of the "widespread and deep dismay on this campus about the way those who refused, on principle, to sign the Feinberg certificate have been proceeded against." Gould replied that he was "greatly interested in the case" and was "sensitive to the need for protection of academic freedom."[61] Once in charge, Gould made sure that Maud, Hochfield, and Garver would keep their jobs pending the outcome of the lawsuit. It was too late for Keyishian and Starbuck, who had already been fired. Keyishian returned to New York City to finish his PhD, and Starbuck went to Iowa to teach in its creative writing program.

Judge Henderson was assigned the new lawsuit. The Supreme Court's *Baggett* decision had not changed his view that there was no constitutional problem with the Feinberg Law. In September, he denied Lipsitz's motion for a preliminary injunction and for a three-judge court, required at that time by federal law when substantial constitutional issues were at stake. Keyishian's reaction was brisk: he wrote to Lipsitz, "Kick Henderson in the balls for me next time you see him."[62]

The next step was the Second Circuit Court of Appeals. In May 1965, the court reversed Henderson, finding a "substantial federal question," and sent the case back to Buffalo so that a three-judge court could be convened. Thurgood Marshall, then a circuit judge, wrote the opinion. *Adler* was not dispositive, he said: it could not have addressed the amendment to the Feinberg Law, applying it to academia; and in any case, in the years since *Adler*, the Supreme Court had rejected the notion that "public employment which may be denied altogether may be subjected to any conditions, regardless of how unreasonable." Both of Lipsitz's main claims—that the Feinberg Law was unconstitutionally vague and that the entire system it created inhibited "vital thought and speech in violation of the First Amendment"—raised serious questions of constitutional law.[63]

Chancellor Gould now persuaded the SUNY trustees to revoke the Feinberg certificate.[64] How much this decision was inspired by the Court of Appeals' reasoning, and how much by a desire to undermine the *Keyishian* litigation by depriving the plaintiffs of the only tangible thing they had objected to, is debatable. Certainly, the state's lawyers would argue that with the oath gone, there was no longer a live controversy. They did not win this argument: Lipsitz had framed his case as a challenge to the whole Feinberg Law, and although he and his clients were to face more hurdles, by the time the case got to the Supreme Court, five justices were ready at last to confront the fundamental problems with loyalty programs.

Keyishian went to trial in June 1965 before a three-judge court; Henderson was one of the three. In January 1966, the court again dismissed the case. The opinion quoted from *Adler*: the classroom is "a sensitive area" where the teacher "shapes the attitude of young minds," and it would be "strangely anomalous" to "proscribe the advocacy of violent overthrow of the government in all parts of the United States, except in the breeding-grounds of the future leaders of the nation."[65]

There was little question that Lipsitz would seek Supreme Court review, which was available directly from a three-judge court decision; the only issue was where to get the money. The national AAUP said that other crises were now draining its funds, and an appeal from the Buffalo chapter brought in only $671—far below the $2,500 that Lipsitz had suggested as his fee. Lipsitz offered to reduce the amount if the AAUP "considered [it] to be out of line" and proceeded to prepare his Supreme Court papers.[66]

At SUNY-Buffalo, the bitterness of the preceding two years had not dissipated. Ralph Maud had been promoted and awarded tenure, but he nevertheless moved to Simon Fraser University in Vancouver in the fall of 1965. He wrote in his resignation letter, "Insofar as this course can be thought not to benefit me professionally as much as staying in this university, my motivation can perhaps be understood in terms of the unprofessional intrusions that this administration has allowed since becoming a state institution." He detailed the depredations: Keyishian was gone; Paul Sporn was gone; and he had been subject to "anxiety about my status here." Maud admitted that it was hard to know "how much the Feinberg certificate will affect recruiting": "I have written this paragraph so that you will have at least one person's opinion."[67]

In the spring of 1965, beat poet Gregory Corso came to Buffalo to teach a course on the English Romantic poet Percy Shelley. Corso lacked traditional academic credentials, but English Department chair Albert Cook was on a mission to expand its scope. Corso was not inclined to sign a Feinberg certificate, and the university fired him. The campus academic freedom committee protested, students and faculty formed a picket line, and the student paper's editors were "appalled" that the university had deprived them "of the privilege of taking classes from a man whose imagination and creativity have been recognized the world over."[68] Corso cheerfully observed, "The great thing is that they were willing to accept me without an academic passport" in the first place. "I never even went to high school."[69]

12

"A Pall of Orthodoxy over the Classroom"

Arizona's Perjury Law

The Supreme Court had one more loyalty case on its docket before it decided *Keyishian*. Since Arizona's beginnings as a territory, it had a typical affirmative oath for all public employees—to swear to support the U.S. and state constitutions, to "bear true faith and allegiance" to them, and to "defend them against all enemies, foreign and domestic." Then in 1961, the state legislature enacted an imaginative variation on the anti-subversive test oath: a "Communist Control Act" that created criminal penalties for perjury for anyone who took the affirmative oath and who "knowingly and willfully" became or remained a member of the Communist Party, "any of its subordinate organizations," or any other group that had as "one of its purposes" the overthrow of the government.[1]

Barbara Elfbrandt, a Tucson schoolteacher and a Quaker, had political and religious objections to the oath. She did not know what it meant, and the state provided no procedure for seeking an interpretation. She brought a class action suit, but the Arizona trial court dismissed it; and in May 1963, the state supreme court affirmed. Elfbrandt was not fired; she simply was not paid. She continued to teach for five years without salary before her case was resolved.[2]

The Arizona Supreme Court acknowledged that the oath, combined with the perjury law, might deter "constitutionally protected conduct" and that it "weighs most heavily on those whose scruples are the most sensitive," but it rejected Elfbrandt's claim by using the Supreme Court's vague balancing test from the 1951 *Dennis* case, which upheld the convictions of CP leaders under the Smith Act: "the gravity of the evil sought to be reached, discounted by its improbability, justifies the invasion." The state's chief justice concurred, but only on the assumption that a hearing would be available at which Elfbrandt could explain her objections. If they turned out to be "based not upon a showing of disloyalty, but upon grounds of religion or conscience," then her punishment would be "arbitrary and discriminatory," he said, because "however much we may disagree with the logic or reasonableness of [her] objections, we must admit that they do not prove disloyalty." He added that the legislature had chosen "a curious method of enforcement" because despite oath refusers' presumptive disloyalty, they could continue to work; they just could not get paid. Thus, "dedicated subversives . . . can continue their nefarious work in sensitive positions of public employment."[3]

Elfbrandt's lawyers appealed to the U.S. Supreme Court, which sent the case back to Arizona for further consideration in light of its recent *Baggett v. Bullitt* decision striking down Washington's two loyalty oaths. But the Arizona Supreme Court again upheld the law, now over the dissent of the chief, whose reading of *Baggett* convinced him that even a hearing at which the state had the burden of proving disloyalty would not make Arizona's combined oath and perjury law constitutional.[4]

The case went back to the U.S. Supreme Court. There were now five votes to reverse; Chief Justice Warren assigned William O. Douglas to write the opinion. This would have seemed to bode well for a decision on grounds more sweeping than the case-by-case method of finding particular oath language too vague, but Douglas's first draft, circulated in early March 1966, was cursory and relied only on vagueness. A different draft four days later contained the essence of Douglas's April 1966 decision in *Elfbrandt v. Russell*, invalidating Arizona's loyalty scheme as an unconstitutional exercise in guilt by association.[5] It was a step beyond the recent rulings in *Baggett* and *Cramp*, but in the process, Douglas lost the votes of their authors, Byron White and Potter Stewart.

Douglas's opinion for the Court explained that Arizona's perjury law was too broad because it punished people who joined a political group without "specific intent" to further the group's illegal aims. The Court had ruled as early as 1951, in its decision upholding Los Angeles's loyalty oath, that people must have knowledge of those illegal aims, or *scienter*, before they can be punished for an organizational affiliation. But this *scienter* rule had done nothing to stop or even to slow the purges based on guilt by association. More recently, the Court had added a further requirement, at least in cases involving criminal laws: the person must not only know of but specifically share the group's unlawful purpose. Douglas in *Elfbrandt* now extended this concept of "specific intent" to a loyalty case.[6]

It seemed like a technical distinction, but it made a huge difference. Tens of thousands of people had joined the CP over the years, probably knowing that it supported violent revolution in some circumstances but not agreeing with that particular tenet, at least not as applied to the United States. They joined instead because it seemed at the time the best way to fight fascism, racism, and other evils, because they believed that a radical overhaul of existing institutions, not just piecemeal reforms, was needed, and because the Party offered a social and cultural community of fellow rebels.

Byron White's dissent in *Elfbrandt*—joined by Clark, Harlan, and Stewart—quarreled with Douglas's distinction between "knowledge" and "specific intent."[7] As the dissenters were well aware, punishments based on guilt by association could not continue if the government had to prove specific intent to further the CP's allegedly violent aims before prosecuting or firing people on the basis of present or past association with the Party. In that sense, *Elfbrandt* was a harbinger of the next loyalty case, in which the Supreme Court finally found in the First Amendment concept of academic freedom a reason to end the teacher purges.

Keyishian at the Supreme Court

Knowing that even a liberal Supreme Court preferred to draw distinctions between cases rather than directly overrule bad precedents, Richard Lipsitz continued relying on academic freedom at the college level as a way of making *Keyishian* look as different as possible from *Adler v. Board of Education*, which had upheld the Feinberg Law. His initial brief to the Court focused on whether the convoluted apparatus of the law was unconstitutional as applied to institutions whose "*raison d'être*," he said, was intellectual freedom. And he stressed other changes since *Adler*: additions to the civil service law in 1958 that made membership in the Communist Party a presumptive ground for firing and that repeated the state education law's disqualification for "treasonable or seditious acts or utterances."[8]

But Lipsitz did not ignore the other possibility: if the Court saw fit, it should overrule *Adler*. This would have the advantage of "at last eliminating the doctrine of guilt by association," which "represents an aberration on the American scene."[9] The state's lawyers, for their part, aggressively defended the law but admitted that the five plaintiffs were sincere conscientious objectors: "there is no indication that any of the appellants are, in fact, members of any communist party."[10]

In June 1966, the Supreme Court met to discuss whether to hear the case; everyone except Potter Stewart voted yes.[11] A new justice, Abe Fortas, whose Washington, D.C., law firm had represented victims of loyalty programs during the '50s, would presumably join the liberals. President Lyndon Johnson had appointed Fortas in 1965 to replace Arthur Goldberg, whom Johnson had persuaded to leave the Court and become U.S. representative at the United Nations.[12]

Both the ACLU and the AAUP submitted *amicus* briefs supporting Lipsitz. Osmond Fraenkel, the ACLU's lead lawyer, took a cautious approach, arguing that under the First Amendment balancing test used in *Adler* and subsequent cases, the Feinberg Law's repressive effects outweighed any ostensible benefit to national security. The AAUP was bolder: it argued that "a major premise of *Adler*—that public employment may be conditioned on the virtual surrender of First Amendment freedoms"—had been "clearly rejected" in later Supreme Court cases. Of course, it also emphasized academic freedom, citing Felix Frankfurter's 1952 encomium to "the priests of our democracy" and Earl Warren's statement five years later that "to impose any strait jacket upon the intellectual leaders in our colleges and universities would imperil the future of our Nation."[13]

Despite Lipsitz's ample experience in labor and civil rights law, this was his first Supreme Court argument. "I did a lot of preparation," he said. "I made up my mind that there were nasty people on the Court, and if they were nasty to me, I wasn't gonna roll over."[14] As it happened, most of the oral argument on November 17, 1966, focused on the convoluted scheme of laws and regulations that Lipsitz said were at the heart of the case. In this way, he finessed the issue of mootness, now that the Feinberg certificate had been rescinded: the plaintiffs and the class of employees they represented were still subject to all the strictures and vague prohibitions of the Feinberg Law. Moreover, the SUNY trustees' order rescinding the certificate only said that an employee would not be "deemed ineligible *solely* because of" failure to sign; the refusals of George Hochfield and Newton Garver, the two plaintiffs left at Buffalo, could still be used against them.

Earl Warren threw Lipsitz a softball question: "I suppose you'll tell us why university students are less subject to subversion than children?" Lipsitz replied that in contrast to 1949, when the legislature enacting the Feinberg Law made extensive "findings" as to the risk of teachers indoctrinating children, the addition of universities to the law in 1953 was unaccompanied by any findings of danger.[15]

Ruth Kessler Toch, the New York assistant attorney general defending the case, had two main arguments: first, that nothing really had changed since *Adler* and, second, that the new sections of the civil service law, providing that CP membership would "constitute *prima facie* evidence of disqualification," did not unconstitutionally shift the burden of proving loyalty to employees, because other parts of the law still gave them a right to challenge their dismissal in court, where the state would bear the burden of proof. Richard Crary, arguing on behalf of the SUNY trustees, also relied on technical points: he said tenured professors had a contractual right to a hearing before termination, where, again, the state would have to prove unfitness. Lipsitz tried to clear away the smokescreen: the Feinberg Law gave accused employees only three narrow ways to rebut the presumption of guilt by association: they could argue that the organization in question was not really subversive—even though the state had already concluded that it was—or that they were not members or that they had no knowledge of the organization's unlawful goals.[16]

All this wrangling over procedural niceties and burdens of proof may have signaled an interest in avoiding more substantive issues, and at the post-argument conference, it was still not clear how the case would turn out. Warren wanted to reverse the three-judge court based on the vagueness of the "statutory scheme as a whole, which, as [an] interrelated framework, violates [the] First Amendment."[17] Black, Douglas, Brennan, and Fortas voted their agreement, but Fortas was tentative. What happened next is best recounted by Brennan's law clerks in the case history they compiled at the end of the Supreme Court term. "It was clear that Justice Fortas was a shaky vote for reversal," they wrote, "and he indicated he did not know which way he would ultimately turn. It was therefore hoped [presumably by Brennan] that Justice Fortas would be assigned the opinion." But Warren assigned it to Brennan instead.[18]

Brennan began his task by trying to emphasize the differences between the facts that were before the Court in *Adler* and the situation now faced by the plaintiffs in *Keyishian*. But, the clerks wrote, after trying "to unravel and delineate the boundaries" set by the Feinberg Law's "complex scheme," Brennan concluded that the "prolixity and profusion" of provisions affecting First Amendment rights made the entire law unconstitutional. Brennan "also decided that *Adler* was not worth saving, and that its interment could be made explicit." The second part of his draft opinion "therefore revealed how the underpinnings of *Adler* had already been demolished." He circulated the draft and received "quick affirmative responses" from Black, Douglas, and Warren. "But there was no word from Justice Fortas." More than two weeks later, Clark circulated a dissent. Its "McCarthyistic" tone "outraged" the wavering Fortas and persuaded him to join Brennan in striking down the law.

Clark was incensed because he had written two of the precedents that Brennan's draft cited in arguing that *Adler* had been undermined by later decisions: *Wieman*, striking down Oklahoma's test oath, and *Slochower*, invalidating New York City's summary firing of a professor for invoking the Fifth Amendment. Clark had written in those cases that although teachers have no "right" to public employment, the government cannot impose unconstitutional job conditions; and this was the context in which Brennan cited them. But as Clark wrote in a draft of his dissent, *Wieman* and *Slochower*, "both written by me," cited *Adler* approvingly. "For the majority to say that these cases undercut *Adler* just won't wash."[19] Clark deleted this passage in the final version of his dissent, but he left in much of the sting. He wrote to his fellow dissenters that if they thought his near-final draft "too tough," they should "strike out" whatever they wished,[20] but this did not lead to any softening of the dissent's bitter tone. The 5–4 decision in *Keyishian* was announced on January 23, 1967, in a courtroom bristling with tension between Brennan and Clark.

Brennan's opinion for the Court in *Keyishian*, although it ended by overruling *Adler*, began by showing how different it was from the case now before the Court. Three parts of the 1939 civil service law that were now up for review had not been challenged in *Adler*. Nor was the SUNY board's elimination of the Feinberg certificate a barrier for the plaintiffs: Starbuck and Keyishian still had claims for back pay arising from their dismissals, and the trustees had made clear that although nobody would now be fired "'solely' because he refused to sign," failure to answer any question relevant to a loyalty investigation would still be grounds for disqualification. "The substance of the statutory and regulatory complex remains and from the outset appellants' basic claim has been that they are aggrieved by its application."[21]

Brennan moved to part 1 of his legal analysis: vagueness. Section 3021 of New York's education law, originally enacted in 1917, mandated job termination for "treasonable or seditious" acts or utterances, and the 1958 amendment to the civil service law incorporated the same vague language. This amendment provided a definition of "treasonable or seditious," though: "treasonable" had the criminal law definition (levying war against the United States or giving aid and comfort to its enemies); "seditious" meant "criminal anarchy," defined as advocating forceful overthrow of the government or assassination of its leaders. But, said Brennan, "our experience under the Sedition Act of 1798 taught us that dangers fatal to First Amendment freedoms inhere in the word 'seditious.'" Even if the terms "treasonable or seditious" in the 1917 law were assumed now to have the definitions in the 1958 amendment, "the uncertainty is hardly removed," for "seditious" could still include abstract advocacy of revolution. "If so, the possible scope of 'seditious' utterances or acts has virtually no limit": it covers the "public display" of any book "containing or advocating, advising or teaching the doctrine that organized government should be overthrown by force, violence or any unlawful means." This led Brennan to the first of *Keyishian*'s memorable rhetorical questions: "Does the teacher who carries a copy of the *Communist*

Manifesto on a public street thereby advocate criminal anarchy? It is no answer to say that the statute would not be applied in such a case. We cannot gainsay the potential effect of this obscure wording on 'those with a conscientious and scrupulous regard for such undertakings.'"[22]

Brennan also found unconstitutional vagueness in the language of the 1939 New York law barring employment of anyone who "advocates, advises or teaches the doctrine of forceful overthrow of government." The provision was "susceptible of sweeping and improper application"; it could "prohibit the employment of one who merely advocates the doctrine in the abstract without any attempt to indoctrinate others, or incite others to action." And "since 'advocacy' of the doctrine of forceful overthrow is separately prohibited," what other meaning might the words "teach" and "advise" have? "Does the teacher who informs his class about the precepts of Marxism or the Declaration of Independence violate this prohibition?" More questions followed: does the librarian who recommends reading "histories of the evolution of Marxist doctrine or tracing the background of the French, American, or Russian revolutions" violate the Feinberg Law? The "very intricacy" of the law's administrative machinery and the "uncertainty as to the scope of its proscriptions" made it "a highly efficient *in terrorem* mechanism."[23]

Brennan paid passing obeisance to "the legitimacy of New York's interest in protecting its education system from subversion." But "even though the governmental purpose be legitimate," he said, it "'cannot be pursued by means that broadly stifle fundamental personal liberties when the end can be more narrowly achieved.'" Now came the most famous lines in *Keyishian*. Brennan borrowed from the "pall over the classroom" imagery of Douglas's *Adler* dissent: "Our Nation is deeply committed to safeguarding academic freedom, which is of transcendent value to all of us and not merely to the teachers concerned. That freedom is therefore a special concern of the First Amendment, which does not tolerate laws that cast a pall of orthodoxy over the classroom."[24]

Brennan proceeded to part 2 of his opinion: guilt by association. The 1958 amendment to the Feinberg Law made CP membership "*prima facie* evidence of disqualification," but the original 1949 enactment had done essentially the same by directing the Board of Regents to create a list of subversive organizations, membership in which would be *prima facie* evidence of unfitness. Brennan acknowledged that *Adler* had upheld the original provision. He had already intimated that "pertinent constitutional doctrines have since rejected" the premises of *Adler*; now he elaborated: the idea that public employment can be subjected to any condition, no matter how obnoxious to the Constitution—that is, the hoary right-privilege distinction—had been rejected in *Wieman, Slochower, Cramp, Baggett,* and other cases. Guilt by association is not an acceptable legal rule unless an individual has "a specific intent to further the unlawful aims of an organization." Should the result be any different because teachers and professors "have captive audiences of young minds?" On the contrary, the First Amendment is especially important in schools: "curtailing freedom of association" has an impermissibly "stifling effect on the academic mind."[25]

Brennan did not specify whether this was true only at the college level or throughout a young person's education. He thus avoided the distinction that Lipsitz and the AAUP had carefully emphasized: academic freedom as the *raison d'être* of higher education. Certainly, elementary and high school teachers also have a right to join organizations of their choosing, but like Brennan's earlier language condemning laws that "cast a pall of orthodoxy over the classroom" without specifying which classrooms he had in mind, his reference to "the academic mind" was to cause confusion in years to come.

Brennan moved inexorably to his conclusion. The Feinberg Law was unconstitutional because it punished associational ties without requiring that a suspect teacher had a specific intent to further an organization's illegal aims. The guilt-by-association provisions thus suffered from "impermissible overbreadth." They barred employment based not only on associations that "legitimately may be proscribed" but on associations "which may not be proscribed consistently with First Amendment rights."[26]

According to Brennan's clerks, the announcement of the majority and dissenting opinions in *Keyishian* was "marked by some of the most impassioned oratory which followers of the Court had ever seen."[27] Clark's dissent, part of which he read aloud on January 23, 1967, attacked the "blunderbuss fashion in which the majority couches its 'artillery of words'" and predicted that "neither New York nor the several States that have followed the teaching of *Adler* for some 15 years can ever put the pieces together again." No court had ever "reached out so far to destroy so much with so little."[28] Brennan "sought to neutralize the inflamed dissent by charging that it 'indulges in richly colored and impassioned hyperbole.'" Clark replied that this showed his dissent "must have hurt."[29] He concluded apocalyptically: the majority opinion had "by its broadside swept away one of our most precious rights, namely, the right of self-preservation. Our public educational system is the genius of our democracy. The minds of our youth are developed there and the character of that development will determine the future of our land. Indeed, our very existence depends upon it."[30]

Clark was right that *Keyishian* was a decisive moment—in the history of the Court, of academic freedom as a part of the First Amendment, and of the heresy hunt that had dominated American politics for 20 years.

Celebration and Backlash

"We had a big party," Lipsitz said. "The English Department threw it. There was a lot of excitement. People were jumping for joy."[31] Herman Orentlicher at the AAUP wrote to him, "News of the victory was indeed wonderful to receive, and I want very much to indicate our appreciation for your splendidly effective contribution to the result. It was a long, hard fight, and this of course makes the result even more heartwarming." Leonard Boudin, who had conveyed such a discouraging assessment of the case to Ralph Maud in 1964, also wrote: "May I congratulate you upon a magnificent victory in *Keyishian*."[32]

From Vancouver, Ralph Maud wrote, "Dear Dick—Harry sent me the *NY Times* and George called me the day before. So we must allow ourselves a little orgy of self-congratulation! . . . I think it only right now that we go after those damages—especially for Harry and George." Professor Tom Connolly and his wife, ardent opponents of the oath who had since left Buffalo, wrote excitedly, "Dear Dick, congratulations! What great news. . . . You must have heard our whoops of joy."[33]

The *New York Times* was more sedate. Initially a supporter of the ideology behind the Feinberg Law, if not its specific provisions, the *Times* now congratulated the Court for rejecting the "often hysterical philosophy of the fifties" and ending "the last vestige in New York State of the unedifying era of witch hunts, guilt by association, and loyalty oaths." It praised Black's and Douglas's dissents in *Adler* 15 years before for accurately predicting "the real and lasting damage" that the Feinberg Law would cause by creating an "atmosphere of implied guilt [and] mandated spying" and a "straitjacket of uniformity." The *Washington Post* was also congratulatory, though more defensive: if the Court had really "swept away" our "right of self-preservation," as Clark claimed, "we should be among the first to protest," said the *Post*. But "the Court did not say that New York may not dismiss teachers who are peddling communist propaganda or seeking to overthrow the government. Rather, it said that in the struggle for national security the state could not destroy academic freedom."[34]

Other journalists were less approving. The *Buffalo Evening News* lamented the end to "our state policy of keeping communists and other subversives from teaching in the public schools" and urged the legislature to try (paraphrasing Clark's dissent) to "put the pieces together again." The *Chicago Tribune* could not understand how, "in the unending fantasy of which the Warren Court is capable," it could grant academic freedom to communists "who do not themselves respect such a principle." A *New York Daily News*

'Get Lost! The Supreme Court Says You're
A Menace To Academic Freedom!'

Cartoonist Charles Brooks's reaction to the *Keyishian* decision. (Copyright, 1967,
The Birmingham News. All rights reserved. Reprinted with permission.)

editorial, "To Russia with Love," called the decision "a handsome present" to
"the Kremlin bandits and murderers" and urged a constitutional amendment
to eliminate the Court's power of judicial review.[35]

Protests poured into the Court. Brennan's papers at the Library of Congress
contain 77 letters of complaint or angry notes scrawled on news clippings.
They range from the rhetorical but polite to the crazed and abusive. Many
cite scripture or accuse the Court of betraying the American soldiers fighting

communism in Vietnam. A Virginia legislator called Brennan and Warren "Judases" whose "despicable judicial record of sympathy" with communism "speaks louder than the sham of words through which they permit the subversion of their country." An eighth grader warned that teachers' subversive ideas "might rub off on their students" and that communists want to remove "In God We Trust" from U.S. coins. A pharmacist who appealed to Brennan as a fellow Catholic called the justices "intellectual morons" and boasted that he would not fill prescriptions for birth control; an anonymous letter to Brennan from St. Petersburg, Florida, said, "Of all human scum balls, you top the list," claimed "the right to put a bullet through your skull" because "my son is in the front lines, fighting for bastards like you in Vietnam," and threatened "to dispose of you when in Washington." Brennan forwarded the threat to J. Edgar Hoover, who responded that an investigation would be conducted.[36]

Back in Buffalo, Lipsitz began negotiating with state attorney John Crary over back pay. Although Crary was cooperative, it was not a quick or easy process. In April 1967, the lawyers agreed on the amounts, but nearly three months later, no checks had arrived. Starbuck, wry as usual, wrote to Crary, "By straining my fiscal imagination to the utmost, I can see that there might be concocted some vaguely plausible rationalization for delaying payment," but "I think it may well be time for that vast state machinery, which gave us such a hard time in the name of Instant Unquestioning Obedience to Law, to show a modicum of grace in accepting a legal determination." To Lipsitz, Starbuck added, "By Saturday we should be on our way to Minnesota for some much-needed isolation from students. . . . I'm not quite as broke as my letter to Crary hints, but I will be if I don't get my half of the take by 1 August. Cheers. We'll send a postcard of a moose or something."[37]

The long-awaited check arrived in mid-July. Starbuck wrote to thank Lipsitz "for getting the money and passing it along at such a ridiculously low fee." He questioned the state's deduction of taxes and promised to "write a fulsome Augustan letter of gratitude to Crary some day." Lipsitz in reply acknowledged that his fee was "ridiculously low" but said, "It represents part of my pleasure in both having represented you and having known you for these last several years." The state "correctly withheld taxes," he added.[38]

Starbuck was by this time director of the University of Iowa's creative writing program. He was writing poignant protest poems against the Vietnam War and continuing to bewitch readers with what one admirer called "such a dazzling display of pun, parody and pyrotechnic wit that critics sometimes seemed too busy laughing out loud to take him seriously." At his premature death in 1996, a critic called him "one of the great geniuses of 20th century American poetry."[39]

George Starbuck, 1982. (Photo
courtesy of Kathryn Starbuck)

Newton Garver remained at Buffalo, a persistent activist and a productive
scholar, expert in the works of Jacques Derrida and Ludwig Wittgenstein. A
few months after *Keyishian* was decided, he led a group of Quakers across
the bridge to Canada with medical supplies for Vietnam. After three hours of
wrangling, customs officers let the parcels through but threatened criminal
charges. The same month, Garver and a fellow pacifist received a letter from
Martin Luther King, Jr., thanking them for a telegram of encouragement. The
Supreme Court had just heard argument in the appeal of King and seven
other ministers from a 1963 conviction for demonstrating against racial
apartheid in Birmingham, Alabama, in violation of a court injunction. "It
was especially heartening," King wrote, "to know that you would take time to
send these kind words to me while you were engaged in your own witness.
If the peaceful dissenters will continue to work together and support each
other, it will make the difficult and lonely road a little easier."[40] Two months
later, in an opinion by Potter Stewart, the Court affirmed the convictions,
and King had to return to Birmingham jail; Brennan, Douglas, Warren, and
Fortas dissented.[41]

Garver was respected on campus for his stand in *Keyishian*. One administrator wrote that his "role in getting rid of the Feinberg certificate did more
to improve the promise and prospects of the university than all the buildings that had been built." In later years, though still a Quaker, he felt "no
longer as wedded to Christian doctrine: the beliefs in miracles and so on."
In retirement, he maintained a website with entries on favorite philosophers,
thoughts about pacifism, and news reports on Bolivia, where a non-violent
revolution had installed the first indigenous president, Evo Morales, in 2005

and which, Garver wrote, has the "third largest number of Quakers in the world, all indigenous and evangelical." In 2011, he still lived with Anneliese in a country house built by his grandparents not far from Buffalo.[42]

Richard Lipsitz also joined the anti-war battles of the late 1960s. He recalled, "I had a lot of experience with arrestees at demonstrations against the war. It never went beyond city court, [but] the university was torn apart. In one incident, 54 faculty members were arrested on the campus with a couple of priests." Lipsitz's opposition to the war perturbed some of his labor union clients: "They didn't leave me, but they made it known that they were upset with me. Twenty years after the end of the war, I was then about to retire, and one of the leaders in the building trades unions I represented came into the office and said, 'By the way Dick, I want to tell you, you were right; we were wrong.'"[43]

The SUNY-Buffalo English Department continued to grow. Chairman Al Cook brought in more creative writers: the poet Robert Creeley, the novelists John Barth and J. M. Coetzee. One former student enthused,

> Other universities had the best English departments for history or criticism or philology or whatever. But UB was the only place where it all went on at once: hot-center and cutting-edge scholarship and creative writing, literary and film criticism, poem and play and novel writing, deep history and magazine journalism. There was a constant flow of fabulous visitors, some here for a day or week, some for a semester or year. . . . There was not a better place to be.[44]

Ralph Maud was a founding member of the English Department at Simon Fraser University when he arrived in the fall of 1965. He published prolifically, including books on ethnography and myth and on the poets Dylan Thomas and Charles Olson. With Olson, he had a special relationship dating from their days at Buffalo. (Keyishian had introduced them, over drinks.) One day in the spring of 1965, he encountered Olson in a café near campus and, he recalled, "asked him a few direct questions" about his celebrated *Maximus Poems*. "After the second session, Olson leaned across the table, his eyes round in his glasses, and said, 'how would you like to be my scholar?' Each participant at the coming Berkeley Poetry Conference had been given a free pass to hand out to his or her 'scholar.' I accepted the title and turned up in Berkeley in July." But the position was, "as it turned out for the next 40-some years, no sinecure": Maud founded the Charles Olson Society and used the *Maximus Poems* every year in his classes.[45]

Maud continued to raise eyebrows: a student in the late '60s remembered him entering the lecture hall one day and asking "who in the class was going to go and see Aretha Franklin that night playing in concert in Vancouver": "A few hands went up. He admonished the rest of us for not taking advantage of seeing in person someone he considered one of the greatest musical talents of our time." Maud played Franklin's music and encouraged the students to dance. "A few walked out but for the most part, it was an hour of great music and song and Ralph was dancing up a storm on the podium."[46]

George Hochfield was also an academic star in the years during and after the litigation: in 1966, he published an anthology of writings by American transcendentalists, then became a translator of Italian literature. In 2006, he won a National Endowment for the Arts fellowship to translate *Songbook*, a collection of poems by the Italian Umberto Saba. Although relatively unknown, *Songbook* was "viewed as a major work in 20th century Italian literature."[47] Hochfield remained at Buffalo until retirement, then returned to Berkeley, California. In 2011, at age 84, he was translating the poems of Pirandello into English.[48]

Harry Keyishian completed his dissertation (on the Elizabethan playwright Thomas Dekker) after he lost his job at Buffalo and in 1965 joined the faculty of Fairleigh Dickinson University in New Jersey, where he became a Shakespeare scholar, an expert on the theme of revenge in English drama, and, in 1976, director of the university press, a job he kept even after his retirement from teaching in 2010. In 1987, he and Hochfield were interviewed by Bill Moyers for his PBS series *In Search of the Constitution*; Keyishian explained that in the early 1950s "a number of my professors had been fired under the terms of the Feinberg Law and they were people I admired very much. What struck me at the time and what I still carried as a kind of burden into the '60s was a sense of frustration and impotence, to watch these very decent, intelligent, talented teachers vanishing from the system, being driven out and being unable to do anything about it." A decade later, "there was an opportunity to do something about it."[49]

Keyishian and Hochfield thought that the litigation would have been unnecessary if a critical mass of the faculty, most of whom opposed the Feinberg certificate, had stood their ground and refused to sign. Keyishian reflected soon after the events, "Suppose there had been 25 or, for that matter, 500? Clearly, the problem would have been so serious that it is doubtful the administration could have taken any action at all. The faculty underestimated its power and allowed itself to be stampeded into signing with unnecessary haste." He blamed the campus AAUP chapter—"faculty messenger boys."[50] Hochfield agreed that "if a large number had refused to sign, the certificate could not have been enforced." Even 100, he thought, "and the state would have had to back down."[51]

13

"A Generation Stopped in Its Tracks"

Belated Vindication

Keyishian v. Board of Regents inspired the New York City teachers who had been fired in the 1950s to begin what turned out to be a laborious process of seeking compensation for actions now recognized as not only politically but legally unjust. In addition, the year after *Keyishian*, the Supreme Court struck down city charter section 903 (now renumbered), which had prohibited employees from invoking the Fifth Amendment when called to testify about city business.[1] Victor Rabinowitz and other lawyers who had been representing beleaguered teachers since the late 1940s now had an argument as well for compensating those whose positions the Boards of Education and Higher Education had deemed "vacant" after they had relied on the Fifth Amendment in refusing to testify about their politics.

Rabinowitz and attorney Benjamin Zelman instituted a new round of petitions and lawsuits arguing that teachers fired for insubordination and conduct unbecoming, for alleged CP membership, or for invoking the Fifth Amendment should be reinstated or, if already at retirement age, granted pension rights. The cases dragged on, in part because of bureaucratic lassitude and Board of Education resistance (the city argued that since none of the teachers had been plaintiffs in *Keyishian*, they had no right to relief), and in part because the board was not sure it had the legal power to reinstate teachers fired long ago under laws that were upheld at the time. Letters and memos to and from Rabinowitz, Zelman, and their clients document alternating moods of impatience, outrage, and despair as the matter sat first at the Board of Education, then at the city's law office, then back at the board, with long periods of somnolence in between. It was not until 1973 that a settlement for 33 teachers was finally signed, awarding pensions to many of them and lump-sum payments to the estates of those who had died.[2]

One of the issues in the negotiations was whether Julius Nash and Irving Mauer should be included. They had refused to name names in 1955, and after the board's forced-informer policy was finally interred by the courts, they were fired for falsely denying past communist affiliation on job applications. The board initially refused to include them, and the other teachers were divided. In early 1968, Nash wrote to Rabinowitz about a recent meeting at which, he said, "the Board of Education accomplished its purpose—the enemy was no longer the Board but Mauer and Nash." Because of "the charged atmosphere that pervaded the room, one thing was never made clear: that we are not asking people to refuse their jobs back as a mere gesture of solidarity and support for us (though perhaps I might have hoped that it would come from them)." Nevertheless, Nash thought that the board's offer was "a minimum" which could be improved and would be premature to accept. Mauer had a more emotional approach: "Our hopes were raised and now to be dashed. . . . We were, if anything, courageous. We fought an evil in our land and helped subdue it. In the process we paid severe penalties and our families suffered terribly."[3]

Rabinowitz wrote to the board's lawyer about Nash and Mauer, "I hope you will not take it amiss if I suggest that the Board is being somewhat vindictive at this point. Their offense was not so terribly grave, given all of the circumstances. They have already been punished far in excess of anything that might be called for."[4] Settlement talks were still at an impasse, however. Alice Citron, whose long service in Harlem before her firing had made her a legend in the community, sent Rabinowitz "a fragile thought from a heat-soaked brain": "I tuned in on Mayor [John] Lindsay's Hour and heard him announce that he had made new appointments to the lousy Board of Education. . . . During our day, he fought with us and is familiar with the battles against racism. . . . Perhaps he would lend a sympathetic ear."[5]

Citron's instinct was right: it was, finally, during Lindsay's administration that the board settled with the teachers it had fired. But it took several more years and numerous letters, phone calls, and legal filings to make it happen. In May 1972, Rabinowitz wrote to Lindsay's Corporation Counsel, "It has been almost six weeks since our conference and, to be perfectly frank, I had hoped for some action on the part of the Board in half that time." He supposed it would "take a week or so" to prepare another lawsuit. This seemed to galvanize the board, which finally voted in September to amend its bylaws to allow the reinstatements. The vote "brought applause from many of the former teachers who were present at the meeting. . . . Some brushed tears from their eyes. . . . Several kissed their long-time lawyer, Benjamin Zelman, on the cheek."[6]

There were still details to work out; another year passed before the settlement was in place, and it included Nash and Mauer. More than 20 years after the purges began, some of its aging victims could collect their pensions. But, as Zelman and Irving Adler noted in an article about the settlement, the city had lost "378 of its best teachers during a critical time when those teachers were badly needed." They were the ones who had "succeeded in building a bridge of understanding between the school and the community"—a bridge that had "yet to be rebuilt."[7]

The Teachers Union, though it fought on through the 1950s, had been fatally weakened by the purge and in particular by the Timone resolution of 1950, which barred it from dealing with the Board of Education. The board, newly constituted after the state legislature fired its scandal-ridden predecessor in 1961, finally decided to hold a collective bargaining election for teachers, but the TU polled only 2,575 votes of the more than 33,000 cast. The newly organized United Federation of Teachers won the election, and the TU advised its remaining members to join the UFT. In 1962, the board lifted the Timone resolution, but it was too late for the TU to recoup its losses. Late in 1963, its executive board voted to dissolve, and the membership ratified the decision the following year.[8]

Rose Russell stayed with the TU until the end. In January 1963, she was given a testimonial dinner at the Waldorf Astoria to commemorate her 20 years of service to education, civil rights, and labor. Milton Galamison, a Presbyterian minister, praised her as "a prophet" who had "brought so much light to a school system lumbering in darkness." Among others who offered tributes were the state attorney general, Louis Lefkowitz, Commissioner of Education James Allen, Coretta Scott King, and writer Langston Hughes.[9] Rose Russell died a year later, at the age of 65. The *New York Times* wrote, "Although she had no legal training, she served brilliantly in courts." Victor Rabinowitz in his memoir called Russell "one of the most greathearted and unselfish persons I have known."[10]

With the TU's demise went the alliance it had built between Jewish teachers and African American parents. The union's advocacy for minority children, for decent facilities, and against racism was history by the time that desegregation battles tore apart the school system in the late 1960s and early '70s. Although speculation is always precarious, one chronicler of the TU's history suggested that had this remarkable union not been destroyed, the subsequent race wars in the schools of New York City might have been avoided.[11]

"Time's Winged Chariot"

By 1958, the purge at the Board of Education was winding down: only 13 teachers were called for questioning, and Saul Moskoff returned to his duties as a lawyer in the city Corporation Counsel's office.[12] He went on to defend the city against a suit by the American Nazi leader George Lincoln Rockwell,

Teachers Union legislative representative Rose Russell and philosopher Barrows Dunham at 17th Annual Education Conference, New York City, April 1953. (Sam Wallach Photographs Collection, Tamiment Library, New York University; photograph by Mildred Grossman)

who had been denied a permit to speak at Union Square; the ACLU represented Rockwell. Moskoff eventually became a family court judge in his home borough of Queens. Michael Castaldi, who directed the Board of Higher Education's purge, also was rewarded for his services with a judgeship.[13]

Julius Nash and Irving Mauer remained good friends in the years of their exile. Nash went to graduate school, then taught at yeshivas. Mauer scraped together a living as a TV repairman, taught at a private school in Queens, and finally returned to teaching physics in the city school system. Nash's son Michael, who eventually became director of the Tamiment Library at NYU, a repository of materials on the American left, remembered that the families vacationed together and that Mauer, the former Jewish all-American, remained impressively athletic.[14] But the years of blacklisting, obloquy, and FBI surveillance were hard on Mauer's wife and children. "My kids were tortured," he said: "'Your father's a commie rat. Go back to Russia.' . . . My wife never recovered." But "they didn't succeed in destroying me. I was wounded. I recovered. I beat the shit out of those bastards."[15]

Irving Adler earned more money after his dismissal and loss of the two cases that bear his name than he ever would have earned as a schoolteacher. He wrote more than 100 books on math and science, many of them for children, while simultaneously contributing to scholarly journals in advanced areas of mathematics. In 1959, he moved to Bennington, Vermont, with his wife, Ruth, began teaching at Bennington College, and renewed his political commitments. He wrote petitions, organized against the Vietnam War, and joined the local school board. His continued activism did not escape the notice of the FBI, which tracked his movements until the mid-1960s, or of local opponents, one of whom wrote to U.S. Senator Winston Prouty of Vermont, asking if this was the same Adler who was a witness before the SISS in the early '50s. "Prouty took his letter to the FBI," Adler recalled, "and the FBI told him, 'We are not permitted to give you any information,' but they gave him the information anyhow, unofficially. I know all about this because I have a copy of my FBI file. He found out I was a member of the executive board of the American Institute for Marxist Studies. That was another bad mark against me."[16]

In 1960, the FBI's New York office recommended that Adler be removed from the Security Index, the agency's list of people to be summarily arrested and detained in case of national emergency, and placed in Section A of its Reserve Index, described as "those individuals whose subversive activities do not bring them within the Security Index criteria but who, in a time of national emergency, are in a position to influence others against the national interest." Included in Section A were "professors, teachers and educators; labor union organizers or leaders; writers, lecturers, newsmen, entertainers and others in the mass media field," as well as "lawyers, doctors or scientists." Individuals on the Reserve Index could also be imprisoned once the government's "Emergency Detention Program" was invoked.[17]

In 2007, the 94-year-old Adler completed a 211-page memoir. He wrote of mass resignations from the Communist Party in 1956 as a result of two traumatic events: Nikita Khrushchev's speech to the Party's 20th Congress exposing Stalin's crimes, and the Soviet invasion of Hungary later that year to suppress an uprising against communist rule. "I at first intended to stay in the Party to try to reform it from within," Adler wrote,

but Ruth insisted that we should both leave. She felt that reforming the Party was hopeless since the Party was dominated by sectarian dogmatists who would continue to be apologists for the Soviet Union. Ruth threatened to divorce me if I did not leave the Party. I certainly didn't want my marriage broken up, so I left. Leaving the Party was not a formal procedure. We simply stopped going to Party meetings. Thus it came about that Ruth, who had gotten me into the Communist movement, was the person who got me out of it.[18]

Among the professors who lost their jobs, Frederic Ewen was prodigiously active in the years after his premature retirement from Brooklyn College. As the FBI was careful to note, he continued to lecture on literature and politics—at the TU's Teacher Center, at meetings sponsored by the International Workers Order and other left-leaning groups, and at events protesting the SISS. An FBI informer reported on the contents of one Ewen lecture: "he pointed out certain revolutionary connotations appearing throughout English literature," including Shakespeare. The talk "sounded more like a lecture in English literature than anything else"; the audience "smiled at each other and shrugged."[19]

Ewen's post-retirement books included a literary biography of Bertolt Brecht and a large tome on the "heroic imagination" of writers and artists in the Romantic era. The theme obviously had resonance for this aging radical: Ewen wrote of a poem by William Blake, for example, that Blake's vision of workers rising against their oppressors "is in a sense the 'final conflict'—a war for the rehabilitation of all of humanity."[20]

Ewen also organized theatrical performances at union halls and other venues, featuring blacklisted actors such as Ossie Davis and Ruby Dee. He staged dramatic adaptations of modern classics, among them James Joyce's *Portrait of the Artist as a Young Man* and Thomas Mann's *The Magic Mountain*. The philosopher Barrows Dunham wrote to Ewen that he was "captivated" by the adaptation of Joyce's *Portrait*; he found it "ennobling, inspiring": "I do not recall the original as being nearly so much so. The stream of consciousness style I have always thought a supreme nuisance, and I'll wager that that was what impeded the awareness of a basic glory. The glory you have now exposed. . . . My congratulations, and my profound respect!"[21]

The FBI kept Ewen on its Security Index. Even though the agency had no evidence—not even the opinions of informants, on which it usually relied—that Ewen was in the CP after 1945, it was sufficiently damning that he continued to teach at the Jefferson School, to give lectures sponsored by other organizations on the Attorney General's List, and to write for journals that had been labeled as communist run. Agents interviewed superintendents at buildings where he lived, one of whom found it indicative of his "communist inclinations" that there were "frequent interracial gatherings" at his apartment.[22] In 1958, he was finally removed from the Security Index.[23]

The FBI also tracked Harry Slochower, at one point considering him "for custodial detention."[24] As early as the Rapp-Coudert hearings, it had an informer who supported the claim of Slochower's colleague Bernard Grebanier that Slochower was "a Communist Party functionary at Brooklyn College."[25] This informant had at least one detail wrong: she told the FBI that

Slochower had "tried to swing the German-American League for Culture to support the Hitler-Stalin Pact." Yet Slochower had publicly disagreed with the pro-Pact Party line: as he told the committee considering his promotion in 1949, he had worked against Nazism, "along with many American liberals, under the auspices of any organization (including communist), so long as it was opposed to fascism," but "this 'united front' broke up with the Non-Aggression Pact, when I publicly supported Great Britain against the communist charge that it was as fascist as was Hitler Germany."[26]

Slochower had, even before his 1957 resignation from Brooklyn College, found other interests to replace the political passions of an earlier time. He had been studying and practicing psychotherapy even while still teaching. After his resignation, he sought further training and expanded his practice: "I sent out business cards to my former students, and within two weeks I had 12 patients."[27] In 1959, he wrote a foreword to a book on "man and his divine nature" and in 1970 published *Mythopoesis: Mythic Patterns in the Literary Classics*. For many years, he was editor of the Freudian *American Imago* magazine. Slochower later said, "The whole thing gave me a kind of rebirth. If this hadn't happened, I would still be in Brooklyn College, still being adored and deified by the girls and boys; it wouldn't have helped me grow."[28]

Sarah Riedman and Melba Phillips, scientists who were also fired from Brooklyn College after their refusals to answer the SISS's political questions, initially turned their talents to authorship. Riedman had been writing science books for children since the late 1940s; by 1983, she had written or co-authored 40 of them, occasionally reminding her readers, in the course of recounting the careers of groundbreaking scientists, that "questioning and nonconformity [are] attitudes of mind worth cultivating."[29] But her academic career was over: she remained a freelance scientific writer, then became director of medical literature at the Hoffman-La Roche drug and medical supply company.[30]

Melba Phillips did get back into the academy, first as associate director of a teacher-training institute at Washington University, then as a professor at the University of Chicago. Later in her career, she undertook an ambitious project of improving high school physics education. Although she won many awards for teaching and service to the profession, she did not continue the brilliant research that she had begun as a young scholar working with J. Robert Oppenheimer.[31]

Oscar Shaftel did not look for another academic job after he was fired from Queens College—"the blacklist was just too strong," he said. Instead, he found work writing for trade magazines, mostly in the construction industry. It was "the lowest kind of hack work," but it paid the bills. One magazine fired him; the editor explained that it was because of "this Queens College stuff." Shaftel asked if the FBI had come around. "He didn't deny it." But his luck turned in 1963 when he was hired by J. Sherwood Weber, chair of the English Department at Pratt Institute in Brooklyn. Weber knew Shaftel as a good scholar; still, "it was a courageous thing to do. He had to face the trustees." But "then again, he was trying to build up the humanities department, and my Harvard PhD would not do him any harm."[32]

The FBI kept an open file on Shaftel. In March 1953, just after his SISS testimony, it added him to the Security Index. In July 1955, finding "no Communist Party membership within the past five years and no leadership in Communist Party front organizations," it removed him. True, his refusal to cooperate with the SISS had been "an overt act" within the criteria created two months earlier to merit inclusion on the Security Index, but it was "not believed that subject's other activities are so extensive as to warrant his retention."[33] He remained on the Reserve Index.

Eventually, Shaftel returned to Queens College, though only as an adjunct professor. The college was starting a religious studies program, and Shaftel had just written *An Understanding of the Buddha* (1974), the product of a lifelong interest in philosophy and religion that had taken a turn toward Asian culture in the years after his exile from Queens.

Vera Shlakman's academic job prospects were, like Shaftel's, non-existent after her firing in 1952. She was unemployed for a year, then found work as a secretary.[34] She taught when she could: at the TU's Teacher Center in 1952 (a course titled "Monopoly and Government"). In 1953, the *Journal of Economic History* published her review of two books, one of them Oscar Handlin's popular history of immigration, *The Uprooted*. Shlakman did not spare Handlin: his "treatment of the unyielding conservatism and docility of the immigrant 'peasant' is pushed to extremes," she wrote. Handlin's thesis, for example, did not "accord with the role of Jewish immigrants (not peasants, exactly, and not inconsequential in number) who built the clothing workers unions; with the socialist workers who helped to build the cigar-makers union and the various socialist parties; with the masses of workers who participated in the great steel strike of 1919."[35]

The FBI placed Shlakman on its Security Index because she "reportedly" was a Communist Party member in 1944–46, was active in the Teachers Union, and had invoked the Fifth Amendment in 1952 before the SISS. In 1955, an agent noted, "subject's case is inherently weak," and even though reliance on the Fifth Amendment was "an overt act which technically brings her within the criteria" for retention, he recommended that her Security Index card be canceled. But the agency continued to follow her movements well into the 1960s.[36]

Shlakman eventually made her way back to academia: first, in 1959, in an administrative position at Adelphi University; a year later, as a teacher in Adelphi's School of Social Work. In 1966, she moved to the Columbia University School of Social Work, where she taught until her retirement as Professor Emeritus in 1978. At an event in her honor 20 years later, she reflected on the importance of social work: "You and I remember the coming of the welfare state, and we thought it was good, because it permitted society to defend itself from the cruel discipline of competition in allegedly free markets. We remember that entitlements were a solemn right and not a denigration. We remember when poverty was a social problem and it was not a sin to be poor."[37]

Shlakman wrote articles during the 1960s and '70s, but she never published another book—never, as the historian Alice Kessler-Harris writes, followed her early social and economic history of the factory town of Chicopee, Massachusetts, with another empirical study. And, "like many volumes written by scholars purged from the academy," Kessler-Harris recounts, the book "faded into obscurity." But it "never quite died": "As economic historians persisted in writing the history of labor through its institutions, the book gathered dust on library shelves. And then, as the trajectory of labor history began to alter in the sixties, and a new generation of historians turned their attention to working people, Shlakman's name reentered scholarly consciousness." Columbia University library's copy of her book was borrowed in 1951, then, apparently, not again until 1966, "when it drew a flurry of readers. It was reprinted by Octagon Books in 1969. I found it in 1971."[38]

Since the '60s, Kessler-Harris says, Shlakman has had "an extraordinary effect" on a "generation of labor historians." No other study from those days "approached the kind of gender inclusive comprehension that Vera Shlakman had reached" in detailing "the active participation of women as workers and boardinghouse keepers as well as family members." Shlakman's book had also documented "the abrasive relationship between capital and labor."

> In a period when the field was dominated by Jeffersonian myths about the harmonious interaction of labor and capital, her detailed explorations of Chicopee confirmed what other data had already begun to suggest: that capital and labor were at odds with one another in fundamental ways. . . . As she followed the twists and turns of capital accumulation and concentration, her skeptical view helped to break down the notion that a community of interest had created a prosperous America.

Although for inquisitors of the 1950s, labor history of this sort was probably communist indoctrination, for others, "*Economic History of a Factory Town* reminds us that in some sense those of us who do labor history remain the intellectual children of Vera Shlakman and those like her who belonged to a generation stopped in its tracks."

Shlakman, Shaftel, Dudley Straus (who had been fired from Queens in 1955), and a handful of others whose academic careers were "stopped in their tracks" continued to seek apologies and compensation. After all, the Supreme Court had invalidated the Feinberg Law in 1967 and section 903 of the city charter, which the BHE had used to fire them, a year later. The Board of Education had finally, in 1973, compensated 33 public school teachers who had been fired for refusing to cooperate with its political interrogations. Bureaucracy, lassitude, politics, and money all played a part in the delays at the higher-education level, but Shaftel, Straus, and their lawyers kept up the pressure. In late 1977, Paul O'Dwyer, president of the city council, wrote to Michael Solomon, a lawyer for the City University of New York, pushing for compensation for nine people who had "waited for upwards of 30 years for justice." Although part of the delay was apparently due to the pendency of separate applications from Shaftel and Riedman, O'Dwyer urged Solomon to "place the matter before the Board without waiting for the other two cases," so that "at least some of those so unjustly treated during our period of hysteria should have what is due them during their lifetimes." Around the same time, Shaftel wrote to the director of alumni relations at Queens, rehearsing the entire history of the controversy and asking that the alumni group urge the BHE to make up its mind. If, "contrary to Board of Education precedent," the BHE refused to compensate the fired professors, "we wish to institute legal suit for full restitution before more of us die."[39]

The Board of Higher Education made conciliatory noises but continued to drag its feet. Solomon wrote a memo to the BHE in March 1978, reviewing the history of the firings and urging the board to "consider a resolution recognizing the inequities suffered by the dismissed teachers and the hope that the repression which permeated McCarthyism will not return." He also suggested that the board "authorize the settlement of any outstanding claims for a certain amount," albeit well below the salaries that Shaftel and the others had lost.[40] But nothing happened for the next two years. In early 1980, Solomon told Rabinowitz's office that "he had a meeting on Straus and other teachers' cases": there was "no definite decision"; the "main question was where to get the money."[41]

March 24, 1980, was a day of at least symbolic progress: the CUNY trustees—the successor body to the BHE—issued a statement formally apologizing "for the moral injustices suffered by the dismissed employees" and resolving "that the repression which permeated the McCarthy era will not again affect this university." But there was no financial compensation, only an expression of support for efforts to obtain the funds "to provide the individuals with equitable pensions or their estates with death benefits." This was slender consolation to the still feisty, and still literary, Shaftel, who mocked the board for merely expressing "in effect the hope that some day my grandchild will reap my death benefits," and who warned, "I hear time's winged chariot hurrying near."[42]

Rabinowitz's files document the frustration. In April 1980, Straus wrote to city councilor Carol Bellamy thanking her for her assistance, noting that the board's apology, "however pleasant, does us very little good," and hoping that "we may continue to count on your support in whatever further action is necessary." Bellamy replied politely: "As you so well know, the process of settling this matter is slow and cumbersome. I hope I can be helpful by bringing all the government agents together necessary for a final settlement." In August, Shlakman and Shaftel collaborated on a biting letter to city comptroller Harrison Goldin: "In quiet desperation, we turn to you in the hope that you will exercise your power to bring to a decent conclusion 28 years of injustice and indifference." The March 24 resolution was all very nice, but how about pensions (or death benefits), "as a small atonement for many years of career displacement, financial disadvantage, and family disruption"?

> Perhaps the Board, in its virtuous euphoria, suffered a touch of the Pish Tush rationale: the Mikado need only make a wish, and that wish is self-executed. In the five months since the Board expressed its wish, there has been some palaver, we are told. Lower ranks among the Trustees' legal staff, the Corporation Counsel, the Comptroller's office, and the Retirement Board have performed a stately quadrille, with every figure ending in an encouraging response to our attorney's pleas for information.

Shaftel and Shlakman were writing, they said, "because the talks seem to be going nowhere. We sense a painful throwback to many years of strung-out hopes and broken promises prior to March 24. . . . We beg you to take up the matter directly, cut the Gordian knot, and find the funds."[43]

The professors also lobbied the *New York Times*, which in January 1981 reported that even though "it has been 14 years since the laws under which they had been discharged were declared unconstitutional" and "over a decade since 11 of them filed legal claims seeking restitution," all the professors had gotten so far was a resolution from the trustees "denouncing past 'moral injustices'"; "meanwhile, three of the 11 have died." The city said it wanted to restore the pensions of the survivors, but the state legislature had not approved the funding.[44]

A changed political climate at CUNY was on the professors' side. While their settlements languished in 1980, a group of faculty was revisiting the even more ancient history of the Rapp-Coudert investigation. At a City College event organized by the ever-resourceful Irving Adler to honor the Abraham Lincoln Brigade, Americans who had volunteered during the late 1930s to fight Franco's fascist uprising in Spain, CCNY acting president Alice Chandler expressed interest in doing something to rectify the firings prompted 40 years before by Rapp-Coudert. In June 1981, the CUNY trustees adopted a resolution expressing "profound regret at the injustice done to former colleagues . . . who were dismissed or forced to resign because of their alleged political associations and beliefs and their unwillingness to testify publicly about them," and pledging in the future "diligently to safeguard the constitutional rights of freedom of expression."[45] Morris Schappes, in a speech before the board vote, recounted the achievements of the CCNY professors who had been fired, among them Philip Foner, author of more than 60 books; Lloyd Motz, a past president of the New York Academy of Science; and Moses Finley, who had emigrated to England and "established such a reputation as an ancient historian that the Queen knighted him." Had they not been driven from campus, Schappes said, "these achievements and others might well have been effected for the benefit of the City College community."[46]

The apology to the Rapp-Coudert victims of 1941–42 seemed to stimulate the city to find the funds to compensate the casualties of the SISS a decade later. In April 1982, a settlement totaling $935,098 was finally announced for Shlakman, Shaftel, Straus, four other ex-professors who were still alive, and three who had died. Checks were distributed at a City Hall ceremony on April 29. "This is a special day for the city," Comptroller Goldin boasted. "This is a day on which we right a wrong." Victor Rabinowitz was more cynical: "we were all treated to self-congratulatory speeches by city officials." Shaftel was grateful that he and his colleagues "will no longer be frayed-cuff retired teachers living on Social Security." But, had he not been forced out of college teaching in 1953, he mused, "I would have been a mild, meek, sheltered, scared teacher hanging on to my job. . . . I'm not sure I regret the vital experiences I had out in the world."[47]

Shlakman received a standing ovation when she walked into a Columbia faculty lounge after the restitution was announced. Straus wrote to Rabinowitz three months later: "Dear Vic: I can't think of any bill I've ever paid with the affection, respect and gratitude that goes with this check. Thanks for all those years. Dudley."[48]

In 2000, the Queens College student newspaper published a history of the school that described the purges of the early 1950s. Shlakman, who according to a former student "never talked about what happened to her," on this occasion wrote gratefully to the editor: "I was particularly impressed and pleased at how this rather unsavory chapter in the College's—and our nation's—history was handled." She was sorry that it could not be shared with "my colleague and dear friend, Oscar Shaftel, who has been ill for some time now. (Dudley Straus, I am unhappy to report, died a few years ago.)"[49]

Shaftel died in 2000. At his memorial service, the historian Alfred Young (Queens College '46) remembered him as faculty advisor to the *Crown*: there was no prior censorship, "no such thing as submitting copy to Oscar in advance." But "after each weekly issue everybody on the staff jammed into the third floor office to hear Oscar do a *post mortem*. He went over each page. Was that story complete? Wasn't that sentence garbled? It was like getting your freshman theme back but the style was all Oscar: casual, soft-spoken, low key, wry jokes, laughter. We hung on every word." According to the *New York Times*, Shaftel was working on "a long study about the changing concepts of God through history when he died." The book's tentative title was *A Plausible God*; in it, he wrote, "Scripture sanctions hearing a voice, whether from burning bush or whirlwind or the B Minor Mass. . . . Our god, like the Buddha, is best understood as a projection of our mind, and he speaks with the wisdom and majesty that we are ready for."[50]

Queens College continued to explore its history. Alumni Day in May 2001 included a panel titled "Can the Future Transform the Past? Academic Freedom and the Firing of Oscar Shaftel, Vera Shlakman and Dudley Straus: How Should Queens College Honor Them Now?" Among the speakers were Shlakman herself and members of the Class of 1951 who had been students of the three.[51] Two years later, former students organized an exhibit, "McCarthyism at Queens College, 1947–1955," in conjunction with a symposium at which historians Ellen Schrecker and Alice Kessler-Harris, among others, spoke.[52] The college president, James Muyskens, offered opening remarks that stressed the importance of academic freedom, especially in politically challenging times. Queens professor Joshua Freeman, who organized the event, thought Muyskens's statement "quite brave, given that 9/11 was not all that long ago and he was relatively new as president." Freeman added, "Vera was there, an amazing act of survival and triumph."[53]

Vera Shlakman, age 102 in 2012, was still living in her Manhattan apartment, cared for by friends who had met her through her sister Ella and her colleague Oscar Shaftel.[54]

At Brooklyn College graduation in 2005, Frederic Ewen received a posthumous Presidential Citation. It praised him as a "celebrated author, literary critic, and champion of the individual's right to self-expression and intellectual freedom" and recounted his activism against the rise of fascism and "the intensity of suffering during the Great Depression," his refusal to cooperate with the SISS, his forced resignation, and his later work writing, teaching, and organizing theatrical performances. Ewen had dedicated his final book, on Maxim Gorky, to his students, "who had made 'teaching a privilege and learning a joy.'" A lecture series bearing his name was inaugurated.[55]

Harry Gideonse was not there to witness this repudiation of the philosophy underlying his presidency of Brooklyn College. He had resigned in 1966 after a dispute with the BHE over the power of the municipal college presidents to charge tuition. His resignation statement was characteristically combative. It was not the tuition issue that forced him to leave, he said, but the board's demand for "fealty." Fealty was a "medieval concept": "It describes the position of a medieval lord in his relation to his feudal serfs. Members of the Board of Higher Education are not medieval lords—and I am not inclined to become a serf." Gideonse died in 1985 in a Long Island nursing home.[56]

14

Academic Freedom after *Keyishian*

Race, Sex, and Judicial Retrenchment

The Supreme Court's 1967 decision in *Keyishian v. Board of Regents* was fatal to loyalty programs across the nation. William Brennan, so often a master of compromise, did not, in this case, craft a middle-ground standard that would allow some anti-subversive programs to continue or encourage the passage of new, arguably narrower laws. There were no linguistic acrobatics justifying loyalty schemes if only they were more limited, provided greater due process, or eschewed test oaths.

Brennan's opinion nonetheless left many questions about the scope of academic freedom unanswered. *Keyishian* became a ubiquitous source of authority for court decisions condemning censorship in school libraries, reading assignments, and classrooms, but it also invited myriad conflicts in local communities, at school board meetings, and among university trustees over where to draw the line.

The Supreme Court initially stood by *Keyishian* despite the political backlash. Later in 1967, it struck down Maryland's loyalty scheme in the case of *Whitehill v. Elkins*. Creative writing professor Howard Whitehill, a Quaker, had been offered a visiting lecturership at the state university but refused to sign a test oath denying that he was engaged, "in one way or another," in "the attempt to overthrow" the government "by force or violence" or that he was a member of an organization involved in such an effort. The Court had upheld the oath in 1951, as Tom Clark pointed out in his *Keyishian* dissent.[1] Now, the decision to strike it down seemed inevitable.

Douglas wrote the opinion for the Court, relying on both vagueness and overbreadth. "We are in the First Amendment field," he said, and "the continuing surveillance which this type of law places on teachers is hostile to academic freedom." He cited his decision the year before in *Elfbrandt*, the Arizona oath case: "even attendance at an international conference might be a trap for the innocent if that conference were predominantly composed of those who would overthrow the Government by force or violence."[2]

Justice Harlan's dissent (for himself, Stewart, and White) complained that Maryland would "doubtless be surprised to learn that its meticulous efforts to conform the state 'loyalty oath'" to the Court's requirements had been "to no avail." Douglas's reasoning, he said, "defies analysis": the only thing "that does shine through the opinion of the majority is that its members do not like loyalty oaths."[3]

In the three years after *Keyishian*, courts in Texas, Kansas, New Hampshire, Illinois, Nebraska, California, Mississippi, Florida, and the District Columbia invalidated public-employee loyalty laws.[4] The California Supreme Court invalidated the anti-communist oath that had caused such a fracas at the state university in 1949.[5] Attorneys general in Vermont, New Jersey, Oregon, New Hampshire, Hawaii, and Oklahoma pronounced their loyalty laws unconstitutional.[6] In 1969, a federal court invalidated the Hatch Act disclaimer oath; the government did not appeal.[7] By the early '70s, courts had applied *Keyishian*, as well as the Washington and Arizona oath cases that preceded it, to strike down nearly every disclaimer oath, as well as the anti-subversive laws of which they were part.[8] Of course, judges have only limited power, and there were states, such as Nebraska, that simply refused to abide by the courts' rulings.[9]

The Supreme Court, meanwhile, expanded on the promise of *Keyishian*, even after Chief Justice Earl Warren retired in 1969 and President Nixon replaced him with the considerably more conservative Warren Burger. In 1972, in an opinion by Nixon appointee Lewis Powell, the Court extended academic freedom to college students. The president of a state college in Connecticut had refused to recognize a campus chapter of the radical Students for a Democratic Society on the grounds that the national SDS organization had engaged in disruptive protests at other colleges and that its "philosophy was antithetical to the school's policies" of allowing open exchange of competing ideas. The rejection meant that the SDS group could not use campus bulletin boards, advertise events in the student newspaper, or meet in any campus building. Writing for a unanimous Court, Powell rejected the college's use of guilt by association to condemn the local group for activities of other SDS chapters, and he quoted *Keyishian* for the proposition that "the college classroom with its surrounding environs is peculiarly the 'marketplace of ideas.' . . . We break no new constitutional ground in reaffirming this Nation's dedication to safeguarding academic freedom."[10]

Keyishian also opened the portals to cases protecting individual teachers and students from censorship. In 1969, a federal court of appeals ruled that a high school teacher who had assigned his senior English class to read an article in the *Atlantic* magazine could not be punished by the school board simply because the article contained, in the delicate words of the court, "a vulgar term for an incestuous son." Quoting Felix Frankfurter's paean to academic freedom in *Wieman*, the 1952 Oklahoma oath case, the court said the chilling effect of punishing a teacher for assigning such a text would be "even more serious" than any arguable infringement of school authorities' right to control the curriculum. Rebutting the argument that no injunction against firing the teacher was warranted because he could recover money damages if he later won his case, Judge Bailey Aldrich quipped, "Academic freedom is not preserved by compulsory retirement, even at full pay."[11]

Seven years later, a different court of appeals ruled that local authorities violated the First Amendment when they ordered Joseph Heller's *Catch 22* and Kurt Vonnegut's *Cat's Cradle* removed from an Ohio high school library. "A library is a mighty resource in the free marketplace of ideas," the judges announced, and they quoted *Keyishian* on the importance of academic freedom. But they split the difference and deferred to the school board's refusal to allow *Catch 22* and Vonnegut's *God Bless You, Mr. Rosewater* as assigned texts.[12]

Courts in these early cases did not say where the line should be drawn between legitimate school board discretion in educational matters and unconstitutional censorship, but most of them gave authorities ample leeway when the subject matter was vulgar or sexual. New York federal courts, for example, rejected a challenge to the removal from junior high school libraries of the Puerto Rican author Piri Thomas's *Down These Mean Streets* because of crude language and realistic depictions of barrio life.[13]

Often, it seemed that the decisive factor in these cases was whether the judges agreed with school officials that the book, article, play, or poem in question was offensive. Subjective responses dominated, lurking not far below the surface of dispassionate legal analysis. And as the federal bench, increasingly staffed by Ronald Reagan and George H. W. Bush appointees, grew more conservative in the 1980s and '90s, the tension between competing philosophies of education became more apparent. The philosophy of free inquiry, of teaching students how to think instead of simply what to think, clashed with a more "inculcative" view—that the purpose of education, at least below the college level, is to impart basic skills and instill values that will promote good citizenship, however that is defined by the school board. The paradox is that both functions are legitimate; the challenge is to reconcile them.

In 1969, the Supreme Court adopted the free-inquiry approach to education when it announced that "neither students nor teachers shed their constitutional right" to free expression "at the schoolhouse gate."[14] But in a school library censorship case 13 years later, the justices' views of education dramatically clashed. The case involved a school board's removal of several books (including *Down These Mean Streets*) from school libraries on the grounds that they were "anti-American, anti-Christian, anti-Semitic, and just plain filthy." William Brennan wrote a plurality opinion for himself, Thurgood Marshall, and John Paul Stevens, asserting that "a school library, no less than any other public library, is 'a place dedicated to quiet, to knowledge, and to beauty'"; he quoted *Sweezy* and *Keyishian*.[15] Thus, Brennan said, the school board violated the students' First Amendment right to receive ideas if it removed the books for partisan reasons, and he sent the case back to the lower courts to decide this question of intent.

Two swing justices, Harry Blackmun and Byron White, went along with the result in this case but not with Brennan's First Amendment theories. Four dissenters—Nixon appointees William Rehnquist, Lewis Powell, and Warren Burger and Reagan appointee Sandra Day O'Connor—insisted that school boards should be able to make these decisions without interference from judges. The warring philosophies of the justices signaled the beginning of a retrenchment that would steadily undermine the notion that students and teachers retain their First Amendment rights inside "the schoolhouse gate." By the first decade of the 21st century, U.S. courts had closed the door to most academic-freedom claims by teachers and students below college level and returned the near-total discretion to school boards and administrators that they had enjoyed before the 1960s.[16]

A good barometer of the change was the Fourth Circuit Court of Appeals' treatment of a First Amendment claim by a high school drama teacher who had been demoted after she coached her students in a controversial play. In 1996, a three-judge panel of the appeals court ruled for the teacher, citing *Keyishian* and other cases, including one that had dismissed as "fantastic" the "notion that teachers have no First Amendment rights when teaching, or that the government can censor teacher speech without restriction."[17] But the full bench of the Fourth Circuit then accepted the case for rehearing, rejected the panel's reasoning, and announced that teachers, like other public workers, have no First Amendment protection for job-related speech.[18]

As to higher education, most courts, at least for several decades, remained responsive to the spirit of *Keyishian*. A 1969 case held that public-college administrators violated the First Amendment when they barred the appearance on campus of the Reverend William Sloane Coffin, a prominent opponent of the Vietnam War. In 1990, a federal court in New York ruled that a professor stated a viable legal claim when his public university denied him tenure because he had characterized Zionism as a form of racism in a class called "The Politics of Race." Another court in 1997 found that a public university violated academic freedom when, responding to pressure from women's rights activists, it removed an exhibit in the history department's display case that included photos of two male professors holding weapons.[19]

The City College of New York had more than its share of academic-freedom battles. In the early 1990s, Professor Michael Levin publicly (not in the classroom) expressed his opposition to affirmative action and his belief that, on average, African Americans are less intelligent than whites. The college administration called his views "odious" and created "shadow sections" of his introductory philosophy course, to be taught by other instructors. Levin alleged in his lawsuit that the college had also done nothing to stop students from disrupting his classes and that, by creating a committee to review his writings and teaching, it had implicitly threatened to revoke his tenure. Indeed, the college president, Bernard Harleston, had said that although "the process of removing a tenured professor is a complicated one," Levin's views were "offensive to the basic values of human equality and decency and simply have no place at City College."[20]

Federal judge Kenneth Conboy found a blatant violation of Levin's First Amendment rights. He relied heavily on *Keyishian*, which, he said, invalidated the Feinberg Law because it "failed to narrowly specify *actual conduct* that could legitimately be proscribed by the state" and thereby created (in the words of *Keyishian*) "a highly efficient *in terrorem* mechanism." Levin's case involved that same fatal ambiguity: the review committee's "secret deliberations were predicated upon no announced or promulgated criteria"; Levin "had no way of knowing which of his statements were being reviewed"; and the committee's report "invites and indeed recommends further and continuing scrutiny of Professor Levin, albeit in its characteristically elliptical and . . . Orwellian double-speak." The whole case, according to Conboy, illustrated that academic tenure, "if it is to have any meaning at all, must encompass the right to pursue scholarship wherever it may lead, . . . without the deadening limits of orthodoxy or the corrosive atmosphere of suspicion and distrust."[21] The court of appeals essentially agreed, though it vacated Conboy's judgment in some particulars.[22]

At the other end of the racial-intellectual divide at CCNY was Leonard Jeffries, who had chaired the Black Studies Department since its creation in 1972. At the same time that Levin was voicing his opinions about the intelligence of African Americans, Jeffries was venting his anti-Semitism and anti-white racism and his bizarre view that "AIDS was created as part of a conspiracy by whites to destroy blacks."[23] At an off-campus symposium in 1991, Jeffries gave a speech that focused on bias in the state educational curriculum, but included comments that Judge Conboy, who again drew the case, described as "hateful and repugnant": he called one educational official a "sophisticated Texas Jew" and asserted that "rich Jews" had financed the slave trade. The speech "ignited a firestorm of controversy," Conboy wrote, the result being that the administration reduced Jeffries's upcoming term as department chair from three years to one.[24]

A jury found that the college violated Jeffries's First Amendment rights; as in Levin's case, despite the professor's provocative statements, there was no claim that his views adversely affected his job performance. The court of appeals initially affirmed the jury verdict but reversed itself in 1995, after the Supreme Court announced a new rule that further limited the steadily shrinking speech rights of public employees: now, to defeat a First Amendment claim, managers would no longer have to show that the plaintiff's expression actually disrupted workplace operations, only that it was "likely to be disruptive." The court of appeals recognized that a different standard might apply to professors because of the importance of free speech at universities but finessed the issue by saying that because the position of department chair at CCNY is administrative, Jeffries's loss of that job did not implicate academic freedom.[25]

Some people might say good riddance to both Levin and Jeffries because their views exceeded the bounds of legitimate academics and entered the realm of racial harassment or intellectual irresponsibility. Certainly, if either of them had submitted as part of a tenure or promotion application an article or book that argued their positions based on substandard scholarship, their cases would have been different. But in the circumstances, Judge Conboy was right both times to follow the wisdom of *Keyishian*, deriving as it did from two decades of experience with firing professors for beliefs that were thought at the time at least as hateful as the racial views of Levin or Jeffries. As the TU and others argued in the 1950s, performance, not political opinions, should be the relevant criterion for an academic job.

None of the decisions of the 1970s–'90s said that First Amendment academic freedom created an absolute immunity for scholars. And far from all cases brought by aggrieved professors were winners. Sometimes a person really was fired, or refused promotion, because of mediocre performance rather than expression of controversial views. Sorting out motives remained difficult, however. As the Ward Churchill case so vividly demonstrated,[26] faculty committees and university administrators can easily claim poor scholarship to mask what are really objections to controversial views. And backlash against a perceived left-wing trend in academia, fueled by such books as Allan Bloom's *The Closing of the American Mind* (1987), drove public attitudes that were not sympathetic to academic freedom.[27]

By the turn of the century, the status of First Amendment academic freedom for professors' research, writing, and teaching was increasingly shaky. A case brought by the ACLU in 1997 on behalf of six Virginia professors gave conservative judges on the Fourth Circuit Court of Appeals an opportunity to extend to higher education their view that public workers' job-related speech is never constitutionally protected. The facts of the case did not help the professors: the Virginia law they challenged barred all public employees—with the interesting exception of state troopers—from accessing anything "sexually explicit" on their office computers without advance permission from their supervisors. The six plaintiffs included Melvin Urofsky, a constitutional scholar who assigned his classes readings in obscenity law; Terry Meyers, an expert in the sometimes kinky poetry of Algernon Swinburne; and Dana Heller, an English professor specializing in gay and lesbian studies.

The ACLU's major dilemma at the outset was whether to limit its claims to the academic-freedom rights of professors to write and conduct research without seeking permission from an administrator—rights that seemed secure under *Keyishian*—or to broaden the case to include all state employees, including, for example, social workers who write reports of sexual abuse or health officials who do research on sexually transmitted diseases. The ACLU chose the broader approach and won the case in the trial court. But the state appealed, and a fractured majority of the 12 judges on the Fourth Circuit rejected First Amendment academic freedom for individual professors. Ignoring *Keyishian* and subsequent cases, they asserted that "to the extent the Constitution recognizes any right of 'academic freedom' above and beyond the First Amendment rights to which every citizen is entitled, the right inheres in the University, not in individual professors."[28]

There were four dissenters in the *Urofsky* case and a separate opinion by the chief judge of the court, J. Harvie Wilkinson, who agreed with the result but disagreed energetically on the question of academic freedom. Quoting *Keyishian*, Wilkinson protested that academic freedom "is of transcendent value to all of us and not merely to the teachers concerned"; it is, he said, "necessary to informed political debate" and "critical to useful social discoveries. . . . One cannot possibly contend that research in socially useful subjects such as medicine, biology, anatomy, psychology, anthropology, law, economics, art history, literature, and philosophy is not a matter of public concern." And, Wilkinson said, "the right to academic inquiry into such subjects cannot be divorced from access to one means (the Internet) by which that inquiry is carried out. By restricting Internet access, a state thus restricts academic inquiry at what may become its single most fruitful source."[29]

Yet Wilkinson joined in the judgment upholding the Virginia law because he felt the state had an overriding interest in restricting access to pornography. It would be an exaggeration to suggest that pornography, by the 1990s in America, occupied the same despised position and inspired the same panic as communism did in the 1950s, but certainly the fact that the Virginia law targeted "sexually explicit" content drove the result in the case.

Only six of the 12 Fourth Circuit judges in the *Urofsky* case went along with the extreme notion that professors have no First Amendment academic freedom in connection with their work. In addition to Wilkinson's disagreement, a sixth judge concurred reluctantly: he felt that the earlier Fourth Circuit case involving the high school drama teacher was a controlling precedent, even though he disagreed with it. The four dissenters thought the majority had simply misinterpreted Supreme Court precedents that made a distinction between public employees' internal office expression and their speech as citizens on matters of "public concern"; almost by definition, they said, scholarly work is of public concern. As the dissenters explained, the Virginia law's definition of "sexually explicit" content included "research and debate on sexual themes in art, literature, history and the law, speech and research by medical and mental health professionals concerning sexual disease, sexual dysfunction, and sexually related mental disorders, and the routine exchange of information among social workers on sexual assault and child abuse. These topics undeniably touch on matters of public concern."[30]

Academic Freedom as an Institutional Right

The Supreme Court in these years did not revisit *Keyishian*. When it next confronted academic freedom, it was in a context more convoluted than the simple claim of professors that their research, teaching, or extramural expression was threatened by the investigatory apparatus of the state. In the late 1960s and early '70s, as the affirmative action plans so deplored by Professor Michael Levin began to proliferate, white applicants for jobs and university admissions brought "reverse discrimination" suits to challenge them. So it was that the case of Allan Bakke, an unsuccessful applicant to the University of California's medical school at Davis, arrived at the Supreme Court in 1977.

The Davis affirmative action plan gave an advantage to minority applicants based on their race. Although the Supreme Court struck it down, an opinion by Lewis Powell announcing the judgment of the Court said that not all race-conscious efforts by universities to increase minority enrollment were necessarily unconstitutional. He based this conclusion on deference to a university's judgment about its need for a diverse student body—an aspect, he said, of academic freedom. Discretion to decide who will be admitted to study, he said—quoting Felix Frankfurter in *Sweezy v. New Hampshire*—is one of the "four essential freedoms" of a university.[31] Twenty-five years later, the Court reiterated this institutional view of academic freedom in a 2003 affirmative action case.[32]

It seemed to make sense, but it was the first sign, in the Supreme Court, of a tension between claims of university autonomy (institutional academic freedom) and teacher autonomy (personal academic freedom). As Ellen Schrecker observes, Justice Powell's citation of *Sweezy* and *Keyishian* "transformed the traditional version of academic freedom from its original function of shielding the professional activities of individual instructors."[33] The Court recognized the conflict in a 1985 case involving a student's unsuccessful challenge to his university's decision to stop his advancement toward a medical degree. Academic freedom, Justice John Paul Stevens noted in passing, "thrives not only on the independent and uninhibited exchange of ideas among teachers and students, . . . but also, and somewhat inconsistently, on autonomous decision making by the academy itself."[34] Stevens did not indicate how the courts were supposed to umpire disputes when these two aspects of academic freedom collided.

Institutional autonomy, of course, had its limits. In the late 1980s, the University of Pennsylvania balked at the Equal Employment Opportunity Commission's demand for documents relating to the denial of tenure to Rosalie Tung, a professor at the university's Wharton School of Business. Tung had charged race, sex, and national-origin discrimination. The university argued that First Amendment academic freedom should protect it from having to reveal confidential peer-review materials. It relied on an institutional view of academic freedom, bolstered by Frankfurter's language in *Sweezy* extolling the "'four essential freedoms' that a university possesses under the First Amendment," among them the right to "determine for itself on academic grounds who may teach."[35]

Justice Harry Blackmun acknowledged all this in the unanimous decision he wrote for the Court, but he rejected the university's argument. He reaffirmed Brennan's statement in *Keyishian* that "our Nation is deeply committed to safeguarding academic freedom, which is of transcendent value to all of us and not merely to the teachers concerned." But here, the university did not claim that the government was trying to control or suppress "particular subjects or points of view." Instead, the university only argued that "the 'quality of instruction and scholarship [will] decline' as a result of the burden EEOC subpoenas place on the peer review process." This was too vague and speculative to persuade a majority of justices. The EEOC was not dictating any criteria—it was not "second-guessing" any "legitimate academic judgments." It was only enforcing the law against race and sex discrimination.[36]

The principle of *Keyishian* thus seemed secure after the Pennsylvania case, but questions proliferated about how to balance professors' First Amendment academic freedom against their universities'—or the government's—rules, whether about discrimination, harassment, grades, curriculum, or countless other issues. Some scholars argued that *Keyishian* had not meant all that it seemed, at the time, to be saying about the rights of individual professors. In retrospect, they thought, *Keyishian* was just the Supreme Court's way of giving some protection to teachers at public institutions at a time when government employees in general had almost no legal recourse if they were punished because of political activity or ideas.[37] Actually, they said, First Amendment academic freedom is about the rights of the institution—the community of scholars—to set its own agenda, to police its employees, and to hire and fire free from interference by the state.[38]

The Persistence of Loyalty Oaths

Justice Harlan was only partly right when he complained in the 1967 *Whitehill* case that the Supreme Court majority simply did "not like loyalty oaths." True, the liberal wing of the Court disapproved negative, or disclaimer, oaths, but affirmative loyalty oaths persisted as requirements for all kinds of jobs and benefits. These affirmative oaths—typically, to support and defend the Constitution and to protect the government against all enemies—are at least as vague as negative oaths, but they are so traditional and widespread that judges examining them tend to abandon fine legal analysis.

A few months after *Keyishian*, a three-judge court rejected a challenge to a New York law that made it illegal to serve as teacher in any public institution in the state, or any private school with a property-tax exemption, without signing an oath to "support the constitution of the United States of America and the constitution of the State of New York."[39] Twenty-seven Adelphi University professors challenged the requirement as unduly vague and a violation of their First Amendment rights.

A commentator ruefully described the case, which "arose on perhaps the most ambiguous record to grace the Supreme Court's files since the celebrated *Adler* litigation of 16 years before." The ambiguity was

> attributable to legal mismanagement rather than statutory desuetude; Adelphi officials had inadvertently overlooked the requirement ever since it was first enacted in 1934, and the Board of Regents seems to have been

equally remiss. Apparently nobody was sure even how to enforce the law: the court was unable to say whether a refusal to sign the oath would lead to prosecution of the teachers, prosecution of the school, suspension of the latter's tax exemption, or some combination of the three.[40]

But the judges in the case of *Knight v. Board of Regents* were sure that the oath was harmless: it simply paralleled the sort of pledge required of state legislators and other public officials. True, the Supreme Court had struck down a mandatory pledge of allegiance to the flag 24 years before when challenged by schoolchildren, but, they argued, the language of the pledge was "far more elaborate" than the New York teacher oath.[41] The judges also dismissed the professors' argument that a promise to "support" the Constitution was unduly vague. Early 1960s cases such as *Cramp* and *Baggett* involved negative oaths that looked to past beliefs and behavior, they said—an assertion that was simply wrong, as *Baggett* had also struck down an affirmative oath to "promote respect for the flag and institutions of the United States" and "reverence for law and order and undivided allegiance to the government" (see chapter 10).

The three-judge court in *Knight* reverted to the right-privilege distinction that the Supreme Court had so roundly rejected by the time of *Keyishian*. "A state does not interfere with its teachers," they opined, "by requiring them to support the governmental systems which shelter and nourish the institutions in which they teach."[42] The reasoning "should have attracted a few raised eyebrows in the Supreme Court,"[43] according to one scholar, but instead, the justices affirmed without writing an opinion.

Four years later, the Court did address affirmative oaths. The case came from Massachusetts, where Lucretia Richardson, a researcher at Boston State Hospital, was presented with a state-mandated oath six weeks into her job. Public employees in Massachusetts had to swear not only to "uphold and defend" the state and federal constitutions but to "oppose the overthrow of the government" of the United States and the state "by force, violence, or any illegal or unconstitutional method." A three-judge court rejected Richardson's challenge to the "uphold and defend" portion of the oath but struck down the promise to "oppose the overthrow of the government" as "hopelessly vague." The deputy attorney general who argued for the state did not help his case when he explained to the court that there were "three standards of obligation to take active steps to 'oppose' the overthrow of the government": the "ordinary citizen who has taken no oath has an obligation to act *in extremis*"; a person who has taken only an affirmative oath "would have a somewhat larger obligation"; and one who has specifically sworn to oppose revolution has the largest obligation of all. This elaborate explanation persuaded the three judges that "such varied standards" made the Massachusetts oath essentially "unintelligible."[44]

Richardson's case generated considerable controversy among the justices when it arrived at the Court in early 1970. The new chief, Warren Burger, agreed with Justice Harlan that Richardson's complaint was trivial. Brennan, Black, and Douglas thought the opposite, at least as to the oath's promise to "oppose the overthrow of the government." Rather than decide the case, the justices tried to avoid it by positing that there might not be a live controversy: perhaps Richardson's job was no longer available. Despite an affidavit from the hospital superintendent assuring that "the project for which Mrs. Richardson was hired 'is still ongoing' and that 'employment consonant with her abilities and qualifications has been and is periodically available,'"[45] a majority of the Court agreed to send the case back to the lower court to decide whether it was moot. Harlan, with Burger joining him, appended a blistering concurrence. He thought the case clearly not moot, but he was "content to acquiesce in the Court's action because of the manifest triviality of the impact of the oath under challenge, a factor that may, I suspect, underlie today's unusual disposition." Harlan thought the oath "no more than an amenity."[46]

Cole v. Richardson returned to the high court in late 1971. Justice Abe Fortas was gone (a financial scandal had cut short his tenure), and President Nixon had appointed a conservative Minnesota judge, Harry Blackmun, to replace him. Black and Harlan had retired in 1971. William Rehnquist and Lewis Powell were to replace them, though they did not participate in the *Cole* decision. After the oral argument, the justices seemed to agree that the mandated promise to "uphold and defend" the Constitution was perfectly acceptable. What remained of the liberal bloc—Douglas, Brennan, and Marshall—wanted to strike down the additional language, the promise to "oppose the overthrow of the government," but they were outvoted. Stewart preferred that the case "go away."[47]

Burger assigned himself to write the opinion for the Court; White, Blackmun, and Stewart joined. With Rehnquist and Powell not participating, that was enough for a majority. Burger started out by acknowledging that public employment cannot, under precedents such as *Elfbrandt* and *Baggett*, "be conditioned on an oath that one has not engaged, or will not engage, in protected speech activities." Nor can employment be conditioned "on an oath denying past, or abjuring future, associational activities within constitutional protection."[48] But affirmative oaths were not an unreasonable condition on employment, he said, and the required promise to "oppose the overthrow" of the government was really just the flip side of the affirmative promise to support the Constitution. Ignoring the state attorney's elaborate explanation of the three levels of obligation to oppose rebellion, Burger said that both promises were merely intended "to assure that those in positions of public trust were willing to commit themselves to live by the constitutional processes of our system. . . . Such repetition, whether for emphasis or cadence, seems to be the wont of authors of oaths. That the second clause may be redundant is no ground to strike it down; we are not charged with correcting grammar but with enforcing a constitution."[49]

Douglas had no patience with this sophistry. He took Burger to task for "emasculat[ing]" the word "oppose" by reading it merely to be the negative side of "support." "Having thus emasculated the word, the majority then labels it as 'redundant.'" Douglas added that advocating fundamental changes in government, "which might popularly be described as 'overthrow,' is within the protection of the First Amendment."[50] For his pains, Douglas received an admonitory postcard from a couple in his home state: loyalty oaths, they said, are "a necessary part of the preservation of our country." By contrast, the *Sacramento Bee* called the *Cole* decision "a sad retrogression to the late 1940s and early 1950s when such spurious declarations were the order of the day and Senator Joseph McCarthy of Wisconsin was terrorizing loyal government employees." In Burger's belief that the oath was "no more than an amenity," the *Bee*'s editorial writer said, he was "attempting to label something bland and insignificant which is neither."[51]

Whatever the flaws and justifications of affirmative "support and defend" oaths, they persist all over America. Many, perhaps most, people consider them at best a worthy ritual, at worst an annoyance. But for conscientious objectors, often Quakers and others with principled dispositions, affirmative oaths pose a real problem. Others who find them oppressive politically, sloppy linguistically, or both tend to hold their noses and sign.[52]

15

September 11 and Beyond

Is Anti-terrorism the New Anti-communism?

At the turn of the 21st century, academic freedom was in a murky state. The Supreme Court had said that as a matter of First Amendment right, it attached to the university as an institution as well as to individual professors, but did not say how to resolve conflicts between the two. Some commentators had argued that academic freedom is fundamentally about institutional autonomy, on the theory that a community of scholars governs the institution in the first place. Another argument was that academic freedom only applies to scholarship and teaching, not to "extramural" political speech, which enjoys the same First Amendment protection regardless of whether a public employee is a professor, a police officer, or a nurse. As a matter of policy rather than law, most universities, public and private, accepted the AAUP's three-part definition of academic freedom (scholarship, teaching, extramural speech), but the strength of their commitment varied; and they were still vulnerable to pressures to avoid or dismiss controversial professors.

Then September 11 happened. Some critics of the censorship that took hold after the attacks on the World Trade Center compared the atmosphere to McCarthyism—that common misnomer for the repression that began well before Senator Joseph McCarthy seized upon Cold War anti-communist panic and that lasted for at least another half dozen years after his 1954 fall from grace. The comparison was no more accurate than it had been in the 1970s and '80s when leveled against left-wing academics for insisting on broad anti-harassment speech codes or against other campus censorship crusades.

Post-9/11 censorship was not nearly as pervasive and deeply rooted as the anti-subversive purges of the 1950s, but there were similarities nonetheless. The epithet "terrorist" became a convenient, and conveniently frightening, term for views or activities that a government agency or private pressure group sought to suppress. If nowhere near the equivalent of "communist" in the 1950s, "terrorist" did become a scare word with no fixed meaning, while government officials' varying deployments of the term were often politically driven and included at times even non-violent dissenters.

One of the most striking examples emerged in October 2008, when the *Washington Times* reported that two nuns who had protested the death penalty and the U.S. invasion of Iraq had been placed on the FBI's Terrorist Watch List; they were among 53 people added to the list "in conjunction with an extensive Maryland surveillance effort of antiwar activists."[1] Police commonly consult the list when making traffic stops, the State Department uses it to vet visa applications, and the Department of Homeland Security uses it to create its No Fly List and to select airport travelers for interrogation.[2] Files produced in response to public-records requests revealed that non-violent environmental groups, anti-abortion activists, and people opposed to biological-warfare research and the manufacture of cluster bombs were also listed as terrorists, along with "activists devoted to such wide-ranging causes as promoting human rights and establishing bike lanes."[3] In May 2009, the Justice Department's inspector general issued a report faulting the FBI Watch List for both including people who posed no risk of terrorism and failing to include people who were genuine suspects.[4]

Part of the problem is simply government overreaching, but part arises from broad legal definitions of terrorism. The State Department uses the definition in U.S. immigration law, much of which comports with ordinary notions of terrorism: hijacking, sabotage, and threats to kill, injure, or detain a person "in order to compel a third person (including a governmental organization) to do or abstain from doing any act." But the definition also covers the use of any weapon "or dangerous device" with intent to endanger either people or property.[5] Obviously, this encompasses a broad range of crimes. The U.S. criminal law definition of terrorism is narrower, covering only acts "dangerous to human life" that "appear to be intended" to intimidate or coerce a civilian population or to influence the policy of a government by intimidation or coercion.[6]

An executive order signed by President George W. Bush 12 days after 9/11 extended the definition of terrorism found in the criminal law: it was not limited to threats to human life but also covered any act dangerous to "property or infrastructure" that "appears to be intended to influence the policy of a government by intimidation or coercion."[7] Under this definition, civil disobedience that involves damage to property—pouring blood, for example, on weaponry or draft files as was done in symbolic protest of the Vietnam War—qualifies as terrorism.

The U.S. government maintains several different but partially overlapping lists of organizations or people that it believes are engaged in terrorism.

The FBI Watch List, with hundreds of thousands of names, is the largest and most error prone, as the experience of the Maryland nuns suggests. The State Department has a Foreign Terrorist Organization, or FTO, list as well as a Terrorist Exclusion List, or TEL, required by the 2001 USA PATRIOT Act. The Treasury Department compiles the Specially Designated Terrorists, or SDT, list. Political considerations go into all of the listings: whether the U.S. government considers an individual or group part of a legitimate liberation movement or an illegitimate terrorist conspiracy depends on our foreign policy. Federal law specifies that "national security," for the purpose of designating foreign terrorist organizations, includes the "national defense, foreign relations, or economic interests of the United States."[8] The African National Congress was on a State Department terrorist list for decades because it used violence, among other tactics, in its struggle against apartheid; eventually, of course, its leader, Nelson Mandela, was released from prison and became president of the country (not to mention a Nobel Peace Prize winner), and the ANC became the leading political party.[9]

One anti-terrorism law particularly relates to academic freedom. The 1996 Antiterrorism and Effective Death Penalty Act (AEDPA) makes it a crime to provide "material support" to any "foreign terrorist organization" and defines "material support" to include expert assistance even for peaceful humanitarian purposes. Congress amended AEDPA several times, largely in response to court decisions striking down parts of the ban on "material support" because they unduly interfered with free speech and association. But in June 2010, the Supreme Court, now led by George W. Bush's appointee as chief justice, John Roberts, upheld the "material support" provisions. The plaintiffs in the case included the Humanitarian Law Project, an organization that wanted to help the Kurdistan Workers' Party (the PKK), a rebel group fighting oppression of the Kurds in Turkey and Iran, with training in peaceful conflict resolution. Ralph Fertig, the project's president and a retired administrative law judge, was also a plaintiff, as was Dr. Nagalingam Jeyalingam, a Sri Lankan–born physician who, with several non-profit groups, wanted to assist the Liberation Tigers of Tamil Eelam, or Tamil Tigers, with peaceful political activities. The Tamil Tigers had unsuccessfully challenged their inclusion on the secretary of state's FTO list.[10]

Writing for the Court majority in the Humanitarian Law Project case, Chief Justice Roberts opined that even under the "strict scrutiny" required by the First Amendment, the material-support ban was justified by compelling government interests. But Roberts did not really scrutinize the government's justifications; instead, he deferred to executive-branch judgments about how to combat terrorism. Roberts rejected the plaintiffs' argument that the 1961 Smith Act case of *Scales v. United States* should apply. In *Scales*, the Court had ruled that members of organizations considered subversive could not be prosecuted unless the government proved that they not only knew of the unlawful aims of the organization but specifically intended to help achieve them.[11] Since the Humanitarian Law Project and the other plaintiffs only intended to assist with peaceful aims of the rebel groups, they argued that the anti-material-support provisions of the law were too broad. Their argument was supported by an *amicus* brief on behalf of 32 "Victims of the McCarthy Era"—individuals, and their family members or close friends, who were blacklisted or otherwise lost their jobs, and in some cases served prison terms, during the 1950s because of associations with the Communist Party, even though they only supported the Party's peaceful aims.

Roberts was not impressed. He said *Scales* was "readily distinguishable" because the Smith Act prohibited "mere membership" in a subversive group; here, the law prohibited "providing 'material support.'"[12] It was a meaningless distinction, since membership ordinarily involves material support, and membership for peaceful aims is no different in substance from material support for peaceful aims. Indeed, criminalizing material support has an even broader effect on freedom of association than criminalizing membership does: in this case, it prevented lawyers and law professors from filing friend-of-the-court briefs on behalf of the PKK, the Tamil Tigers, or any other listed group. But much like the Vinson Court in the early 1950s, the Roberts Court was not about to apply the First Amendment too rigorously when the case involved claims of national security.

Justice Stephen Breyer's dissent in *Humanitarian Law Project*, joined by Ruth Bader Ginsburg and Sonia Sotomayor, argued that the First Amendment does not permit the government to prosecute people for teaching and advocacy with lawful aims, even if it is coordinated with a group branded as terrorist. The government did not show that banning peaceful advocacy was necessary to fight terrorism; and the activities the plaintiffs wanted to pursue, such as helping the groups file petitions with the United Nations, involved the communication "of political ideas and lawful means of achieving political ends."[13] The *New York Times*, one among many critics of the Court's decision, urged Congress to repair the damage by writing the standard of specific intent into the law, since the Supreme Court was not willing to do so.[14] As one scholar pointed out, if the material-support provisions had been on the books in the 1980s, the thousands of Americans who donated to the African National Congress would have been criminals.[15]

The events of September 11 undoubtedly influenced the Supreme Court's 2010 decision in *Humanitarian Law Project*, but the repercussions of the

World Trade Center attacks were far broader than legal restrictions on peaceful aid to rebel organizations. Shortly after 9/11, White House press secretary Ari Fleisher warned that Americans must now "watch what they say,"[16] and at schools and colleges, where debate about the causes of the disaster and America's image in the Arab world should have been most vigorous, there were innumerable incidents of punishment for allegedly unpatriotic ideas. In Albuquerque, New Mexico, two high school teachers and a guidance counselor were suspended without pay for displaying posters and other artwork expressing opposition to the U.S. invasion of Iraq. One of them had refused to remove student posters that the principal considered "not sufficiently pro-war." In Dearborn, Michigan, a student was sent home after refusing to turn inside out a T-shirt with an image of George W. Bush and the words "International Terrorist."[17]

Teach-ins were held at many colleges; the AAUP reported that most of them "represented academia at its best," providing forums to "explore difficult questions, and debate ideas." But at CCNY, a brouhaha ensued after the *New York Post* attacked a post-9/11 teach-in as a "peacefest" run by "academics who are too blind, stupid, or intellectually dishonest to tell the difference between the divisive war in Vietnam and the coming war against terrorism that's uniting Americans." Professors named in the article received hate mail, and administrators joined the melee. CUNY's chancellor excoriated "those who seek to justify or make lame excuses for the attacks . . . based on ideological or historical circumstances," and two trustees denounced the teach-in, which neither they nor the chancellor had attended.[18]

Teach-in fallout gave way to more sustained attacks on professors specializing in the Middle East. Stanford professor Ahmad Dallal recounted that, after 9/11,

> many scholars of Islam and the Middle East were called upon to explain these tragic events and help the public understand their background. Yet the handful of commentators, mostly on university campuses, who dared to expand their search for an explanation beyond a sinister focus on terror and security came under vicious attacks and were accused of blaming the victims and rationalizing and justifying terrorism.

The mainstream media, Dallal added, presented "an army of 'experts'" who actually knew little about Islam but who claimed it was an inherently violent religion. And "in the name of unity and patriotism," anyone seeking to understand the crisis "in all of its complexities and go beyond the simplistic cultural polarities widely circulated among policy makers and apologetic media pundits" was excluded from public debate. Little was said about "the disastrous effects of an American foreign policy that has supported many twisted dictatorships in the Muslim world and helped thwart democratic reforms, or about the American-Saudi partnership that used Afghanistan to defeat the Soviet Union and in the process turned the country into a breeding ground for misery and monstrosity."[19]

The argument here is not about whether the Middle East scholars or the "army of experts" who demonized Islam as a terrorist religion were right; it is about open debate and access to information. As in the 1950s, ideological pressures suppressed views and perspectives that the American people needed in order meaningfully to evaluate our foreign-policy options.

Most of the pressure on Middle East studies came from private groups. Shortly after 9/11, the American Council of Trustees and Alumni, or ACTA, founded in 1995 by Senator Joseph Lieberman and former National Endowment for the Humanities chair and vice presidential wife Lynne Cheney, published a report that attacked the teach-ins for "moral equivocation" and "condemnation of America," criticized course offerings in "Islamic and Asian cultures," and appended a list of 117 "un-American" professors, staff, and students who had made statements of which it disapproved. The report's enumeration of "un-American" statements was remarkable for its breadth and its apparent expectation that the role of universities was to promote a uniformly bellicose response to 9/11. Among the statements that ACTA found reprehensible were:

- "There is a terrible and understandable desire to find and punish whoever was responsible for this. But as we think about it, it's very important for Americans to think about our own history, what we did in World War II to Japanese citizens by interning them."
- "What happened on September 11 was terrorism, but what happened during the Gulf War was also terrorism."
- "[We should] build bridges and relationships, not simply bombs and walls."
- "The responsible thing for the President and Congress to do would be to lower the rhetorical temperature in Washington and halt the contest to sound more bellicose and patriotic than the last politician or official."
- "I'm not sure which is more frightening: the horror that engulfed New York City or the apocalyptic rhetoric emanating daily from the White House."[20]

Protests from the academic establishment and mainstream press persuaded ACTA to delete individuals' names from the online version of its report, although it retained the institutional affiliations of the quoted professors and students.[21] ACTA had already promised to send its list to 3,000 trustees at colleges nationwide, and pressure groups, including most prominently the website Campus Watch, created in 2001 to monitor Middle East studies, began to recruit students and faculty to report on colleagues whom they perceived as "un-American, anti-Semitic, or pro-terrorist."[22]

Continued agitation prodded the House of Representatives in 2003 to pass a bill to police Middle East studies. The proposed "International Studies in Higher Education Act" died in the Senate but was passed again by the House in 2005: it would have subjected federally funded academic resource centers, about 17 of which studied the Middle East, to oversight by a committee of political appointees, including two representing "national security agencies" and four chosen by House and Senate leaders. The bill was opposed by the AAUP, the American Anthropological Association, the Middle East Studies Association, the American Council on Education, and the ACLU. It did not become law—an indication that academic freedom was more robust in the first decade of the 21st century than in the 1950s—but it was a reminder of the perils confronting scholars when political passions intervene.[23]

Major foundations such as Ford and Rockefeller were also under pressure after 9/11, in particular, to withdraw support for any group or individual thought to oppose Israeli policy in its occupied territories. "Terrorism" was the language of the prohibitions in the grants that resulted, but the funding restrictions were broader: they included "violence," "bigotry," or "the destruction of any state"—the last being code words for opposition to Israel. As Jonathan Cole, former provost of Columbia University, recounted, there was "no direct evidence" that the Ford Foundation, the initial target of the pressure, had supported terrorism, "unless one applies the broadest possible definition of both 'terrorism' and 'support'"; this was an "effort to silence criticism of the Sharon government" in Israel.[24] Activities banned under the broad terms of the foundation grants could include films and poetry readings at universities as well as courses or conferences about anarchism, Marxism, white supremacy, the French Resistance, or the works of Malcolm X.[25]

Some foundations required grantees to assure that no funds would go toward assisting individuals or organizations on government terrorist lists, a restriction that one scholar, Beshara Doumani, argued would prevent a college from allowing a student or professor involved with a funded project to speak "in favor of the right of indigenous people to use violence against a foreign military occupation" or to advocate "the right of Islamist organizations" such as Hezbollah to participate in the Lebanese political system.[26] (Hezbollah, like Hamas—the elected government of Gaza—was on the State Department's Specially Designated Terrorist List.) Cole added that even "putting aside the

vagueness of the conditions," Ford's restrictions pressured universities "to compromise some of their most fundamental values of free inquiry and discourse,
their belief that there is no single way to view the world or discuss it."[27] Again,
the question here is not whether Israeli policy is right or wrong; it is whether
we can have informed debate on this tragically difficult subject.

In 2002, a group called the Family Policy Network sued the University of
North Carolina for assigning an introductory text about Islam to incoming
students. The state legislature then voted 64–10 to forbid the university to
use public funds to teach the book. The university resisted the pressure, and
a court of appeals eventually dismissed the suit;[28] but local politicians and
some trustees continued to agitate. In 2003, Senate Republicans led by Rick
Santorum floated plans for an "ideological diversity" law that would terminate federal funding to universities that allowed students or faculty members
to criticize Israel, on the assumption, Doumani writes, "that such criticism
is necessarily anti-Semitic." He concludes, "It is difficult to sustain a rational
and productive discourse when criticisms of U.S. or Israeli government policies are routinely stigmatized as treasonous or anti-Semitic. In the post-9/11
political climate, there is no field more radioactive than Middle East studies
and nothing more frowned upon than expression of support for Palestinian
rights."[29]

A number of campaigns were launched against individual professors in
these years. Joseph Massad at Columbia was one prominent target: in early
2002, pro-Israel students and auditors participated aggressively in his class
titled "Palestinian and Israeli Politics and Societies," then filed complaints,
the most serious of which was that he had responded angrily to a student's
question about whether the Israeli military sometimes gave warnings "before
bombing certain areas and buildings so that people could get out and no one
would get hurt." The complaint averred that Massad shouted, "If you're going
to deny the atrocities being committed against Palestinians, then you can get
out of my classroom!" Massad denied the accusation, and his graduate assistants backed him up.[30] As the battle flamed on, an advocacy group called the
David Project produced and distributed a film, *Columbia Unbecoming*, that
emotionally publicized pro-Israel students' complaints against Massad and
other professors in the school's Middle East and Arab Languages and Cultures Department.[31]

The university assembled a grievance committee, which reported in 2005
that two witnesses corroborated "the main elements" of the complaint against
Massad; one was "a registered student; another was a visitor for the day." The
student asserted that Massad had "leaned over the lectern, raised his voice
considerably, and said 'I will not stand by and let you sit in my classroom and

deny atrocities.'" But the committee found "little doubt" of Massad's "dedication to, and respectful attitude towards, his students whatever their confessional or ethnic background or their political outlook" and of his continuing "friendly relations with students who questioned him regularly and critically in class."[32]

Columbia's grievance committee concluded with the understatement that after 9/11, "the involvement of outside organizations in the surveillance of professors teaching the Middle East increased." People on Campus Watch's list of suspect professors received hate mail. In the spring of 2004, someone began filming in a Columbia class without permission, "and left after being challenged. The inhibiting effect upon classroom debate was noted by a number of students." Teaching assistants "reported that they no longer felt able to express their views freely for fear of retribution from outside bodies." Students in Massad's class, meanwhile, "found no signs" of bias but instead "a professor who was constantly harassed by outside agitators"—unregistered auditors who frequently interrupted and made hostile asides.[33]

Massad's upcoming tenure vote was delayed; he finally did receive tenure in 2009, two years after publishing a much-acclaimed book, *Desiring Arabs*, a literary history of Arab sexual attitudes and, according to one reviewer, a brilliant corroboration of his mentor Edward Said's thesis "that orientalist writing [that is, Western writing about the Middle East] was racist and dehumanizing."[34] But the attacks continued. Fourteen of Massad's colleagues protested the tenure decision and asked the university to reconsider.[35]

Massad was not driven out of Columbia, but a campaign against DePaul University professor Norman Finkelstein was more successful. Finkelstein was an outspoken critic of Israel and of what he called "the Holocaust industry": he argued that Israel uses the Nazi genocide against Jews to justify its current policy toward Palestinians and its poor human rights record. In 2007, when Finkelstein was up for tenure, Harvard law professor Alan Dershowitz wrote an attack letter to DePaul faculty and ultimately pressured the university into rejecting his tenure bid, despite favorable votes from his department (political science) and the College of Arts and Sciences personnel committee. The *New York Times* described it as "a full-court press" in which Dershowitz "lobbied professors, alumni and the administration of DePaul"; many faculty there and elsewhere "decried what they called Mr. Dershowitz's heavy-handed tactics." Finkelstein called the decision "transparently political" and "an egregious violation" of academic freedom, given that he clearly met the university's standards for publishing and teaching.[36]

Looking back at the repressive atmosphere for free speech on campuses after 9/11, one might conclude that it dissipated fairly soon, that ACTA did not succeed in blacklisting the professors whose comments on the World Trade Center attack it felt insufficiently patriotic, and that Middle East studies survived; hence, academic freedom is alive and well. Indeed, this was the AAUP's conclusion after surveying the teach-ins and the assaults on Middle East scholars.[37] It is true that the cries of a new McCarthyism after 9/11 were exaggerated and that nothing resembling the pervasive, systemic repression of the 1950s ensued. Still, the chill imposed by the "war on terror" and the marginalization of views denigrated as pro-terrorist has narrowed the scope of acceptable debate in the United States over Islamic jihadism, its underlying roots, and options for addressing it.

Academic Freedom in Judicial Purgatory

Well before 9/11, the Supreme Court was narrowing First Amendment protection for public employees. Its 1968 decision in *Pickering v. Board of Education* had ruled that firing a teacher because he criticized school board policies in a letter to the local newspaper violated his First Amendment rights. The Court created a balancing test that weighed the interest of public employees, "as citizen[s], in commenting upon matters of public concern" against "the interest of the State, as an employer, in promoting the efficiency of the public services it performs through its employees."[38] But a different lineup of justices in 1983 limited public workers' right to be free of retaliation for exercising free speech in a case involving an assistant district attorney who had circulated a questionnaire around the office to address concerns about the boss's policies. The Court majority said the complaint was merely a personnel issue, not speech by a citizen on a matter of "public concern," and therefore not protected by the First Amendment.[39] The Court's desire to close judicial doors to at least some of the vast range of public employees' disputes with their bosses was understandable, but from this tricky distinction between private and public concern some courts reached the questionable conclusion that anything said by government workers in the course of performing their jobs was not speech by a citizen on a matter of public concern and therefore lacked First Amendment protection.

This notion had devastating implications for academia, where the job of professors—scholarship and teaching—inherently embraces matters of public concern. The Fourth Circuit Court of Appeals was aggressive in applying it against high school teachers (in the *Boring* case), then against college professors (in *Urofsky*). (Both cases are described in chapter 14.)

The federal judiciary did not uniformly fall into line with the Fourth Circuit's extreme interpretation of the "public concern" doctrine. In 2001, a year after the ruling in *Urofsky*, a different set of appellate judges (on the Sixth Circuit) rejected as "fantastic" the idea that professors have no First Amendment rights in the classroom or that government can censor their on-the-job expression.[40] Yet other courts, content to rid their dockets of academic-freedom claims that seemed to involve administrative rather than intellectual disputes, followed the lead of the Fourth Circuit and dismissed suits by individual professors. One of them said, "The only way to preserve academic freedom is to keep claims of academic error out of the legal maw."[41] It was a sentiment far distant from the Supreme Court's solicitude for dissident professors in the 1960s.

In 2006, the Supreme Court decided a public-employee free-speech case that dramatically heightened fears for First Amendment academic freedom. *Garcetti v. Ceballos* involved a prosecutor who was punished after he reported that a deputy sheriff had made false statements in an affidavit in support of a search warrant. Writing for the majority, Justice Anthony Kennedy reasoned that the prosecutor had merely made a complaint about an internal work-related matter; hence, he had no First Amendment protection from the retaliation he experienced after blowing the whistle on the fraud. "When public employees make statements pursuant to their official duties," Kennedy said, "the employees are not speaking as citizens for First Amendment purposes, and the Constitution does not insulate their communications from employer discipline."[42]

Justice David Souter was alarmed by the breadth of Kennedy's language: the Court's creation of an "ostensible domain beyond the pale of the First Amendment is spacious enough to include even the teaching of a public university professor," he wrote. Souter hoped that the majority did not "mean to imperil First Amendment protection of academic freedom in public colleges and universities, whose teachers necessarily speak and write 'pursuant to . . . official duties.'" He quoted *Keyishian* and *Sweezy* on the "transcendent value" of academic freedom. In response, Kennedy inserted a caveat into his majority opinion:

> Justice Souter suggests today's decision may have important ramifications for academic freedom, at least as a constitutional value. There is some argument that expression related to academic scholarship or classroom instruction implicates additional constitutional interests that are not fully accounted for by this Court's customary employee-speech jurisprudence. We need not, and for that reason do not, decide whether the analysis we conduct today would apply in the same manner to a case involving speech related to scholarship or teaching.[43]

The Court's once full-bodied appreciation of academic freedom as essential to the educational enterprise and to democracy was now reduced to a querulous and ambiguous aside.

The AAUP responded with trepidation to *Garcetti*, which threw into question what had previously been well established, and commentators attempted to lay out the constitutional interests that make academic expression a poor fit for the Court's cramped public-employee free-speech rules. Lower courts, meanwhile, were at sea. Some ignored Kennedy's caveat and simply applied a rigid rule that job-related expression has no First Amendment protection.

Suits involving disputes over university governance were particularly hard hit. When an engineering professor at the Irvine campus of the University of California claimed that administrators denied him a salary increase in retaliation for his criticism of hiring and promotion decisions, a federal judge dismissed his case, following *Garcetti*. Professor Juan Hong's criticisms involved "internal hiring, promotion and staffing practices," which the judge thought were "of very little concern to the public"; more broadly and ominously, he ruled that because all of Hong's criticisms "were made in the course of doing his job as a UCI professor, the speech is not protected from discipline."[44] (Ironically, the fact that faculty participation in governance was an intrinsic part of academic life at Irvine undermined Hong's legal claim, for his criticisms could be considered part of his job duties.)

The dispute in Hong's case seemed trivial to the judge, but scholarship and teaching are also, of course, part of "doing [one's] job" as a professor; and the blithe assertion that anything job related is off-limits for First Amendment protection understandably alarmed the AAUP, which organized an *amicus* brief as the case went up on appeal. It argued that Hong's concerns about candidate qualifications and his protest against excessive reliance on part-time teachers were both related to the quality of the academic experience, which the Supreme Court in *Garcetti* recognized might call for constitutional protection. But the Ninth Circuit Court of Appeals avoided the First Amendment issue by ruling that the university officials involved were all legally immune from suit.[45]

The next post-*Garcetti* case to cause alarm was arguably closer to the core of academic freedom, but still it involved bureaucratic issues. The University of Wisconsin had reduced the pay of a professor and returned his National Science Foundation funding after disputes over administration of the grant proved unresolvable. Again, a trial court found this was merely an internal matter—not of public concern—and the Court of Appeals for the Seventh Circuit agreed, citing *Garcetti*. A similar case from the Third Circuit had the same result: the plaintiff professor had changed the grades of student athletes, allegedly without authorization, and was suspended. He filed suit, claiming that the suspension was really in retaliation for his objection to the selection of the university president and other internal disagreements. The court saw no First Amendment violation even assuming these were the reasons for the professor's treatment, but it took note of the caveat in *Garcetti* that "expression related to academic scholarship or classroom instruction" may "implicate additional constitutional interests." The plaintiff's speech was not "related to scholarship or teaching," and thus, according to the court, his punishment did not "imperil First Amendment protection of academic freedom in public colleges and universities."[46]

None of these cases had strongly sympathetic facts or involved the core of academic freedom—research, writing, and teaching. Nor did the professors' expression address social or political matters that were clearly of public concern. When such a case did come along, a federal judge pushed the distinction between on-the-job speech and First Amendment–protected speech to an absurd point, but the appeals court reversed and, in the process, made the first judicial use of the academic-freedom caveat in *Garcetti*. The case involved a popular teacher of criminology and devout Christian whose off-campus writings on civil rights, campus culture, sex, feminism, abortion, homosexuality, and religion had raised hackles among some of his University of North Carolina colleagues. Michael Adams was denied a promotion because, according to his department chair, his "scholarly research productivity" was weak—a credible judgment, given that he had spent most of his energies since his religious conversion on newspaper columns and non-scholarly advocacy. But the district court did not deny his claim on this basis: instead, relying on *Garcetti*, it accepted the university's argument that Adams's constitutionally protected extramural speech—his news articles and broadsides—somehow lost their constitutional protection and became job related once Adams had listed them in his application for promotion. This was a surreal stretch: protected speech was converted into unprotected speech on the basis of its use after the fact in a job application. The AAUP weighed in with an *amicus* brief in Adams's Fourth Circuit appeal.

This was not a hospitable forum for academic-freedom claims by professors: it was the same federal circuit that decided the *Urofsky* case, and the judges were disinclined to wade into a dispute over Adams's academic qualifications. Quoting one in the Supreme Court's line of cases viewing academic freedom as a matter of deference to university administrations, they said that a federal court is not "suited to evaluate the substance of the multitude of academic decisions that are made daily by faculty members of public educational institutions."[47] But this set of Fourth Circuit judges did correct the lower court on the meaning of *Garcetti*. Its error, the appellate judges said, was thinking that Adams's speech, which the university acknowledged had First Amendment protection initially, "was converted into unprotected speech based on factors that came into play only after the protected speech was made." Furthermore, *Garcetti* did not apply where writings are "intended for and directed at a national or international audience on issues of public importance." Most important, the court rejected the university's argument that "because Adams was employed as an associate professor, and his position required him to engage in scholarship, research, and service to the community," his articles lacked First Amendment protection within the meaning of *Garcetti*. On the contrary, they were "not tied to any more specific or direct employee duty than the general concept that professors will engage in writing, public appearances, and service within their respective fields," and this "thin thread" did not make them part of his "official duties, as intended by *Garcetti*."[48] This was, at least implicitly, a rejection of the extreme position taken by six other judges on the Fourth Circuit in *Urofsky*, that professors have no First Amendment academic-freedom protection for their writing and teaching.[49]

How, if at all, the Supreme Court will ultimately resolve the question of First Amendment protection for individual teachers' academic freedom remains unknown at this writing. Probably, the issue will always be in flux, as the political context changes and as the Court's makeup changes. Academic freedom as a matter of institutional autonomy seems secure; judges like it because in conflicts between university administrations and wayward professors, they can simply defer, with the institution's First Amendment rights as justification. Nevertheless, it is a distortion of the spirit and purpose of *Keyishian*, which protected individuals, not their university employers, from political repression by the state.

Loyalty Oaths after 9/11

Negative or disclaimer oaths were mostly gone in America by the 21st century, but affirmative oaths of loyalty remain pervasive. Despite the Supreme Court's assurances in the Massachusetts oath case, *Cole v. Richardson*, that such oaths are just ceremonial and not to be taken literally,[50] there are people who do take them literally and are accordingly confused or who have conscientious objections and cannot sign.

American Studies professor Wendy Gonaver was not told about the required loyalty oath when she accepted a job at California State University's campus at Fullerton in 2007. Like Newton Garver at SUNY-Buffalo half a century before, Gonaver was a Quaker and pacifist. California's oath is mandatory for all state, city, and county workers, except non-citizens and those "as may be by law exempted." They must not only swear to do their jobs faithfully and to "support and defend" the state and federal constitutions "against all enemies, foreign and domestic," but they must agree that they "take this obligation freely, without any mental reservation."[51]

Anyone who thinks before signing the California oath must wonder at its meaning. The U.S. Constitution is a complex, detailed document, and the California Constitution contains 35 articles and hundreds of sections. As the journalist Jessica Mitford wrote several decades earlier in explaining her own refusal to sign the oath, the annotated California Constitution "runs to three hefty volumes and covers all manner of subjects. Do I uphold and defend, for example, Article 4, Section 25¾, limiting championship boxing and wrestling matches to 15 rounds?"[52]

For Gonaver, the sticking point was the part about defense against "all enemies." She explained her objection to college officials and asked to append a statement that she could not agree to bear arms. Other branches of the state's public university system had made this accommodation; indeed, as one journalist reported, the University of California (as opposed to the state colleges) advised its employees "on how they can register their objections yet still sign the pledge."[53] But Cal State–Fullerton would not budge, and Gonaver lost her job for the 2007–8 academic year.

In the spring of 2008, the *Los Angeles Times* picked up Gonaver's story. Another conscientious objector, at Cal State–Hayward, had been in the news a few months before. Responding to the ensuing publicity, as well as demands from Gonaver's pro bono lawyers, the college now changed its mind. For unlike the communists and suspected communists who had been widely despised during the heyday of loyalty oaths in the 1950s, Gonaver was a sympathetic victim. About three weeks after the publicity began, Fullerton allowed Gonaver to append her statement. She added a general objection to the compelled signing of the oath, as a violation of her right to free speech.[54]

Negative oaths have also returned to the political scene. While Congress's main response to 9/11 was to expand the government's search and surveillance powers through the hastily enacted USA PATRIOT Act, in one state, the terrorist attacks inspired a new variant on the old disclaimer oath. A 2006 Ohio law requires every new public employee, along with certain contractors and licensees, to answer six questions concerning material support to any organization listed by the State Department as terrorist or compensation to any person that the employee, contractor, or licensee "knew to be engaged in planning, assisting, or carrying out an act of terrorism."[55] On the surface, the questions may have seemed innocuous: material support for terrorism was already a crime. But apart from its inefficacy in fighting the terrorist threat, Ohio's required declaration had all the flaws of the Cold War–era loyalty oaths. That is, as William O. Douglas pointed out long ago, the declaration wrongly places "the burden of proving loyalty on the citizen."[56] People who, for whatever reason, refuse to swear their innocence are presumed guilty. Failure to answer any of six questions posed by Ohio about organizational affiliations, material support, or employment of a person planning a terrorist act is a disqualification from public employment, from a contract with a public agency, and from a license to practice many trades. And like the loyalty oaths of the 1950s, Ohio's requirement is broad and vague. It takes its definition of "material support" from federal law, which does not require specific intent to assist an organization's violent aims.

The state of Ohio and four of its major public university campuses had no record—at least, nothing made available to this author under the state public-records law—of any teacher or professor who resisted the anti-terrorist oath.[57] The only legal challenge was filed by an attorney who contracted with the state to represent indigent defendants. He won, but on a technical ground that did not get at the heart of the problem: the Ohio Supreme Court ruled that the law only applied to those who had contracts with the government worth more than $100,000 a year.[58] This author's public-records request revealed that two other people—a heating contractor and a water-supply operator—had refused on principle to sign the oath. One of them had pasted onto the form a statement: "This is in conflict with my USA, Constitutional rights to privacy, free association, free speech and self-incrimination. Therefore, I have chosen not to provide any responses to this waste of paper and government employee time." His license was eventually renewed despite his continuing refusal to sign.[59]

A test-oath relic of the 1950s also turned up in Georgia in 2008. The performance artist Karen Finley, after accepting a visiting professorship at Georgia State College, was confronted with a questionnaire requiring her to state whether she was or within the past 10 years had been "a member of any organization that to your knowledge at the time of membership advocates, or has as one of its objectives, the overthrow of the government of the United States or of the government of the State of Georgia by force or violence." The question was unconstitutional under the Supreme Court decisions in *Elfbrandt* and *Keyishian*, and it had been reworded twice in response to declarations of its unconstitutionality (the first time, in a case brought by the AAUP); but Georgia's legislature persisted in reenacting it with different wording, and Finley could find no one on the Georgia State faculty interested in joining her in a lawsuit to strike it down yet again. As the chair of the English Department explained, "Given the economy, the last thing people want to do is get into a fight with the state." Finley refused to answer the question, and the job offer was revoked.[60]

Conclusion

Political Repression and the American Left

The story of academic freedom in the United States is intimately tied to the story of the American left. It was as a result of the heresy hunts of the 1950s that the Supreme Court enshrined academic freedom as a special concern of the First Amendment. And although that era of repression has been largely repudiated, its effects persist. We remain a society in which the range of acceptable views is remarkably narrow and where emotional appeals often overwhelm coherent discussion of political issues.

The problem, of course, is not entirely due to political repression. Despite energy and idealism, the American left in the 20th century made its share of grievous errors. By "the left," I include a broad range of beliefs, from social reform to revolution. Leftists differ on many questions—indeed, doctrinal hairsplitting has been an occupational disease on this end of the political spectrum—but they share a vision of radical social change. "The left" does not necessarily denote a belief in socialism, but it is, unlike liberalism, fundamentally at odds with existing social and economic arrangements. (Here, I mean liberalism in its classic form, as distinct from the "neo-liberalism" that opposes social welfare and government regulation.)

Traditional American liberalism seeks essentially to preserve the prevailing system but to improve it by expanding civil rights, civil liberties, and economic justice. In the early 20th century, as one scholar puts it, liberalism "was devoted to saving capitalism by regulating it,"[1] and this aspect of old-fashioned liberalism has not changed significantly since. The distinction between leftism and liberalism can be hazy at the margins, but a critique more comprehensive than that offered by liberalism has been essential in the past to pushing America into correcting deeply entrenched systems of prejudice and exploitation. It was the left—indeed, for a period in the '30s, it was primarily the Communist Party—that pioneered support for racial equality among whites in America and pushed for economic reforms that made capitalism more just and stable.

People are frequently drawn leftward because of humanitarian and egalitarian concerns. They may start out as liberals, but resistance from those in power, failures of capitalism, and continuing suffering and injustice may turn them into radicals or revolutionaries. This was one reason for the rise of socialism in the late 19th century. Before the Bolshevik Revolution, socialism was a legitimate and popular topic of discussion in America, even though it never achieved the clout and status of European socialist movements; and afterward, the Communist Party, with its network of affiliated or front organizations, attracted brilliant scholars, writers, and artists, as well as tens of thousands of ordinary idealistic Americans.

The failures of the Party—in particular, its refusal to question even the most horrific aspects of Stalinism—greatly contributed to the decline of the American left and its contemporary near absence from mainstream political debate. Stalin's purge trials, the Nazi-Soviet Pact of 1939, and the many shifts in the Party line took their toll even before the Cold War, with its spy scandals and anti-communist panic. Nikita Khrushchev's 1956 speech at the 20th Communist Party Congress, describing Stalin's crimes, and the USSR's invasion of Hungary the same year were the final revelations of totalitarian reality for nearly all the American leftists who still cherished fantasies of the communist utopia.

The Party's secrecy also contributed to the debacle. It may have been an understandable response to the severe repression that began even before the post-World War I Palmer raids, and it also fed a certain romantic vision of revolutionary change, but it was peculiarly unsuited to American democracy. One disastrous consequence—that some professors in New York City perjured themselves before the Rapp-Coudert Committee in 1941 when they denied Party membership—disillusioned liberal defenders of civil liberties and bolstered reactionaries who used the charge of communist deception to stigmatize all manner of progressive movements because the CP also supported them. At the same time, doctrinal rigidity and the shifting Party line drove people out of the CP as rapidly as idealism and anger at injustice drew them in.

Harvey Klehr, an unremitting critic of the Old Left in America and the scholars who today, he feels, unjustifiably try to ennoble it, nevertheless acknowledges that communists "fought many good fights and exhibited large doses of courage and idealism." This is precisely why their lives had "a tragic dimension": the CP-USA "used and misused the idealism of a generation."[2] On this, left-leaning historian Maurice Isserman agrees with Klehr: the CP's intolerance of dissent in its ranks and its obeisance to Stalin's demands "may well have stunted the development of a viable socialist tradition in America."[3]

By the 1960s, when a new generation of radicals emerged, indignant at the contradictions between the celebrations of American political virtue that permeated their public schools and communities and the awful realities of racial apartheid in the American South and escalating war in Vietnam, there was no credible surviving left-wing tradition to guide them. Isserman writes movingly of the resulting disaster: "The Communist Party stood in hostile isolation from most of the new currents that grew up on the left in the United States during the 1960s. This 'New Left,' centered in the Students for a Democratic Society (SDS), began its political history by repudiating the traditions and outlook of the Communist movement." But because there was no surviving left tradition, the young radicals' "search for a comprehensive political strategy" led many of them to repeat the CP's mistakes:

> By the end of the decade, competing factions at SDS conventions were chanting the name of one or another Third World revolutionary leader to drown out their opponents—an exercise in "proletarian internationalism" that left observers from the Old Left shaking their heads in dismay. . . . It had taken the Communists a quarter of a century to learn that the American left could not be built on foreign models; that civil liberties and democratic institutions should be at the center of any vision of an American socialist future. . . . When these lessons were finally learned, they came too late to be of any use to the generation that had learned them, and too early to be of use to the generation that followed.[4]

But the collapse of the Old Left and then, less than two decades later, of the New Left as well were only partly due to their internal weaknesses. Waves of political repression, in particular the phenomenon still commonly called McCarthyism, did the major damage. The chill is difficult to measure, but personal experiences yield numerous examples. One of the three University of Washington professors placed on probation as a result of the 1948 Canwell Committee hearings put the matter succinctly: "If I was going to make a living here in the U.S., I had to shut up—that was part of the job." Another of the three recounted that "throughout the remainder of his teaching years he would not sign anything even remotely political."[5]

As Ellen Schrecker writes, the 1950s Red Scare not only helped "destroy whatever influence communism had within American society, but it silenced the rest of the left as well. For over a decade, at the height of the Cold War, meaningful dissent had been all but eliminated." One consequence was that "the fear of a replay of Joe McCarthy's attacks on the State Department probably helped pull American policymakers into the Vietnam quagmire."[6] And repressive, often illegal techniques deployed by the government against the New Left undermined dissent from other domestic and foreign policies.[7]

The outcome of this history is a continuing vacuum in American political discourse. Socialism remains a curse word in our vocabulary, and in the early 21st century, the United States still lacked a consensus on progressive values that other industrialized democracies took for granted—the need for universal health care perhaps being the most glaring example. The historian Robert Goldstein summarizes the anomaly: despite the wealth of the United States, it has "among the least adequate" government social programs of all industrialized democracies and "the most unequal distribution of wealth." Political repression alone is not responsible, Goldstein says, but "it has significantly contributed to the shaping of a political system that is exceptionally narrow in the kinds of ideas that can be 'safely' propounded and considered."[8]

The narrowness of vision in American politics, and the substitution of platitudinous slogans for informed thought, was well illustrated after 9/11, when the perceived need to circle the ideological wagons resulted in accusations of un-Americanism against anyone who offered contextualized explorations of the causes of jihadism and ferocious retaliation against those who, like Professor Ward Churchill of Colorado, engaged in angry and provocative rhetoric that challenged the national consensus.[9]

How to revitalize the left critique of our basic social and economic arrangements, how to expand political discourse and thereby push our society toward needed reforms, are questions well beyond the scope of this book. But the story told here does suggest the lasting impact that anti-subversive purges have had on education, academic freedom, and a viable tradition of progressive social change.

The Universities and the Liberals

Three notable characteristics of the assault on academic freedom in the 1950s were guilt by association, the response of the educational establishment, and the part played by liberals. The first, guilt by association, was the pivot around which the Cold War witch hunt turned. Membership in or—in the vague words of President Truman's 1947 loyalty order—"sympathetic association" with the Communist Party or indeed any organization on the Attorney General's List was a *prima facie* disqualification from employment. But whatever a person's reasons may have been for joining or "sympathetically associating" with an organization that was thought to have revolutionary beliefs—and they ranged from the intellectual's fascination with Marxism to the unemployed worker's desire for a job—the great majority of American communists and fellow travelers, whatever their illusions and blind spots, were not trying to overthrow the government; they were working to stop fascism, to ameliorate poverty, to get rid of racist textbooks, and to promote scores of other worthy causes. The Supreme Court ultimately condemned guilt by association as an unacceptable departure from the traditional rule of personal guilt, but massive damage ensued before it did so.

There is relevance here for the 21st-century war on terrorism. The Supreme Court in 2010 upheld a law criminalizing sympathetic association, in the form of "material support," for even the peaceful work of groups condemned by the U.S. government as terrorist.[10] The ban was only questionably related to national security and arguably was counterproductive because it isolated liberation movements and discouraged their use of peaceful routes to change. But the Court majority was not about to question the judgment of Congress and the State Department. It was an unfortunate retreat from rulings that, once the Red hunt receded, rejected guilt by association.

A second aspect of the 1950s purge—the acquiescence of educational institutions—remains equally pertinent. With very few exceptions, university administrators either eagerly embraced guilt by association or were pressured into embracing it. As we know from the few examples of defiance— Robert Maynard Hutchins at Chicago, Harold Taylor at Sarah Lawrence (see chapter 8)—there is at least a strong possibility that if the higher-education establishment had put up unified resistance, much of the damage to individuals, to free inquiry on campus, and to political dissent by intellectual leaders in the wider society could have been avoided.

Since the 1970s, university administrations have been apologizing for the injuries to teachers, to education, and to academic freedom caused by the anti-communist purges. In New York, as we have seen, the Board of Education and, more belatedly, the Board of Higher Education gave apologies and compensation to fired teachers; memorial exhibits were mounted, and awards were presented to those who had resisted or been victimized.[11] Nationwide, universities were similarly acknowledging their failure of nerve and promising it would not happen again. In 1990, the University of Michigan established an Academic Freedom Lecture Fund to honor three professors whom it had punished for refusing to cooperate with HUAC, and in 1994, the University of Washington, site of the first explicit firing of professors during the Cold War simply for being communists, issued a public apology.[12]

In University of Washington president William Gerberding's speech on that occasion, he acknowledged that it had been wrong to fire Professors Ralph Gundlach, Joseph Butterworth, and Herbert Phillips in 1949.[13] It was "a dark day in our history," he said, "and we must make sure that it doesn't happen again." Then he had a moment of self-reflection:

> I don't wish to be judgmental or pious about this. I don't know what I would have done had I been there. . . . Presidents are under some considerable pressure. But whatever the *ex post facto* justifications or explanations may be, the basic, simple truth is that what happened to those professors . . . was an outrage. It was a disgrace. It was, in the dictionary sense, not in the perverted sense, un-American.[14]

Perhaps universities remembered some of this history when, in the panicky post-9/11 climate, they mostly resisted pressures against scholars who departed from the national consensus or who questioned simplistic but widely accepted views about Islam, the Israel-Palestine conflict, and the Arab world. The AAUP has also been far more vigorous in recent academic-freedom battles than it was in the 1950s. Regardless of one's views on multiculturalism, Islam, or Israel and Palestine, it strengthens democracy to hear information and arguments on all sides. Judges as different as William O. Douglas and Felix Frankfurter pointed out more than half a century ago that democracy depends on free inquiry and critical thinking; therefore, it depends on academic freedom.

Related to the acquiescence of universities is another pertinent aspect of the Cold War purge: the collaboration of moderates and liberals. Anti-communist liberals were understandably appalled at Soviet totalitarianism and its American apologists, but in their rush to distance themselves they greatly augmented the breadth and power of the purge. Indeed, their active participation was likely the pivotal factor in making the repression of the 1950s as pervasive, long, and successful as it was.

From Ordway Tead to Harry Gideonse, anti-communists who claimed liberal credentials from time to time bemoaned the recklessness and anti-intellectualism of demagogues like Joseph McCarthy and deceived themselves into thinking that a gentler, fairer witch hunt was possible. They were wrong. Saul Moskoff, fair and decent person though he thought he was, caused serious human and moral harm and robbed the New York City school system of some of its best and most dedicated teachers. The Board of Higher Education, with its arbitrary and hasty use of section 903 of the city charter to derail the careers of talented, admired professors, was little better. Tead, who in 1938 had so forthrightly defended free speech and diversity on campus, by 1964 was retrospectively justifying the BHE's cooperation with the Rapp-Coudert investigation of 1940–42 by attributing to it "the salutary effect of getting rid of certain people who were using their instructional posts for indoctrination, . . . whose instruction was not animated by what we may be allowed to call truth-seeking, but was animated by a desire to convert to a communist point of view"[15]—allegations that were never proven, that were belied by evidence from students, and that in any case singled out "a communist point of view" (as opposed to a capitalist point of view, a libertarian point of view, or for that matter a vegetarian point of view) as uniquely beyond the pale of acceptable teaching or scholarship.

Attorney Victor Rabinowitz summed up the difference between the New York City purges and the anti-communist antics of such national figures as Roy Cohn, Joseph McCarthy's assistant, or Richard Arens, staff director of HUAC in the early '60s. Cohn and Arens, he said, "came out ready to kill. Moskoff was not a killer. The brutality of the congressional committee approach was not ever present here." But "it made no difference. After a very short period everybody was aware that the interview with Moskoff would turn out to be exactly the same thing."[16]

Academic Freedom as Educational Policy

We come to the question of academic freedom as an essential component of American liberty. Even though most professors are neither activists nor political radicals, they are the "priests of our democracy" because, in Felix Frankfurter's words, they nurture the "habits of open-mindedness and critical inquiry which alone make for responsible citizens."[17]

There is a big distinction between academic freedom as a matter of educational policy and of First Amendment right. The two are often confused because some of the same questions about this complex and murky subject arise in both the policy and legal arenas. What should academic freedom really mean? What should be its limits? What is needed, given the realities of the 21st-century university, to protect it?

The standard definition of academic freedom as a matter of educational policy was articulated by the AAUP in 1915 and refined but not basically changed in the near century since. It has three components: freedom in classroom teaching, freedom in research and writing, and freedom in extramural expression unrelated to teaching and scholarship. The AAUP rightly says that these principles should apply to both public and private institutions. In modified form, they should apply to college students as well. In still more modified form, they should apply to education below college level.[18]

At universities, moreover, the AAUP contends that to secure academic freedom, professors must participate in governance: they must make the critical decisions about course offerings, new hires, promotions, and many other administrative matters. As legal scholar Judith Areen puts it, academic freedom "is not only about faculty research and teaching; it is also about the freedom of faculties to govern their institutions in a way that accords with academic values whether they are approving the curriculum, hiring faculty, or establishing graduation requirements for students."[19]

All of these propositions are controversial, except perhaps for teaching and scholarship as the core of academic freedom. Many commentators have questioned whether extramural speech unrelated to teaching or scholarship should be part of academic freedom; why cannot teachers simply have the same free-speech rights as other citizens, subject to the same sorts of reasonable limitations that their jobs may demand? As for governance, some would say it is an ideal that depends on an unrealistically utopian view of today's university as a community of scholars deciding how the institution will be run and who will be admitted to membership. The contemporary university is managed by administrators and headed by chief executives whose major qualification, in many cases, is their talent for fund-raising; it is increasingly beholden to corporate and foundation funders; and it increasingly employs part-time and adjunct instructors who have no chance for tenure and no role in governance.

Since the 1980s, American universities have been steadily replacing tenured and tenure-track faculty with adjuncts and part-timers. In 1975, 57% of university teachers were tenured or on a tenure track; by 2007, that number was down to 31%.[20] The majority of undergraduate classes are now taught by part-time or non-tenure-track employees—the exploited "contingent workers" whom the journalist Jennifer Washburn aptly calls "the hamburger flippers of the academic world." By 2010, according to former AAUP president Cary Nelson, "of the roughly 1.4 million faculty members teaching in the United States nearly 1 million [were] contingent."[21] In these circumstances, faculty governance leaves out most of the people who are actually teaching classes, and despite its importance as an ideal, it risks exacerbating the divide between a privileged academic élite and the rest of the college community.

The contemporary university also increasingly relies on corporate funds and is correspondingly subject to corporate demands—to keep research results secret, to value profit-making enterprises over humanistic learning, and to tailor scholarship to the funders' ideological goals.[22] As Washburn observes, corporatization is closely related to the transformation of teaching ranks from tenured to contingent: universities lure superstar professors who can bring in grant money with promises of light teaching loads.[23] Such institutions are fully as likely to rein in faculty members who do not conform as were state legislatures or politically driven investigating committees in the days of Frederic Coudert or George Timone.

A model of academic freedom centering around faculty governance presents a further dilemma: its resemblance to the vision of institutional autonomy that Justice Lewis Powell articulated in *Bakke*, the Supreme Court's 1978 affirmative action case, and that lower courts have since seized upon to dismiss individual claims of professors against their university employers. Locating academic freedom in the ideal of a collective community of scholars leaves out the maverick professor who may be a brilliant teacher and expert in her field but who does not satisfy the standards of what may be a more hidebound, or frankly jealous, committee of her peers. What if the community of scholars is sexist or racist? What about the individual scholar's freedom to break new ground or to teach Marxist texts in the face of a virulently anti-communist majority on the faculty senate—or, for that matter, to teach conservative texts when faculty committees are dominated by left-wingers? What of the Middle East scholar who is fired or denied tenure by faculty decision-makers who have collaborated or acquiesced in pressures from lobbying groups or legislative committees? As a matter of educational policy, academic freedom should provide protection. Professor Judith Butler argues that "new challenges to academic freedom cannot be easily referred to a community of like-minded professionals, not only because such communities are often defined by disagreement about which academic norms ought to be brought to bear on a given case" but also because the academic norms are themselves in flux and subject to political pressures.[24]

Academic Freedom as First Amendment Right

How do these policy questions about faculty governance, institutional autonomy, and individual rights translate to the separate sphere of constitutional law—academic freedom as a First Amendment right? The Supreme Court's seminal decisions in *Sweezy* and *Keyishian* recognized academic freedom as essentially adhering to individuals. The Court reiterated that perception, as the political scientist Philippa Strum points out, in its 1972 decision rejecting a university's claim that its denial of recognition to a campus chapter of Students for a Democratic Society was justified because of "the asserted freedom of the institution to decide that SDS was antithetical to its aims and therefore had no place on a college campus."[25] Even in its 2006 opinion in *Garcetti v. Ceballos*, which greatly restricted public employees' First Amendment right to on-the-job speech, the Court majority assumed that if academic freedom created an exception to this general restriction, the right would adhere to the "scholarship or teaching" of individual professors.[26]

The status of academic freedom as, in the words of *Keyishian*, "a special concern of the First Amendment" has been under attack for decades. Law professor J. Peter Byrne argued in an influential 1989 article that, at least as to individual professors, academic freedom should not be seen as a part of the First Amendment: courts are not competent, he said, to umpire disputes over university decision-making. The only First Amendment concern (with some minor exceptions), said Byrne, should be protecting the university from interference by the state. Yale Law School dean Robert Post similarly has concluded that since the constitutional law of academic freedom emerged in response to political attacks from outside the universities in the 1950s, its only real function is to keep government, including courts, out of academic decisions.[27]

But, like the vision of academic freedom as primarily a matter of collective governance, not an individual's right to be different, this model of First Amendment academic freedom gives little or no protection to the idiosyncratic professor—he who does not "do lunch well" in the view of the administration or his colleagues but who might just be the most brilliant scholar around. Former AAUP general counsel and Texas law professor David Rabban writes that "the broad institutional immunity advocated by Byrne would heighten the danger that administrators and trustees might violate the academic freedom of professors." That is, although "it makes sense to derive institutional academic freedom from the same value of independent critical inquiry that underlies individual academic freedom, it perverts the First Amendment and the concept of a bill of rights to subordinate individual academic freedom to broad institutional autonomy from judicial review."[28] It is individual scholars, after all—not administrators or faculty committees—who are the source of the inquiry, research, and teaching needed for a dynamic culture and body politic.

A practical anomaly may partly explain proposals to eliminate the individual teacher from First Amendment academic freedom. Because the First Amendment applies only to "state action"—that is, generally speaking, to the actions of government officers, including public school and university administrators—it protects teachers at public institutions from retaliation by their employers but only protects teachers at private institutions from actions by outside government forces—legislative investigating committees, for example. Recognizing academic freedom as a matter of First Amendment right for teachers thus favors those at public institutions over those at private ones. The imbalance may seem unfair, especially in an era when public universities increasingly resemble private ones in their reliance on a mix of corporate, foundation, and government funding. But it is an imbalance at the core of our constitutional system, which leaves a large measure of autonomy to private entities. It is not, in any event, a reason to abandon First Amendment protection for those who labor at public universities and schools.

My argument here relies not only on the need for courts to enforce the Bill of Rights against sometimes repressive government agencies, including school boards, administrators, and boards of trustees, but also on the role that courts in America play beyond adjudicating specific legal disputes. Some of our greatest literature and most profound moral imperatives are found in Supreme Court opinions—from the condemnation of "separate but equal" in *Brown v. Board of Education* to William Brennan's warning in *Keyishian* that loyalty programs cast a "pall of orthodoxy over the classroom." A court decision technically applies only to the participants in the case, but its rhetoric and arguments resonate. The Supreme Court's language in *Sweezy* about the importance of academic freedom—"teachers and students must always remain free to inquire, to study and to evaluate; otherwise our civilization will stagnate and die"—suggests a principle equally applicable to private and public schools. Indeed, as the role played by Justices Black and Douglas on the Vinson Court so vividly showed, prophetic dissents are also part of our tradition and literature.

How, then, should academic freedom apply—how broad should it be—as a matter of First Amendment right? Even in the core areas of classroom teaching and scholarship, there are obvious limits—sexual and racial harassment are not protected, nor are sloppy scholarship and plagiarism. Rabban points out that academic freedom restrains as well as enhances free speech: "A professor who plagiarizes a scholarly paper may be disciplined for a gross violation of professional ethics, while a prisoner, who in many respects has fewer First Amendment protections than other citizens, could probably not be punished for copying verbatim the clemency petition of a fellow inmate." Likewise, "grossly inaccurate speech about the Holocaust, for example, could be cause for dismissing a historian for incompetence, but not for taking any adverse action against a professor in the school of engineering or an employee of the municipal utility commission."[29] This is not to say that delineating the limits is always easy; deciding what amounts to incompetence, or what constitutes harassment, in class or elsewhere on campus, can sometimes be a tough call. Many a well-intentioned campus speech code has been fatally overbroad and vague, inhibiting legitimate expression and even backfiring against groups that are supposed to be its beneficiaries. But again, the occasional difficulty of drawing lines is not a reason to give up on academic freedom.

My argument so far has been to defend First Amendment academic free-dom at its core: teaching and scholarship. But what about teachers' off-cam-pus activity? Such extramural speech became part of the AAUP's definition and the Supreme Court's embrace of academic freedom in eras when pub-lic employees in general had no First Amendment shield against being fired or otherwise punished for their off-work activities. But as we have seen, the year after the Supreme Court enshrined constitutional protection for teach-ers' extramural speech in *Keyishian*, it decided *Pickering v. Board of Educa-tion*, recognizing First Amendment protection for all public employees, sub-ject to a balancing test that asks whether the employee's speech addressed a matter of public concern and, if so, whether the authorities were justified in concluding that it interfered with workplace efficiency.[30]

Thus, the argument goes, although core research and teaching—"on-the-job" speech—still needs special protection, there is no longer a need to treat teachers' extramural speech differently from political activity off the job that is the right (within limits) of every public employee. And subjecting teachers to the same First Amendment standards as everyone else would do much to combat charges of élitism and special pleading and thus make courts and the public more hospitable to core academic-freedom claims. As Rabban argues, "the distinctive professional functions of professors" justify special First Amendment protection, but the same justification does not exist for treat-ing their "aprofessional speech" differently from anyone else's. Instead, the *Pickering* balancing test can protect public-university teachers provided that courts accept the principle that intellectual inquiry and dissent, not unifor-mity and obeisance to official pronouncements, are the essential components of a healthy—and efficient—academic workplace.[31]

So, for example, the anti-affirmative-action sentiments of a Michael Levin at CCNY or the pro-Palestinian views of a Joseph Massad at Columbia, whether expressed on campus or off, would not interfere with the efficient operation of the university unless the professor actually violated standards of good scholarship or discriminated against students holding contrary views. Mere institutional discomfort, or administrators' dislike for particular ide-ologies, would not qualify as workplace inefficiency.

A final question about the scope of First Amendment academic freedom brings us back to the issue of faculty governance. How should courts deal with claims that a public university violated a professor's rights by inflict-ing punishment for comments about grading policies, hiring practices, corporate contracts, or myriad other administrative disputes? Many schol-ars have defended participation in governance as critical to First Amend-ment academic freedom, and the AAUP has argued eloquently to the same effect. Indeed, administrative and academic issues are often hard to separate: deciding whether to promote a professor, how to structure the curriculum, or whether to embark on a joint research venture with a pharmaceutical company are inherently academic questions. But Rabban makes a good point when he argues that extending First Amendment academic freedom to administrative matters poses the same danger of "overgeneralization" as applying it to extramural speech: it risks confusing general public-employee First Amendment rights with the educational core of teaching and scholarship.[32]

After the Supreme Court's decision in *Garcetti*, several lower court judges ruled that the First Amendment does not protect professors against retaliation when they protest university policies. As these cases (described in chapter 15) suggest, courts are not inclined to wade into disputes between professors and administrators about such matters as grading, hiring, conditions on research grants, or the funding of the athletic team. Indeed, a 1984 Supreme Court decision, dismissing a challenge by community-college instructors to a law that required their administration to "meet and confer" only with a designated employee organization, explicitly rejected governance as a part of First Amendment academic freedom. Although "faculty involvement in academic governance has much to recommend it as a matter of academic policy," Justice Sandra Day O'Connor wrote for the Court, "it finds no basis in the Constitution."[33]

One argument for leaving governance out of the First Amendment concept of academic freedom, then, is a practical one: courts are more likely to protect the core (teaching and scholarship) if the periphery is not spread too thin. This does not necessarily mean that retaliation against a professor at a public institution who protests an administrative decision would not violate the First Amendment. As with extramural speech, so with governance, the value of a free exchange of ideas on campus becomes part of the First Amendment balancing test that the Supreme Court outlined in the 1968 *Pickering* case. That is, when professors at public universities speak out on significant issues of governance, then by definition they are speaking about matters of public concern, and workplace efficiency is not damaged but enhanced by the debate.

Below the college level, the balance is necessarily different, but the core values of academic freedom should not be ignored. Especially when disputes arise at high schools, courts should not be too deferential to administrators' or school boards' ideas of what is suitable. Too often, what is suitable translates to a narrow concept of education: no texts with vulgar words, for example, or presumed unpatriotic sentiments or tolerant attitudes toward minority lifestyles. The tension between free expression as an educational principle and public school boards' desire to inculcate their version of civic values is an ever-challenging one, but judges should not forget that students are not simply "closed circuit recipients of only that which the state chooses to communicate"[34] and should not abdicate their role in protecting academic freedom even for the underappreciated and underpaid "priests of our democracy" who labor in the nation's public schools.

Final Thoughts

Courts in America may be the "least dangerous branch" of government, but precisely because of federal judges' life tenure and tradition of judicial review, they are crucial players in the continuing saga of free speech and democracy. The debate is not, as pundits so often claim, between judicial restraint and judicial activism; even Felix Frankfurter, who proclaimed the virtues of restraint loudly and often, was activist when he thought the Constitution demanded it; and the Court majorities headed by William Rehnquist and John Roberts in the 1990s and 2000s were astoundingly activist in striking down legislation or intervening in the political process when it suited them.[35]

The Supreme Court is ineluctably a political player. It should have responded sooner and more aggressively to the violations of due process and free speech in the late 1940s and the 1950s, but even in the worst days of the Vinson Court, it set some limits—condemning the summary procedures used by the attorney general to create his list of subversive organizations, invalidating a loyalty oath in Oklahoma because it lacked a "*scienter*" requirement. And the dissents of Douglas and Black in those years provided rhetorical ammunition for defenders of academic freedom. Liberty depends on the understanding and support of the public—when it dies in "the hearts of men and women," as Judge Learned Hand memorably said, "no constitution, no law, no court can save it."[36] But courts also have a role to play, especially in times of public intolerance.

As at other moments in our history, in the 21st century it is sometimes argued that the need for political loyalty trumps free speech, including—or especially—speech by teachers. Meanwhile, some courts and commentators have sought to ignore, distinguish, or interpret out of existence the academic-freedom principles announced by Justice Brennan in *Keyishian*. A primary lesson of the history recounted in this book is that the American political system is all too vulnerable to political repression and to demonizing the dissenter, both on campus and off. I hope the story told here helps make the case for a renewed appreciation of academic freedom and of the role played by teachers as priests of our democracy. Just as the anti-communist panic of the Cold War triggered a political, and eventually a judicial, recognition of academic freedom, so in our post-9/11 world teachers, students, universities, judges, and the whole body politic should adhere to the promise of *Keyishian*.

"The past is never dead," William Faulkner wrote, and Barack Obama liked the line enough to quote it. "It's not even past."[37]

ACKNOWLEDGMENTS

Thanks to the Frederic Ewen Academic Freedom Center at New York University for awarding me a fellowship in 2011 to complete the research and writing for this book. Its directors, Michael Nash and Marilyn Young, were wonderfully supportive scholars, brimming with knowledge and perspective about radical history and the Cold War heresy hunts. Double thanks to Marilyn, who, with NYU professor and former graduate school dean Catharine Stimpson, enabled me to become a visiting scholar after my Ewen fellowship ended.

Ellen Schrecker, dean of historians of the McCarthy era, has been especially generous—in her encouragement, wise counsel, and aid, even to the point of lending her interview notes for some of the people, now deceased, whose stories figure in this book.

Thanks to the staff of NYU's Tamiment Library, where the Ewen Center makes its home and where I spent many hours unearthing archival treasures. The history of the American left is underrepresented in standard textbooks, but its substance and spirit permeate the Tamiment.

Archivists at other libraries were also consistently helpful; this is truly a committed profession. Thanks to those at the University of Buffalo Library, which houses materials on the *Keyishian* case; to David Ment at the New York City Municipal Archives, home to the Board of Education's anti-communist files, to Gerard McCarthy of CUNY, which maintains the Board of Higher Education papers, and to the staff at Princeton's Mudd Library, the Library of Congress, the National Archives and Records Administration, the Yale University Library (home of Justice Stewart's papers), the Harvard Law School Library (the papers of Justice Frankfurter), the Columbia University Oral History Project, and Brooklyn College (the papers of Harry Slochower).

One of my great pleasures in researching and writing this book was getting to know Lisa Harbatkin and Lori Styler, who have kept alive the documentary film project "Dreamers and Fighters: the NYC Teacher Purges" and in the process have sustained a community of aging left-wing idealists and their (also aging) children. Lisa and Lori generously shared the fruits of the project's research, including an original drawing by Teachers Union cartoonist Bernard Kassoy, reproduced in this book, and taped interviews of teachers and professors conducted by the late founder of "Dreamers and Fighters," Sophie-Louise Ullman.

Thanks also to Clarence Taylor, author of *Reds at the Blackboard*, an insightful history of the Teachers Union, who gave me a copy of *Bias and Prejudice*, the TU's historic attack on racism in New York City textbooks; to Judith Podore Ward and Bernard Tuchman, who shared memories and materials of Oscar Shaftel and Vera Shlakman; to Andrew Feffer, who sent me copies of the hard-to-find December 1940 Rapp-Coudert hearing transcripts; to Joshua Freeman, who provided information about the 2003 symposium on the McCarthy era at Queens College; to Stephen Leberstein, who shared Board of Higher Education materials and recollections of CCNY's belated apology to the victims of anti-communist purges; to Carol Smith, who shared the knowledge she acquired while compiling the exhibit "The Struggle for Free Speech at CCNY, 1931–42"; to Ann Shaftel, who generously loaned a photograph of her father during his Queens College years; and to Ellen Holahan, Vera Shlakman, Kathryn Starbuck, and Herb Dorfman and Albert Lasher of the Brooklyn College *Vanguard* alumni group, all of whom took time out to search through memorabilia and provide me with photographs.

Thanks especially to the surviving *Keyishian* plaintiffs—George Hochfield, Newton Garver, Ralph Maud, and Harry Keyishian—and to their intrepid lawyer, Richard Lipsitz, for consenting to be interviewed after these many years. Thanks to Harry, George, Ralph, and Newton for sending me photographs of their younger selves. A special hug for Harry, who lent me his trove of papers about both Queens College and SUNY-Buffalo and who has become not only an admirable research subject but a valued friend.

I am grateful to everyone who read parts or all of the manuscript and offered comments: Phillip Deery, Harry Keyishian, Stephen Leberstein, Michael Nash, Ellen Schrecker, Michael Schudson, Carol Smith, Philippa Strum, Clarence Taylor, Bernard Tuchman, Judith Podore Ward, and John Wilson. Thanks also to good friends who gave me food and lodging while I labored in archives far from home: George Kannar and Ellen Weissman, Paul DiMaggio and Carol Mason, Richard and Joan Zorza, Philippa Strum, Betty Vorenberg, Ann Lambert, and Steven Come.

Finally, thanks to Michael Schudson for being a loving, supportive, and understanding partner as I struggled through the many drafts that preceded the book you are holding in your hands.

NOTES

NOTES ON ABBREVIATIONS AND STYLE

See pages 327-328 for abbreviations used in citations to archives and interviews. For citations to archives, box and folder numbers are denoted with a colon; for example, Box 1, Folder 1 is 1:1. For microfilm, —:— refers to part number and reel number.
Abbreviations for legislative materials cited in full in the bibliography are as follows:

Hartley hearings	U.S. House of Representatives, Special Subcommittee of the Committee on Education and Labor, 1948.
Rapp-Coudert hearings	Joint Legislative Committee to Investigate the Educational System of the State of New York, 1940–41.
SISS hearings	U.S. Senate, Subcommittee to Investigate the Administration of the Internal Security Act and Other Internal Security Laws of Senate Committee on the Judiciary, 1952–53.

In quotations, I have used ellipsis dots to indicate a break of more than a few words and supplied missing words in brackets, but I have made minor grammatical adjustments or dropped a few words without using brackets or ellipsis dots. Nowhere have I changed the meaning.
Some writers use a capital "C" to denote not only the Communist Party but also its members and its doctrines. I use a lower-case "c" throughout, except in referring to the Party itself and except in quotations where the capital letter is used.

NOTES TO THE INTRODUCTION

1. Schrecker-Shlakman interview.
2. HK interview.
3. SISS hearings, 2/10/1953, 431.
4. Editorial, *Queens College Crown*, 2/13/1953, 2.
5. Shaftel Statement to BHE, 3/16/1953, pamphlet published by Students for Freedom in Schools, HK papers.
6. *Adler I*, 492–3; see chapters 4 and 5 for details on the Feinberg Law, and chapter 6 for more on the *Adler* case.
7. *McAuliffe*, 220.
8. *Adler I*, 508–11.
9. See Hyman, 1–60.
10. Moyers interview.
11. *Keyishian III*, 603; see chapter 12.
12. The phrase is I. F. Stone's: *Haunted Fifties*.

13. See Haynes and Klehr.

14. See chapters 14 and 15 for detail and further rumination on these themes.

15. Byrne, 253.

16. *E.g.*, Robert Post, "The Structure of Academic Freedom," in Doumani, 61; and generally, Finkin and Post. The First Amendment prohibits Congress from "abridging the freedom of speech"; over the years, the Supreme Court has expanded its application to any action of federal, state, or local government.

17. FIRE.

18. *Jeffries I* and *II*; see chapter 14.

19. Thus, according to Churchill, if "any of them were unaware of the costs and consequences to others of what they were involved in, . . . it was because of their absolute refusal to see. More likely, it was because they were too busy braying, incessantly and self-importantly, into their cell phones, arranging power lunches and stock transactions, each of which translated, conveniently out of sight, mind and smelling distance, into the starved and rotting flesh of infants." Churchill; see also Eron, Hudson, and Hulen, 27–9, for the political context of the essay.

20. The Colorado Supreme Court affirmed the ruling: *Churchill*; see also Schrecker, *Lost Soul*, 126–53; Eron , Hudson, and Hulen; Ward Churchill, "The Myth of Academic Freedom," in Schueller and Dawson, 253.

21. *Wieman*, 196–7 (Frankfurter concurrence); see chapter 6.

22. *Sweezy*, 250; see chapter 10.

23. AAUP Commission, 12.

24. *Tinker*, 511.

25. Chamberlain, 2.

26. Eliot, 59.

27. See discussion of the lasting effect of successive waves of repression in the conclusion.

NOTES TO CHAPTER 1

1. Gruber, 15.

2. Benjamin Rader, "'That Little Pill': Richard T. Ely and the Emerging Parameters of Professional Propriety," in Hansen, 102.

3. *Id.*, 103.

4. Robert Church, "Economists as Experts: The Rise of an Academic Profession in the United States, 1870–1920," in L. Stone, 572–3.

5. Gruber, 42–3.

6. Rader, *op cit.*, 105.

7. *Id.*

8. "Edward Bemis," *The Encyclopedia of Cleveland History*, http://ech.cwru.edu/ech-cgi/article.pl?id=BEW (accessed 5/10/2011).

9. Hofstadter and Metzger, 427.

10. *Id.*, 427–8.

11. "Edward Bemis," *op. cit.*

12. Church, *op cit.*, 586.

13. John Buenker, "Sifting and Winnowing: The Historical Context," in Hansen, 19–23.

14. "The Moral of Carnot's Assassination," *Nation*, 6/28/1894, 480. The catalyst for these comments was the anarchist-inspired assassination of the president of France.

15. Wells, 27; "An Ethical Professor Rebuked," *Nation*, 7/19/1894, 41.

16. Theodore Herfurth, "Sifting & Winnowing: A Chapter in the History of Academic Freedom at the University of Wisconsin," in Hansen, 61–3.

17. *Id.*, 64.

18. Theron Schlabach, "An Aristocrat on Trial: The Case of Richard T. Ely," in Hansen, 50–1.

19. *Id.*, 52.

20. W. Lee Hansen, "Introduction," in Hansen, 3; Hofstadter and Metzger, 427; Sifting and Winnowing: An Independent News and Opinion Page for the UW-Madison Community, "Mission Statement," http://siftingandwinnowing.org/about (accessed 12/5/2011).

21. Schlabach, *op cit.*, 52.

22. Hansen, "Introduction," *op cit.*, 3.

23. Hofstadter and Metzger, 438–9.

24. Mohr, 48; see also Schrecker, *No Ivory Tower*, 17 (the case "became a sensation").

25. Mohr, 52.

26. Hofstadter and Metzger, 442.

27. *Id.*, 442–3; Mohr, 58–9.

28. Ross, 290; see also Herfurth, *op cit.*, 71.

29. Buenker, *op cit.*, 29. Ross did, however, express anti-Semitic and racist views, for example, attacking Jews from eastern Europe as "moral cripples." Dinnerstein, 65.

30. Weinstein, 93–107. Wisconsin elected Victor Berger in 1910; New York elected Meyer London in 1914.

31. Howe, 321.

32. Nearing, 89; "Report of the Committee of Inquiry on the Case of Professor Scott Nearing," in Metzger, 157.

33. Metzger, 135–8; see also Nearing, 82–4.

34. Nearing, 85.

35. "How to Gag the Professors," *World*, 6/23/1915, 8.

36. "The Philadelphia Martyr," *NY Times*, 10/10/1915, 29.

37. Nearing, 84–5; "Colleagues Rally to Nearing's Cause," *NY Times*, 6/20/1915, 8.

38. Nearing, 96–103; Gruber, 175.

39. The AAUP investigation found violations of academic freedom both in the reasons for Nearing's firing and the absence of any procedure for him to address the charges against him. Summary firings were a particular threat to the new organization's view that knowledgeable faculty, not the laymen populating boards of trustees, should decide academic qualifications. Metzger, 127–71.

40. Hofstadter and Metzger, 475–6.

41. *Id.*, 478.

42. *Id.*, 477.

43. AAUP, "1915 Declaration."

44. Gruber, 477.

45. Kathleen Frydl notes that the AAUP's "ultimate recognition" of *lernfreiheit* came only in 1964, "after the era of student protests had arrived." "Trust to the Public: Academic Freedom in the Multiversity," in Doumani, 177.

46. AAUP, "1915 Declaration."

47. *Id.*

48. *Id.*; see also Gruber, 22–3.

49. Pfannestiel, 7 (on war propaganda); Goldstein, *Political Repression*, 118–20; G. Stone, 135–232 (on the Espionage and Sedition Acts).

50. Howe, 319.

51. Gruber, 54; see also A. W. Coats, "Economists, the Economics Profession, and Academic Freedom in the United States," in Hansen, 134.

52. Gruber, 199, quoting Butler's speech at Columbia alumni luncheon, 6/6/1917.

53. Gruber, 199, quoting Seligman, "Report of the Committee of Nine in re: Participation of Columbia Professors at the Meeting of the Anti-Militaristic League on May 8, 1917."

54. AAUP Committee, 41. A three-man committee led by Arthur Lovejoy drafted the report, which was approved at the AAUP's annual meeting in December 1917. *Id.*, 47.

55. Gruber, 170–1.

56. *Id.*, 104, 116.

57. *Id.*, 207–8, citing the petition, in Presidents' Papers, University of Wisconsin Archives, Madison.

58. *Id.*, 254.

59. *Id.*, 130–3.

60. *Id.*, 1–2, citing Charles Angoff, "The Higher Learning Goes to War," *American Mercury*, June 1927, 177, and C. Hartley Grattan, "The Historians Cut Loose," *American Mercury*, Aug. 1927, 414.

61. See Rabban, *Free Speech*.

62. The Court's first major First Amendment decisions were *Schenck* and *Abrams*, decided a few months apart in 1919. Holmes created the "clear and present danger" test in *Schenck* but upheld the conviction of an anti-war leafletter without any showing that the danger he posed to the war effort was either clear or present. In *Abrams*, Holmes dissented from a decision affirming the convictions of young radicals who distributed leaflets calling for a general strike and protesting U.S. military attempts to defeat the new Bolshevik government.

63. *McAuliffe*, 220.

64. Laws of 1917, ch. 416, §3.

65. Ottanelli, 10; Weinstein, 213n94.

66. Chamberlain, 9.

67. Pfannestiel, 13.

68. "Bolsheviki in This State," *NY Times*, 3/22/19, 14.

69. Pfannestiel, 26–7.

70. There is a large literature on the Palmer raids; see, *e.g.*, Preston, 208–37; G. Stone, 220–6.

71. Pfannestiel, 37–74.

72. *Id.*, 75–9; "Raid Rand School, 'Left Wing,' and I.W.W. Offices," *NY Times*, 6/22/1919, 1.

73. "Raid Rand School," *op cit.*

74. Chamberlain, 27; see also "Moves to Close the Rand School," *NY Times*, 6/28/1919, 1, 3. The document in question was an article sent in by a black socialist, William Domingo, which the school did not intend to publish. Lusk also publicized a letter from a school official that, he said, urged a young man to "arm himself" and "take over the state"; the letter actually asked the young man: "are you arming yourself with the knowledge of the foundations of our society?" Pfannestiel, 85–6.

75. Quoted in "Attacks Charter of Rand School," *NY Times*, 7/9/1919, 15.

76. Pfannestiel, 88–95; "Rand School Wins Temporary Writ," *NY Times*, 7/17/1919, 17; "Will Ask Delay in Rand School Case," *NY Times*, 7/29/1919, 6; "Court Dismisses Rand School Case," *NY Times*, 7/31/1919, 15.

77. Pfannestiel, 103–5; Chamberlain, 40–1.

78. "The Lusk Bills," *NY Times*, 4/22/1920, 10. Three weeks earlier, the legislature voted to expel its five socialist members. They were reelected; their colleagues again voted to oust three of them, and the other two "resigned immediately after the fate of their three comrades had been announced." "Oust 5 Socialists; Will Compel Party to Purge Itself," *NY Times*, 4/2/1920, 1; "Assembly Again Expels Three Socialists; Decides to Oust Them by Vote of 90 to 45; DeWitt and Orr Seated, but Resign," *NY Times*, 9/22/1920, 1.

79. Quoted in "Gov. Smith Vetoes Six Bills Aimed at Socialist Party," *NY Times*, 5/20/1920, 1, 5.

80. Slayton, 138–9.

81. Pfannestiel, 106–17.

82. Quoted in "Lusk Laws Repealed by Smith's Approval," *NY Times*, 5/26/1923, 17.

NOTES TO CHAPTER 2

1. Ottanelli, 19.

2. *Id.*, 28–36.

3. Howard Johnson, "A Communist in Harlem," in Schrecker, *Age of McCarthyism*, 111. There is a large literature on the appeal of communism in the 1930s and '40s; see, *e.g.*, Gornick; Isserman; Naison.

4. Quoted in Epstein, 38.

5. Klehr, 6.

6. C. Taylor, 87, 291–2, 352.

7. Saul Moskoff interview of Harry Adler, 2/10/1954, Tam-RB, 97:5.

8. Ottanelli, 101.

9. Maurice Isserman, "Communism," in Jackson, 295.

10. "The Moscow Trials—A Statement by American Progressives," *New Masses*, 5/3/1938, 19.

11. Klehr, xi.

12. Annette Rubinstein, "The Cultural World of the Communist Party," in M. Brown *et al.*, 241, 229.

13. Notes, William Canning file, n.d., Rapp-Coudert hearings, reel 47 (notes on Professor Lloyd Motz).

14. See Barrett, 275; Ottanelli, 2–3.

15. Schrecker, *No Ivory Tower*, 31. Because the CP was secretive, Schrecker says, one cannot be sure about membership numbers; she based her estimate on her sample of about 200 communist academics. *Id.*, 363n15; see also Johnson, 567.

16. Zitron, 16.

17. *Id.*, 17; see also C. Taylor, 60; Hartman, 34–5.

18. Zitron, 10; see C. Taylor, 237–71, for the union's civil rights work.

19. Johnson, 567; Hartman, 36 (educational reform), 84 ("problems they preferred to ignore").

20. Ann Matlin interview, D&F, n.d.

21. Zitron, 571–6; C. Taylor, 34–60; Naison.

22. Iverson, 36–59; C. Taylor, 11–33.

23. Iverson, 114, gives the date as 1938; the Local 537 constitution is dated 11/29/1937.

24. Dodd, 36, 65, 71.

25. C. Taylor, 273–7.

26. Dodd, 93.

27. Zitron, 572, 584; C. Taylor, 61–74; "Teachers Union Fights Charges," *NY Times*, 1/21/1941, 1; "Federation Votes 3 Teachers Unions Out as Red-Ruled," *NY Times*, 6/7/1941, 1; letter from TU president Charles Hendley to CIO Industrial Council of New York City, 10/12/1943, Tam-Hendley, 8:28.

28. Ottanelli, 182.

29. Goldstein, *American Blacklist*, 21. Ottanelli writes that only 15% of the members left, but recruitment was down from an average of 3,000 per month in 1937 to about 700 two years later (198).

30. Quoted in Schrecker, *No Ivory Tower*, 55.

31. Marc Ferris, "City College of New York," in Jackson, 255–6; Van Nort.

32. Coulton, 6–7, 18; Fischel, 114–6.

33. "Queens College," *Wikipedia*, http://en.wikipedia.org/wiki/Queens_College,_City_University_of_New_York (accessed 6/24/2011). Konrad Gries, Chair of the Department of Classics, authored this entry.

34. Columbia University's undergraduate population, for example, was 40% Jewish before World War I, but newly instituted quotas brought the number down to 17% by 1934. Holmes, 13.

35. Quoted in Kenneth Gross, "Payment for an Injustice Long Borne," *NY Newsday*, 5/3/1982, 6.

36. Liben, 65, 66.

37. By the end of the 1920s, Jews constituted 26% of the New York City population and were the best-educated group in the city, but 90% of professional job openings were not available to them. Dinnerstein, 89.

38. Leberstein, "Morris Schappes" (Shelley); Iverson, 153–6; Schappes interview, D&F, n.d.; Douglas Martin, "Morris Schappes Dies at 97; Marxist and Jewish Scholar," *NY Times*, 6/9/2004, C15. For more on President Robinson and political battles at CCNY, see "Struggle for Free Speech."

39. Fischel, 90–8.

40. *Id.*, 16, 93–8, 130–2.

41. Ordway Tead testimony, 12/1/1941, Tam-RC, 4, reel 50; Holmes, 25. (Boylan had no higher-education experience but evidently got his job because he was a favorite of Mayor Jimmy Walker.)

42. Coulton, 13 ("social opportunities"); Fischel, 135 ("more cosmopolitan").

43. L. Friedman.

44. See chapter 7.

45. Fischel, 158–9.

46. Fischel, 168–70; Coulton, 115–7; "Riotous Reds Raided Classes, Cowed Pupils, Says Gideonse," *Brooklyn Eagle*, 12/4/1940, 1, 4.

47. Iverson, 142 (Selsam), 160; Holmes, 32 (citing 1984 interview with former Brooklyn College CP member Alex Novikoff); Report on Frederic Ewen, 5/21/1953 (interview with Harry Albaum), and Memo to Director, 9/15/1955 (interviews with [names

redacted]), FBI-Ewen, 73, 92 (informers' reports that Ewen was on the executive committee of the CP unit at Brooklyn College).

48. Coulton, 99.

49. Fischel, 167–8; Iverson, 161.

50. Coulton, 101; see also Holmes, 40 ("almost all of the Party members were committed scholars, with deep-seated respect for the search for truth in their academic fields and for methods of dispassionate inquiry").

51. Fischel, 159–60; Teller, 182.

52. Johnson, 567.

53. Fischel, 159–60; see also C. Taylor, 197.

54. Telegram from Abraham Cahan, editor of the *Jewish Daily Forward*, to Mayor LaGuardia, 6/26/1939 (pogroms), and letter from Jewish National Workers Alliance to LaGuardia, 7/19/1939, MA-LaG, subject files, "Christian Front" ("buy Christian," etc.).

55. Dinnerstein, 121. Coughlin's weekly radio address had 3.5 million American listeners. *Id.*, 118. For a time, it was the largest radio audience in the world. Mark Naison, "Remaking America: Communists and Liberals in the Popular Front," in M. Brown *et al.*, 55.

56. Patrick McNamara, "A People Set Apart: The Church Grows in Brooklyn . . . and Queens," in Golway, 49 (Catholics); Horowitz and Kaplan, 22 (857,000 Jews in Brooklyn in 1940; 851,000 in 1930, or 33% of the borough's population).

57. Naison, 49.

58. Coulton, 13.

59. ACLU, *Gag on Teaching*, 25; see also Hyman, 325.

60. ACLU, *Gag on Teaching*, 25. The law was repealed in 1935. *Id.*

61. *Id.*, 24–5.

62. Chamberlain, 53–5.

63. NY Education Law, §3002; see C. Taylor, 285.

64. Mitgang, 221, 258.

65. Chamberlain, 55–60.

66. "Lehman Is Asked to Remove Isaacs," *NY Times*, 3/9/1938, 10; "Lehman Rejects Plea to Remove Isaacs," *NY Times*, 3/11/1938, 1; see also Chamberlain, 58. Timone spoke at a pro-fascist meeting that year of the Fire Department's Holy Name Society. "Priest Sees Soviet as Real Foe of U.S.," *NY Times*, 5/23/1938, 20.

67. "Tead Defends College," *NY Times*, 8/24/1938, 7. Also, in 1939, the BHE overturned Brooklyn College President Boylan's decision not to renew the teaching contract of the leftist biology teacher Alex Novikoff. Novikoff's biographer comments, "It appears that the Board resisted the rising winds of anti-communist sentiment." Holmes, 52.

68. Stephen Leberstein, "Fragile Promises: Academic Freedom at the City University of New York," in Schueller and Dawson, 97n. 4; see also Fischel, 121–4.

69. Chamberlain, 154–5.

70. Col-Tead.

71. The Hatch Act, available at Legal Information Institute, Cornell University Law School, "CRS Annotated Constitution," http://www.law.cornell.edu/anncon/html/art2frag26_user.html (accessed 6/25/2011); Bontecou, 284–6.

72. *West Virginia State Board*, 642.

73. The Alien and Sedition Acts criminalized "any false, scandalous, and malicious" writing against the U.S. government, including the President and Congress, with the intent to defame them or bring them "into contempt or disrepute." G. Stone, 36.
74. Fischel, 198–9, quoting the *Tablet*, 2/26/1940, 1; see also Kessner, 474.
75. LaGuardia to Tead, 3/5/1940, MA-LaG, 2582.
76. Chamberlain, 71–2.
77. *Id.*, and appendix 4, 235–6 (Dunnigan Resolution); "Senate Gets Plan for School Inquiry," *NY Times*, 3/26/1940, 15.
78. Horace Kallen, "Behind the Bertrand Russell Case," in Dewey and Kallen, 20.
79. *Id.*
80. *Kay*, 950–1.
81. *Id.*, 950, 946.
82. *Gitlow.*
83. *Hague.*
84. Kallen, *op. cit.*, 23–4; Weidlich, 143–66; Kessner, 475.
85. "The Russell Case," *NY Times*, 4/20/1940, 10 (quoting NYU Chancellor Harry Chase). The *Times* found McGeehan's ruling "dangerously broad" but also criticized Russell for not withdrawing from the appointment "as soon as its harmful [political] results became evident." *Id.*
86. Ginsberg, 62.
87. AAUP, "1940 Statement" (with "1970 Interpretive Comments"). The Association of American Colleges later became the Association of American Colleges and Universities. *Id.*
88. *Id.*

NOTES TO CHAPTER 3

1. Dodd, 116–7.
2. "Rally Will Protest Blows to Education," *NY Times*, 4/7/1940, 42.
3. "The Right Man," *NY Times*, 4/2/1940, 14.
4. See Feffer, 32, 35 (Windels could "selectively quote [the transcripts] out of context to distort the public record").
5. Rapp-Coudert hearings, 10/23/1940, 2.
6. "Prof. Grebanier Reveals Stalinite Intrigue at Brooklyn College," *New Leader*, 11/30/1940, 2, 7.
7. Rapp-Coudert hearings, 10/23/40, 16.
8. *Id.*, 11/18/1940, 62; 1/30/1941, 135–8. Grebanier did not repeat the 23 additional names at the public hearings. Undated memo, Grebanier folder, Tam-RC, reel 9.
9. Holmes, 32; Guide to the Frederic Ewen Papers, NYU-Tam, http://dlib.nyu.edu/find-ingaids/html/tamwag/ewen2.html (accessed 3/28/2011); see also "Coudert Subpoenas More Active Unionists," *College Newsletter* (publication of NY College Teachers Union), 11/25/1940, 1, Tam-Hendley, 11:7; FBI-Ewen, 6/24/1942, 2–3, 8.
10. FBI-Ewen; Ewen Rapp-Coudert file, Tam-RC, reel 8.
11. Michael Castaldi notes, n.d., CUNY-BHE, TN-139.
12. Rapp-Coudert hearings, 2/28/1941, 21.
13. Fischel, 399–401. Grebanier told Coudert subcommittee investigators that his CP unit was reluctant to admit Slochower because "they felt he was unsafe." Report of Grebanier interview, 11/26/1940, Tam-RC, reel 9.

14. Fischel, 401.
15. Selsam questionnaire, Princeton-Tillett.
16. Rapp-Coudert hearings, 2/28/1941, 4.
17. *Id.*, 12/2/1940, 3–7.
18. *Id.*, 8–11.
19. "A Sound Approach," *NY Herald Tribune*, 12/3/1940, 26.
20. Rapp-Coudert hearings, 12/2/1940, 14–5.
21. *Id.*, 12/3/1940, 138.
22. *Id.*, 12/2/1940, 21–4, 35–6.
23. *Id.*, 12/3/1940, 75–9; letter from "Brooklyn College Branch of the Communist Party" to Grebanier, 8/19/1939, and Grebanier's reply, reprinted in *Brooklyn Eagle*, 12/3/1940, 1.
24. Rapp-Coudert hearings, 12/2/1940, 29–31, 34–5. White had since left teaching to fight for the Loyalists in Spain.
25. *Id.*, 12/3/1940, 44, 63.
26. "Brooklyn Teacher Accuses 9, as Reds on College Staff," *NY Times*, 12/3/1940, 1; "Red Tutors Incited Students in Outbreaks, Quiz Reveals," *Brooklyn Eagle*, 12/3/1940, 1, 2. Despite the *Times* headline, Grebanier named only eight (in addition to himself).
27. Rapp-Coudert hearings, 12/4/1940, 155–65.
28. *Id.*, 172–5.
29. "Journal Writers Exposed Red Teachers," *NY Journal American*, 12/3/1940, 3; "Demand Ouster of Red Teachers," *NY Journal American*, 12/3/1940, 1.
30. "'We're with You, Prof,' Class Tells Grebanier," and "Left-Wing Units Call Grebanier 'Stool Pigeon,'" *Brooklyn Eagle*, 12/4/1940, 4.
31. "Students Resent Red Disclosure as Blow to Them," *NY Herald Tribune*, 12/4/1940, 1, 22.
32. *Id.*, quoting Robert Bruce, Jr., and Alice Pokorny.
33. Editorial, *Vanguard*, 12/6/1940, 1, Tam-Ewen, 1:18.
34. "Inquiry Cites 25 in Schools for Defiance," *NY Herald Tribune*, 12/5/1940, 1, 18; "Teachers Battle Jail Threat," *Brooklyn Eagle*, 12/26/1940, 1, 22; *Joint Legislative Committee Application to Punish Charles Hendley; Teachers Union v. Joint Legislative Committee*, filed 10/1940, and *Joint Legislative Committee Application to Punish Howard Selsam, et al., for Contempt*, filed 12/18/1940, Tam-RC, reel 35.
35. "Huge Rally Applauds Testimony That Coudert Refused to Hear," *Teacher News*, 1/10/1941, 4, Tam-Ewen, 1:19.
36. Kenneth Johnston, "Teachers Quit Union in Rush as State Probes Link to Reds," *Brooklyn Eagle*, 12/6/1940, 1; "Teachers Union Head Denies Mass Desertion," *Brooklyn Eagle*, 12/7/1940, 1.
37. "Action on Suit to Oust Teachers Set for Friday," *Brooklyn Eagle*, 12/24/1940, 2.
38. Slochower affidavit, in *Joint Legislative Committee Application to Punish Howard Selsam, et al., for Contempt*, 12/24/1940, CUNY-BHE, TN-139.
39. Order in *Joint Legislative Committee Application to Punish Howard Selsam, et al., for Contempt*, 2/11/1941, Tam-RC, reel 38.
40. "Hendley Arrest Ordered to Get Union Roster," *NY Herald Tribune*, 1/25/1941, 9.
41. *Joint Legislative Committee.*
42. *Id.*, 4–5, citing briefs of the Cafeteria Employees Union, the Greater New York Industrial Council, and other unions. The National Lawyers Guild, the ACLU, and the "New York Conference for Inalienable Rights" also filed supporting briefs.

43. *Id.*, 7–10. Two judges dissented on the last point: "properly construed," they thought, the resolution did "not authorize the committee or appoint a subcommittee of one," even assuming it had the power to do so. *Id.*, 10.

44. Chamberlain, 91.

45. "Teachers to Yield Roster to Inquiry," *NY Times*, 1/27/1941, 1, 16.

46. *NAACP*, 462.

47. "New Teacher Lists Asked in Inquiry," *NY Times*, 2/12/1941, 23.

48. Dodd, 122–3.

49. See chapter 7.

50. Stephen Leberstein, "Purging the Profs: The Rapp Coudert Committee in New York, 1940–42," in M. Brown *et al.*, 117.

51. Countryman, 240 (advice to Melville Jacobs). A 7/15/1948 letter from Jacobs identified his attorney as Edward Henry: All Powers Project.

52. Leberstein, *op. cit.*, 116; Holmes, 76. Novikoff left Brooklyn in 1948 to accept a position as a professor and cancer researcher at the University of Vermont Medical School; he was fired in 1953 for refusing to answer questions posed by the SISS. Eventually, and with the personal support of Albert Einstein, he was able to return to academia as a "research professor" at Yeshiva University's Albert Einstein College of Medicine. *Id.*, 97, 138–60, 227–8.

53. "Education Board Moves for Ouster of 21 Teachers," *Daily Worker*, 12/7/1940, 1, 4.

54. "Inquiry in Schools Upheld by Chanler," *NY Times*, 12/12/1940, 22.

55. "Rival City Probe Hunts Reds in College System," *Brooklyn Eagle*, 12/24/1940, 1, 5.

56. BHE resolutions of 1/20/1941 and 4/21/1941, entered in record by Joseph Cavallaro, SISS hearings, 6/7/1953, 1137; resolution of 3/17/1941, BHE Special Committee on Section 903, the Feinberg Law, and Related Matters, Final Report, Mar. 1958, MA-BE, series 591, 32:3.

57. See chapter 2.

58. Rapp-Coudert hearings, 3/6/1941, 338–9.

59. "Schappes Indicted, Held as Perjurer," *NY Times*, 3/19/1941, 1; "Schappes Is Guilty of Perjury Charge," *NY Times*, 6/29/1941, 1.

60. Dodd, 129.

61. Schappes interview, D&F, n.d.

62. Quotations from Canning questioning are from Rapp-Coudert hearings, 3/6/1941, 400, 425–33.

63. The four additional witnesses were Annette Sherman, Abraham Goodhartz, and Oscar Zeichner of City College and Mark Graubard of Columbia.

64. "City College Head Backs Red Inquiry," *NY Times*, 3/13/1941, 23.

65. *In the Matter of Charges Preferred against Philip S. Foner*, 8/20/1941, 181–2, CUNY-BHE, 2:16.

66. *Id.*, Report of the Trial Committee, 11/6/1941, concurring opinion of Woolf, 4, CUNY-BHE, 2:17.

67. Rapp-Coudert, *Final Report*, 340.

68. Freeman.

69. Gettleman, 22; Freeman.

70. Freeman.

71. FBI-Foner.

72. Schappes questionnaire, Princeton-Tillett.

73. All quotations from Ewen questioning are from Rapp-Coudert hearings, 2/28/1941, 4.

74. Slochower to Whyte, 6/29/1941, CUNY-BHE, TN-139.

75. Whyte to Slochower, 7/8/1941, CUNY-BHE, TN-139.

76. Notes of interview, Tam-RC, reel III, side 2, 7/14/1941, CUNY-BHE, TN-139.

77. Chamberlain, 204, 217–8.

78. *Id.*, 185.

79. The number 33 is from Zitron, 199. Schrecker reports that the BHE fired 20 people, that 11 others "resigned while their cases were pending," and that all but three of those dismissed were from City College. Schrecker, *No Ivory Tower*, 82. Her total of 31 is close to Zitron's 33 and identical with Chamberlain (169). Another author puts the number fired by the BHE at 24, with 11 resignations, for a total of 35, in addition to "a number of others" who were later not reappointed. Caute, 432. His source is the memoir of Bella Dodd. Among those fired was Max Yergan, the first African American on the City College faculty and teacher of its first black studies course. Leberstein, *op cit.*, 110.

80. Selsam questionnaire, Princeton-Tillett.

81. "Communist Teachers," *New Republic*, 3/17/1941, 359.

NOTES TO CHAPTER 4

1. Winston Churchill, "The Sinews of Peace," in Kishlansky, 298–302.

2. Timone co-sponsored a pro-Franco mass meeting in 1939; among the other sponsors were representatives of the anti-Semitic radio priest Charles Coughlin and a propagandist whose works inspired the fascistic Christian Front. "Timone a Sponsor of Two Rallies Boomed by Christian Fronters," *PM*, 3/10/1946, 11; see also "The New Man on School Board—Pro-Christian Fronter Named by O'Dwyer to School Board," *PM*, 3/8/1946, 1, 8 (reprinting a leaflet for the mass meeting, with Timone as a sponsor); "Asks Ousting of Timone," *NY Times*, 3/15/1946, 24. Timone denied he was a member of the Christian Front: "Denies Joining Group," *NY Times*, 3/19/1946, 23.

3. "Asks Ousting of Timone," *op. cit.* (quoting Citizens Union founder William Schieffelin).

4. "Confirmation Needed!" *NY Post*, 3/9/1946, 11.

5. Murray Illson, "Superintendents Ban 'The Nation' from Schools as Anti-Catholic," *NY Times*, 6/24/1948, 1; Lou Baldwin, "Pious Prejudice: Catholicism and the American Press over Three Centuries," in Lockwood, 77 ("George Timone, who acted as a Catholic spokesman, launched a violent attack on two series of articles"); Blanshard, "Roman Catholic Church"; Blanshard, "Paul Blanshard Replies"; Hovde.

6. Fischel, 313–4.

7. Iverson, 23, quoting Board of Education Brief, *Matter of Thompson*, 7–8.

8. *Application of BHE for Leave to Reargue Appeal of Francis Thompson*; "Gideonse Attacks Ruling on Teacher," *NY Times*, 9/8/1948, 31.

9. "Hirschmann Asks Gideonse Inquiry," *NY Times*, 9/19/1948, 13; "Hirschmann Charges Denied by Gideonse," 9/21/1948, 9. The BHE sided with Gideonse: "Board Bars Action on Knickerbocker," *NY Times*, 9/28/1948, 29.

10. Bontecou; on the long and tortuous history of the Attorney General's List, see Goldstein, *American Blacklist*.

11. McWilliams, 159; see also Schrecker, *No Ivory Tower*, 93–106.

12. McWilliams, 173; on the hearings, see Sanders, 24–47; Countryman, 75–138.

13. Quoted in Sanders, 44.

14. Countryman, 275, and, detailing the administrative proceedings, 186–285; see also Sanders, 47–75, and on Gundlach's political advocacy, 56; Lawrence Davies, "Communist Ouster Upsets University," *NY Times*, 2/8/1949, 5. The three put on probation were E. Harold Eby, Garland Ethel, and Melville Jacobs. Another of the targeted professors, Melvin Rader, persuaded the county prosecutor to file perjury charges against one of the committee's star witnesses, George Hewitt, who had sworn that Rader was at a secret communist training school in the summer of 1938. Rader scrupulously collected evidence that he had been elsewhere that entire summer. Hewitt was never extradited from New York to stand trial, but Rader's proof persuaded President Allen ultimately to issue a statement exonerating him. Honig and Brenner, 26–7; Countryman, 286–326.

15. Sanders, 96–7; Wick, "Seeing Red: The Aftermath."

16. Sidney Hook, "Should Communists Be Permitted to Teach?," *NY Times Magazine*, 2/27/1949, 7; Alexander Meiklejohn, "Should Communists Be Allowed to Teach?," *NY Times Magazine*, 3/27/1949, 10; see also Sidney Hook, "Heresy, Yes—but Conspiracy, No," *NY Times Magazine*, 7/9/1950, 7.

17. Gardner, 13, quoting the AAUP's *Bulletin* 34:1 (Spring 1948): 127–8; AAU Statement, in Emerson, Haber, and Dorsen, 1003. On the academic establishment's overall acquiescence, see Schrecker, *No Ivory Tower*.

18. Barth, *Loyalty*, 213.

19. *Id.*; Schrecker, *No Ivory Tower*, 117–25; Gardner.

20. *Vogel*; McWilliams, 102–20.

21. "Loyalty Oaths," *NY Times*, 6/14/1949, 30.

22. McWilliams, 104–5.

23. The Ten were directors, producers, and screenwriters, among them Dalton Trumbo and Ring Lardner, Jr., who refused to answer HUAC's questions, were convicted of contempt of Congress, and served prison terms.

24. NY Laws of 1917, ch. 416, adding §3021 to NY Education Law; NY Laws of 1939, ch. 547, adding §12-a to NY Civil Service Law.

25. Leo Egan, "Dewey Signs Bill to Oust Reds and 'Fellow Travelers' in Schools." *NY Times*, 4/2/1949, 1.

26. NY Laws of 1949, ch. 360, §1.

27. *Id.*, §2, adding §3022 to NY Education Law.

28. "Blunderbuss at Albany," *NY Times*, 3/28/1949, 20.

29. "Dewey Signs Bill to Oust Red Teachers," *NY Herald Tribune*, 4/2/1949, 1, 10.

30. Zitron, 213.

31. Leo Egan, "Disloyalty Purge Voted by Regents." *NY Times*, 4/23/1949, 18.

32. Murray Illson, "Regents Are Split on Communist Bar," *NY Times*, 7/6/1949, 11. The five were already on the Attorney General's List: the CP-USA, the Trotskyist Socialist Workers Party, another leftist faction called the Workers Party, the near-moribund Industrial Workers of the World, and the Nationalist Party of Puerto Rico.

33. Legal challenges to the Feinberg Law prevented the board from completing its list making. After the litigation ended in 1952 with the Supreme Court's decision in *Adler v. Board of Education*, the board decided to name only the CP-USA and the CP of New York State. Parsons, 42–3.

34. Regents Rules on Subversive Activities, 7/15/1949, reprinted in Parsons, 297–302.

35. *Id.*, 11.
36. *Id.*
37. Chamberlain, 198.
38. Zitron, 213.
39. *Id.*; "Teachers to Fight New Feinberg Law," *NY Times*, 4/3/1949, 63.
40. "Communist Party Wins Court Stay," *NY Times*, 9/14/1949, 1, 23.
41. "Text of Jansen Order on Teacher-Loyalty Reports," *NY Times*, 9/13/1949, 32.
42. "Testing Future Teachers for Loyalty Is Considered by City's Four Colleges," *NY Times*, 9/16/1949, 14.
43. Benjamin Fine, "Charges of Freedom Curbs Rising in Nation's Colleges," *NY Times*, 5/29/1949, 1, 4.
44. "Irate House Group Members Deny They Approved Textbook Inquiry," *NY Times*, 6/19/1949, 1.
45. John Fenton, "Wellesley's Head Cites Age of Fear," *NY Times*, 6/14/1949, 26; Benjamin Fine, "Education in Review," *NY Times*, 6/19/1949, E9 (Vassar); "Textbook Request Assailed by Tead," *NY Times*, 6/22/1949, 16.
46. "Textbook Request Assailed," *op cit.*
47. *Gitlow.*
48. *Whitney*, 374–5.
49. *Fiske*, 387.
50. On the fierce battles among these four, see Feldman. Roosevelt also appointed James Byrnes in 1941, but he left the Court a year later to head the War Mobilization Board. *Id.*, 213.
51. Dunne, 85–106; Newman, 241 (Black told a fellow senator, "I had no affiliations of any kind with the Klan since I had come to the Senate").
52. *Tinker*, 524–5.
53. Adam Cohen, "Jousting Justices," *NY Times Book Review*, 11/5/2010, 12 (review of Feldman).
54. Michael Parrish, "Felix Frankfurter," in Urofsky, *Supreme Court Justices*, 171; see also Feldman, 5–9.
55. Feldman, 261, citing Douglas oral history interview with Walter Murphy (law school class); Douglas to Frankfurter, 5/29/1954, LC-Black, 317: October Term 1953 Conference memoranda.
56. Feldman, 112.
57. *Stromberg.*
58. Kalven, 167.
59. *DeJonge*, 363–5.
60. *United States v. Carolene Products*, 184n4.
61. Murphy, 71.
62. *Hague.*
63. *West Virginia State Board*, 642, overruling *Minersville School District v. Gobitis*, 310 U.S. 586 (1940).
64. *Schneiderman*, 137–9. Other important First Amendment cases in this period included *Thornhill v. Alabama*, 310 U.S. 88 (1940) (striking down an Alabama law that criminalized peaceful picketing), and *Thomas v. Collins*, 323 U.S. 516 (1945) (striking down a Texas law that required union organizers to get permission from state authorities before recruiting members).

65. Frankfurter to Stone, 5/31/1943; Frankfurter to Murphy, 5/31/1943; and Frankfurter to Reed, 12/5/1951, Harvard-FF, 3:2.

66. *United States v. Lovett*, 308–13.

67. *Cummings*, 328. A companion case, *Ex parte Garland*, struck down a loyalty oath for public officials and attorneys practicing before the federal courts. Article 1, §10 of the Constitution bans bills of attainder.

68. *Lovett*, 316–8.

69. *Id.*, 326.

NOTES TO CHAPTER 5

1. *Lederman*, 196 Misc. at 875.

2. *Id.*, 875–6, citing *United Public Workers*.

3. IA interview.

4. *Thompson*, 196 Misc. at 688.

5. *Id.*, 695–706.

6. *McAuliffe*, 218.

7. *Thompson*, 196 Misc. at 694.

8. *Id.*, 706.

9. *Lederman*, 196 Misc. at 879, 877.

10. *Lederman*, 276 A.D. at 529–30.

11. Rose Russell testimony, Hartley hearings, 10/1/1948, 364–5.

12. William Campbell testimony, Hartley hearings, 9/27/1948, 37.

13. *Id.*, 35–6; Stanley Levey, "CIO Teachers Union Called Subversive at U.S. Inquiry," *NY Times*, 9/28/1948, 1.

14. C. Taylor, 116.

15. Hartley hearings, 9/28/1948, 72 (Clauson), 76–7 (Jansen); Stanley Levey, "City's School Heads Deny Infiltration by Communists." *NY Times*, 9/29/1948, 1.

16. Hartley hearings, 9/28/1948, 93–103 (Timone); Levey, "City's School Heads," *op cit.*

17. Hartley hearings, 10/1/1948, 317; Stanley Levey, "Teacher Risks Loss of Job to Defy Red Query on Union," *NY Times*, 10/2/1948, 1.

18. Hartley hearings, 10/1/1948, 366–7, 375–6.

19. Levey, "Teacher Risks," *op cit.* Wallach was fired in 1952 for resisting a Board of Education interrogation.

20. "Subversive Groups Scored at Hearing," *NY Times*, 10/24/1947, 25.

21. *Stanton*, 1016; C. Taylor, 158–60.

22. Jansen cross-examination in *Matter of Louis Jaffe*, 10/20/1950, 53–60, MA-BE series 593, 2:VII.

23. Quoted in C. Taylor, 110.

24. National Council of Arts, Sciences, and Professions, "The Case of Mr. Louis Jaffe: A Factual Report," 1948; and TU, "The Case of Mr. Louis Jaffe: A Threat to the Security, Tenure, and Academic Freedom of All Teachers," flyer, 1948, both in Tam-Hendley, 11:23; C. Taylor, 104–15.

25. TU, "The Case of Mr. Louis Jaffe," *op cit.*

26. TU, "What's Happening in Our Schools?" flyer, n.d., Tam-Hendley, 11:15; see also "Teacher's Suicide Is Laid to Inquiry," *NY Times*, 12/25/1948, 28.

27. "Teacher's Letter Protesting Quiz Gives Clue to Her Suicide," *NY Post*, 12/27/1948, 5; see C. Taylor, 126–9.

28. Unsigned memos to Jansen, n.d., MA-BE, series 591, 33:17.

29. Unsigned memos to Jansen, n.d., MA-BE, series 591, 33:17. Whether or not Citron and Begun were married at the time, they were reported to have been man and wife in her obituary, *NY Times*, 1/23/1988, 9; Markowitz, 202n62, says the same.

30. "Peace Fight Keys May Day March," *Daily Worker*, 5/1/1949, 3. "The war parade will march under the windows of the millionaires of Fifth Avenue while the peace forces march through the working-class streets of the West Side," the paper presaged in its none-too-subtle style. On the 1949 Smith Act trial, see chapter 6.

31. Postcards to Jansen, 5–10/1949, MA-BE, series 471, 4.

32. Quoted in Zitron, 236.

33. *Id.*, 228–9; *Matter of Charges Preferred by William Jansen v. Alice Citron et al.*, transcript, 10/16/1950, MA-BE, series 593, 2:VI, 10–5, 123–38.

34. Zitron, 229; see also "College Suspends 4 Student Groups," *NY Times*, 5/20/1950, 7.

35. "21 Students on Probation," *NY Times*, 5/30/1950, 9.

36. CUNY-BHE, B20–3. The Timone resolution provided that "the Board of Education and its supervisors and administrators shall not negotiate, confer or deal with the Teachers Union, Local 555, United Public Workers, or its agents or representatives, in relation to any teacher grievances, or any personnel or professional problems." *Id.*

37. C. Taylor, 171.

38. Russell statement on Timone resolution, 4/6/1950, Tam-Hendley, 10:6.

39. C. Taylor, 36.

40. "Teacher Union Ban Is Voted by Board," *NY Times*, 6/2/1950, 1, 12.

41. NYC Teachers Union, *Bias and Prejudice in Textbooks in Use in New York City Schools: An Indictment*, 1950; see C. Taylor, 239–45.

42. Hartman, 84.

43. Johnson, 584.

44. *Appeal of Teachers Union, Local 555*, 42.

45. David Margolick, "Osmond Fraenkel Dies at 94." *NY Times*, 5/17/1983, B6.

46. *Matter of Charges Preferred by William Jansen v. David Friedman*, transcript, 9/18/1950, MA-BE, series 593, 1:II, 4. Budenz continued his lucrative career as a professional witness, testifying at least 60 times before legislative committees, courts, and loyalty boards and earning $70,000, by his own estimate, from the FBI and various committees between 1946 and 1953. His charges became increasingly reckless and his claimed expertise increasingly questioned as the years went by. Robert McFadden, "Editor of *Daily Worker*" (Budenz obituary), *NY Times*, 4/28/1972, 44; see also Caute, 123–5.

47. Friedman transcript, *op cit.*, 34–5.

48. *Id.*, 10/5/1950, MA-BE, series 593, 2:V, 1769–1802.

49. *Id.*, 1814–19; see also Zitron, 231; Iversen, 265; C. Taylor, 140–52.

50. Zitron, 237, quoting *NY Teacher*, 6/23/1951.

51. NYC Board of Education, "Findings of Fact and Declaration of Policy Concerning Communist Party," 12/6/1951, MA-BE, series 591, 2:7.

52. *Bailey* (federal loyalty program); *Garner* (Los Angeles oath); *Adler I* (Feinberg Law); see chapter 6.

53. Saul Moskoff summary, 1951, MA-BE, series 591, 30:1.

54. Iversen, 265.

55. Zitron, 237.

56. *Id.*; Moskoff to Jansen, 11/22/1955, MA-BE, series 591, 2:7 (33 were fired, 207 resigned or retired, and 18 were the "subject of automatic vacating of their positions by virtue of section 903" of the city charter—that is, also fired; see chapter 7).

57. Lawrence Martin, "School's Out for Teacher Who Wouldn't Answer 'Baseless' Charges," *Denver Post*, 9/28/1954, 2. This article reported that 62 teachers had been fired, 33 for refusing to answer questions, and that the board had revoked the substitute or probationary licenses of 16 more.

58. Zitron, 237; see also "Schools Query 59 about Red Links," *NY Times*, 11/26/1956, 19.

59. Zitron, 238; Matusow, 87–94.

60. Jansen to Deputy Superintendent Frederic Pertsch, outlining the questions to be asked, 9/11/1952, Tam-RB, 98:16.

61. Moskoff interview of Maurice Kurzman, 6/25/1953, 25–7, Tam-RB, 96:17.

NOTES TO CHAPTER 6

1. On the *Lovett* decision, see chapter 4.

2. *Shelley.*

3. *McLaurin; Sweatt; Henderson.*

4. Burns, 174.

5. Horwitz, 56.

6. George Goodman, Jr., "Ex-Justice Stanley Reed, 95, Dead," *NY Times*, 4/4/1980, A23.

7. "Harold Burton," The Oyez Project at IIT Chicago-Kent College of Law, http://www.oyez.org/justices/harold_burton (accessed 2/4/2011).

8. Gavin, 218; "Café Society," ByrdNest Productions, http://byrdnestproductions.com/Files/cafe.htm (accessed 12/7/2011).

9. *Josephson*, 86–8.

10. *Id.*, 93–6.

11. See *Joint Anti-Fascist Refugee Committee* (hereafter cited as "*JAFRC*"), 130–1.

12. Deery, 2.

13. In mid-1949, the D.C. Circuit affirmed contempt-of-Congress convictions of 10 screenwriters and directors who had refused to cooperate with HUAC; in 1950, the Supreme Court refused to accept their appeal, with Black and Douglas dissenting. *Lawson.*

14. *Barsky*, 244, 246.

15. *Id.*, 254.

16. The Court did accept review of another contempt-of-Congress appeal, by the Austrian-born communist Gerhard Eisler; but Eisler fled the United States, and the Supreme Court dismissed the case. *Eisler.*

17. The officer had to swear that he was "not a member of the Communist Party or affiliated with such party, and that he does not believe in, and is not a member of or supports any organization that believes in or teaches, the overthrow of the United States Government by force or by any illegal or unconstitutional methods." *American Communications Association v. Douds* (hereafter cited as "*Douds*"), 385–6.

18. Rabinowitz, 55.

19. *Id.*, 52, 54.

20. *Douds*, 388–9.

21. *Id.*, 399, 408, 411.

22. *Id.*, 419–22.

23. Quoted in Urofsky, *Douglas Letters*, 120.

24. *Douds*, 435, 422–4, 427.

25. *Id.*, 422–3, 439.

26. Docket sheet, *Douds*, 10/15/1949, LC-Jackson, 151:1.

27. Schlesinger to Jackson, 6/16/1950, and Jackson to Schlesinger, 6/29/1950, LC-Jackson, 159:3.

28. *Douds*, 446–8 (Black dissent).

29. A. Hamilton, 269–70.

30. Hyman, 94 ("rendered a whit stronger"; describing "multiple conflicting oaths" of Revolutionary War era), 139–66 (detailing use of anonymous informers and other abuses, some of which Lincoln opposed, during Civil War era), 169 (Union army commanders used loyalty tests to decide who could "travel, buy food and clothing, engage in business, plead cases of law, preach, teach, marry, or vote, and those who could not").

31. *Bailey*, 67 (Edgerton dissent).

32. *Id.*, 50, 61, 65.

33. *Id.*, 66–71.

34. Bench memo, *Bailey*, LC-Jackson, 167:2.

35. Docket sheet, *Bailey*, 10/14/1950, LC-Jackson, 167:2.

36. Jaffe, 112.

37. *JAFRC*, 125.

38. *Id.*, 127, 175 (Douglas, concurring).

39. Draft "Addendum," 4/12/1951, LC-Jackson, 165:9.

40. *JAFRC*, 136, 141–2.

41. Douglas, 95.

42. *JAFRC*, 170.

43. Coudert to Frankfurter, 7/2/1951, Harvard-FF, 1:47.

44. *JAFRC*, 178–9, quoting (as to the "village idiot") Barth, *Loyalty*, 109.

45. *Id.*, 142–5. Vinson, Minton, and Reed dissented in *JAFRC*, citing statistics on the many thousands of investigations and 3,166 firings under the loyalty program to argue that the system was fair. *Id.*, 207.

46. Goldstein, *American Blacklist*, 148–204; see also Sabin, 74 (the victory was "entirely pyrrhic: it changed nothing").

47. *Dennis*, 499–510.

48. *Id.*, 525, quoting George Kennan, "Where Do You Stand on Communism?," *NY Times Magazine*, 4/27/1951, 7, 53.

49. *Id.*, 570.

50. *Id.*, 582, 588–9.

51. *Id.*, 589, 581.

52. A total of 140 CP officers or members were prosecuted under the Smith Act, yielding 93 convictions. Daniel Levin, "Smith Act," in Finkelman, 1488.

53. Frankfurter to Jackson, 5/24/1951, Harvard-FF, 3:1.

54. Draft opinions of Frankfurter, 5/25/1951, and Jackson, 5/17/1951, LC-Jackson, 170:6.

55. *Garner*, 720–3, citing *Gerende*.

56. *Id.*, 723–4.

57. *Id.*, 724–8.

58. Burton said the oath left "no room for a change of heart" because it operated "retrospectively as a perpetual bar to those employees who held certain views" as long as five years before the ordinance went into effect. *Id.*, 729.

59. Alexander Hamilton, "Federalist No. 78," in Rossiter, 465.

60. *Thompson*, 301 N.Y. at 488–94.

61. *Id.*, 494.

62. Docket sheet, *Adler I*, LC-Jackson, 171:7.

63. *Adler I*, 504.

64. Luther Huston, "High Court Scans the Feinberg Law," *NY Times*, 1/4/1952, 21.

65. *Id.*

66. Fraenkel to Court clerk, 1/16/1952, LC-Jackson, 171:7.

67. *Adler I*, 497.

68. Frank, 67 (in the Court's 1951–51 term, Minton decided "against the claimed civil liberty in every divided civil rights case in which he participated").

69. *Adler I*, 492–4. The famous Holmes dictum was in *McAuliffe*, 220; Minton did not cite the case.

70. Frank, 67, 23.

71. *Adler I*, 496–7.

72. *Id.*, 508–9.

73. *Id.*, 509–11.

74. Irving Dillard to Black, n.d., and Mrs. L. E. Trachsel to Black, May 1952, LC-Black, 310:Adler.

75. "Free to Go Elsewhere," *NY World-Telegram and Sun*, 3/4/1952, 18; "The Feinberg Law Upheld," *NY Times*, 3/5/1952, 28.

76. *Wieman*, 196–7.

NOTES TO CHAPTER 7

1. Fischel, 336.

2. *Id.*, 336–8.

3. Coulton, 133; Fischel, 338–9.

4. Fischel, 339, 370n50.

5. *Id.*, 342–3; Stevens, quoting Herb Dorfman (on the *Vanguard* article); W. Taylor, 2 (faculty advisor); ACLU Academic Freedom Committee, 6–7 (equal viewpoints rule).

6. ACLU Academic Freedom Committee, 7–8.

7. Fischel, 350.

8. Stevens.

9. Fischel, 348–9; ACLU Academic Freedom Committee, 9.

10. ACLU Academic Freedom Committee, 9–10 (Taylor's comment to press); W. Taylor, xvi (quoting from his FBI file). Taylor recounts that his civil rights education began as a teenager witnessing the racist threats and invective aimed at Brooklyn Dodger Jackie Robinson, the first African American to play major league baseball. *Id.*, 2–3.

11. ACLU Academic Freedom Committee, 2, 11–14.

12. *Id.*, 17.

13. Fischel, 358–61. Gideonse studied for two years at a Calvinist school. *Id.*, 3.

14. Karen Arenson, "College Honors Man It Tried to Discredit," *NY Times*, 6/2/2001, B3.

15. W. Taylor, 218–9.

16. Arenson, *op cit.*

17. *Id.*

18. Brooklyn College; "Vanguard-Plaque Celebration"; Stevens; Grinberg. A number of *Vanguard* staffers went on to notable journalism careers, among them Mitchel Levitas

(*NY Times*), Albert Lasher (*Wall Street Journal*), and Joe and Shirley Wershba (CBS News; see the 2005 movie *Good Night, and Good Luck*, which lightly fictionalizes the Wershbas' work at CBS for Edward R. Murrow).

19. See chapter 6.

20. Oshinsky, 207–8.

21. Zitron, 241.

22. On the second-witness problem, see chapter 3.

23. SISS hearings, 9/8/1952, 1.

24. *Id.*, 12–3; on Dodd's emotional state, see *id.*, 9/9/1952, 30 (describing her "physical [and] emotional fears" upon leaving the Party; "you are beset by the fact that the old world that you lived in, the friends that you had, are cutting away from you, . . . and you are left alone").

25. *Id.*, 9/8/1952, 5–6; 9/9/1952, 36. The Lovestoneites were communists who left the Party after Stalin decided that their leader, Jay Lovestone, had departed from orthodoxy.

26. *Id.*, 9/9/1952, 40–4.

27. *Id.*, 45–8.

28. BHE Resolution, 9/22/1952, entered in record by Joseph Cavallaro, SISS hearings, 6/17/1953, 1147.

29. Iverson, 314–5.

30. "Lena Shlakman," in Avrich, 325–7.

31. "Mark Blaug," in Backhouse and Middleton, 203.

32. Alfred Young, talk at Oscar Shaftel Memorial Tribute, 10/21/2000, Tam-AAUP, "Queens-Memorials" folder. Similarly, a member of the Queens College Economics Department told an FBI agent that Shlakman "enjoy[ed] an exceptional reputation as an outstanding teacher" and that her courses were consistently popular with students. FBI-Shlakman, 10/8/1953.

33. SISS hearings, 9/24/1952, 170.

34. *Id.*

35. Shlakman, "Dear Colleagues" letter, 9/30/1952, published in "A Purged Teacher Says Farewell to Her Colleagues," *Daily Compass*, 10/12/1952, 11, Tam-Shaftel, 1:3. On HUAC's attempted textbook investigation, see chapter 4.

36. See *Shlakman II*.

37. See *Slochower*, 564–5; Zitron, 244–5.

38. Shaftel interview in Fariello, 430.

39. Holmes, 53.

40. All quotations from Albaum questioning are from SISS hearings, 9/25/1952, 209–22.

41. "The $64 question" referred to a popular radio quiz show, originally called *Take It or Leave It*. By the early 1950s, it was shorthand for "Are you now or have you ever been a member of the Communist Party?"

42. I. Stone, "Must Teachers," 2.

43. *In the Matter of Charges v. Jerauld McGill, et al.*, report of BHE trial committee, 9/17/1954, 44, Tam-BHE, 2:10.

44. "Boot Reds to Save Schools—'Kingsman,'" *Brooklyn Eagle*, 10/3/1952, 1; "Brooklyn College Paper's Firm Stand on Reds," *Brooklyn Eagle*, 10/6/1952, 8.

45. *Brooklyn Eagle*: William Dahut and August Franza, "Nation's Hopes Fly with Them," 11/10/1952, 1; Claire Thomas, "Studies Blend with Social, Religious Life," 11/11/1952, 1;

Elly Kempler, "26,000 Graduates Rank B.C. High in Academic Standings," 11/18/1952, 4.

46. "Girl Editor Speaks," *NY Journal American*, 11/15/1952, 10; Judith Crist, "No Demonstrations Today," *NY Herald Tribune*, 10/12/1952, sec. 2, p. 6.

47. *Matter of Adler*, 135.

48. *Adler II*, 458, 462.

49. Fischel, 390.

50. SISS hearings, 3/11/1953, 571–2. Alex Novikoff's biographer identifies the professor in question as Harry Albaum. Holmes, 113–4.

51. Fischel, 402–9, quoting Slochower's written account of 1/16/1947 meeting with Gideonse.

52. *Id.*, 422nn49–50 (letters in possession of Fischel).

53. Slochower to Joseph Pearl, 2/7/1947, CUNY-BHE, TN-139.

54. Cirino-Slochower interview.

55. All quotations from Slochower questioning are from SISS hearings, 9/24/1952, 199–203.

56. Leonard Buder, "3 Silent Professors Suspended By City," *NY Times*, 10/4/1952, 1.

57. Slochower to Tead, 10/4/1952, CUNY-BHE, TN-139.

58. BHE minutes, 10/6/1952, CUNY-BHE, TN-139.

59. *Id.*; see also "Final Report, BHE Special Committee on Section 903 of the City Charter, the Feinberg Law, and Related Matters," Mar. 1958, 5, MA-BE, series 591, 32:3; Schrecker, *No Ivory Tower*, 169–70. Two BHE members who voted for the firings would have preferred to give the teachers hearings first.

60. U. of Chicago (quoting Stuart Rice). Phillips attended Oakland City College in Indiana. Sopka.

61. U. of Chicago; see also Sopka. Whatever political engagement Phillips had, it likely began at Berkeley: one Oppenheimer biography reports that "for a short time, Robert dated his doctoral student Melba Phillips" and that during the 1934 general strike in San Francisco, she went with Oppenheimer to a rally in support of striking longshoremen. Bird and Sherwin, 95, 106.

62. "Ousted Prof Tells of His Faith in Future," *Daily Compass*, 10/19/1952, Tam-Shaftel, 1:3.

63. Cirino-Slochower interview.

64. Lillian Tudiver to Ewen, 9/23/1952, and Charles Nichols to Ewen, 9/27/1952, Tam-Ewen, 1:4.

65. Beatrice Hunter to Ewen, 10/6/1952, Tam-Ewen, 1:4.

66. Statement of Frederic Ewen, *Daily Nebraskan*, 10/14/1952, reprinted from *Kingsman*, 9/26/1952, Tam-Ewen, 1:4.

NOTES TO CHAPTER 8

1. Shaftel interview in Fariello, 429 (protest meeting, "ran out of time"); Schrecker-Shaftel interview ("euphoria").

2. Douglas Martin, "Oscar Shaftel, Fired after Refusing McCarthy, Dies at 88," *NY Times*, 5/24/2000, B11. The *Times* eventually corrected the erroneous reference to McCarthy in this obituary.

3. Martin, *op cit.* (combined PhD); Kenneth Gross, "Payment for an Injustice Long Borne," *NY Newsday*, 5/3/1982, 6 (military intelligence); Navy Department memo,

8/30/1943 ("cultivating the underprivileged"), War Department Military Intelligence Division Report, 1/4/1944 ("at least a fellow-traveler"), and War Department memo, 12/24/1943 ("a finer fellow"), Tam-Shaftel, 1:6.

4. Martin, *op. cit.* (Henry Wallace); "Shaftel Testifies before Sen Group," *Crown*, 2/13/1953, 1 (two children), HK papers.

5. "Shaftel Testifies," *op cit.*

6. "Who's Next?," *Crown*, 2/13/1953, 2, HK papers.

7. HK interview; communication with author, 1/1/2011.

8. "Shaftel Testifies," *op cit.*

9. Martin, *op cit.*

10. See chapter 3.

11. Statement of Oscar Shaftel, SISS hearings, 2/10/1953, 418. Harold Velde was chair of HUAC; see also C. P. Trussell, "4 in City Colleges Reject Red Query," *NY Times*, 2/10/1953, 1, 16.

12. Statement of Dr. Oscar Shaftel to the Board of Higher Education, 3/16/1953, HK papers; see the introduction for Shaftel's quotation from "Lycidas."

13. See *Shlakman II*; *Austin*, 435.

14. *Daniman I*, 922.

15. *Burstyn*; Heins, "Miracle."

16. Cirino-Slochower interview.

17. *Daniman I* (A.D.); *Shlakman I* (A.D.), 719.

18. Schrecker-Shaftel interview ("loss of nerve"); Shaftel questionnaire, Princeton-Tillett, 3:6 ("no movement of support"); Shaftel interview in Fariello, 431 ("nothing happened").

19. "Harry Says Goodbye," *Crown*, 1/8/1954, 2, HK papers.

20. SISS hearings, 2/10/1953, 433–5.

21. SISS, *Subversive Influence*, 7.

22. All quotations from Young questioning are from SISS hearings, 2/24/1953, 477–8.

23. All quotations from Gideonse questioning are from SISS hearings, 3/11/1953, 549–61.

24. Cavallaro wrote of McCarthy in response to a *New York Times* survey, "I like his courage and his patriotism. . . . In helping to get rid of Communist influence in our midst, he most certainly is benefitting the country." Cavallaro to Russell Porter, 6/16/1953, CUNY-BHE, B20-3.

25. SISS hearings, 6/17/1953, 1135–6.

26. *Id.*, 1137–51.

27. *Id.*, 1150–1.

28. Cavallaro to Jenner, 3/17/1954, CUNY-BHE, B20-3.

29. Shoup to Cavallaro, 11/19/1953, CUNY-BHE, B20-3.

30. Tead to Cavallaro, 9/8/1955, CUNY-BHE, B20-3.

31. "13 in Red Inquiry at City Colleges," *NY Times*, 12/1/1956, 13. In 1958, the BHE announced that it had cleared 63 suspects, dismissed 39 or forced them to resign or retire while under investigation, and gotten rid of another 18 who left their jobs before being questioned. BHE Special Committee on Section 903 of the City Charter, the Feinberg Law, and Related Matters, Final Report, MA-BE, series 591, 32:3.

32. Matusow, 96 ("extremely intense"); Matusow interview in Fariello, 105 ("bullshit"). Matusow's book, *False Witness*, published in 1955, documented his career as an ex-communist prevaricator.

33. "Theobald Denies Matusow Charge," *NY Times*, 4/1/1955, 7.

34. Lawrence Kaplan, quoted in Carl MacGowan, "Textbook McCarthyism: Former Students Curate exhibit on Blacklisted Professors," *NY Newsday*, 9/29/2003, A37.

35. *Amicus curiae* brief of Public Education Association in *Daniman* and *Shlakman*, 3/20/1953, CUNY-BHE, B20-3.

36. *Daniman I; Shlakman I*, 306 N.Y. at 538–41, quoting *McAuliffe*, 220.

37. *Shlakman I*, 306 N.Y. at 544–6.

38. *Daniman II; Shlakman II*.

39. Urofsky, *Douglas Letters*, 112 (next vacancy); Douglas to Black, 9/12/1953, in *id.*, 111–2 ("best possible appointment"); Pollack, 138 (actively campaigning). Contrary to some reports, Warren did not deliver the votes of the California delegation to Eisenhower at the 1952 Republican Convention. Burger 7–8.

40. Ambrose, 30 ("S.O.B."); Fox; "The Law" ("damn-fool mistake").

41. *Pennsylvania v. Nelson*.

42. Oshinsky, 497.

43. Douglas notes, 10/21/1955, LC-Douglas, 1164: O.T. 1955.

44. Douglas notes, 3/8/1956, LC-Douglas, 1164: O.T. 1955.

45. *Slochower*, 555–9.

46. *Id.*, 558–9.

47. *Id.*, 559, 560–6.

48. See chapter 10.

49. Murphy, 87, citing 102 *Congressional Record* 6063–4 (McCarthy); *id.*, 89, citing Internal Security Subcommittee, "Hearings on S. 3603 and S. 3617, 84th Cong., 2d Sess., 5/11/1956, Vol. XXXVII of subcommittee's unprinted hearings, 2510–1 (Eastland).

50. Sidney Hook, "The Slochower Decision," *New Leader*, 4/22/1957, 18–20; AAUP, "Academic Freedom and Tenure in the Quest for National Security," 42 *AAUP Bulletin* 339 (1956), in Emerson, Haber, and Dorsen, 1009–14.

51. Minutes, BHE 903 Committee, 10/13/1955, CUNY-BHE, TN-139.

52. Minutes, BHE 903 Committee, 1/17/1956, CUNY-BHE, TN-139.

53. Minutes, BHE 903 Committee, 4/10/1956, CUNY-BHE, TN-139. Shlakman's co-plaintiffs were Bernard Riess and Henrietta Friedman of Hunter College, and Sarah Riedman and Melba Phillips of Brooklyn. The six covered by the stipulation were Oscar Shaftel of Queens; Murray Young, Joseph Bressler, and Elton Gustafson of Brooklyn; and Richard Austin and Hyman Gold of CCNY. BHE 903 Committee, Final Report, MA-BE, series 591, 32:3, 6.

54. Leonard Buder, "Slochower to Get and Lose Old Job," *NY Times*, 4/10/1956, 17.

55. BHE hearing, 1/5/1957, CUNY-BHE, TN-139.

56. BHE press release, 2/27/1957, CUNY-BHE, TN-139.

57. Castaldi notes, n.d., CUNY-BHE, TN-139. Harry Albaum told Castaldi that Slochower "was upset over [the Hitler-Stalin] pact and gave up going to meetings after '39." Castaldi memo to file, 12/2/1953, CUNY-BHE, TN-139.

58. Castaldi notes, n.d., CUNY-BHE, TN-139: folder labeled "exhibits—hrg on 1/8/57."

59. See chapter 3.

60. "Slochower, on Eve of New Trial, Resigns from Brooklyn College," *NY Times*, 2/27/1957, 14.

61. Two decades later, the Supreme Court backed away from *Slochower*, ruling that it was not unconstitutional for authorities to draw adverse inferences in a civil

proceeding from a witness's use of the Fifth Amendment. (The case involved inmates in a prison disciplinary proceeding.) Justice Brennan dissented on the ground that the ruling was inconsistent with *Slochower* and numerous other cases. *Baxter*, 327.

62. *Shlakman III*; *Austin*.

63. *Austin*, 445.

64. Schrecker, *No Ivory Tower*, 189.

65. Association of American Universities, "The Rights and Responsibilities of Universities and Their Faculties," 3/24/1953, in Emerson, Haber, and Dorsen, 1008.

66. Schrecker, *No Ivory Tower*, 94.

67. A. W. Coats, "Economists, the Economics Profession, and Academic Freedom in the United States," in Hansen, 139; see also Holmes, 166–7 (although some people attributed AAUP inaction during the early 1950s "to a reluctance to meet the McCarthy challenge squarely, the major factor was probably the general ineffectiveness and inefficiency of the office").

68. Schrecker, *No Ivory Tower*, 336.

69. G. Stone, 316–8, quoting Hutchins, "The President's Report to the Alumni," *U. of Chicago Magazine*, Mar. 1935, 171–2.

70. *Id.*, 423–5, quoting Hutchins testimony before Illinois Subversive Activities Committee, 4/21/1949, 10–18.

71. Schrecker, *No Ivory Tower*, 213.

72. Price.

73. *Id.*, 21.

74. Schrecker, *No Ivory Tower*, 337.

75. AAU, *op cit.*, 1007.

76. See Heins, *Sex, Sin*, 117–36; Bolton.

77. Schrecker, *No Ivory Tower*, 340–1. Precisely calculating the extent of the chill on academic freedom is impossible. As the historian Peter Novick observes, "Documented cases of the repression of dissidence in this period are, presumably, the tip of the iceberg. In the case of icebergs we know that the total mass is nine times what we see above water. What multiplier do we use in cases of repression? . . . With respect to the consequences of repression one confronts the paradox that the measure of its effectiveness is the scarcity of overt instances" (331). But see Lazarsfeld and Thielens (discussed in the conclusion, note 5).

NOTES TO CHAPTER 9

1. Third World Traveler ("most excruciating"); Parks testimony quoted in Bentley, 333–4; see also Navasky, 236.

2. Hellman to HUAC, 5/19/1952, in Schrecker, *Age of McCarthyism*, 227.

3. Miller was convicted of contempt of Congress and fined $500—a mere slap on the wrist compared to the jail sentences imposed on the Hollywood Ten and others. His conviction was reversed on appeal. Meyers, 149.

4. Navasky, vii (characterizing Chambers's viewpoint). Navasky's chapter "The Reasons Considered" evaluates the arguments commonly made in favor of informing. *Id.*, 279–313.

5. Holmes, 113, citing Albaum interview with Murray Horowitz, 10/10/1979; *id.*, 158, quoting Novikoff letter to Van Potter, 6/26/1953.

6. Navasky, ix.

7. Barth, *Government by Investigation*, 128–9; see also Navasky, 322 (the "degradation ceremonies" were "pseudo-events" that simultaneously profited the investigating committees and served the mass media's thirst for sensation).

8. All quotations from Adler questioning are from Saul Moskoff interview of Harry Adler, 2/10/1954, 20–33, Tam-RB, 97:5.

9. As recounted in memo from Mr. Burke to Mr. Larkin, 3/3/1954: MA-BE, series 591, 2:9.

10. Moskoff to Timone, 8/19/1954, MA-BE, series 591, 19:3.

11. Moskoff to Timone, 9/15/1953, MA-BE, series 591, 19:3.

12. Jansen, "Statement," 9/20/1954, MA-BE, series 591, 6:14.

13. Moskoff to Corporation Counsel, 9/8/1954, MA-BE, series 591, 2:9.

14. Moskoff to Board of Education, 9/24/1954, MA-BE, series 591, 6:14, citing "Should Ex-Red Teachers Be Made to Sing?," *NY World-Telegram and Sun*, 9/21/1954, 26.

15. Memo to Teacher Interest Committees, 9/17/1954, MA-BE, series 591, 2:9.

16. Statements of Matthew Shevlin and Rabbi Benjamin Schultz, Board of Education meeting, 2/24/1955, MA-BE, series 591, 16:12.

17. Statements of Rose Russell, George Ferrell, Charles Hendley, *id.*

18. "Ex-Red Teachers Must Give Names," *NY Times*, 3/18/1955, 18. Cammer was right: The U.S. Office of Education and the National Education Association reported that "they had no record of such a mandate anywhere else in the nation." Gene Currivan, "Education in Review," *NY Times*, 8/12/1956, 157. Another board member, Charles Bensley, was known to oppose the policy but was absent from the meeting because of illness. Judith Crist, "Teachers Must Tell on Reds," *NY Herald Tribune*, 3/18/1955, 1, 25.

19. Board of Education Resolution, 3/17/1955; see *Board of Education v. Allen*, 454. The policy as originally proposed would have "authorized and directed" the superintendent to require informing; the final resolution deleted the words "and directed," thus ostensibly giving Jansen discretion. "Ex-Red Teachers Must Give Names," *op cit.*

20. Alistair Cooke, "Informers Wanted—Must Be Able to Teach," *Manchester Guardian*, 3/19/1955, 1.

21. Quoted in *Bulletin* of Jewish Center of Kew Garden Hills, 4/22/1955; Tam-Hendley, 10:15; and Brief for Appellants in *Matter of Benjamin Baronofsky et al.*, 3/25/1955, 12, Tam-RB, 96:16.

22. Council of the Diocese of NY to Board of Education, 3/15/1955, excerpted in Appendix to Respondents' Brief, *Board of Education v. Allen* (3/11/1958), Tam-RB, 97:15; "Teachers as Informers," *NY Times*, 3/17/1955, 44. Other opponents (totaling 14 organizations) included the United Parents Associations, the New York Association of Teachers of Social Studies, B'nai B'rith, and the American Jewish Congress; supporters included 11 veterans' and religious groups. Crist, "Teachers Must Tell on Reds," *op cit.*

23. *Matter of Benjamin Baronofsky et al.*, 34.

24. Brown, Opinion No. 103,538, n.d., MA-BE, series 591, 2:9.

25. All 16 of the first two groups of teachers fired for insubordination and conduct unbecoming were Jewish. The TU accused the board of anti-Semitism or at least a double standard, since it dealt leniently with Christian teachers such as the notorious May Quinn, who repeatedly promoted racism and anti-Semitism in her classroom. C. Taylor, 7, 75–94, 185; Markowitz, 151; *Matter of May Quinn*.

26. Moskoff interview of Julius Nash, 3/10/1954, 5, and Moskoff interview of Irving Mauer, 12/1/1954, 4–6, Tam-RB, 97:5. The Moskoff-Nash transcript gives the date of his permanent license as 1945, but Nash's son states that it was 1941 and adds that his father had been failed on the oral portion of the exam twice, after which, on the advice of one of the examiners, he changed his name from the Jewish-sounding Nachimovsky to Nash and passed the oral on the third try. MN interview.

27. Quoted in "Open Letter to the Teaching Staff from Adler, Mauer, Feinstein, and Nash," 9/27/1955, Tam-RB, 97:13.

28. Moskoff interview of Julius Nash, 3/10/1954, 24–9, Tam-RB 97:5.

29. Moskoff interview of Irving Mauer, 4/26/1955, 3–7, Tam-RB 97:5.

30. Grossman to Members of Congregation Agudas Israel, 4/21/1955, MA-BE, series 591, 1:6.

31. Moskoff to Grossman, 4/25/1955 and 4/26/1955, MA-BE, series 591, 1:6.

32. Boudin to Moskoff, 4/25/1955, MA-BE, series 591, 1:6.

33. Petition of Nash, Feinstein, and Mauer in *Board of Education v. Allen*, 9/7/1955, Tam-RB, 97:15; Jansen to Board, 9/9/1955, MA-BE, series 591, 28:3.

34. *Application of Harry Adler et al.*, 54.

35. TU press release, 8/9/1956, Tam-RB, 97:15.

36. Moskoff to Jansen, 1/20/1958, MA-BE, series 591, 2:7.

37. *Board of Education v. Allen.*

38. "Teachers as Informers," *NY Times*, 4/30/1958, 32; Murray Kempton, "What Is Wrong with Our Schools?" *NY Post*, 3/28/1958, M6; "Meanwhile, in Our Town," *NY Post*, 6/5/1958, M5; "Vendetta," *NY Post*, 6/8/1958, M9.

39. *Hughes*; "Two School Cases Pend in Red Study," *NY Times*, 12/1/1958, 25.

40. *Board of Education v. Allen*, 6 N.Y.2d at 138–40.

41. Eleanor Roosevelt, "My Day," *NY Post*, 9/23/1959, 47.

42. "The Exiles," *NY Post*, 11/12/1959, 57.

43. "Conditional Surrender," *NY Post*, 12/11/1959, 49.

44. "School Scandals," *NY Post*, 6/1/1961, 28.

45. "Persecution by Administration," *NY Times*, 6/14/1961, 18.

46. Warren Weaver, "State to Replace Any New Board," *NY Times*, 8/16/1961, 1; Warren Weaver, "Reform Ordered—Democrats Are Beaten on Amendments, and All but 7 Yield," *NY Times*, 8/22/1961, 1.

47. *Jansen v. Mauer et al.* and *Theobald v. Douglas et al.*, 8/22/1962, Tam-RB, 97:1.

48. *Appeal of Julius Nash and Irving Mauer*, 32.

49. Complaint, *Nash and Mauer v. Allen* (S.Ct. Albany Cty, 12/10/1963), Tam-RB, 97:2.

50. Petitioners' Reply Memorandum, *Matter of Deborah Douglas and Ethel Levine v. Allen*; and *Julius Nash and Irving Mauer v. Allen* (S.Ct. Albany Cty), n.d., 19–27, Tam-RB, 97:1.

51. See C. Taylor, 178–202; Markowitz, 151–69; Caute, 435–8.

NOTES TO CHAPTER 10

1. See chapter 6.

2. *Peters*, 351. A memo from Douglas's law clerk had urged reconsideration of *Bailey*, "as the practices condoned there were shocking." Conference memo, 11/4/1954, LC-Douglas, 1156: O.T. 1954.

3. *Cole v. Young.*

4. Douglas, 64.

5. *Schware*, 244. Frankfurter, Clark, and Harlan filed a concurrence distancing themselves from Black's political ruminations and simply finding Schware's rejection on
account of long-ago Party membership unjustified; the same three justices dissented
in Konigsberg's case. California still refused to admit Konigsberg to the bar, and four
years later, the Supreme Court let that ruling stand. *Konigsberg II.*

6. *Jencks*, 665n9 ("Matusow recanted as deliberately false the testimony given by him
at the trial. On the basis of this recantation, the petitioner moved for a new trial. . . .
The District Court denied the motion").

7. Stern and Wermiel, 126.

8. *Id.*, 127.

9. *Jencks*, 681–2.

10. Stern and Wermiel, 127–8. After much legislative maneuvering, the compromise
"Jencks Act" provided that the trial judge should decide whether information must
be turned over and that the penalty for non-disclosure would be to strike the witness's testimony, not to dismiss the case. See Murphy, 152–3; Sabin, 151.

11. Schwartz, 228.

12. *Service; Yates.*

13. Sabin, 6–12, 192–8.

14. *Watkins*, 200.

15. Frankfurter to Warren, 5/31/1957, LC-Warren, 580:261,175.

16. *Sweezy*, 243–4.

17. Curtis Reitz to Warren, n.d., 8–11, LC-Warren, 174:151–75.

18. *Sweezy*, 250.

19. Judge Arthur Suzman to Frankfurter, 5/15/1957; and Hon. Albert Van de Sandt
Centlivres, "Freedom," *The Forum*, Mar. 1957, in Harvard-FF, 2:25.

20. Frankfurter to Warren, 6/3/1957, LC-Warren, 174:151–75.

21. *Sweezy*, 261–3, quoting University of Cape Town and University of the Witwatersrand, *The Open Universities in South Africa* (Johannesburg: Witwatersrand U.
Press, 1957), 10–12.

22. To be sure, Frankfurter had started out as a liberal: his philosophy of judicial
restraint grew out of liberals' frustration with the Supreme Court's property-rights
activism in the early 1930s. But he stuck to the doctrine over decades when deferring to the other branches of government meant acquiescing in multiple violations of
individual rights. Eventually, "it became impossible as a matter of political reality to
trumpet judicial restraint while remaining a liberal." Feldman, 419.

23. *Sweezy*, 266.

24. Kalven, 497.

25. *Sweezy*, 270.

26. "High Court Scored in Senate and House," *NY Times*, 6/25/1957, 15 (constitutional
amendment); Murphy, 154–7 (jurisdiction). Opposition from the legal establishment
and the Justice Department, the likelihood of a presidential veto, and the political
skills of Senate Majority Leader Lyndon Johnson combined to defeat the Jenner bill,
but as Murphy notes, these legislative assaults were "symbols of congressional repudiation of the moral authority of the Warren Court." *Id.*, 157–71, 183.

27. I. Stone, 199–204.

28. *Lerner*, 476. Warren, Douglas, Black, and Brennan dissented. The teacher case was *Beilan*.
29. Murphy, 64.
30. *Speiser*, 526. Harlan and Frankfurter joined the 7–1 decision; Warren did not participate because, as California governor, he had signed the tax-exemption law. Only Clark dissented.
31. Stern and Wermiel, 136.
32. *Speiser*, 528n. 8.
33. *Barenblatt*, 113.
34. Kalven, 498.
35. Douglas, 100. The other two cases were *Braden* and *Wilkinson*.
36. "Bar Bids Congress Tighten Red Laws," *NY Times*, 2/25/1959, 1; "Text of Bar Association's Stand on Communists," *NY Times*, 2/25/1959, 25.
37. Justice Charles Whittaker, whom Eisenhower had appointed in 1957 to replace Stanley Reed, did not participate in *Watkins* but accounted for the fifth vote approving HUAC's questioning of Barenblatt.
38. Stewart, at news conference announcing his retirement in 1981, quoted in "Guide to the Potter Stewart Papers," Yale-Stewart, 4, http://drs.library.yale.edu:8083/fedora/get/mssa:ms.1367/PDF (accessed 12/9/2011).
39. Quoted in Charns, 14–15.
40. Stern and Wermiel, 155. The pornography case was *Jacobellis*.
41. *NAACP*; see chapter 3.
42. *Uphaus*, 79–80, 77.
43. Stewart to Clark, 2/23/1959; and Harlan to Clark, 2/10/1959, Yale-Stewart, 167:1466. Stewart and Harlan urged Clark to make clear that the state had no power to subpoena guest lists without "grounds for believing that the Fellowship was a subversive organization" (Harlan); as originally written, Clark's draft "could permit a state to subpoena everyone in the telephone book and ask them to give the names of their house guests for the past two years" (Stewart).
44. Frankfurter to Brennan, 1/7/1959, LC-Brennan, I:19:3.
45. *Shelton*, 485–7. Frankfurter, Harlan, Clark, and Whittaker dissented, with Frankfurter asserting, as he frequently did, his personal opposition to "crude intrusions by the state into the atmosphere of creative freedom" but, unlike in *Sweezy*, adopting the mantle of judicial restraint. *Id.*, 490.
46. *Cummings*; *Ex parte Garland*.
47. A. W. Coats, "Economists, the Economics Profession, and Academic Freedom in the United States," in Hansen, 138.
48. Walker, 188.
49. *Garner*; see chapter 6.
50. Hyman, 338 (42 states); Goldstein, *Political Repression*, 351–2 (Aristotle).
51. Roger Revelle, Oral History, Scripps Institute of Oceanography Library, 3:7, 1984, http://scilib.ucsd.edu/sio/oral/Revelle%20Volume%203.pdf (accessed 8/17/2010); see also Tiersten, 27.
52. Kennedy, "Loyalty Oath," 25; see also Kennedy, "Let's Get Rid," 89 ("Loyalty oaths, especially in education, have never contributed to our security. Traitors and liars will easily take them. But frequently, principled people will refuse.")

53. See Griswold; Bess Furman, "Hot Fight Likely on Student Oath," *NY Times*, 2/7/1960, 51; Ben Franklin, "President Signs Repealer of Student Non-Red Oath." *NY Times*, 10/18/1962, 1.

54. Cramp to ACLU, 11/6/1959, Princeton-ACLU, 1318.

55. Simon to Ennis, 12/23/1959, Princeton-ACLU, 1318.

56. *Cramp I*, 558–9.

57. Jurisdictional Statement, *Cramp II*, 2/1/1961, 9–11.

58. Howard Dixon to Lawrence Speiser, 10/6/1961, Princeton-ACLU, 1318.

59. *Cramp* docket book, Yale-Stewart, 383:4690.

60. *Cramp II*, 286; undated draft, Yale-Stewart, 15:144.

61. *Cramp II*, 286–7, 293.

62. *Cramp III*.

63. Wulf to Simon, 3/6/1962; and Simon to Wolf, 3/12/1962, Princeton-ACLU, 1318. A decade later, a federal court invalidated most of the Florida oath, leaving only an affirmative promise to support the Constitution and an agreement not to "believe" in the forceful overthrow of the government. The state did not appeal, but the teacher-plaintiff did, and in a terse unsigned opinion, the U.S. Supreme Court struck down the "believe" provision because it denied employees a hearing before being fired. *Connell*. Simon and Wulf were co-counsel for the teacher.

64. Washington Laws, 1931, ch. 103.

65. Washington Laws, 1955, ch. 377, defining a "subversive person" as anyone who commits, aids, or advocates any act "intended to overthrow, destroy or alter, or to assist in the overthrow, destruction or alteration," of the state or federal government by "revolution, force, or violence" or who knowingly joins a group with such an aim.

66. *Nostrand v. Balmer*, 467, 467n11.

67. *Nostrand v. Little*.

68. Honig and Brenner, 32.

69. Levi Pulokinen, "Arval Morris, 1928–2008: UW Lawyer Won Loyalty Oath Case," *Seattle Post-Intelligencer*, 9/17/2008, http://www.seattlepi.com/local/379590_obitmorris18.html (accessed 4/23/2010).

70. "The Legendary Giovanni Costigan," in *UW Showcase*, comp. Deborah L. Illman, http://www.washington.edu/research/showcase/1934a.html (accessed 1/24/2011); "Fair Play and a Free Press: The Triumph of Melvin Rader," in *id.*, http://www.washington.edu/research/showcase/1950a.html (accessed 1/24/2011); Jurisdictional Statement, *Baggett II* (6/20/1963), 25–33.

71. Jurisdictional Statement, *op cit.*, 25–33.

72. *Baggett I*, 446. The Black quotation was from his concurrence in *Speiser v. Randall*, the 1958 case striking down a test oath required by California for certain property-tax exemptions; see *supra* note 30 and surrounding text.

73. *Baggett I*, 446–7.

74. *Id.*, 454.

NOTES TO CHAPTER 11

1. Parsons, 46–50, citing SUNY Trustees Minutes, 10/11/1956; NY Laws, 1953, ch. 681.

2. Feinberg certificate, Buff-Lipsitz, 2:2.

3. Samuel Capen, "The Responsibilities of Boards of Trustees for the Preservation of Academic Freedom,"1935, quoted in Hicks, 12, and in AAUP-Buffalo resolution,

5/15/1962, Buff-Connolly, 4:3 ("any subject"); Capen, *Management of Universities*, v ("rabbit hutch").

4. Schrecker, *No Ivory Tower*, 205–7.

5. *Egan*, 152; Bob Balme, "Aptheker Can Speak at UB, Court Rules; Voids Previous Ban," *Buffalo Evening News*, 12/28/1963, 1. Aptheker was the last of five speakers in a program titled "Political Spectrum in the Contemporary World"; the series also included the fascist Oswald Mosley. "Freedom of Inquiry Principle Upheld—Appellate Division Reverses Aptheker Speech Ban," *State University of New York Newsletter*, 1/13/1964, 1, Buff-Connolly, 4:1.

6. Parsons, 59–61; NG interview; Furnas to faculty, 12/23/1963, Buff-Garver, 1:1.1.

7. Executive committee to members, 1/3/1964, Buff-Lipsitz, 2:10.

8. "The Non-Communist Disclaimer Requirement: Report of AAUP Committee on Academic Freedom and Tenure," Jan. 1964, Buff-Lipsitz, 2:10.

9. RL interview.

10. HK interview (1/21/1964 meeting); RL interview (needed some money); GH interview (fees may have deterred).

11. AAUP Resolutions, 1/24/1964, Buff-AAUP-AF.

12. NG interview.

13. Starbuck Payroll and Personnel Transaction form, 10/28/1963, Buff-Lipsitz, 2:5.

14. Robert Thomas, Jr., "George Starbuck, Wry Poet, Is Dead at 65," *NY Times*, 8/17/1996, 26.

15. Parsons, 143–5.

16. Starbuck Payroll and Personnel Transaction form, *op cit.*

17. Starbuck to "Mark," 1/10/1964, Buff-Starbuck, 1:1.

18. RL interview.

19. Starbuck to Morgan, 3/24/1954, Buff-Lipsitz, 2:4.

20. HK phone interview; Keyishian, unpublished paper, 7.

21. HK phone interview.

22. Moyers interview.

23. RM interview.

24. HK interview; RM interview.

25. Maud to Murray, 6/29/1964, Buff-AAUP:11.

26. GH interview.

27. Yasmin Anwar, "Leonard Nathan, Distinguished Poet, Dies at 82," *UC Berkeley News*, 6/7/2007, http://berkeley.edu/news/media/releases/2007/06/07_nathan.shtml (accessed 1/29/2011) (describing Hochfield's friendship with the fellow poet); GH interview.

28. Moyers interview.

29. HK phone interview.

30. NG interview.

31. Garver to J. Lawrence Murray, 6/8/1964, Buff-Lipsitz, 1:1.21.

32. NG interview.

33. The change was negotiated by medical school professor Peter Nicholls: Frank Nugent, "The Feinberg Certificate at Buffalo," Apr. 1965 (pamphlet), Buff-Lipsitz, 2:11. ("Frank Nugent" was a pen name used by Ralph Maud; RM interview.)

34. GH interview.

35. Schrecker, *Lost Soul*, 77, citing in part Ohmann, xxiii.

36. Parsons, 64, quoting Handy to SUNY Vice President for Personnel David Price, 1/27/1964.
37. Maud to Associate Dean Myles Slatin, 1/13/1964, Buff-Lipsitz, 1:1.23.
38. Boudin to Maud, 1/29/1964, Buff-Lipsitz, 1:1.23.
39. See chapter 10.
40. Starbuck to Lipsitz, 2/13/1964, quoted in Parsons, 152–3.
41. Decision and Order, *Starbuck v. Board of Regents*, 4/17/1964, Buff-Lipsitz, 1:1.15.
42. Maud to Murray, 3/14/1964, Buff-Lipsitz, 1:1.23.
43. "Dr. Furnas Deplores Red Inferences Made since HCUA Hearing," *Buffalo Evening News*, 5/26/1964, 39. On resistance to HUAC, see, *e.g.*, "HUAC: May 1960."
44. Keyishian, unpublished paper, 9.
45. *Id* ; see also Parsons, 218–28; Nugent, "Feinberg Certificate," *op cit*. Sporn went on to a successful career at Wayne State University; his 2004 obituary noted that before academia, he had been a factory worker and labor organizer who "saw capitalism as an unjust system that bred poverty and racism. These views led him to join the Communist Party as a young man, and later to help found the Progressive Labor Party." "Paul Sporn," *Chicago Tribune*, 3/7/2004, http://www.legacy.com/obituaries/chicago-tribune/obituary.aspx?n=paul-sporn&pid=86724211 (accessed 7/18/2011).
46. Jurisdictional Statement, *Baggett II*, 6/20/1963, 37–8, 73, citing Lazarsfeld and Thielens, 84–5, 240, 192, 218, 197.
47. *Id.*, citing R. Brown, 498.
48. *Id.*, 41–5.
49. *Baggett* docket book, Yale-Stewart, 387:4765.
50. *Baggett II*, 368–70.
51. *Id.*, 371.
52. *Id.*, 372. The three-judge court had dismissed the four student plaintiffs from the case, and the Supreme Court did not revisit this decision. *Id.*, 366n5.
53. *Id.*, 382–3. The Maryland case was *Gerende*, which upheld an oath required of candidates for office, after the state attorney general assured the Court that it applied only to "knowing" membership in subversive organizations.
54. Morgan to Keyishian, 6/3/1964, Buff-Lipsitz, 1:1.18; Morgan to Maud, 6/3/1964, Buff-Lipsitz, 1:1.24; Morgan to Starbuck, 6/3/1964, Buff-Lipsitz, 1:1.26.
55. NG interview.
56. Garver to Murray, 6/8/1964, Buff-Lipsitz, 1:1.21.
57. Parsons, 90–1.
58. Garver to Price, 7/1/1964, Buff-Lipsitz, 1:5.
59. Price to Garver, 7/8/1964, Buff-Garver, 4; Victor Paschkis to Garver, 8/1/1964, Buff-Garver, 4.
60. NG interview.
61. Handy to Gould, 6/5/1964; and Gould to Handy, 6/9/1964, Buff-AAUP-AF.
62. Keyishian to Lipsitz, 9/4/1964, Buff-Lipsitz, 1:1.18.
63. *Keyishian I*, 238–9.
64. "Gould Announces Unanimous Decision," *Spectrum*, 6/15/1965, Buff-AAUP, 14:3; Gould, "Statement for Prospective Appointees," July 1965, Buff-AAUP, 11:11.
65. *Keyishian II*, 986.
66. E. Friedman, 49, citing Minutes, 1/27/1966, Buff-AAUP, 14:4 (other crises), and "Campaign to Raise Funds," n.d., and "The Voluntary Fund," n.d., Buff-AAUP, 13:9

(only $671); Lipsitz to Herman Orentlicher, AAUP, 1/22/1966, Buff-Lipsitz, 1:1.42 ("out of line").

67. Maud to Albert Cook, 2/23/1965, Buff-Lipsitz, 1:1.25.

68. "Corso Dismissed, Academic Freedom Committee to Picket," *Spectrum*, 4/5/1965, 1 (quoting the committee and the editorial); "History of Feinberg and the University," *Spectrum*, 6/15/1965, 2, Buff-Lipsitz, 2:9.

69. Murray Schumach, "Students Decry Corso Dismissal, *NY Times*, 4/9/1965, 30. Lipsitz recalled that Allen Ginsberg had also been invited to campus, as "a guest lecturer or something": "They didn't want to pay him unless he signed. I convinced them to pay him. It was kind of foolish of the administration." RL interview.

NOTES TO CHAPTER 12

1. *Elfbrandt III*, 12–3.
2. Sager, 60.
3. *Elfbrandt I*, 7–16, 24n. 2.
4. *Elfbrandt II*, 147–8.
5. Draft opinions, 3/11/1966, 3/15/1966, Yale-Stewart, 215:2283.
6. *Elfbrandt III*. The previous cases were *Scales* and *Aptheker*.
7. *Id.*, 22–3.
8. Jurisdictional Statement, *Keyishian III*, 3–4, 19.
9. Answer to Motion to Dismiss, *Keyishian III*, 9.
10. Motion to Dismiss and Brief for SUNY Trustees, *Keyishian III*, 5/16/1966, 2.
11. *Keyishian* docket sheet, Yale-Stewart, 394:4856.
12. Burns, 197.
13. Brief of ACLU and New York CLU, 10/25/1966, 21; Brief of AAUP, 9/28/1966, 25, *Keyishian III*, citing *Wieman* (see chapter 6) and *Sweezy* (see chapter 10).
14. RL interview.
15. Recording of oral argument in *Keyishian III*, 11/17/1966, NARA, tape no. 267-608.
16. *Id.*
17. *Keyishian* docket sheet, Yale-Stewart, 394:4856.
18. All quotations from the law clerks' case history are from Goodman and Sofaer, VIII.
19. E. Friedman, 57, citing draft opinion, n.d., Tom Clark Papers, A204:1, Tarlton Law Library, Austin, Texas.
20. Clark to Harlan, Stewart, and White, 1/18/1967, Yale-Stewart, 222:2411.
21. *Keyishian III*, 594–6.
22. *Id.*, 597–9, quoting *Baggett*, 374.
23. *Id.*, 599–602.
24. *Id.*, 602–3, quoting *Adler*, 510.
25. *Id.*, 595, 605–7.
26. *Id.*, 609.
27. Goodman and Sofaer, IX.
28. *Keyishian III*, 622–4.
29. Goodman and Sofaer, IX.
30. *Keyishian III*, 628–9.
31. RL interview.
32. Orentlicher to Lipsitz, 1/24/1967; and Boudin to Lipsitz, 1/25/1967, Buff-Lipsitz, 1:1.52
33. Maud to Lipsitz, 1/28/1967; and Connolly to Lipsitz, 1/28/1967, Buff-Lipsitz, 1:1.54.

34. "End of the Feinberg Law," *NY Times*, 1/26/1967, 32; "Overbroad Sweep," *Washington Post*, 1/26/1967, A20.

35. "End of Feinberg Law," *Buffalo Evening News*, 1/25/1967, 32; "The Baby Goes Out with the Bathwater," *Chicago Tribune*, 1/24/1967, 16; "To Russia with Love," *NY Daily News*, 1/25/1967, 19.

36. C. Harrison Mann, Virginia House of Delegates, to Clark, 1/24/1967; Sandi Gray to Brennan, 1/28/1967; Charles Earhart to Brennan, 1/25/1967; copy of unsigned threat, 1/24/1967; Brennan to Hoover, 1/26/1967; and Hoover to Brennan, 1/31/1967, all in LC-Brennan, I:153:4.

37. Starbuck to Crary, 6/20/1967; and Starbuck to Lipsitz, 6/20/1967, Buff-Starbuck, 1:1-5.

38. Starbuck to Lipsitz, 7/18/1967; and Lipsitz to Starbuck, 7/21/1967, Buff-Starbuck, 1:1-5.

39. Robert Thomas, Jr., "George Starbuck, Wry Poet, Is Dead at 65," *NY Times*, 8/17/1996, 26 ("dazzling display"); McHenry ("geniuses").

40. NG interview; Garver to *Buffalo Courier-Express*, 4/4/1967, 14 (medical supplies); King to Garver, 4/4/1967, Buff-Garver, 2:1.

41. *Walker.*

42. NG interview (describing letter from Myles Slatin; country house); "Newton Garver," http://newtongarver.com (accessed 3/15/2011) (Bolivia).

43. RL interview.

44. Bruce Jackson, "Buffalo English: Literary Glory Days at UB," *Buffalo Beat*, 2/26/1999, http://www.acsu.buffalo.edu/~bjackson/englishdept.htm (accessed 8/23/2011).

45. Maud, 206–7; Keyishian to author, 9/22/2011 (introduced over drinks).

46. June Maynard, "I Didn't Come Back for the Coffee," Read SFU Memories, http://www.sfu.ca/40th_anniversary/read/Maynard_June.html (accessed 1/27/2010).

47. Hochfield; NEA ("major work").

48. GH interview.

49. Moyers interview.

50. Keyishian, unpublished paper, 11–4.

51. GH interview.

NOTES TO CHAPTER 13

1. *Uniformed Sanitation Men*; *Gardner.* The *Slochower* decision had not, technically, invalidated section 903 but only invalidated the summary firing of a tenured professor without any semblance of due process.

2. Settlement and Discontinuance, *Matter of Grossman et al.*, 11/15/1973, Tam-RB, 97:9.

3. Nash to Rabinowitz, 1/6/1968, Tam-RB, 96:22; Mauer to Rabinowitz, n.d., Tam-RB, 97:6.

4. Rabinowitz to Sidney Nadel, 1/9/1968, Tam-RB, 96:22.

5. Citron to Rabinowitz, 7/15/1968, Tam-RB, 96:22.

6. Rabinowitz to Norman Redlich, May 1972, Tam-RB, 96:23; Leonard Buder, "City Acts to Rehire 31 Teachers Ousted in McCarthy Era," *NY Times*, 9/21/1972, 1.

7. Adler and Zelman, 436.

8. C. Taylor, 311–4.

9. Sara Slack, "Reading, Writing, & Arithmetic," *NY Amsterdam News*, 1/18/1964, 4.

10. "Rose Russell, 65, Unionist, Is Dead," *NY Times*, 1/3/1965, 84; Rabinowitz, 149.

11. CT interview.

12. Leonard Buder, "126 Former Reds Kept as Teachers," *NY Times*, 11/6/1958, 39.

13. Peter Flint, "Liberty Debated at Nazi's Hearing," *NY Times*, 8/25/1960, 8; Leslie Oelsner, "Juvenile Justice: Helpless Frustration Grips Many," *NY Times*, 4/3/1973, 1 (Moskoff judgeship); Wolfgang Saxon, "Michael Castaldi, Ex-Special Prosecutor, Dies," *NY Times*, 1/12/1995, B11.

14. MN interview.

15. Mauer interview, D&F, 1998.

16. IA interview.

17. FBI memo, 2/17/1961 (describing Security Index and Reserve Index), Tam-Shaftel, 2:2; FBI memo, 9/1/1960, in Adler, appendix; Rothschild (describing provision for interrogation and detention of people on the Reserve Index).

18. Adler, 103.

19. FBI report, 5/21/1953, FBI-Ewen.

20. Ewen, 60.

21. Introduction, Frederic Ewen Papers, Tam-Ewen (theatrical ventures); Dunham to Ewen, 1/23/1962, Tam-Ewen, 1:1.

22. FBI report, 12/30/1952, FBI-Ewen.

23. From SAC, NY, to Director, FBI, 2/24/1958, FBI-Ewen.

24. J. Edgar Hoover to Lawrence Smith, Chief, Special War Policies Unit, 1/23/1943, FBI-Slochower.

25. FBI report, 6/27/1942, FBI-Slochower.

26. Quoted in FBI report, 5/9/1949, FBI-Slochower.

27. Cirino-Slochower interview.

28. Schrecker-Slochower interview.

29. Mickenberg, 221 (in Riedman's biography of the chemist Antoine Lavoisier, she "makes note of his involvement with the French Revolution; in her biography of Charles Darwin (1959), she emphasizes his support of the American Revolution and his revulsion for slavery").

30. Sarah Riedman Papers, de Grummond Collection, U. of Southern Mississippi, http://www.lib.usm.edu/~degrum/html/research/findaids/riedman.htm (accessed 11/2/2011).

31. U. of Chicago; Sopka.

32. Shaftel interview in Fariello, 432–3. Shaftel retired from Pratt as Professor Emeritus in 1977 and continued to teach there as Visiting Professor of Oriental Studies until 1990. Shaftel CV, n.d. (courtesy of Judith Podore Ward, 11/15/2011).

33. FBI memos, 3/23/1953 and 8/11/1955, Tam-Shaftel, 2:1.

34. Shlakman to Avi Muchnick, 4/14/2000, Tam-AAUP, "Vera Shlakman 52" folder; Alice Murray, "QC Profs Seek to Wipe Out McCarthy Era Stain," *NY Daily News*, 3/19/1980, 3xQ (secretary).

35. Shlakman, 241–4; FBI report, 5/21/1953, FBI-Ewen (TU course).

36. FBI memo, 8/18/1955, FBI-Shlakman.

37. Vera Shlakman CV, n.d.; remarks sent to silver anniversary event, Columbia School of Social Work, 6/7/1998 (both documents courtesy of Judith Podore Ward).

38. Quotations in this and the next paragraph are from Kessler-Harris, 195–200.

39. O'Dwyer to Solomon, 10/21/1977; and Shaftel to Jim Meyer, 10/18/1977, Tam-RB, 97:10.

40. Solomon to Mary Bass, 3/10/1978, 20 (courtesy of Stephen Leberstein).

41. Gordon Johnson to file, 1/22/1980, Tam-RB, 97:10.

42. E. R. Shipp, "The 'Shameful Era' Begins to End for Professors Dismissed by City U," *NY Times*, 3/26/1980, B1; Murray, *op cit.*

43. Straus to Bellamy, 4/23/1980; Bellamy to Straus, 4/29/1980; and Shaftel and Shlakman to Goldin, 8/25/1980, Tam-RB, 97:12.

44. Clyde Haberman, "Ex-City U. Teachers Still Await Restitution for Dismissal in '50s," *NY Times*, 1/18/1981, A34.

45. Stephen Leberstein, "Purging the Profs: The Rapp Coudert Committee in New York, 1940–42," in M. Brown *et al.*, 119.

46. Schappes, 23.

47. Paul Montgomery, "Ten Teachers Ousted in 50s Given Restitution by City," *NY Times*, 4/29/1982, B3 (Goldin and Shaftel quotes); see also Office of the Comptroller, press release, 4/28/1982, Tam-RB, 97:10; Rabinowitz, 152. The others who received pensions were Richard Austin, Joseph Bressler, Sarah Riedman Gustafson, and Bernard Riess. There were lump-sum settlements to the estates of Elton Gustafson, Myron Hoch, and Murray Young.

48. Carl MacGowan, "Textbook McCarthyism: Former Students Curate Exhibit on Blacklisted Professors," *NY Newsday* (Queens ed.), 9/29/2003, A37 (standing ovation—quoting recollection of former student Dorothy Pita); Straus to Rabinowitz, 6/21/1982, Tam-RB, 97:10.

49. MacGowan, *op cit.* ("never talked"—quoting Dorothy Pita); Shlakman to Avi Muchnick, 4/14/2000, Tam-AAUP, "Vera Shlakman 52" folder.

50. Alfred Young, talk at Shaftel Memorial Tribute, 10/21/2000, Tam-AAUP, "Queens-Memorials" folder; Douglas Martin, "Oscar Shaftel, Fired after Refusing McCarthy, Dies at 88," *NY Times*, 5/24/2000, B11; communication from Judith Podore Ward, 11/15/2011 (quotation from *A Plausible God*). On the *Times* obituary's mistaken reference to Senator McCarthy, see chapter 8, note 2.

51. Queens College Alumni Day announcement, 5/5/2001 (courtesy of Judith Podore Ward).

52. MacGowan, *op cit.*; Queens College; "McCarthyism at Queens College." All this activity at Queens was followed by an exhibit at CCNY, organized by Carol Smith, which focused on the Rapp-Coudert era. "Struggle for Free Speech."

53. Joshua Freeman to author, 11/16/2011.

54. JPW/BT interview.

55. Brooklyn College Commencement Exercises, June 2005, Tam-Ewen, 1:22.

56. Walter Waggoner, "Dr. Harry D. Gideonse Dead; Ex-Head of Brooklyn College," *NY Times*, 3/14/1985, D27; Fischel, 519 ("medieval lord"—quoting Gideonse to Gustave Rosenberg, 11/19/1965).

NOTES TO CHAPTER 14

1. *Gerende.*

2. *Whitehill*, 59–60.

3. *Id.*, 62–3. Tom Clark had by this time retired and been replaced by Thurgood Marshall, who joined the majority.

4. See Sager, 77, for citations.

5. *Vogel.*

6. Sager, 77.

7. *Stewart.* On the Hatch Act, see chapter 2.

8. Sager, 68.

9. *Id.*, 57–8.

10. *Healy*, 180–1. Then-Justice (not yet Chief Justice) William Rehnquist wrote a concurrence stressing that the case was simply being sent back to the lower courts to decide whether in fact the students were willing to abide by reasonable campus regulations.

11. *Keefe*, 361–2. The court entered a preliminary injunction against the school board, finding that the teacher would most likely win his case.

12. *Minarcini*, 580–3.

13. *Presidents Council.*

14. *Tinker*, 511 (holding that public school students have a right to wear black armbands in silent opposition to the Vietnam War and establishing a balancing test under which school officials can only suppress student expression if they have a well-grounded fear that it would materially disrupt the educational process).

15. *Board of Education, Island Trees*, 868, quoting *Brown v. Louisiana*, 383 U.S. 131, 142 (1966).

16. In 1986, the Court rejected a student's First Amendment challenge to his punishment for delivering an off-color speech at a school assembly (*Bethel*); in 1988, it allowed a principal to censor a student newspaper published as part of a journalism class (*Hazelwood School District*); and in 2007, it ruled that a student had no First Amendment right to hold a banner reading "Bong Hits 4 Jesus" across the street from his high school because its arguably pro-drug message violated school policy (*Morse*).

17. *Boring*, 98 F.3d at 1480.

18. *Boring*, 136 F.3d at 369.

19. *Brooks*; *Burnham*; *Dube.*

20. *Levin*, 770 F. Supp. at 910–1.

21. *Id.*, 898, 919–20, 925.

22. *Levin*, 966 F.2d at 87.

23. *Levin*, 770 F. Supp. at 914.

24. *Jeffries I*, 1241–2.

25. *Jeffries II*, 17. The intervening Supreme Court case was *Waters*.

26. See the introduction.

27. See Schrecker, *Lost Soul*, 89–122, for a good summary of the backlash.

28. *Urofsky v. Gilmore*, 410. This author was lead counsel in the case. By the time of the appeal, the Virginia legislature had amended its law to cover only "lascivious" sexually explicit content.

29. *Id.*, 428.

30. *Id.*, 425–6 (Hamilton [the sixth judge] concurring), 438 (dissent).

31. *Regents of the University of California*, 312. Four justices—Marshall, Brennan, Blackmun, and White—would have upheld the plan as a legitimate effort to remedy past discrimination; four others—Burger, Rehnquist, Stewart, and Stevens—wanted to strike it down without considering whether some other race-conscious plan might be acceptable.

32. *Grutter*, 328.

33. Schrecker, *Lost Soul*, 21.

34. *Regents of the University of Michigan*, 226n. 12.

35. *University of Pennsylvania*, 196.

36. *Id.*, 196–200.

37. It was not until 1968 that the Supreme Court extended free-speech protection to all public employees, in *Pickering*; see the discussion of *Pickering* in chapter 15 and the conclusion.
38. Peter Byrne was a leading proponent of this position. Byrne, 264. See the conclusion for more on contemporary scholars' differing views on academic freedom.
39. NY Education Law §3002.
40. Note, "Loyalty Oaths," 759.
41. *Knight*, 340–1, referring to *West Virginia State Board*.
42. *Id.*, 342.
43. Note, "Loyalty Oaths," 761.
44. *Richardson*, 1322.
45. Brennan to conference, 2/13/1970, LC-Brennan, 220:6.
46. *Cole I*, 240–1.
47. Douglas notes of conference, 11/19/1971, LC-Douglas, 1544: O.T. 1971.
48. *Cole II*, 680.
49. *Id.*, 684.
50. *Id.*, 688–9.
51. Hazel and Alberg Hansen to Douglas, 7/19/1972, LC-Douglas, 1544; Cole; "High Court's Endorsement of Loyalty Oath Is a Regressive Turnabout," *Sacramento Bee*, 4/21/1972, A22.
52. See chapter 15 for 21st-century controversies over affirmative oaths and the revival of the negative disclaimer oath after 9/11/2001.

NOTES TO CHAPTER 15

1. Tom LoBianco, "Protesting Nuns Branded Terrorists," *Washington Times*, 10/10/2008, 1.
2. Singel.
3. Lisa Rein and Josh White, "Many Groups Spied Upon in Md. Were Nonviolent," *Washington Post*, 11/19/2008, B1; Rein and White, "More Groups than Thought Monitored in Police Spying," *Washington Post*, 1/4/2009, 1 (human rights and bike lanes).
4. Singel; see also Charlie Savage, "Even Those Cleared of Crimes Can Stay on F.B.I.'s Watch List," *NY Times*, 9/27/2011, A1.
5. 8 U.S. Code §1182(a)(3)(B)(iii).
6. 18 U.S. Code §2331(5).
7. Executive Order 13224, §3, 9/23/2001, http://www.treasury.gov/resource-center/sanctions/Programs/Documents/terror.pdf (accessed 9/7/2011). The purpose of the order was to enable the government to effect quick seizures of the assets of any person or entity it thought might contribute to terrorism.
8. 8 U.S. Code §1189(d).
9. See, *e.g.*, Robert Pear, "U.S. Report Stirs Furor in South Africa: The Pentagon Calls the A.N.C. a Terrorist Group," *NY Times*, 1/14/1989, 3; Mimi Hall, "U.S. Has Mandela on Terrorist List," *USA Today*, 4/30/2008, http://www.usatoday.com/news/world/2008-04-30-watchlist_N.htm (accessed 12/9/2011); Moran.
10. *People's Mojahedin.*
11. *Scales*, 221–2.
12. *Holder*, 2718.

13. *Id.*, 2732.

14. "A Bruise on the First Amendment," *NY Times*, 6/21/2010, A26.

15. D. Cole, 8–14. Cole was lead attorney in *Holder*.

16. Fleisher made the statement at a September 26, 2001, press briefing, in response to TV commentator Bill Maher's televised remark that the World Trade Center terrorists were not "cowards"; see, *e.g.*, Hitchens.

17. ACLU, *Freedom under Fire*, 14, 15.

18. Andrea Peyser, "Once-Proud Campus a Breeding Ground for Idiots," *NY Post*, 10/3/2001, available at http://www.greenspun.com/bboard/q-and-a-fetch-msg. tcl?msg_id=006Z26 (accessed 2/22/2012); AAUP, "Responses" (professors received threats). Participants objected that the *Post* "misquoted some speakers, took the remarks of others out of context, and virtually ignored the multiplicity of views represented." *Id.*

19. Dallal, quoted in AAUP, "September 11."

20. Martin and Neal.

21. Emily Eakin, "On the Lookout for Patriotic Incorrectness," *NY Times*, 11/2/2001, A1; Burgan; Joel Beinin, "The New McCarthyism: Policing Thoughts about the Middle East," in Doumani, 245.

22. Beshara Doumani, "Between Coercion and Privatization: Academic Freedom in the 21st Century," in Doumani, 23–4; see "Campus Watch," http://www.campus-watch. org (accessed 6/3/2011); Scigliano (3,000 trustees). On ACTA and Campus Watch, see Roy.

23. Doumani, "Between Coercion and Privatization," *op cit.*, 13; H.R. 509 (109th Cong.), 2/2/2005; Malini Johar Schueller, "Area Studies and Multicultural Imperialism," in Schueller and Dawson, 121–3; Roy.

24. J. Cole, 414–6.

25. Some of these examples are from Philippa Strum, "Why Academic Freedom? The Theoretical and Constitutional Context," in Doumani, 159.

26. Doumani, "Between Coercion," *op cit.*, 31–2.

27. J. Cole, 417.

28. Doumani, "Between Coercion," *op cit.*, 26–7.

29. *Id.*, 31; see also Timothy Starks, "Universities Resist Efforts to Require Ideological Diversity on Campuses," *NY Sun*, 4/15/2003, 2; "Santorum," *In These Times*, 6/9/2003, 6 ("Santorum, [Sam] Brownback and a handful of conservative Christian senators met with representatives of several Jewish organizations, including the campus organization Hillel, to discuss anti-Israel and anti-Semitic behavior on campus. A Hillel official later leaked Santorum's plan in the *New York Sun*"). A search of the Library of Congress "Thomas" website for tracking legislation does not show that Santorum introduced the contemplated legislation.

30. Columbia University, "Ad Hoc Grievance Committee Report."

31. See Senior.

32. Columbia University, "Ad Hoc Grievance Committee Report."

33. *Id.* Massad contested the grievance committee's one adverse conclusion: that the classroom incident had occurred as claimed by the complaining student. His denial, he pointed out, was "corroborated by three students, two graduate Teaching Assistants and one registered undergraduate student," whereas the complaint was only supported by one student and one alleged auditor. Massad. On a similar campaign,

ultimately unsuccessful, against the Barnard scholar Nadi Abu El-Haj, see Kramer, 50.

34. John Bradley, "Arabian Nights," *Financial Times*, 8/25/2007, http://www.ft.com/cms/s/2/d69aa534-4ed3-11dc-85e7-0000779fd2ac.html#axzz1dPSnYIqo (accessed 11/11/2011).

35. Alix Pianin, "Professors Protest Massad's Tenure," *Columbia Spectator*, 9/22/2009, http://www.columbiaspectator.com/2009/09/22/professors-protest-massads-tenure (accessed 11/10/2011).

36. Patricia Cohen, "Outspoken Political Scientist Denied Tenure at DePaul," *NY Times*, 6/11/2007, 2. Finkelstein later reached a settlement with the university in which it acknowledged that he was "a prolific scholar and outstanding teacher." "Professor Norman Finkelstein."

37. AAUP, "September 11."

38. *Pickering*, 568.

39. *Connick.*

40. *Hardy*, 680, quoting *Scallet*, 1013–4. *Hardy* involved a professor whose contract was not renewed because he uttered the terms "bitch" and "nigger" in a class discussion on the impact of offensive and disparaging words.

41. *Feldman*, 497 (denying First Amendment claim by a mathematician who alleged that his contract was not renewed in retaliation for his charge of misconduct against another professor).

42. *Garcetti*, 421.

43. *Id.*, 438–9 (Souter dissent), 425 (Kennedy). Justices Stevens, Ginsburg, and Breyer also dissented.

44. *Hong*, 1161.

45. Brief *amicus curiae* of AAUP and Thomas Jefferson Center for Freedom of Expression in *Hong*, 6; *Hong* (9th Cir., unpublished).

46. *Renken; Gorum*, 186. The court in *Gorum* also found that the plaintiff's arguments were "makeweight attempts to counter his dismissal for doctoring student grades." *Id.*, 151.

47. *Adams*, 557.

48. *Id.*, 560–5. The case was remanded to the district court to decide whether Adams's First Amendment–protected writings were in fact the reason he was not promoted.

49. Later in 2011, a federal judge rejected Louisiana State University's claim that a professor had no First Amendment protection from retaliation after he made public statements, and eventually wrote a book, charging that the U.S. Army Corps of Engineers' negligence in maintaining New Orleans's levees was to blame for the devastation wrought by Hurricane Katrina. The university argued that the statements were part of the professor's job as head of the school's Hurricane Center and therefore were not protected under *Garcetti*. The judge found that the professor "was not acting within his official duties" when he spoke with reporters about Katrina or when he wrote his book, thereby avoiding the question whether there is "an academic's exception to *Garcetti*." But the judge added that he "shares Justice Souter's concern that wholesale application of the *Garcetti* analysis to the type of facts presented here could lead to a whittling-away of academics' ability to delve into issues or express opinions that are unpopular, uncomfortable or unorthodox. Allowing an institution devoted to teaching and research to discipline the whole of the academy for their failure to adhere to

the tenets established by university administrators will in time do much more harm than good." *Van Heerden*, 15–20.

50. See chapter 14.
51. Cal. Constitution, art. XX, §3.
52. Mitford, 90, 94.
53. Richard Paddock, "Loyalty Oath Poses Ethical Dilemmas," *Los Angeles Times*, 5/11/2008, http://articles.sfgate.com/2008-05-11/news/17152368_1_loyalty-oath-wendy-gonaver-speech-and-religious-freedom (accessed 9/7/2011).
54. Jaschik.
55. Ohio Rev. Code §§2909.32–4.
56. *Speiser*, 532 (Douglas concurrence).
57. Responses to the author's public records requests, Apr.–June 2009. In addition to the Ohio Department of Public Safety, requests were sent to Ohio State University, Kent State University, the University of Akron, and Bowling Green State University.
58. *State ex rel. Triplet*.
59. The other objector did not pursue his license renewal for unrelated reasons; see Heins, "What Makes a Conscientious Objector?"
60. Heins, "Guilt by Association."

NOTES TO THE CONCLUSION

1. Feldman, 177.
2. Klehr, 157.
3. Maurice Isserman, "Communism," in Jackson, 295.
4. *Id.*, 255–6.
5. Sanders, 96, quoting E. Harold Eby ("had to shut up") and Melville Jacobs ("even remotely political"). A survey by Columbia sociologists in 1955 found that almost half of the professors interviewed were apprehensive about what they said and wrote, though "relatively few" admitted to self-censoring; 63% thought there was a "greater threat to intellectual activity in America than a decade ago." Lazarsfeld and Thielens, 35. The actual numbers were probably higher, given that caution infected the interview process: one professor denied self-censoring but in separate comments acknowledged refraining from writing letters to the editor about racial segregation; another who claimed no apprehension nevertheless said, "I have to be careful about socialized medicine. If I do refer to it, I refer to a conservative reference." *Id.*, 87–8.
6. Schrecker, "Political Tests" ("meaningful dissent"); Schrecker, "McCarthyism and the Red Scare," in Agnew and Rosenzweig, 380 ("Vietnam quagmire").
7. See G. Stone, 429–526, for a detailed summary of New Left-era repression.
8. Goldstein, *Political Repression*, xiii.
9. See the introduction (on Churchill) and chapter 15 (on other post-9/11 repression).
10. *Holder*; see chapter 15.
11. See chapter 13.
12. Academic Freedom Lecture Fund, http://www.umich.edu/~aflf/history.html (accessed 8/1/2011) (Michigan); Wick, "Seeing Red: The Aftermath" (Washington).
13. See chapter 4.
14. Wick, "Seeing Red: The Apology."
15. Col-Tead, 66. On Tead's 1938 statement, see chapter 2.
16. Harbatkin.

17. *Wieman*, 197.

18. See AAUP, "Policy Documents and Reports," http://www.aaup.org/AAUP/pubsres/ policydocs (accessed 7/31/2011), for the AAUP's policy statements, many of which also appear in its printed "Redbook."

19. Areen, 947; see also Thomas Haskell, "Justifying the Rights of Academic Freedom in the Era of 'Power/Knowledge,'" in Menand, 54 ("the heart and soul of academic freedom lie not in free speech but in professional autonomy and collegial self-governance").

20. AAUP, "Trends in Faculty Status."

21. Washburn, 203; Nelson, *No University Is an Island*, 81.

22. See Washburn; Schrecker, *Lost Soul*, 158–86 (corporate conditions on funding) and 97–105 (detailing how infusion of money from right-wing foundations has affected scholarship).

23. Washburn, xii–xiii.

24. Judith Butler, "Academic Norms, Contemporary Challenges: A Reply to Robert Post on Academic Freedom," in Doumani, 132.

25. Philippa Strum, "Why Academic Freedom?," in Doumani, 149–50, citing *Healy* (described in chapter 14).

26. *Garcetti*, 425; see chapter 15.

27. Byrne; Finkin and Post, 8. Another prominent scholar, Rodney Smolla, seems to go further than Byrne, Post, and his co-author Finkin, arguing that academic freedom should not be recognized as "an 'implied' First Amendment right" at all. Smolla, 18–25. But the quarrel here is largely semantic: Smolla agrees that the concept of academic freedom should infuse judicial interpretation of the First Amendment in the campus context. That is all the Supreme Court claimed in *Keyishian*.

28. Rabban, "Functional Analysis," 284.

29. *Id.*, 255, 242.

30. *Pickering*, 568; see chapter 15.

31. Rabban, "Functional Analysis," 244.

32. *Id.*, 295.

33. *Minnesota State Board for Community Colleges*, 288. Justice Brennan's dissent, citing *Keyishian*, *Sweezy*, and other cases, argued that "First Amendment freedom to explore novel or controversial ideas in the classroom is closely linked to the freedom of faculty members to express their views to the administration concerning matters of academic governance." *Id.*, 296–7. But Brennan had lost the allies who formed a majority in *Keyishian*: Stevens and Powell also dissented but not on grounds of academic freedom.

34. *Tinker*, 511.

35. *E.g.*, *Bush* (stopping vote recount and handing presidential election to George W. Bush) and *Citizens United* (striking down laws that limited corporate spending on election campaigns).

36. Learned Hand, "The Spirit of Liberty," in Hand, 144.

37. Faulkner, 92; see Obama.

BIBLIOGRAPHY

ARCHIVES

BC-Slochower   Harry Slochower Papers, Brooklyn College Library
Buff-AAUP   AAUP-Buffalo chapter, University Archives, State University of New
                    York (SUNY)-Buffalo
Buff-AAUP-AF   AAUP-Buffalo chapter, Academic Freedom files, SUNY-Buffalo
Buff-Connolly   Thomas Connolly Papers, University Archives, SUNY-Buffalo
Buff-Garver   Newton Garver Papers, University Archives, SUNY-Buffalo
Buff-Handy   Rollo Handy Papers, University Archives, SUNY-Buffalo
Buff-Lipsitz   Richard Lipsitz Papers, University Archives, SUNY-Buffalo
Buff-Starbuck   George Starbuck Papers, University Archives, SUNY-Buffalo
Col-Jansen   Reminiscences of William Jansen, Oral History Research Office,
                    Columbia University, 1964
Col-Tead   Reminiscences of Ordway Tead, Oral History Research Office,
                    Columbia University, 1964
CUNY-BHE   Board of Higher Education Archives, City University of New York
                    (located at LaGuardia Community College, Queens)
Harvard-FF   Felix Frankfurter Papers, Harvard Law School Library
HK papers   Papers of Harry Keyishian, on file with the author
LC-Black   Hugo Black Papers, Manuscript Division, Library of Congress,
                    Washington, D.C.
LC-Brennan   William J. Brennan Papers, Manuscript Division, Library of
                    Congress, Washington, D.C.
LC-Douglas   William O. Douglas Papers, Manuscript Division, Library of
                    Congress, Washington, D.C.
LC-Jackson   Robert Jackson Papers, Manuscript Division, Library of Congress,
                    Washington, D.C.
LC-Warren   Earl Warren Papers, Manuscript Division, Library of Congress,
                    Washington, D.C.
MA-BE   Board of Education Papers, New York City Department of Records/
                    Municipal Archives
MA-LaG   Fiorello LaGuardia Papers, New York City Department of Records/
                    Municipal Archives
NARA   National Archives and Records Administration, College Park, MD
NYU-Tam   Materials in the Tamiment Library, New York University, where not
                    cited more specifically

Princeton-ACLU   ACLU Archives, Manuscript Division, Department of Rare Books
                      and Special Collections, Princeton University Library
Princeton-Harlan   John M. Harlan Papers, Manuscript Division, Department of Rare
                      Books and Special Collections, Princeton University Library
Princeton-Tillett   Paul Tillett Papers, Manuscript Division, Department of Rare Books
                      and Special Collections, Princeton University Library
Tam-AAUP   American Association of University Professors, Academic Freedom
                      Committee, Tamiment Library, New York University
Tam-BHE   New York City Board of Higher Education Papers, Tamiment Library,
                      New York University
Tam-Ewen   Frederic Ewen Papers, Tamiment Library, New York University
Tam-Hendley   Charles Hendley Papers, Tamiment Library, New York University
Tam-RB   Rabinowitz Boudin Law Firm Papers, Tamiment Library, New York
                      University
Tam-RC   Microfilms of Rapp-Coudert Committee files, Tamiment Library,
                      New York University (including some hearing transcripts)
Tam-Shaftel   Oscar Shaftel Papers, Tamiment Library, New York University
Yale-Stewart   Potter Stewart Papers (MS 1367), Manuscripts and Archives, Yale
                      University Library

INTERVIEWS BY AUTHOR

CT interview   Clarence Taylor, 4/29/2011
NG interview   Newton Garver, 4/29/2010
GH interview   George Hochfield (telephone), 2/6/2011
HK interview   Harry Keyishian, 5/14/2010
HK phone interview   Harry Keyishian (telephone), 11/20/2008
IA interview   Irving Adler, 7/21/2008
JPW/BT interview   Judith Podore Ward and Bernard Tuchman, 9/13/2011
MN interview   Michael Nash, 4/14/11, 2/7/2012
RL interview   Richard Lipsitz, 4/30/2010
RM interview   Ralph Maud (telephone), 5/16/2010

OTHER INTERVIEWS

Cirino-Slochower interview   Linda Cirino interview with Harry Slochower (taped),
                                 1/19/1984 (courtesy of Lisa Harbatkin)
D&F   "Dreamers and Fighters" film project, video interviews by
                                 Sophie-Louise Ullman. n.d. (courtesy of Lori Styler)
Moyers interview   Bill Moyers. "In Search of the Constitution." PBS,
                                 1987 (interview with Harry Keyishian and George
                                 Hochfield)
Schrecker-Shaftel interview   Ellen Schrecker interview with Oscar Shaftel (handwritten
                                 notes), 4/13/1978 (courtesy of Ellen Schrecker)
Schrecker-Shlakman interview   Ellen Schrecker interview with Vera Shlakman (handwritten
                                 notes), 3/28/1979 (courtesy of Ellen Schrecker)
Schrecker-Slochower interview   Ellen Schrecker interview with Harry Slochower
                                 (handwritten notes), 12/19/1980 (courtesy of Ellen
                                 Schrecker)

OTHER SOURCES

Abrams v. United States, 250 U.S. 616 (1919).

Adams v. Trustees of University of North Carolina-Wilmington, 640 F.3d. 550 (4th Cir. 2011).

Adler, Irving. *Kicked Upstairs: A Political Autobiography of a "Blacklisted" Teacher*. N. Bennington, VT: Adler House, 2007.

Adler, Irving, and Benjamin Zelman. "New York's 'Subversive' Teachers." *Nation*, 4/9/1977, 434.

Adler v. Board of Education, 342 U.S. 485 (1952) (*Adler I*); *Adler v. Wilson*, 203 Misc. 456 (S.Ct. Albany Cty), affirmed, 282 A.D. 418 (N.Y. 3d Dept.), leave to appeal denied, 306 N.Y. 981 (1953) (*Adler II*).

Agnew, Jean-Christophe, and Roy Rosenzweig. *A Companion to Post-1945 America*. Malden, MA; Blackwell, 2002.

All Powers Project. "Melvin Jacobs Letter to President Allen." In *"Yours, in Dread of the Hot Seat*—Anti-Communist Investigations in Seattle, 1947–1949," virtual exhibit, University of Washington Libraries, Jan.–Mar. 1998. http://www.lib.washington.edu/exhibits/allpowers/Exhibit/jacobs.html (accessed 7/8/2011).

Ambrose, Stephen. "The Ike Age." *New Republic*, 5/9/1981.

American Association of University Professors. "1915 Declaration of Principles on Academic Freedom and Academic Tenure." http://www.aaup.org/AAUP/pubsres/policydocs/contents/1915.htm (accessed 7/12/2010).

———. "1940 Statement of Principles on Academic Freedom and Tenure," with "1970 Interpretive Comments." http://www.aaup.org/AAUP/pubsres/policydocs/contents/1940statement.htm (accessed 8/6/2011).

———. "Responses to September 11, 2001." *Academe*, Jan.–Feb. 2002. http://www.aaup.org/AAUP/pubsres/academe/2002/JF/911/911.htm (accessed 5/30/2011).

———. "September 11 and the Academic Profession: A Symposium." *Academe*, Jan.–Feb.2002. http://www.aaup.org/AAUP/pubsres/academe/2002/JF/Feat/scot.htm (accessed 5/30/2011).

———. "Trends in Faculty Status, 1975–2007." http://www.aaup2.org/research/TrendsinFacultyStatus2007.pdf (accessed 10/18/2011).

American Association of University Professors, Commission on Academic Freedom and Pre-College Education. "Liberty and Learning in the Schools." 1986.

American Association of University Professors, Committee on Academic Freedom in Wartime. "Report of the Committee on Academic Freedom in Wartime." 4 *AAUP Bulletin* 29 (Feb.–Mar. 1918).

American Civil Liberties Union. *Freedom under Fire: Dissent in Post-9/11 America*. 5/8/2003. http://www.aclu.org/national-security/freedom-under-fire-dissent-post-911-america (accessed 8/6/2011).

———. *The Gag on Teaching: The Story of the New Restrictions by Law on Teaching in Schools*. 3rd ed. Jan. 1940. Princeton-ACLU, 1887:9.

———. *The Story of the Bertrand Russell Case*. Jan. 1941, Princeton-ACLU, 1887:9.

American Civil Liberties Union Academic Freedom Committee. "Report on the 'Vanguard' Problem at Brooklyn College." 4/5/1951. Princeton-ACLU, 1189:5.

American Communications Association v. Douds, 339 U.S. 382 (1950).

Anwar, Yasmin. "Leonard Nathan, Distinguished Poet, Dies at 82." Press release, UC Berkeley News Center. 6/7/2007. http://berkeley.edu/news/media/releases/2007/06/07_nathan.shtml (accessed 1/29/2011).

Appeal of Julius Nash and Irving Mauer, 3 NY Education Dept. Reports 29 (1963).

Appeal of Teachers Union, Local 555, 73 NY State Dept. Reports 41 (1952).

Application of Board of Higher Education for Leave to Reargue Appeal of Francis Thompson, 69 NY State Dept. Reports 48 (1948).

Application of Harry Adler et al., 77 NY State Dept. Reports 53 (1956).

Aptheker v. Secretary of State, 378 U.S. 500 (1964).

Areen, Judith. "Government as Educator: A New Understanding of First Amendment Protection of Academic Freedom and Governance." 98 *Geo. L.J.* 945 (2009).

Austin v. Board of Higher Education, 5 N.Y.2d 430 (1959).

Avrich, Paul. *Anarchist Voices*. Princeton: Princeton U. Press, 1995.

Backhouse, Roger E., and Roger Middleton, eds. *Exemplary Economists*, vol. 2, *Europe, Asia and Australia*. Cheltenham, UK: Edward Elgar , 2000.

Baggett v. Bullitt, 215 F. Supp. 439 (W.D. Wash. 1963) (*Baggett I*); 377 U.S. 360 (1964) (*Baggett II*).

Bailey v. Richardson, 182 F.2d 46 (D.C. Cir. 1950), affirmed without opinion, 341 U.S. 918 (1951).

Barenblatt v. United States, 360 U.S. 109 (1959).

Barsky v. United States, 167 F.2d 241 (D.C. Cir. 1948).

Barrett, James. *William Z. Foster and the Tragedy of American Radicalism*. Urbana: U. of Illinois Press, 1999.

Barth, Alan. *Government by Investigation*. New York: Viking, 1955.

———. *The Loyalty of Free Men*. New York: Viking, 1952.

Baxter v. Palmigiano, 425 U.S. 308 (1976).

Beilan v. Board of Public Education, 357 U.S. 399 (1958).

Bentley, Eric. *Thirty Years of Treason: Excerpts from Hearings before the House Committee on Un-American Activities*. New York: Viking, 1971.

Bethel School District v. Fraser, 478 U.S. 675 (1986).

Bird, Kai, and Martin Sherwin. *American Prometheus: The Triumph and Tragedy of J. Robert Oppenheimer*. New York: Knopf, 2005.

Blanshard Paul. "Paul Blanshard Replies to Robert Fitzgerald." Letter. *Nation*, 7/24/1948, 110.

———. "The Roman Catholic Church and Fascism." *Nation*, 4/10/1948, 390.

Board of Education v. Allen, 6 Misc.2d 453 (S.Ct. Albany Cty, 1957), affirmed, 5 A.D.2d 1038 (3d Dept., 1958), affirmed, 6 N.Y.2d 127 (1959).

Board of Education, Island Trees School District v. Pico, 457 U.S. 853 (1982).

Bolton, Richard, ed. *Culture Wars*. New York: New Press, 1992.

Bontecou, Eleanor. *The Federal Loyalty-Security Program*. Ithaca: Cornell U. Press, 1953.

Boring v. Buncombe County Board of Education, 98 F.3d 1474 (4th Cir. 1996), vacated on rehearing *en banc*, 136 F.3d 364 (1998).

Braden v. United States, 365 U.S. 431 (1961).

Brooklyn College. "Veterans of Brooklyn College Student Newspaper, Shut Down by School Officials in 1950, Return for Gala Reunion." http://www.brooklyn.cuny.edu/bc/spotlite/news/index.php?link=041906 (accessed 7/5/2011).

Brooks v. Auburn U., 412 F.2d 1171 (5th Cir. 1969).

Brown, Michael, Randy Martin, Frank Rosengarten, and George Snedeker, eds. *New Studies in the Politics and Culture of U.S. Communism*. New York: Monthly Review Press, 1993.

Brown, Ralph. *Loyalty and Security: Employment Tests in the United States*. New Haven: Yale U. Press, 1958.

Burgan, Mary. "Shoddy Scholarship." *Academe*, Mar.–Apr. 2002, 104.

Burger, Warren, "The 1952 Republican Convention," an oral history conducted in 1975 by Amelia Fry, Regional Oral History Office, The Bancroft Library, University of California, Berkeley, 1987.

Burnham v. Ianni, 119 F.3d 668 (8th Cir. 1997).

Burns, James MacGregor. *Packing the Court*. New York: Penguin, 2009.

Burstyn v. Wilson, 343 U.S. 495 (1952).

Bush v. Gore, 531 U.S. 98 (2000).

Byrne, J. Peter. "Academic Freedom: A 'Special Concern of the First Amendment.'" 99 *Yale L.J.* 251 (1989).

Capen, Samuel. *The Management of Universities*. Buffalo: Forster and Stewart, 1953.

Caress, Barbara, and Stephen Leberstein. "Forty Years after Firings." *NY Times*, 6/2/1981, A15.

Caute, David. *The Great Fear: The Anti-Communist Purge under Truman and Eisenhower*. New York: Simon and Schuster, 1978.

Chamberlain, Lawrence. *Loyalty and Legislative Action: A Survey of Activity by the New York State Legislature, 1919–1949*. Ithaca: Cornell U. Press, 1951.

Charns, Alexander. *Cloak and Gavel: FBI Wiretaps, Bugs, Informers, and the Supreme Court*. Urbana: U. of Illinois Press, 1992.

Churchill v. University of Colorado, No. 2012 CO54 (2012), affirming No. 06CV11473 (Denver Dist. Ct., 2009).

Churchill, Ward. "Some People Push Back: On the Justice of Roosting Chickens." 9/12/2001. Available at http://www.kersplebedeb.com/mystuff/s11/churchill.html (accessed 5/9/11). Later revised and republished in Ward Churchill, *On the Justice of Roosting Chickens: Reflections on the Consequences of U.S. Imperial Arrogance and Criminality*. Oakland: AK Press, 2003.

Citizens United v. Federal Election Commission, 558 U.S 50 (2010).

Cole, David. "The New McCarthyism: Repeating History in the War on Terrorism." 38 *Harv. C.R.-C.L. L. Rev.* 1 (Winter 2003).

Cole, Jonathan. *The Great American University*. New York: Public Affairs, 2009.

Cole v. Richardson, 397 U.S. 238 (1970) (*Cole I*); 405 U.S. 676 (1972) (*Cole II*).

Cole v. Young, 351 U.S. 536 (1956).

Columbia University. "Ad Hoc Grievance Committee Report." 3/28/2005. http://www.columbia.edu/cu/news/05/03/ad_hoc_grievance_committee_report.html (accessed 6/3/2011).

Connell v. Higginbotham, 403 U.S. 207 (1971), affirming in part and reversing in part 305 F. Supp. 445 (M.D.Fla. 1969).

Connick v. Myers, 461 U.S. 138 (1983).

Coulton, Thomas. *A City College in Action: Struggle and Achievement at Brooklyn College, 1930–1955*. New York: Harper, 1955.

Countryman, Vern. *Un-American Activities in the State of Washington*. Ithaca: Cornell U. Press, 1951.

Cramp v. Board of Public Instruction, 125 So.2d 554 (Fla. 1960) (*Cramp I*); 368 U.S. 278 (1961) (*Cramp II*); 137 So.2d 828 (Fla. 1964) (*Cramp III*).

Cronin, Audrey. "The 'FTO List' and Congress: Sanctioning Designated Foreign Terrorist Organizations." Congressional Research Service, 10/21/2003.

Cummings v. Missouri, 4 Wall. 277 (1866).

Daniman v. Board of Education, 202 Misc. 915 (S.Ct. Kings Cty, 1952), affirmed, 282 A.D. 717
(2d Dept., 1953), affirmed, 306 N.Y. 532 (1954) (*Daniman I*); 307 N.Y 806 (1954) (*Daniman II*); 23 Misc. 2d 664 (S.Ct. Kings Cty, 1959) (*Daniman III*).

Deery, Phillip. "The AAUP, Academic Freedom, and the Cold War." 1 *AAUP Journal of Academic Freedom* (2010). Available at http://www.academicfreedomjournal.org/VolumeOne/Deerey.pdf (accessed 10/19/2010).

DeJonge v. Oregon, 299 U.S. 353 (1937).

Dennis v. United States, 341 U.S. 494 (1951).

Dewey, John, and Horace Kallen, eds. *The Bertrand Russell Case*. New York: Viking, 1941.

Dinnerstein, Leonard. *Anti-Semitism in America*. New York: Oxford U. Press, 1994.

Dodd, Bella. *School of Darkness*. New York: P. J. Kenedy & Sons, 1954.

Douglas, William O. *The Court Years*. New York: Vintage, 1981.

Doumani, Beshara, ed. *Academic Freedom after September 11*. New York: Zone Books, 2006.

Dube v. State University of New York, 900 F.2d 587 (2d Cir. 1990).

Dunne, Gerald. *Hugo Black and the Judicial Revolution*. New York: Simon and Schuster, 1977.

Egan v. Moore, 20 A.D.2d 150 (N.Y., 3d Dept., 1963), affirmed, 14 N.Y.2d 775 (1964).

Eisler v. United States, 335 U.S. 857 (1949).

Elfbrandt v. Russell, 94 Ariz. 1 (1963) (*Elfbrandt I*); 97 Ariz. 140 (1964) (*Elfbrandt II*); 384 U.S. 11 (1966) (*Elfbrandt III*).

Eliot, T. S. "Little Gidding." In *Four Quartets*. New York: Harcourt, Brace, 1943.

Emerson, Thomas, David Haber, and Norman Dorsen. *Political and Civil Rights in the United States*. Vol. 1. 3rd ed. Boston: Little, Brown, 1967.

Epstein, Helen. *Joe Papp: An American Life*. Boston: Little, Brown, 1996.

Eron, Don, Suzanne Hudson, and Myron Hulen. "Report on the Termination of Ward Churchill." Colorado Conference of the AAUP. 11/1/2011.

Ewen, Frederic. *Heroic Imagination: The Creative Genius of Europe from Waterloo to the Revolution of 1848*. Secaucus, NJ: Citadel, 1984.

Ex parte Garland, 4 Wall. 333 (1866).

Fariello, Griffin. *Red Scare: Memories of the American Inquisition*. New York: Norton, 1995.

Faulkner, William. *Requiem for a Nun*. New York: Random House, 1951.

Federal Bureau of Investigation. Files, Frederic Ewen. Author's Freedom of Information Act request; page numbers are those on the CD (FBI-Ewen).

———. Files, Philip Foner. Author's Freedom of Information Act request (FBI-Foner).

———. Files, Vera Shlakman, Author's Freedom of Information Act request (FBI-Shlakman).

———. Files, Harry Slochower. Author's Freedom of Information Act request (FBI-Slochower).

Feffer, Andrew. "Subversion in the Schools." *New York Archives*, Winter 2011, 32–5.

Feldman, Noah. *Scorpions: The Battles and Triumphs of FDR's Great Supreme Court Justices*. New York: Twelve, 2010.

Feldman v. Ho, 171 F.3d 494 (7th Cir. 1999).

Finan, Christopher. *From the Palmer Raids to the Patriot Act: A History of the Fight for Free Speech in America*. Boston: Beacon, 2007.

Finkelman, Paul, ed. *Encyclopedia of American Civil Liberties*. Vol. 2. New York: Routledge, 2006.

Finkin, Matthew, and Robert Post. *For the Common Good: Principles of American Academic Freedom*. New Haven: Yale U. Press, 2009.

FIRE (Foundation for Individual Rights in Education). "Brandeis University: Professor Found Guilty of Harassment for Protected Speech." http://www.thefire.org/case/755.html (accessed 6/23/2010).

Fischel, Jacob. "Harry Gideonse: The Public Life." PhD dissertation, U. of Delaware, 1973.

Fiske v. Kansas, 274 U.S. 380 (1927).

Fox, John. "Biographies of the Robes: Earl Warren." In *The Supreme Court: The Court and Democracy*, PBS online, http://www.pbs.org/wnet/supremecourt/democracy/robes_warren.html (accessed 1/17/2011).

Frank, John. "The United States Supreme Court, 1951–52 Term." 20 *U. Chi. L. Rev.* 1 (1952).

Freeman, Joshua B. "In Memoriam: Philip S. Foner." 33 *Perspectives* (American Historical Association) (April 1995). https://www.historians.org/perspectives/issues/1995/9504/9504INM.cfm (accessed 7/23/2010).

Friedman, Elliot. "From *Adler* to *Keyishian*: Academic Freedom and the Fight for the Rights of Public Employees." Schottenstein Honors Program thesis, Yeshiva University, 2011.

Friedman, Larry. "The Early Days of Vanguard." *Brooklyn College Vanguard*, n.d. http://www.brooklyn.cuny.edu/bc/offices/vanguard/?link=20060220_history (accessed 4/3/2010).

Garcetti v. Ceballos, 547 U.S. 410 (2006).

Gardner, David. *The California Oath Controversy*. Berkeley: U. of California Press, 1967.

Gardner v. Broderick, 392 U.S. 273 (1968).

Garner v. Board of Public Works, 341 U.S. 716 (1951).

Gavin, James. *Stormy Weather: The Life of Lena Horne*. New York: Simon and Schuster, 2009.

Gellhorn, Walter. *The States and Subversion*. Ithaca: Cornell U. Press, 1952.

Gerende v. Board of Supervisors of Elections, 341 U.S. 56 (1951).

Gettleman, Marvin. "Communists in Higher Education: C.C.N.Y. and Brooklyn College on the Eve of the Rapp-Coudert Investigation, 1935–1939." Unpublished paper, 1977.

Ginsberg, Allen. "Death to Van Gogh's Ear." In *Kaddish and Other Poems*. San Francisco: City Lights, 1961.

Gitlow v. New York, 268 U.S. 652 (1925).

Goldstein, Robert. *American Blacklist: The Attorney General's List of Subversive Organizations*. Lawrence: U. of Kansas Press, 2008.

———. *Political Repression in Modern America—From 1870 to 1976*. Champaign: U. of Illinois Press, 2001.

Golway, Terry, ed. *Catholics in New York*. New York: Fordham U. Press, 2008.

Goodman, Stephen, and Abraham Sofaer. "Opinions of William J. Brennan, Jr., October Term, 1966." VIII–IX, in LC-Brennan II:6:9.

Goodman, Walter. *The Committee*. Baltimore: Penguin, 1964.

Gornick, Vivian. *The Romance of American Communism*. New York: Basic Books, 1977.

Gorum v. Sessoms, 561 F.3d 179 (3d Cir. 2009).

Grinberg, Henry. "The Legacy: Vanguard Staffers: Constitutionally Loyal and True." *Brooklyn College Vanguard*, n.d. http://www.brooklyn.cuny.edu/bc/offices/vanguard/?link=20060220_history (accessed 7/6/2011).

Griswold, A. Whitney. "'Loyalty': An Issue of Academic Freedom." *NY Times Magazine*, 12/20/1959, 18.

Gruber, Carol. *Mars and Minerva: World War I and the Uses of the Higher Learning in America*. Baton Rouge: Louisiana State U. Press, 1975.

Grutter v. Bollinger, 539 U.S. 306 (2003).

Hague v. Committee for Industrial Organization, 307 U. S. 496 (1939).

Hamilton, Alexander. "Letters from Phocion: Letter 2." In *The Works of Alexander Hamilton*, vol. 4, edited by Henry Cabot Lodge. New York: G. P. Putnam's Sons, 1904.

Hamilton, Neil. *Zealotry and Academic Freedom*. New Brunswick: Transaction, 1995.

Hand, Learned. *The Spirit of Liberty*. New York: Knopf, 1959.

Hansen, W. L., ed. *Academic Freedom on Trial*. Madison: U. of Wisconsin Press, 1998.

Harbatkin, Lisa. "Linda Cirino: The People & the Records." 2009. "Dreamers and Fighters" website, http://www.dreamersandfighters.com/history/lindacirino.aspx (accessed 8/1/2011).

Hardy v. Jefferson Community College, 260 F.3d 671 (6th Cir. 2001).

Hartman, Andrew. *Education and the Cold War: The Battle for the American School*. New York: Palgrave Macmillan, 2008.

Haynes, John, and Harvey Klehr. *Venona: Decoding Soviet Espionage in America*. New Haven: Yale U. Press, 1999.

Hazelwood School District v. Kuhlmeier, 484 U.S. 260 (1988).

Healy v. James, 408 U.S. 169 (1972).

Heins, Marjorie. "Guilt by Association: Georgia's Anti-Subversive Test Oath." Free Expression Policy Project. 8/17/2010. http://www.fepproject.org/commentaries/georgiaoath.html (accessed 7/27/2011).

———. "'The Miracle': Film Censorship and the Entanglement of Church and State." Free Expression Policy Project. 10/28/2002. http://www.fepproject.org/commentaries/the-miracle.html (accessed 7/9/2011).

———. *Not in Front of the Children: "Indecency," Censorship, and the Innocence of Youth*. New Brunswick: Rutgers U. Press, 2007.

———. *Sex, Sin, and Blasphemy: A Guide to America's Censorship Wars*. New York: New Press 1998.

———. "What Makes a Conscientious Objector? Ohio's Anti-Terrorist Oath." Free Expression Policy Project. 6/9/2009. http://www.fepproject.org/commentaries/ohiooath.html (accessed 7/27/2011).

Henderson v. United States, 339 U.S. 816 (1950).

Hicks, Granville. "Are Loyalty Oaths Necessary?" *NY State Education* (publication of New York State Teachers Ass'n), Jan. 1967, 10.

Hitchens, Christopher. "Fear Factor." *Slate*, 9/11/2006. http://www.slate.com/id/2149377 (accessed 6/3/2011).

Hochfield, George, ed. *Selected Writings of the American Transcendentalists*. New Haven: Yale U. Press, 1966.

Hoffman, Hallock. *Loyalty by Oath*. Pendle Hill Pamphlet No. 94. 1957. http://www.pendlehill.org/resources/files/pdf%20files/php094.pdf (accessed 11/7/2008).

Hofstadter, Richard. *Anti-intellectualism in American Life*. New York: Vintage, 1963.

Hofstadter, Richard, and Walter Metzger. *The Development of Academic Freedom in the United States*. New York: Columbia U. Press, 1955.

Holder v. Humanitarian Law Project, 130 S.Ct. 2705 (2010).

Holmes, David. *Stalking the Academic Communist: Intellectual Freedom and the Firing of Alex Novikoff*. Hanover, NH: University Press of New England, 1989.

Hong v. Grant, 516 F. Supp. 2d 1158 (C.D. Cal. 2007), affirmed, 403 Fed. Appx. 236 (9th Cir. 2010) (unpublished).

Honig, Douglas, and Laura Brenner. *On Freedom's Frontier: The First Fifty Years of the ACLU of Washington*. Seattle: ACLU, 1987.

Horowitz, Morris, and Lawrence Kaplan. *The Jewish Population of the New York Area, 1900–1975*. New York: Federation of Jewish Philanthropies of New York, 1959.

Horwitz, Morton. *The Warren Court and the Pursuit of Justice*. New York: Hill & Wang, 1998.

Hovde, Bryn. "The Banning Has Injured the Church." Letter. *Nation*, 7/24/1948, 110.

Howe, Irving. *World of Our Fathers*. New York: Harcourt Brace, 1976.

"HUAC: May 1960." Free Speech Movement Archives. n.d. http://www.fsm-a.org/stacks/AP_files/APHUAC60.html (accessed 12/8/2011).

Hughes v. Board of Higher Education, 309 N.Y. 319 (1955).

Hyman, Harold. *To Try Men's Souls: Loyalty Tests in American History*. Berkeley: U. of California Press, 1959.

In re Summers, 325 U.S. 561 (1945).

Isserman, Maurice. *Which Side Were You On? The American Communist Party during the Second World War*. Middletown, CT: Wesleyan U. Press, 1982.

Iverson, Robert. *The Communists and the Schools*. New York: Harcourt Brace, 1959.

Jackson, Kenneth, ed. *The Encyclopedia of New York City*. 2nd ed. New Haven: Yale U. Press, 2010.

Jacobellis v. Ohio, 378 U.S. 184 (1964).

Jaffe, Louis. "The Supreme Court, 1950 Term." 65 *Harv. L. Rev.* 107 (1951).

Jaschik, Scott. "Loyalty Oath Compromise." *Inside Higher Ed*, 6/3/2008. http://www.inside-highered.com/news/2008/06/03/oaths (accessed 8/20/2008).

Jeffries v. Harleston, 21 F.3d 1238 (2d Cir.), vacated and remanded, 513 U.S. 996 (1994) (*Jeffries I*); 52 F.3d 9 (2d Cir. 1995) (*Jeffries II*).

Jencks v. United States, 353 U.S. 657 (1957).

Johnson, Lauri. "'Making Democracy Real': Teacher Union and Community Activism to Promote Diversity in the New York City Public Schools, 1935–1950." 37.5 *Urb. Ed.* 566 (Nov. 2002).

Joint Anti-Fascist Refugee Committee v. McGrath, 341 U.S. 123 (1951).

Joint Legislative Committee to Investigate the Educational System of the State of New York (Rapp-Coudert). *Final Report of the Subcommittee Relative to the Pubic Educational System in the City of New York*. NYS Legislative Documents, 165th Sess., 1942.

———. *Hearings before the Committee in the Matter of Investigation into the Educational System of the State of New York Pursuant to Joint Resolution of the Senate and Assembly Adopted March 29, 1940*, 10/1940–6/1942.

———. *Interim Report and Conclusions of the New York City Subcommittee Relative to Subversive Activity among Students in the Public High Schools and Colleges in the City of New York*. NYS Legislative Documents, 164th Sess., 1941.

Joint Legislative Committee v. Teachers Union and Hendley, 285 N.Y. 1 (1941).

Josephson v. United States, 165 F.2d 82 (2d Cir. 1947).

Kalven, Harry, Jr. *A Worthy Tradition: Freedom of Speech in America*. New York: Harper, 1988.

Kay v. Board of Higher Education, 173 Misc. 943 (S.Ct. NY Cty), affirmed without opinion, 259 A.D. 879; leave to appeal denied, 259 A.D. 1000, 284 N.Y. 578 (1940).

Keefe v. Geanakos, 418 F.2d 359 (1st Cir. 1969).

Kennedy, John F. "Let's Get Rid of College Loyalty Oaths." *Coronet*, Apr. 1960, 89.

———. "The Loyalty Oath: An Obstacle to Better Education." 45.1 *AAUP Bulletin* 25 (Mar. 1959).

Kessler-Harris, Alice. "Classics Revisited: Vera Shlakman: *Economic History of a Factory Town.*" 69 *Int'l Labor & Working-Class History* 195 (2006).

Kessner, Thomas. *Fiorello LaGuardia and the Making of Modern New York.* New York: McGraw-Hill, 1989.

Keyishian, Harry. Unpublished paper on the *Keyishian* case, 1965. In the author's files.

Keyishian v. Board of Regents, 345 F.2d 236 (2d Cir. 1965) (*Keyishian I*); 255 F. Supp. 981 (W.D.N.Y. 1966) (*Keyishian II*); 385 U.S. 589 (1967) (*Keyishian III*).

Kishlansky, Mark, ed. *Sources of World History.* New York: Harper Collins, 1995.

Klehr, Harvey. *The Heyday of American Communism: The Depression Decade.* New York: Basic Books, 1984.

Knight v. Board of Regents, 269 F. Supp. 339 (S.D.N.Y. 1967), affirmed without opinion, 390 U.S. 36 (1968).

Konigsberg v. State Bar, 353 U.S. 252 (1957) (*Konigsberg I*); 366 U.S. 36 (1961) (*Konigsberg II*).

Kramer, Jane. "The Petition." *New Yorker,* 4/14/2008, 50.

"The Law: Earl Warren's Way." *Time,* 7/22/1974. http://www.time.com/time/magazine/article/0,9171,942946-3,00.html (accessed 1/17/2011).

Lawson and Trumbo v. United States, 176 F.2d 49 (D.C. Cir. 1949).

Lazarsfeld, Paul, and Wagner Thielens. *The Academic Mind: Social Scientists in a Time of Crisis.* Glencoe, IL: Free Press, 1958.

Leberstein, Stephen. Book review, *Reds at the Blackboard,* by Clarence Taylor. 14.3 *WorkingUSA: The Journal of Labor and Society* 434 (Sept. 2011).

———. "Morris Schappes: An Activist's Life." *Clarion* (newspaper of the Professional Staff Congress, City University of New York), Nov. 2004, 11.

Lederman v. Board of Education, 196 Misc. 873 (N.Y. S.Ct. Kings Cty, 1949), reversed, 276 A.D. 527 (2d Dept.), 301 N.Y. 476 (1950).

Lerner v. Casey, 357 U.S. 468 (1958).

Levin v. Harleston, 770 F. Supp. 895 (S.D.N.Y. 1991), affirmed in part, vacated in part, 966 F.2d 85 (2d Cir. 1992).

Liben, Meyer. "CCNY-A Memoir." *Commentary,* Sept. 1965, 64.

Lockwood, Robert, ed. *Anti-Catholicism in American Culture.* Huntington, IN: Our Sunday Visitor, 2000.

MacIver, Robert. *Academic Freedom in Our Time.* New York: Columbia U. Press, 1955.

Markowitz, Ruth. *My Daughter, the Teacher: Jewish Teachers in the New York City Schools.* New Brunswick: Rutgers U. Press, 1993.

Martin, Jerry, and Anne Neal. *Defending Civilization: How Our Universities Are Failing America and What Can Be Done about It.* ACTA, 2002.

Massad, Joseph, "Response to Ad Hoc Grievance Committee Report." 4/5/2005. http://www.columbia.edu/cu/mealac/faculty/massad (accessed 11/11/2011); also available at http://electronicintifada.net/content/ei-exclusive-joseph-massads-response-ad-hoc-grievance-committee-report/5541 (accessed 5/20/12).

Matter of Irving Adler et al., 73 NY State Dept. Reports 134 (1952).

Matter of Benjamin Baronofsky et al., 76 NY State Dept. Reports 32 (1955).

Matter of May Quinn, 67 NY State Dept. Reports 7 (1946).

Matter of Francis Thompson, 68 NY State Dept. Reports 68 (1947).

Matusow, Harvey. *False Witness.* New York: Cameron & Kahn, 1955.

Maud, Ralph. *Charles Olson at the Harbor*. Vancouver: Talonbooks, 2008.

Maynard, June. "I Didn't Come Back for the Coffee." *Read SFU Memories*. http://www.sfu. ca/40th_anniversary/read/Maynard_June.html (accessed 1/27/2010).

McAuliffe v. Mayor of New Bedford, 155 Mass. 216 (1892).

"McCarthyism at Queens College Digital Exhibit." Queens College. n.d. http://qcmccarthyism.blogspot.com (accessed 11/16/2011).

McHenry, Eric. "Starbuck the Great: The Forgotten Poet Who Made Loyalty Oaths Illegal." *Slate*, 9/13/2004. http://www.slate.com/toolbar.aspx?action=print&id=2106536 (accessed 11/7/2008).

McLaurin v. Oklahoma State Regents, 339 U.S. 637 (1950).

McWilliams, Carey. *Witch Hunt: The Revival of Heresy*. Boston: Little, Brown, 1950.

Meiklejohn, Alexander. *The Least Dangerous Branch: The Supreme Court at the Bar of Politics*. Indianapolis: Bobbs Merrill, 1962.

Menand, Louis. ed. *The Future of Academic Freedom*. Chicago: U. of Chicago Press, 1996.

Metzger, Walter, ed. *Professors on Guard: The First AAUP Investigations*. New York: Arno, 1977.

Meyers, Jeffrey. *The Genius and the Goddess*. Urbana: U. Illinois Press, 2010.

Mickenberg, Julia. *Learning from the Left: Children's Literature, the Cold War, and Radical Politics in the United States*. New York: Oxford U. Press, 2006.

Minarcini v. Strongsville City School District, 541 F.2d 577 (6th Cir. 1976).

Minnesota State Board for Community Colleges v. Knight, 465 U.S. 271 (1984).

Mitford, Jessica. "My Short and Happy Life as a Distinguished Professor." *Atlantic*, Oct. 1974, 90.

Mitgang, Herbert. *The Man Who Rode the Tiger: The Life and Times of Judge Samuel Seabury*. Philadelphia: Lippincott, 1963.

Mohr, James. "Academic Turmoil and Public Opinion: The Ross Case at Stanford." 39.1 *Pac. Historical Rev.* 39 (Feb. 1970).

Moran, Michael. "Terrorist Groups and Political Legitimacy." *Backgrounder* (Council on Foreign Relations), 3/16/2006. http://www.cfr.org/terrorism/terrorist-groups-political-legitimacy/p10159 (accessed 12/9/2011).

Morse v. Frederick, 551 U.S. 393 (2007).

Murphy, Walter. *Congress and the Court*. Chicago: U. Chicago Press, 1962.

NAACP v. Alabama ex rel. Patterson, 357 U.S. 449 (1958).

Naison, Mark. *Communists in Harlem during the Depression*. New York: Grove, 1983.

National Endowment for the Arts (NEA). "FY2006 Grant Awards: Literature Fellowships for Translation Projects." http://www.nea.gov/grants/recent/06grants/LitTranslation. html (accessed 11/20/2008).

Navasky, Victor. *Naming Names*. New York: Viking, 1980.

Nearing, Scott. *The Making of a Radical*. White River Junction, VT: Chelsea Green, 2000.

Nelson, Cary. "Defining Academic Freedom." *Inside Higher Ed*, 12/21/2010. http://www. insidehighered.com/layout/set/print/views/2010/12/21/nelson_on_academic_freedom (accessed 6/6/2011).

———. *No University Is an Island*. New York: NYU Press, 2010.

Newman, Roger. *Hugo Black: A Biography*. New York: Fordham U. Press, 1997.

Nostrand v. Balmer, 53 Wn.2d 460 (1959).

Nostrand v. Little, 362 U.S. 474 (1960); on remand, 58 Wn.2d 111, appeal dismissed, 368 U.S. 436 (1962).

Note. "Loyalty Oaths." 77 *Yale L.J.* 739 (1968).

Novick, Peter. *That Noble Dream: The "Objectivity Question" and the American Historical Profession*. New York: Cambridge U. Press, 1998.

Obama, Barack. "A More Perfect Union." Remarks in Philadelphia, 3/18/2008. Transcript at http://my.barackobama.com/page/content/hisownwords/ (accessed 6/6/2011).

Ohmann, Richard. *English in America*. Middletown, CT: Wesleyan U. Press, 1995.

Oshinsky, David. *A Conspiracy So Immense: The World of Joe McCarthy*. New York: Oxford U. Press, 2005.

Ottanelli, Fraser. *The Communist Party of the United States: From the Depression to World War II*. New Brunswick: Rutgers U. Press, 1991.

Parsons, Jerry. "The Feinberg Law: A Case History of the Challenge." PhD dissertation, State University of New York at Buffalo, 1970.

Pedlosky v. Massachusetts Institute of Technology, 352 Mass. 127 (1967).

Pennsylvania v. Nelson, 350 U.S. 497 (1956).

People v. Schappes, 264 A.D. 917 (1st Dept. 1942), affirmed, 291 N.Y. 575 (1950).

People's Mojahedin v. Dept of State, 182 F.3d 17 (D.C. Cir. 1999).

Peters v. Hobby, 349 U.S. 331 (1955).

Pfannestiel, Todd. *Rethinking the Red Scare: The Lusk Committee and New York's Crusade against Radicalism, 1919–1923*. New York: Routledge, 2003.

Pickering v. Board of Education, 391 U.S. 563 (1968).

Pollack, Jack Harrison, *Earl Warren: The Judge Who Changed America*. Englewood Cliffs: Prentice-Hall, 1979.

Presidents Council, District 25 v. Community School Board No. 25, 457 F.2d 289 (2d Cir. 1972).

Preston, William, Jr. *Aliens and Dissenters: Federal Suppression of Radicals, 1903–1933*. New York: Harper & Row, 1963.

Price, David. "Standing Up for Academic Freedom: The Case of Irving Goldman." 20.4 *Anthropology Today* 16 (Aug. 2004).

"Professor Norman Finkelstein and DePaul End Tenure Dispute, but Effect on Academic Freedom Remains." Radio broadcast. *Democracy Now*, 9/10/2007. Transcript at http://www.democracynow.org/2007/9/10/professor_norman_finkelstein_and_depaul_end (accessed 9/16/2009).

Queens College. "Exhibit, Symposium and Video at Queens College Explore McCarthy Era on Campus." Press release. 9/5/2003. http://www.qc.cuny.edu/communications/news_services/releases/Pages/NewsArchive.aspx?ItemID=1200 (accessed 3/16/2011).

Rabban, David. *Free Speech in Its Forgotten Years*. Cambridge: Cambridge U. Press, 1997.

———. "A Functional Analysis of 'Individual' and 'Institutional' Academic Freedom under the First Amendment." 53 *Law & Contemp. Probs.* 227 (1990).

Rabinowitz, Victor. *Unrepentant Leftist*. Urbana: U. of Illinois Press, 1996.

Rader, Melvin. *False Witness*. Seattle: U. of Washington Press, 1998 (reprint of 1969 edition).

Regents of the University of California v. Bakke, 438 U.S. 265 (1978).

Regents of the University of Michigan v. Ewing, 474 U.S. 214 (1985).

Renken v. Gregory, 541 F.3d 769 (7th Cir. 2008).

Richardson v. Cole, 300 F. Supp. 1321 (D.Mass. 1969), vacated and remanded, 397 U.S. 238 (1970).

Ross, Edward. *Seventy Years of It*. New York: D. Appleton, 1936.

Rossiter, Clinton, ed. *The Federalist Papers*. New York: New American Library, 1961.

Rothschild, Matthew. "The FBI's File on Howard Zinn." *The Progressive*, July 31, 2010. http://
progressive.org/wx073110.html (accessed 5/18/2012).

Roy, Sara. "Strategizing Control of the Academy." *NEA Higher Ed. J.*, Fall 2005, 147.

Sabin, Arthur. *In Calmer Times: The Supreme Court and Red Monday*. Philadelphia: U. of
Pennsylvania Press, 1999.

Sager, Alan. "The Impact of Supreme Court Loyalty Oath Decisions." 22 *Am. U. L. Rev.* 39
(1972–3).

Sanders, Jane. *Cold War on the Campus: Academic Freedom at the University of Washington, 1946–64*. Seattle: U. of Washington Press, 1979.

Scales v. United States, 367 U.S. 203 (1961).

Scallet v. Rosenblum, 911 F. Supp. 999 (W.D.Va. 1996).

Schappes, Morris. "Later—but Not Too Late." *Jewish Currents*, Apr. 1982, 12. http://www.
jewishcurrents.org/wp-content/uploads/2010/02/jcarchive0911.pdf (accessed 4/30/2011).

Schauer, Frederick. "Is There a Right to Academic Freedom?" 77 *U. Colo. L. Rev.* 909 (2006).

Schenck v. United States, 249 U.S. 47 (1919).

Schneiderman v. United States, 320 U.S. 118 (1943).

Schrecker, Ellen, ed. *The Age of McCarthyism*. 2nd ed. Boston: Bedford/St. Martin's, 2002.

———. *The Lost Soul of Higher Education*. New York: New Press, 2010.

———. *No Ivory Tower: McCarthyism and the Universities*. New York: Oxford U. Press, 1986.

———. "Political Tests for Professors: Academic Freedom during the McCarthy Years."
Lecture at University Loyalty Oath Symposium, University of California–Berkeley,
10/7/1999. http://sunsite3.berkeley.edu/uchistory/archives_exhibits/loyaltyoath/sympo-
sium/schrecker.htm1 (accessed 2/27/2009).

Schueller, Malini Johar, and Ashley Dawson, eds. *Dangerous Professors: Academic Freedom
and the National Security Campus*. Ann Arbor: U. of Michigan Press, 2009.

Schware v. Board of Bar Examiners, 353 U.S. 232 (1957).

Schwartz, Bernard. *Super Chief*. New York: NYU Press, 1983.

Scigliano, Eric. "Naming—and Un-naming—Names." *Nation*, 12/31/2001, 16.

Senior, Jennifer. "Columbia's Own Middle East War." *New York*, 5/21/2005. http://nymag.
com/nymetro/urban/education/features/10868 (accessed 11/11/2011).

Service v. Dulles, 354 U. S. 363 (1957).

Shelley v. Kraemer, 334 U.S. 1 (1948).

Shelton v. Tucker, 364 U.S. 479 (1960).

Shlakman v. Board of Higher Education, 202 Misc. 915 (S.Ct. Kings Cty, 1952), affirmed, 282
A.D. 718 (2d Dept., 1953), affirmed, 306 N.Y. 532 (1954) (*Shlakman I*); 307 N.Y. 806 (1954)
(*Shlakman II*); 5 Misc. 2d 901 (S.Ct. Kings Cty, 1957) (*Shlakman III*).

Shlakman, Vera. "Review." 13.2 *Journal of Economic History* 241 (1953).

Singel, Ryan. "Report: FBI Mishandles Terror Watch List." *Wired*, 5/6/2009. http://www.
wired.com/threatlevel/2009/05/fbi-gets-f-in-handling-terror-watch-list-ig-finds
(accessed 6/1/2011).

Slayton, Robert. *Empire Statesman: The Rise and Redemption of Al Smith*. New York: Free
Press, 2001.

Slochower v. Board of Higher Education, 350 U.S. 551 (1956).

Smolla, Rodney. *The Constitution Goes to College: Five Constitutional Ideas That Have
Shaped the American University*. New York: NYU Press, 2011.

Sopka, Katherine. "Oral History Transcript: Dr. Melba Phillips." Niels Bohr Library and
Archives, 12/5/1977. http://www.aip.org/history/ohilist/4821.html (accessed 11/3/2011).

Speiser v. Randall, 357 U.S. 513 (1958).

Stanton v. Board of Education, 190 Misc. 1012 (S.Ct. Kings Cty, 1948).

State ex rel. Triplet v. Ross, 111 Ohio St. 3d 231 (2006).

Stern, Seth, and Stephen Wermiel. *Justice Brennan: Liberal Champion*. Boston: Houghton Mifflin, 2010.

Stevens, Geri (Cohen). "Remarks on the Occasion of the Dedication of the Vanguard Plaque on April 28, 2006." *Brooklyn College Vanguard*, n.d. http://www.brooklyn.cuny.edu/bc/offices/vanguard/?link=20060825_events (accessed 4/10/2010).

Stewart v. Washington, 301 F. Supp. 610 (D.D.C. 1969).

Stone, Geoffrey. *Perilous Times: Free Speech in Wartime, from the Sedition Act of 1798 to the War on Terrorism*. New York: Norton, 2004.

Stone, I. F. *The Haunted Fifties*. New York: Random House, 1963.

———. "Must Teachers Become Informers to Keep Their Jobs?" *I. F. Stone's Weekly* 2, no. 36 (10/11/1954).

Stone, Lawrence, ed. *The University in Society*. Princeton: Princeton U. Press, 1974.

Stromberg v. California, 283 U.S. 359 (1931).

"The Struggle for Free Speech at CCNY, 1931–42." Online exhibition, CCNY. http://www.vny.cuny.edu/gutter/panels/panel1.html (accessed 4/30/2011).

Sweatt v. Painter, 339 U.S. 629 (1950).

Sweezy v. New Hampshire, 354 U.S. 234 (1957).

Taylor, Clarence. *Reds at the Blackboard: Communism, Civil Rights, and the New York City Teachers Union*. New York: Columbia U. Press, 2011.

Taylor, William. *The Passion of My Times*. New York: Carroll & Graf, 2004.

Teller, Judd. *Strangers & Natives: The Evolution of the American Jew from 1921 to the Present*. New York: Delacorte, 1968.

Third World Traveler. "HUAC and the Rise of Anti-Communism." http://www.thirdworldtraveler.com/McCarthyism/HUAC_Rise_AntiCommun.html (accessed 9/28/2011).

Thompson v. Wallin, 196 Misc. 686 (N.Y. Albany Cty 1949), reversed, 276 A.D. 463 (3d Dept.), 301 N.Y. 476 (1950).

Tiersten, Sylvia. "Roger Revelle." *@UCSD Magazine*, May 2009.

Tinker v. Des Moines Independent School District, 393 U.S. 503 (1969).

Traub, James. *City on a Hill: Testing the American Dream at City College*. Reading, MA: Addison Wesley, 1994.

Uniformed Sanitation Men v. Commissioner of Sanitation, 392 U.S. 280 (1968).

United Public Workers v. Mitchell, 330 U.S. 75 (1947).

United States v. Carolene Products, 304 U.S. 144 (1938).

United States v. Lovett, 328 U.S. 303 (1946).

University of Chicago. "Melba Phillips, Physicist, 1907–2004." Press release. 11/16/2004. http://www-news.uchicago.edu/releases/04/041116.phillips.shtml (accessed 11/3/2011).

University of Pennsylvania v. Equal Employment Opportunity Commission, 493 U.S. 182 (1990).

Uphaus v. Wyman, 360 U.S. 72 (1959).

Urofsky, Melvin, ed. *The Douglas Letters*. Bethesda, MD: Adler & Adler, 1987.

———, ed. *The Supreme Court Justices—A Biographical Dictionary*. New York: Garland, 1994.

Urofsky v. Allen, 995 F. Supp.2d 634 (E.D. Va. 1998), reversed as *Urofsky v. Gilmore*, 216 F.3d 401 (4th Cir. 2000).

U.S. House of Representatives, Committee on Un-American Congress Activities (HUAC). *Report on the Civil Rights Congress as a Communist Front Organization.* U.S. Gov't Printing Office, Sept. 1947.

U.S. House of Representatives, Special Subcommittee of the Committee on Education and Labor (Hartley hearings). *Hearings before the Subcommittee.* 80th Congress, 2d Session, Pursuant to House Resolution 111, New York City, 9–10/1948.

U.S. Senate, Subcommittee to Investigate the Administration of the Internal Security Act and Other Internal Security Laws of Senate Committee on the Judiciary (SISS). *Hearings before the Subcommittee: Subversive Influence in the Educational Process.* 82d Congress, 2d session, Sept. 1952–June 1953. Some, but not all, of the transcripts are available at http://academic.brooklyn.cuny.edu/english/melani/bc/senate_1952/ and links (accessed 7/6/2011).

———. *Subversive Influence in the Educational Process.* Report, 7/17/1953.

Van Alstyne, William. "Academic Freedom and the First Amendment in the Supreme Court: An Unhurried Historical Review." 53 *Law & Contemp. Probs.* 79 (1990).

"Vanguard-Plaque Celebration, Friday, April 28, 2006." *Brooklyn College Vanguard,* n.d. http://www.brooklyn.cuny.edu/bc/offices/vanguard/?link=20060825_events (accessed 7/6/2011).

Van Heerden v. Board of Supervisors, 2011 U.S. Dist. LEXIS 121414 (2011).

Van Nort, Sydney C. "Townsend Harris," *The Latin Library,* http://www.thelatinlibrary.com/chron/civilwarnotes/harrist.html (accessed 6/24/2011).

Vogel v. County of Los Angeles, 68 Cal.2d 18 (1967).

Walker, Samuel. *In Defense of American Liberties: A History of the ACLU.* New York: Oxford U. Press, 1990.

Walker v. City of Birmingham, 388 U.S. 307 (1967).

Washburn, Jennifer. *University, Inc.: The Corporate Corruption of Higher Education.* New York: Basic Books, 2005.

Waters v. Churchill, 511 U.S. 661 (1994).

Watkins v. United States, 354 U.S. 178 (1957).

Weidlich, Thom. *Appointment Denied: The Inquisition of Bertrand Russell.* Amherst, NY: Prometheus, 2000.

Weinstein, James. *The Decline of American Socialism.* New York: Vintage, 1969.

Wells, Oliver. "The College Anarchist." *Nation,* 7/12/1894.

West Virginia State Board of Education v. Barnette, 319 U.S. 624 (1943).

Whitehill v. Elkins, 389 U.S. 54 (1967).

Whitfield, Stephen. *The Culture of the Cold War.* Baltimore: Johns Hopkins U. Press, 1991.

Whitney v. California, 274 U.S. 357 (1927).

Wick, Nancy. "Seeing Red." University of Washington, Dec. 1997. http://www.washington.edu/alumni/columns/dec97/red1.html (accessed 6/30/2011).

———. "Seeing Red: The Aftermath." University of Washington, Dec. 1997. http://www.washington.edu/alumni/columns/dec97/red5.html (accessed 6/30/2011).

———. "Seeing Red: The Apology." University of Washington, Dec. 1997. http://www.washington.edu/alumni/columns/dec97/red6.html (accessed 6/30/2011).

———. "Seeing Red: The Firings." University of Washington, Dec. 1997. http://www.washington.edu/alumni/columns/dec97/red4.html (accessed 6/30/2011).

Wieman v. Updegraff, 344 U.S. 183 (1952).

Wilkinson v. United States, 365 U.S. 399 (1961).

Yates v. United States, 354 U.S. 298 (1957).

Zitron, Celia. *The New York City Teachers Union, 1916–1964.* New York: Humanities, 1968.

INDEX

Marjorie Heins is a civil liberties lawyer, writer, and teacher and the founding director of the Free Expression Policy Project. From 1991 to 1998, she directed the American Civil Liberties Union's Arts Censorship Project. More recently, she was a fellow at the Brennan Center for Justice and at the Frederic Ewen Center for Academic Freedom, both at New York University. Her previous books include *Strictly Ghetto Property: The Story of Los Siete de la Raza*; *Cutting the Mustard: Affirmative Action and the Nature of Excellence*; *Sex, Sin, and Blasphemy: A Guide to America's Censorship Wars*; and *Not in Front of the Children: "Indecency," Censorship, and the Innocence of Youth*, which won the American Library Association's 2002 Eli Oboler Award for best published work in the field of intellectual freedom. She is a graduate of Harvard Law School.